ONE WEEK

16 MAY 2005

Lesbian, Gay, and Bisexual Identities and Youth

Psychological Perspectives

Edited by

Anthony R. D'Augelli

Charlotte J. Patterson

OXFORD
UNIVERSITY PRESS

2001

OXFORD
UNIVERSITY PRESS

Oxford   New York
Athens   Auckland   Bangkok   Bogotá   Buenos Aires   Calcutta
Cape Town   Chennai   Dar es Salaam   Delhi   Florence   Hong Kong   Istanbul
Karachi   Kuala Lumpur   Madrid   Melbourne   Mexico City   Mumbai
Nairobi   Paris   São Paulo   Shanghai   Singapore   Taipei   Tokyo   Toronto   Warsaw

and associated companies in
Berlin   Ibadan

Library of Congress Cataloging-in-Publication Data
Lesbian, gay, and bisexual identities and youth : psychological perspectives /
edited by Anthony R. D'Augelli and Charlotte J. Patterson.
p. cm.
Includes bibliographical references and index.
ISBN 0-19-511952-5; ISBN 0-19-511953-3 (pbk.)
1. Gay youth—United States—Psychology.   2. Lesbian youth—United
States—Psychology.   3. Bisexual youth—United States—Psychology.   4. Gay
youth—Psychology.   5. Lesbian youth—Psychology.   6. Bisexual youth—Psychology.
I. D'Augelli, Anthony R.   II. Patterson, Charlotte.
HQ76.2.U5 L45 2000
305.235—dc21   00-026622

1   3   5   7   9   8   6   4   2

Printed in the United States of America
on acid-free paper

Preface

The reviews in this volume demonstrate the emergence of social scientific interest in the careful study of sexual orientation during adolescence. Historically, research on sexual orientation focused mainly on adults, with findings based on samples in their late 20's and early 30's. From decades of such work, an image of adult sexual orientation was created, one that debunked earlier views equating same-sex sexual orientation with maladjustment. This normalization, however, served to anchor sexual orientation squarely within the domain of young adulthood, leaving underdescribed the lives of middle-aged and older lesbian, gay, and bisexual adults. It also ignored adolescents. This process led to the invisibility in psychological research of lesbian, gay, and bisexual identity processes during the years between childhood and adulthood. The invisibility of these issues in our culture, moreover, put little pressure on researchers, particularly developmental scientists, to include an examination of the development of sexual orientation during adolescence in their research. The consequent lack of an empirical knowledge base would prove problematic when early studies of nonheterosexually identified youths suggested that these youths might be at special risk for social, emotional, or behavioral problems. Without information obtained on large samples of adolescents such findings were subject to questions of generalizability. One purpose of this volume is to summarize our current knowledge about lesbian, gay, and bisexual identities and adolescence, with the hope that increasing numbers of developmental researchers will enter this research domain. The rich information summarized provides, we hope, a strong basis upon which future research can be based.

The volume is divided into three major sections, dealing with theoretical viewpoints, psychological challenges, and specific areas deserving the attention of those involved with intervention and social change.

In Part I, Conceptual Frameworks, Julia A. Graber and Andrea Bastiani Archibald review research on adolescent sexual development and link sexual orientation development to pubertal processes. Scott L. Hershberger presents a current analysis of research on biological factors in the development of sexual orientation. Finally, Daryl J. Bem proposes an integrating theoretical approach to sexual orientation that has considerable potential to generate further conceptual developments, as well as specific research hypotheses.

The three reviews in Part II provide commentary on core psychological challenges faced by lesbian, gay, and bisexual youths and by researchers studying them. Margaret S. Schneider describes the achievement of lesbian identity for adolescent females. Mary Jane Rotheram-Borus and Kris A. Langabar provide a developmental trajectory analysis. Eric M. Dubé, Ritch C. Savin-Williams, and Lisa M. Diamond reflect on how intimacy, gender, and ethnicity operate in the development of sexual identities in adolescence.

Part III contains six chapters devoted to issues in the lives of lesbian, gay, and bisexual youths that are deserving of social intervention and policy change. A comprehensive review of research on HIV/AIDS among young lesbian, gay, and bisexual people is provided by Arnold H. Grossman. Nancy J. Evans describes how lesbian, gay, and bisexual youths on college campuses cope with the special pressures of higher education. The nature and consequences of victimization based on youths' sexual orientation are detailed by Ian Rivers and Anthony R. D'Augelli. Drawing on much of the work described in other chapters, Caitlin Ryan suggests crucial issues for those who are involved in counseling youths. In a cultural analysis of an effort at change in public schools, Janice M. Irvine shows the importance—and difficulty—of educational reform to be inclusive of diverse sexual identities. Finally, Gilbert Herdt contributes an essay on cultural changes in the United States that suggest a growing acceptance of sexual complexity.

Ranging from analyses of puberty to predictions of progressive social change, these reviews demonstrate the breadth of factors affecting sexual orientation during adolescence and early adulthood. Researchers and scholars can build upon the foundation presented here to articulate new conceptual approaches, suggest methodological innovations, design increasingly sophisticated research, and use the ever-growing body of literature to improve the lives of young people. Extending the psychological study of sexual orientation to adolescence clearly has generated important findings, as well as significant challenges to our previous understanding of sexual orientations over the life span.

Anthony R. D'Augelli and Charlotte J. Patterson

Contents

I
CONCEPTUAL FRAMEWORKS

1

Psychosocial Change
at Puberty and Beyond

Understanding Adolescent Sexuality and Sexual Orientation

Julia A. Graber and Andrea Bastiani Archibald

Development of a sexual identity, or formation of an identity that includes seeing oneself as a sexual being, is the process of engaging in sexual behaviors, forming attitudes about sexual experiences and sexuality, and navigating the social, emotional, and physical challenges of sexual behavior (Graber, Brooks-Gunn, & Galen, 1998). For most youths, much of this developmental work occurs over the course of the adolescent decade. Hence, the study of adolescent sexuality has typically been embedded in the context of the biological and psychosocial changes accompanying the transition to and through adolescence (Brooks-Gunn & Furstenberg, 1989; Brooks-Gunn & Paikoff, 1997; Paikoff & Brooks-Gunn, 1994). These investigations of adolescent sexuality have generally focused on the development and experiences of heterosexual youths. Lacking in this literature is thorough consideration of the emerging sexuality of lesbian, gay, and bisexual youths (see D'Augelli, 1998; Graber & Brooks-Gunn, 1995; Savin-Williams 1995; for some exceptions). In order to better understand the developing sexuality of these youths, it is important also to contemplate their sexual development within the larger context of the transition to adolescence. In this way, researchers and practitioners alike will begin to acknowledge those processes that are similar for all adolescents regardless of eventual sexual orientation. As well, identification of the potentially unique experiences and/or challenges for lesbian, gay, and bisexual adolescents will aid in the creation of developmentally appropriate intervention services for these youths and their families. Consideration of comparable developmental processes for all adolescents may also serve as a connection for these youths to other adolescents through their shared experiences.

An increasing number of adolescents are describing themselves as lesbian, gay, or bisexual (Deisher, 1989; Savin-Williams, 1990; Remafedi, Resnick, Blum, & Harris, 1992). Deisher (1989) estimates that approximately 3 million of all 10- to 20-year-old adolescents in the United States are predominantly or exclusively lesbian or gay. While some adolescents exclusively define themselves as lesbian or gay, a greater number report same-sex attractions, fantasies, and experiences (Remafedi et al., 1992). Remafedi and his colleagues (1992) conducted a large demographic study of the sexual orientation of a diverse sample of 35,000 students in grades 7 through 12. These researchers found that only a small percentage of students self-defined as lesbian/gay (1.1%) or bisexual (0.9%). Another 11% of these adolescents reported that they were "unsure" of their sexual orientation. While the number of "unsure" adolescents was highest in the lower grades, the percentage of adolescents defining as lesbian or gay remained fairly consistent across the years. A slightly greater proportion of adolescents reported homosexual sexual activity. However, these percentages increased over the high school years from 1% at age 12 to nearly 3% at age 18. Just over a quarter of these adolescents (27%) identified as lesbian, gay, or bisexual. A larger number of adolescents report same-sex attractions (2% at age 12 and 6% at 18 years old) and fantasies (almost 3% of all youths). Interestingly, while only 5% of the adolescents reporting same-sex attraction defined themselves as lesbian, gay, or bisexual, 30% of youths with same-sex fantasies self-identified as lesbian or gay (Remafedi et al., 1992).

Clearly, it is difficult to identify young people as lesbian, gay, or bisexual without their labeling themselves as such. As most demographic studies of adolescents have been conducted in high schools, it is likely that an underreporting of lesbian, gay, or bisexual orientation occurred owing to the larger societal culture of homophobia (Savin-Williams, 1994a). However, according to Remafedi's conceptualization (1987), self-identifying as lesbian, gay, or bisexual is only one of four criteria for defining one's sexual orientation. Remafedi asserts that in addition to self-labeling, an adolescent's sexual orientation is composed of her or his patterns of same-gender sexual attraction, arousal to erotic stimuli, and actual sexual behaviors. Each of these four criteria can then be seen as on a continuum ranging from exclusively opposite-sex to exclusively same-sex (Remafedi, 1987). For purpose of the present chapter, we adopt the conceptualization of Remafedi (1987) as we explore the biological and psychosocial events of the transition to adolescence with a particular focus on the emergence of same-sex sexual orientation and the experiences of lesbian, gay, and bisexual youths.

However, our focus is not on the development of sexual orientation per se but rather on developmental experiences during adolescence that may be relevant to emerging sexual experiences and identity. We have thought of sexual identity formation as "the process of mastering emerging sexual feelings and forming a sense of oneself as a sexual being" (Brooks-Gunn & Graber, 1999, p. 158). We have previously proposed that this process occurs within multiple contexts including intra-personal, interpersonal, and societal contexts (Brooks-Gunn & Graber, 1999). At the intrapersonal level, adolescents are working to integrate their sexual feelings and experiences and sexual identities with the larger, more integrated identity they are forming at this time. At the interpersonal level, sexual identities are also shaped by experiences within relationships with either romantic or sexual partners who may have a direct influence on behavior or by experiences with parents and peers who may shape attitudes, beliefs, and expectations about sexuality. Regulation of adolescent sexual behavior has been a continued societal concern, with most societies seeking to limit and structure the sexual behavior of youths (Brooks-Gunn & Paikoff, 1997); as such, sexual identities are shaped by societal norms, values, and constraints.

Adolescent Transitions

As indicated, the period of adolescence is a particularly important one in the life course for the process of defining or forming a sexual identity. Adolescence is characterized by multiple transitions and developmental challenges. The entry into and exit from adolescence are both developmental periods that have been defined in terms of multiple transitions and role changes. The term "transition" is used repeatedly in adolescent research and in developmental psychology more generally. Transitions are thought to be conceptually distinct from life events in that transitions require reorganization at the structural or functional level (Kagan, 1984; Rutter, 1994). However, many events in the course of development approximate developmental transitions but do not result in reorganizations and/or discontinuities of behavior. Consequently, one might use the term "transition" to include the potential for reorganization and behavioral change rather than only the overt occurrence of such change. In this sense, transitions afford the potential for change for some individuals but need not result in change for all individuals. It is the interaction of personal characteristics with the individual's environment at the time of the transition that predicts whether or not behavior changes and how behavior changes at that transition. Along a similar line, Rutter (1994) has used the term "turning point" to refer to times in life when individuals make key decisions that alter the course of their subsequent development. We have incorporated Rutter's concept of developmental turning points with the concept of transition; the result is a model for adolescent development that emphasizes the importance of developmental transition periods as times that are most likely to actually be turning points for behavior (Graber & Brooks-Gunn, 1996).

Often commensurate with turning points and/or transitions are changes in roles. Part of the process of becoming an adult is defining for oneself what adult roles are and which ones are salient in one's life. Behavioral change is in part motivated by an individual's desire to alter behavior to be in line with his or her perceptions of what it means to be an adolescent or what it means to be an adult. As adolescents define themselves as sexual beings and integrate sexuality into their identities, they behave in ways consistent with their perceptions of what this means. The framework for examining behavioral change at transitions is particularly useful as it highlights developmental possibilities but acknowledges that the nature of the change, or whether change occurs at all, varies by individual. Yet such models have the potential to apply to larger groups of adolescents facing particular developmental challenges.

The transition into adolescence is crucial to the development of sexual behaviors and identities (Katchadourian, 1990). Entry into adolescence is marked by pubertal development, changes in cognitive capacities, changes in school contexts, and changes in relations with family and peers. It is noteworthy that the "sexual" transition (i.e., the process of forming a sexual self) may be shaped by each of the psychological and contextual factors associated with the entry into adolescence.

Although many of these transitions define the early adolescent period, most research on sexuality, either behaviors or beliefs, focuses on the mid- to late adolescent years (Brooks-Gunn & Paikoff, 1997; Katchadourian, 1990). Certainly, preadolescent sexual activity occurs, most often in the form of self-exploration and similar exploratory behaviors with same-sex or other-sex peers. Childhood or early adolescent experiences with same-sex peers are often episodic and are not necessarily indicative of consistent and persistent attraction to same sex peers (Bell, Weinberg, & Hammersmith, 1981). Whereas exploratory behaviors in childhood (e.g., playing doctor with either/both same-sex or opposite sex peers) are more common, sexual behaviors such as intercourse have also been reported in the late childhood years. However, these incidents are often linked to the experience of abuse. There are less common situations where prepubertal intercourse occurs in nonabuse situations (Paikoff, 1995; Moore, Nord & Peterson, 1989).

For most individuals, the hormonal and external changes of puberty that typify the entry into adolescence promote increases in sexual feelings, thoughts, and activities. In this sense, puberty serves as a transition or turning point when sexual identity clearly changes. Lesbian, gay, and bisexual adolescents and adults generally trace their awareness of their sexual orientation to their early-adolescent years (Bell et al., 1981; D' Augelli & Hershberger, 1993; Gibson, 1989; Herdt & Boxer, 1993; Strommen, 1989). While some of these individuals report having had a homosexual experience in their youth, many recall generalized feelings of being different during early adolescence (D'Augelli, 1998; Savin-Williams, 1990; Troiden, 1988). No research to the authors' knowledge has investigated sexual orientation prior to the pubertal transition.

Because of the salience of the pubertal transition to increases in sexual interest and behaviors, as well as to the process of forming a sexual identity, the following section provides an overview of links between puberty and sexuality. These connections are not limited to biological links with behavior but also include the interpersonal and intrapersonal experiences of puberty; that is, the individual and those around him or her respond to the individual's changing physical appearance. Thus, both adolescents and those around her or him have expectations for behavior based on what their own notions of appropriate roles are for an adolescent or for an adult. Expectations for sexual feelings and behaviors are an integral part of both adolescent and adult roles.

Pubertal Development

Pubertal development is not a singular transition but rather a series of interrelated processes that ultimately lead to the attainment of adult reproductive capacity. The physical changes of puberty produce the outward appearance of an individual who can no longer be viewed as a child. The changes in external appearance signal to the adolescent and those around her or him that this person will soon assume adult roles.

Pubertal processes include growth spurts in height and weight, alterations in the distribution of body fat, the development of secondary sexual characteristics (e.g., breasts and pubic hair growth), alterations in cardiovascular functioning, and alterations in the central nervous system regulating pubertal development (Marshall & Tanner, 1986). Pubertal development is controlled by the reproductive endocrine system via the hypothalamus-pituitary-adrenal (HPA) axis and the hypothalamus-pituitary-gonadal (HPG) axis. These systems develop and are active prenatally (and perhaps for a short period postnatally), after which neural pathways and structures are in place but hormone levels drop. The reproductive endocrine system does not seem to be "activated" until mid-childhood and the onset of pubertal development occurs (Grumbach & Styne, 1998; Reiter & Grumbach, 1982). Activation involves increases in sex-steroid hormone secretion (e.g., estrogen and testosterone) through two closely linked but independent processes: (1) adrenarche, or the maturation of the adrenal glands, which results in a rise in adrenal steroids (occurring around age 7), and (2) gonadarche, or the maturation of the testes and ovaries (occurring two years later).

Attainment of reproductive capability is indicated by menarche for girls and spermarche for boys, although continued maturation of the reproductive system occurs after these events. The timing of the onset of development and the rate of progress through puberty vary greatly among individuals. For example, the average age at menarche for white girls in the United States is usually around 12.5–12.8 years of age (Brooks-Gunn & Reiter, 1990; Herman-Giddens et al., 1997). Recent studies have reported that African-American girls are reaching menarche about 6–8 months earlier than their White counterparts (e.g., Herman-Giddens et al., 1997), with Hispanic/

Latina girls falling in between (National Survey of Family Growth, 1997). Very little is known about the extent of variation in timing in boys' pubertal development by race. Within race, there is still enormous variation in pubertal timing. The causes of variation among individuals include nutrition and exercise patterns, hereditary factors, and psychosocial experiences such as stressful emotional contexts (Brooks-Gunn, 1988; Brooks-Gunn & Graber, 1994).

The initial hormonal changes of puberty will be unnoticed by most youths, with the first signs most often being the initial appearance of breast buds for girls or genital growth for boys (Marshall & Tanner, 1986). However, it has often been suggested that these unseen hormonal changes are at the root of changing interest in sexual behavior (e.g., McClintock & Herdt, 1996; Udry, Talbert, & Morris, 1986). Attaining reproductive capacity and having a more adult body do not inherently change the experience of sexual feelings or behaviors. However, individuals may begin to see themselves as sexual beings in response to recognizing signs of maturity. Pleasurable aspects of sexual behavior such as orgasm occur for both boys and girls prepubertally, although the nature of orgasm changes significantly at puberty for boys. Of interest are feelings and behaviors that do change at puberty, such as increased sexual fantasies, increased masturbation, and sexual activities that involve partners. Much of this work focuses on the motivators for sexual behavior (e.g., Udry et al., 1986). Links between pubertal development and sexual behavior and feelings have been made for both hormonal changes and external signs of development.

Hormonal Changes and Sexual Behavior

While increases in hormonal activity have long been cited as the cause for increased interest in sexual activity, if not all behavioral change at adolescence, formal tests of these assertions have only recently begun (Brooks-Gunn, Graber, & Paikoff, 1994). Much of this work has focused on the hormonal correlates of arousal, especially sexual arousal. An extensive literature linking sexual behavior and hormones, specifically androgens, exists for adult behavior. However, this literature has been plagued by the difficulty in ascertaining whether hormones differentiated behavior or behavior affected hormonal activity.

Udry and his colleagues (1986) are perhaps the only group to examine the effects of androgens at the time of their rise at puberty. An initial cross-sectional study of boys found a direct effect of increases in testosterone level on the age of initiation of heterosexual intercourse. Comparable findings were reported for other forms of sexual experiences, including thoughts about sex, masturbation, and sexual arousal by stimuli such as music or books (Udry, Billy, Morris, Groff, & Raj, 1985). Thus, for boys, testosterone has a direct effect on behavior, although the link to behavior appears to be through increased arousal. Effects for girls in this study were quite different, such that nonintercourse sexual behaviors such as masturbation, kissing, and petting were correlated with changes in testosterone; however, heterosexual intercourse was influenced more strongly by social factors such as parental control and peer norms (Udry et al., 1986). Longitudinal examination of these samples suggested that direct hormone-behavior links were not as strong as first thought. That is, having higher testosterone at younger ages for boys resulted in a long-term influence on sexual behavior owing to the social advantage of being more physically mature when one's peers are not (Udry & Campbell, 1994). Overall, for both boys and girls, testosterone seemed to lead to arousal and to some sexual behaviors.

McClintock and Herdt (1996) recently noted that several studies find a sharp increase in sexual attraction around age 10. They hypothesize that this may be the result of increasing adrenal activity associated with adrenarche, specifically increases in dihydroepiandrosterone (DHEA). It should be noted that testosterone rises with adrenarche (from the adrenal glands) prior to maturation of the gonads; thus, identifying a specific hormone that accounts for behavioral change in late childhood is likely premature at this time. Unfortunately, none of the studies reviewed by McClintock and Herdt (1996) examined both hormones and behavior in the same samples. Adrenal hormones begin to increase in girls during the middle childhood years as early as ages 6–7 and about two years later for boys. Hormone and behavior studies are virtually nonexistent for children of this age. It would be quite interesting to ascertain whether increased arousal occurred with girls during these young ages and how such feelings are experienced. Prior reports of "prepubertal" sexual activity in terms of exploration or masturbation may in fact have hormonal components. Girls of this age, especially girls who mature earlier than their peers and have higher hormonal levels at earlier ages than other girls, may be so unprepared—cognitively and emotionally—for feelings of sexual desire and arousal that arousal must be channeled into other affective and behavioral expressions. Thus, an array of individual and contextual factors, such as gender, likely influence how arousal is expressed. Perhaps the strongest conclusion that Udry and others have drawn from the studies to date is that hormonal changes of puberty in and of themselves do not explain individual differences in sexual (or other) behavior.

Controversy exists over the validity of a biological component (incorporating genes and prenatal hormones) of sexual orientation development (DeCecco & Elia, 1993). While evidence supporting a biological component to sexual orientation in adult males has been found (Hamer, Hu, Magnuson, Hu, & Pattatucci, 1993; Levay, 1991), it has also been challenged (Bem, 1996; this volume; Byne & Parsons, 1993). Moreover, no such studies have prospectively investigated sexual development, or included children and adolescents. The chapter by Bem in this volume discusses causal explanations of sexual orientation, and this issue will not be reviewed here. Of note for those concerned with pubertal development and homosexual youth is that, although internal and external physiological changes accompanying the pubertal transition may accelerate same-sex orientation, the accompanying social pressures of these years and the larger society may inhibit the expression of same-sex sexual orientation (D'Augelli, 1998). Similar to experiences described above for some girls who mature earlier than their peers, lesbian, gay, or and bisexual youths may be emotionally and cognitively unprepared for feelings of sexual arousal and desire for same-sex peers. For some of these youths, sexual desire and arousal may be channeled into alternate affective behaviors and expressions, or channeled to activities indicative of heterosexual interest (Savin-Williams, 1994a).

Adolescents' Responses to the Social Signs of Puberty

As indicated, hormonal changes at puberty are not the only causes of changes in sexual feelings and behaviors. The most commonly examined pubertal changes are those that are visible to the adolescent and those around her or him. Changes in secondary sexual characteristics and changes in body shape, distribution of fat and muscle mass, and growth in height all serve as cues to oneself and to others that the change from child to adult is occurring. The significance to the individual of pubertal changes has mainly been studied in the context of whether puberty is viewed as a negative, a positive, or an embarrassing phase of development. Much of this work has centered on girls' experiences of menarche, with few studies of the experience of other aspects of girls' development (Brooks-Gunn & Reiter, 1990). Across cultures, menarche has been posited as a pivotal pubertal event often combined with rites of passage specifically designating the change from child to adult. Individual differences in responses to menarche are associated with the extent to which girls felt prepared for the transition and the timing of the event—factors that are interrelated in that girls who mature earlier are less likely to have been prepared for it (Petersen, 1983; Rierdan & Koff, 1985; Ruble & Brooks-Gunn, 1982). Breast development is one of the more socially observable pubertal changes and appears to elicit responses from others (to be discussed in the next section). Feelings about breast development are also mixed in that many girls report being teased about their development and the teasing causes discomfort (Brooks-Gunn, 1984). Recent work connecting pubertal changes to feelings about sexuality indicates that girls consider many of the physical changes of puberty to be signs of themselves becoming sexual beings. O'Sullivan, Meyer-Bahlburg, and Watkins (in press, b) report that girls use their physical development as a cue for other behaviors such as dating or sexual exploration with partners; there are some indications that girls link pubertal development to feelings of arousal and desire for sexual contact. Virtually no research has considered how girls interpret their changing bodies in connection to sexuality and forming a lesbian or bisexual identity.

    In contrast, much less attention has focused on how boys feel about different aspects of their pubertal development. One of the dilemmas of this research is ascertaining which aspects of puberty are psychologically significant for boys. First ejaculation, like menarche, has been a sign across cultures of adulthood or part of the rite of passage to adulthood (McClintock & Herdt, 1996). In the few studies of first ejaculation, the experience was generally positive for boys (as might be expected) with negative feelings like fear or even surprise being reported less frequently (Gaddis & Brooks-Gunn, 1985). In contrast to the pubertal experiences of girls, first ejaculation experiences had most often not been discussed with parents or peers prior to their occurrence. Virtually no boys report talking about their first ejaculation with anyone, although boys report feeling prepared for the experience. The few boys who cited reasons for their feelings of preparedness stated they had read about the experience in magazines (e.g., *Playboy*) or books.

Understanding how puberty and feelings about one's sexuality develop has not been well explored for boys. As an exception, Savin-Williams (1995) has connected retrospective accounts of pubertal development and sexual experiences in a unique study that not only describes the context of first ejaculation but also the nature of ejaculatory experiences in the junior and senior high school years as adolescent boys made the transition to other sexual activities (i.e., those involving partners). One of the more striking aspects of the study is the documentation of the frequency of masturbation, with a substantial number of young males indicating that they masturbated daily or several times per week. Also of note is that the Savin-Williams study concerned gay and bisexual young adult men, indicating that this is perhaps the only area of development in which more is known about the developmental experiences of gay and bisexual youths than of other youths.

Puberty and Sexuality in Social Context: Parental Responses

Puberty is not experienced only by adolescents but also by their families and peers. The visual signs of development are a stimulus for both parents and other adults to begin to reevaluate their expectations of the adolescent's behavior. As adolescents go through puberty they begin to seek greater independence from adults and are expected to take on greater responsibilities in preparation for the transition to adulthood. Physical maturation also cues parents that the child is becoming a sexual being. However, while parents acknowledge and accept puberty as a potentially tumultuous period of development for adolescents, they rarely acknowledge or accept an adolescent's transition into sexual behavior. Although experiencing heterosexual intercourse by age 18 appears to be normative for many if not most adolescents, parental responses to it are often in contrast to this fact (Graber, Brooks-Gunn, & Galen, 1998). Given the polarization of the reality of the adolescent's world and parental beliefs and expectations, parent-adolescent relationships may involve significant change around this transition.

Numerous studies have shown that parent-child conflict increases during the pubertal years (Paikoff & Brooks-Gunn, 1991), peaking at around mid-puberty (Steinberg, 1987). The focus of the increased conflict is often household responsibilities and rules, with adolescents seeking more involvement in establishing guidelines for their behavior. Observational study of the content and nature of mother-daughter conflict indicates that dating and staying out late are common sources of conflict for mothers and postpubertal daughters (Brooks-Gunn & Zahaykevich, 1989). In these discussions, daughters sought greater freedom in regulating their own social behaviors while mothers endeavored to maintain control, with particular attention to the supervision and restriction of potential sexual situations. Whereas this work infers that relational changes between mothers and daughters are in part the result of puberty and its link to sexual behavior, O'Sullivan and her colleagues (in press, a) provide more direct evidence of the meaning of girls' development to their mothers. In focus groups with African-American and Latina women, mothers very strongly indicated an increased monitoring of their daughters after menarche. Some mothers felt that their daughters were not as mature psychologically as they were physically. Mothers were also concerned about the attention that the girls received from older boys who might take advantage of their daughters' naiveté.

Such concerns on the part of parents are not unfounded, in that many adolescents are engaging in sexual behaviors. In fact, Rodgers (1996) reports that the majority of adolescents, regardless of their ethnic background or gender, have intercourse for the first time either in their own home or in the home of their partner. Presumably, the couple's parents are unaware of this activity. However, supervision and restriction are not the only mechanisms through which parents shape the development of adolescent sexuality in the early and mid-adolescent years. Parents also influence sexual attitudes and often the timing of initiation of sexual activity during adolescence (Brooks-Gunn & Furstenberg, 1989). Parental influence is exerted through several avenues. First, many parents do discuss sexual behaviors and sexuality with their adolescents, although both parents and adolescents report feeling uncomfortable with these topics (Hofferth & Hayes, 1987). However, in their discussions of sexuality, few parents discuss sexual orientation, assuming that their adolescent is heterosexual and/or perhaps fearing that discussing same-sex or bisexual orientation would lead to the encouragement of such expressions. Reports on how parents and adolescents feel about discussing sexuality are strikingly similar to reports on how parents and adolescents feel about discussing puberty. Second, families transmit value systems such as religious beliefs that also serve to regulate behavior, although it is clear that despite adolescents' endorsement of basic value systems these beliefs may not be the most salient factors in determining their behavior (Devany & Hubley, 1981). Third, parents may model sexual behaviors. Burton, Allison, and Obeidallah (1995) found that for some single mothers who are dating, discussions with daughters about dating and related behaviors seem more characteristic of discussions that young women might have with peers than with their daughters; in some cases, mothers who are dating may be modeling less healthy sexual choices. Modeling of sexual behaviors by parents seldom occurs for lesbian and gay adolescents, as these youths rarely have parents who provide role models for the adolescents' emerging behavior (Krystal, 1987). Finally, the quality of parent-adolescent relationships clearly influences adolescent sexual behavior as well as other behaviors and adjustment. The positive effects of warm and supportive parent-child relationships, especially when coupled with structured behavioral guidelines and controls, have been documented across childhood and adolescence and likely exist across the life span (Steinberg, 1987). In contrast, the absence of warmth and acceptance from parents predicts the development of unhealthy behaviors.

Unfortunately for adolescents who are developing a gay, lesbian, or bisexual identity, parent-adolescent and family relationships, as a whole, are frequently characterized by negative interactions, intolerance, and rejection. Rotheram-Borus, Hunter, and Rosario (1994) reported that some of the most common gay-related stressors were being discovered as gay by parents or siblings and coming out to parents and siblings. Parents typically respond negatively to their adolescent's disclosure of lesbian, gay or bisexual orientation (Cramer & Roach, 1988; Strommen, 1989), and families often experience periods of disruption or turmoil following disclosure (Boxer, Cook, & Herdt, 1991). In a study of lesbian, gay, and bisexual youths and their families, D'Augelli and Hershberger (1993) found that only 11% of these adolescents received positive parental responses after disclosing their sexual orientation to parents. A number of lesbian, gay, and bisexual adolescents are verbally and/or physically assaulted by family members because of their sexual orientation. Pilkington and D'Augelli (1995) found that over a third of their lesbian, gay, or bisexual youths had been verbally assaulted by a family member because of their sexual orientation. Ten percent of the adolescents in this sample had been physically assaulted by a family member. The extremely negative family relationships—those that involve abuse, neglect, or rejection—may result in adolescent homelessness and emotional and physical health risk (e.g., Rotheram-Borus et al., 1994; Savin-Williams, 1994b).

As noted earlier, most parents are not pleased with facing the realities of their children's developing sexuality. The extreme responses encountered by gay, lesbian, and bisexual youths may fall at one end of a continuum of behavior; a better understanding of the range of factors associated with parental responses to sexuality is needed for helping all parents cope with this transition.

Puberty and Sexuality in Social Context: Peer Responses

Parallel to the range of ways in which parents respond to puberty and shape the development of sexuality in the pubertal and postpubertal years are peer responses to an adolescent's changing form. More important, same-age peers are usually the partners with whom adolescents explore and engage in sexual behavior. During the entry into adolescence peer relations demonstrate several positive changes, as exemplified through the expression and understanding of intimacy, mutual understanding, and equality in relationships (Youniss, 1980). Girls frequently discuss their developmental and sexual experiences with close female friends (Simon, Eder, & Evans, 1992). These interactions are a mechanism for obtaining support and reassurance, but also for learning group norms for behavior. For boys, it is clear that they do not discuss pubertal development among themselves (Gaddis & Brooks-Gunn, 1985). The development of intimacy in boys' relationships more often centers on shared interests and activities rather than through the discussion of feelings or experiences (Camarena, Sarigiani, & Petersen, 1990).

PEER GROUP INFLUENCES

Despite the many healthy interactions that positive peer relationships can afford in adolescence (and across life), the larger peer environment also has the potential to impart negative messages to adolescents that in turn influence sexual attitudes and behaviors. Orenstein (1994), in the book *School Girls*, documents the day-to-day experiences of adolescent girls attending two middle schools in California. Although Orenstein is a journalist with an investigative agenda rather than an ethnographer or researcher, the descriptions of the two school environments and comments from young adolescent girls provide a window onto the daily experience of girls in the larger peer environment. For purposes of the present chapter, there are two striking themes that emerge from this work. First, girls' pubertal development is a stimulus for sexual comments by peers, both by other girls and by boys. Second, these comments often have a very negative connotation. For example, physical changes of puberty such as breast development were a source of teasing, harassment, and actual assault of girls by boys in their classes. One of the girls describes her experiences in gym class, where she had frequently been taunted about her breast development: "The boys began to walk by . . . , their hands cupped a few inches away from their chests, . . . saying, 'You've got competition, Jeanie. Connie is bigger than you are, but we'll always remember that you're second!' A few days later, one of the boys reached out and grabbed Jeanie's breasts" (Orenstein, 1994, p. 112).

In addition to obtaining reports from girls, Orenstein personally observed boys grabbing girls' thighs, rears, and breasts; these events are taking place not only in hallways between classes or at lunch when supervision is low but during English and Math classes. Orenstein and others (American Association of University Women, 1993) have observed that African-American and Latina girls are more likely to respond to harassment with both verbal and physical aggression (e.g., name calling or slapping) whereas white, middle-class girls rarely defend themselves.

Such activities combine aggressive and sexual elements and commonly play out as traditional scripts for gender-appropriate behavior. This group behavior reinforces what is perceived to be gender-appropriate behavior in sexual experiences and, as such, could be similar to the types of taunting and harassment of adolescents whose sexual orientation has come into question. Rein-forcement of sexual norms is not limited to boy-girl interactions; same-sex adolescents also frequently use sexual derogations in their interactions with one another. In Orenstein's discussions with girls, some girls made it a point to identify which of their classmates were "sluts." Name calling in connec-tion to sexual orientation (e.g., "fag," "dyke") is also common among children and adolescents, indicating the strength of homophobia and negative stereo-typing that still pervades U.S. culture (Savin-Williams, 1994a, b). Name call-ing also clearly marks the expression of same-sex interests as nonnormative and subject to verbal and physical sanction. Of course, being harassed about engagement in behaviors that are not considered appropriate by group stan-dards (e.g., being called a fag or slut) need not be based on an adolescents' actual behavior or identification of a particular orientation. Whether or not labels correspond to youths' behavior patterns, their derogatory quality rein-forces norms and creates a climate that may discourage meaningful discus-sions about sexuality among peers for fear of harassment and abuse.

Therefore, the peer and greater societal culture of homophobia make it difficult for adolescents to label themselves as nonheterosexual, for fear of harassment and peer rejection (Savin-Williams, 1994b). Unfortunately, these fears are not unfounded. In a study of gay and lesbian adults, Gross, Aurand, and Addessa (1988) found that 50% of their male sample reported verbal or physical assaults because of their sexual orientation in junior high school; rates of abuse increased in high school. Twelve percent of the les-bians sampled reported being verbally or physically assaulted in junior high school, while 21% of lesbians reported being assaulted in high school owing to their sexual orientation.

Peer relationships can be particularly difficult and/or complicated for lesbian, gay, and bisexual adolescents, beyond those that involve direct peer harassment. In detailing some of these challenges, Savin-Williams (1994a) notes that some of lesbian, gay, and bisexual adolescents reported fear of developing close, same-sex, platonic friendships. There can be anxiety over the larger peer group's discovering an adolescent's sexual orientation. Simi-larly, there may be a fear of appearing "overly friendly" or having platonic feelings misinterpreted as romantic interest. If feelings become stronger for once-platonic friends, adolescents may terminate the friendship as opposed to making the feelings known for fear of rejection. Adolescents might also terminate the relationship when feelings become more intense in order to attempt to disconfirm their own uncertainties about their same-sex orienta-tion. In response to these challenges, lesbian, gay, and bisexual adolescents may seek out opposite-sex friendships in the expectation that they will be easier or less risky. Having opposite-sex friends can help a lesbian, gay, or bisexual adolescent appear heterosexual to the larger peer group, thus avoid-ing harassment or ostracism (Savin-Williams, 1994a).

During the young adolescent years, and within these peer groups, many individuals begin to engage in dating behaviors and further exploration of sexual activities. Connolly and Goldberg (1999) have noted that, much like close friendships, initial romantic relationships of adolescents are affiliative in nature, providing companionship and a sense of belongingness, and potentially social status. As suggested, adolescent girls appear to develop their concepts of both sexual behavior and romance through discussions with their close friends (Simon et al., 1992). These discussions occur in the larger contexts of family, media, and culture. Hence, intimacy is acquired in close friendships and these relationships form a basis for constructing a concept of romantic relations that integrates physical and emotional desires. Some adolescents form romantic relationships that involve minimal sexual experiences, whereas other adolescents form sexual relationships that provide little emotional connection (Graber, Britto, & Brooks-Gunn, 1999).

A common mechanism for forming either sexual or romantic relationships is dating. However, despite indications that dating and/or romantic relationships may fulfill affiliative needs for some adolescents, these early experiences do not necessarily promote healthy development for all adolescents. Managing a physical and/or romantic relationship can be particularly challenging especially when this activity coincides with other developmental challenges (e.g., puberty). By mid-adolescence, romantic relationships may have even stronger effects on adolescent well-being. Many adolescents, both boys and girls, report that breaking up with a partner led to the onset of a depressive episode (Hammen, 2000). For adolescents who have experienced high levels of rejection with parents during childhood, the transition into dating may be particularly challenging (Downey, Rincon, & Bonica, 1999). In general, poorer social skills prior to adolescence will likely be exacerbated by the demands of forming romantic relationships that include both physical and emotional intimacy.

Dating and/or romantic relationships are no less complicated for lesbian, gay, and bisexual adolescents. While dating affords many adolescents time and context to practice and experiment with sexual relationships and companionship (Feiring, 1996), lesbian, gay, and bisexual adolescents have less opportunity for dating and romantic relationships with those individuals to whom they are most attracted. Lesbian, gay, and bisexual adolescents frequently date members of the opposite sex, engaging in same-sex dating less frequently, if at all (D'Augelli, 1991; Herdt & Boxer, 1993; Remafedi, 1987; Savin-Williams, 1990, 1994a). Heterosexual dating may serve to hide a lesbian, gay, or bisexual adolescent's orientation from others. These experiences can also serve to validate or invalidate feelings of hetero- or homosexual interests (Diamond, 1998; Herdt & Boxer, 1993; Savin-Williams, 1994a).

Studies have also shown that a number of lesbian, gay, and bisexual adolescents engage in heterosexual sexual behavior (D'Augelli, 1991; Diamond, 1998; Herdt & Boxer, 1993; Remafedi, 1987; Savin-Williams, 1990, 1994a). These sexual experiences may not always occur within the context of romantic relationships, a situation that is not atypical of adolescent sexual behavior, in general. Importantly, same-sex dating is constrained by the availability of accessible peer partners. Even if adolescents have acknowledged their same-sex sexual interests, it is difficult to find others who are not only out to themselves but are also willing to admit their orientation or interests to others. Further, as many adolescents are still questioning their feelings, any positive feelings derived from same-sex dating or sexual experiences might be coupled with feelings of guilt and/or confusion (Savin-Williams, 1994a). (See Dubé, Savin-Williams, & Diamond, this volume, for a detailed discussion of romantic relationship issues.)

Forming a Sexual Identity

We have taken the position that changes in sexual behavior during the transition to adolescence and beyond are in part stimulated by pubertal development, as well as by the changes in the adolescent's social environment. Clearly, changing parental and peer relationships, as well as changes in physical form, are interconnected experiences for young adolescents. As adolescents reflect upon these experiences and try to make sense of their emerging sexuality, they are also forming a sexual identity. Development of a coherent identity has long been considered a primary activity of each adolescent (Erikson, 1968) and forming a sense of self is shaped by the factors we have discussed thus far—pubertal development, family and peer interactions—but also by factors that we have not reviewed here (e.g., cognitive and social cognitive changes at adolescence). Formation of a coherent identity has often been conceptualized as forming many identities and integrating them into an overarching notions of self (Baumeister, 1998; Markus & Cross, 1990). As adolescents explore new roles and anticipate taking on the role of adults, they define and redefine the identities that go along with these roles. This developmental process is associated with developmental changes that form the transition into adolescence, such as the increased cognitive ability to think of oneself in the future (Lewin, 1939), better decision-making skills, increased independence from parents and self-regulation of behavior, more intimate relationships with peers, and attainment of the physical appearance of an adult. Researchers are beginning to define sexual identity as one domain of the adolescent's identity, rather than just using the term to refer to sexual orientation, or preferences for same-sex or opposite-sex partners.

Recent work by Rosenthal and her colleagues (Buzzwell & Rosenthal, 1996; Moore & Rosenthal, 1993) has employed this approach to articulate a multi-faceted approach to sexual identity. They propose that sexual identity is composed of three components: (1) sexual self-esteem, (2) sexual self-efficacy, and (3) sexual attitudes. Sexual self-esteem includes feelings about one's attractiveness to others, perceptions of the adequacy of one's sexual behaviors with a partner, and feelings about one's body. Sexual self-efficacy involves feelings of confidence in sexual situations, ranging from confidence in being able to refuse sexual activity, to use a condom effectively, to making sexual requests of a partner. Sexual attitudes include arousal, interests in exploring different sexual behaviors, anxiety, and commitment in a sexual relationship.

Five identity patterns emerged from this research: Sexually Idealistic, Sexually Unassured, Sexually Competent, Sexually Adventurous, and Sexually Driven. Groups tended to vary by age, gender, sexual efficacy, arousal, and esteem. Idealistic and Unassured youths were younger and more likely to be virgins. Sexually Competent youths were to be older, more likely to have had sexual experiences, and had high sexual self-esteem and sexual self-efficacy, and intermediate attitudes toward exploration, arousal, and commitment. The Adventurous youths tended to be older males with high sexual self-efficacy, sexual self-esteem, arousal levels, and interest in exploration. Individuals in this group were also the most likely group to report having had a same-sex sexual experience (14%). The smallest group, the Sexually Driven cluster, was most likely to be males who reported great difficulty in refusing unwanted sexual activity, had the lowest sexual anxiety and sexual commitment scores, and had the highest sexual arousal and exploration scores. Although some of the groups had higher percentages of older versus younger adolescents, boys versus girls, or virgins versus nonvirgins, each group included some virgins, adolescents of both genders, and youths of different ages. Although most adolescents identified as heterosexual, each group contained youths who were unsure of their sexual orientation, and some who considered themselves heterosexual but had had a same-sex sexual experience. Adolescents who identified themselves as gay or lesbian were found only in the Sexually Unassured and Sexually Competent groups.

The approach taken by Buzwell and Rosenthal (1996) is particularly valuable in that it describes different groups of youths, all of whom may react quite differently to sexual situations and may have somewhat different motivations for having sex. The findings also highlight some of the comparability or commonality of sexual identities among youths regardless of emerging sexual orientation. Youths may be struggling with many of the same sexual issues, most prominently the development of self-efficacy in expressing sexual desires and in managing sexual relationships. This conceptual approach to the study of adolescent sexuality is appealing as it moves beyond simple categorization into orientation groups and considers issues that are likely salient to all youths.

Considerations for a Better Understanding of Youth

As has been reiterated throughout this chapter and by others, lesbian, gay, and bisexual adolescents share more developmental experiences and challenges with their heterosexual counterparts than is often recognized. As indicated, adolescence is a time of challenge for all youths. The strain of developmental challenge in the adolescent decade is exemplified by, among other things, dramatic increases in the rates of depression, eating disorders, and conduct disorders during adolescence (Colten & Gore, 1991). Clearly, many youths have difficulty coping with the multiple challenges they face regardless of their emerging sexual identities.

Unfortunately, experiences that tend to distinguish lesbian, gay, and bisexual adolescents from other youths are often experiences that provide even greater challenges for these youths. For example, as we have noted, parent-child relationships undergo changes during adolescence with periods of increased conflict. For most youths, the conflict happens in the context of continued warmth and support. In contrast, lesbian, gay, and bisexual youths may lack parental support and have potentially more challenging relationships with parents. Also, lesbian, gay, and bisexual adolescents have less opportunity to explore and develop dating and intimate relationships. The truncation of opportunity for the more normative experience (e.g., going out on a date) influences the adolescent's ability to engage in safer sexual experimentation. Without such opportunities, some youths may be making less healthy choices and increasing their risk for serious health concerns such as HIV infection (see Grossman, this volume).

These challenges for lesbian, gay, and bisexual youths highlight the need for comprehensive and developmentally appropriate programs and interventions not only for lesbian, gay, and bisexual adolescents but also for heterosexual youth who form the larger peer context. Perhaps the most difficult hurdle to overcome is not implementation of programming that provides support and resources to lesbian, gay, and bisexual adolescents, but the initiation of prevention efforts that reduce the culture of homophobia in schools and increase awareness about lesbian, gay, and bisexual issues. One logical place to integrate information would be into existing school-based programs on sexuality. In addition, support programs for lesbian, gay, and bisexual youths and their parents might be implemented in schools and in other community settings (see Ryan, this volume). Such suggestions are certainly not new to those experienced in this area. What we have found to be most enlightening is the response of others when such suggestions are made. In discussions of this chapter with colleagues, the most common response was that the integration of lesbian, gay, and bisexual issues into school-based programming was idealistic, if not completely unrealistic. Given that the quality of current school programs addressing adolescent sexuality issues is abysmal, with few programs addressing any relevant developmental issues or consideration of sexual feelings and beliefs, it is not surprising that we received such a response. However, these discussions highlight the impediments that those who work with and/or study adolescents face, especially if they have an interest in addressing the development of diverse groups of youths rather than just a subset of adolescents.

One of the challenges is finding methodologies that are feasible and provide useful information in the pursuit of a better understanding of adolescent sexuality. Research that focuses exclusively on lesbian, gay, and bisexual youths has often lacked a longitudinal component and may not have been particularly comparable to other developmental studies. It can be assumed that of the longitudinal studies of adolescent development that were instituted over the past 20 years all included some lesbian, gay, and bisexual youths. However, very few of these studies have ever reported the developmental experiences of these youths either independent of or in comparison to the rest of the sample. Efforts by Petersen, Leffert, and Graham (1995) to conduct such analyses were greatly limited by an extremely small subsample of youths who acknowledged they were not exclusively heterosexual.

Why is it so difficult to find these youths in existing or even newly begun studies? There are certainly more reasons than can be covered here, but we will highlight a few that may speak more to developmental scientists. The most obvious reason that lesbian, gay, and bisexual individuals are unidentified in these studies is that the questions that would identify them are never asked (Savin-Williams, 1998). As indicated above, when asked at all, inquiries about sexual orientation may be limited to a single question asked only once the adolescent has reached adulthood (e.g., Petersen et al., 1995). Individuals who go through a period of questioning and experimentation are missed completely, as are individuals who have not self-identified in a manner that would fit the "single-question" approach.

The next obvious question is why a more comprehensive set of questions are not being asked. Most researchers would likely assume that inclusion of such questions would not be feasible. Clearly, issues of homosexuality or bisexuality are typically not embedded within studies of "normal" development because of broad-based homophobia and reluctance to confront that homophobia. Schools often do not want researchers to ask questions about sexuality in the first place, and would be even more resistant to questions about lesbian, gay, and bisexual issues. If these issues are not perceived as central to the study, or even the primary focus of the study, the questions may be quickly dropped to avoid rejection of the study by school administrators. Fear of including questions targeting lesbian or gay experiences or feelings in non-school-based studies of families also occurs for much the same reason; it is believed that families, or even adolescents themselves, may be offended by such questions and will not participate if such questions are included. Again, the pervasiveness of homophobia in the United States supports these fears. Fortunately, there is an emerging group of researchers who have successfully overcome these biases not only in research in school settings (e.g., Remafedi et al., 1992) but also in implementation of school-based programming (e.g., Ryan, this volume).

The barriers faced in conducting research on sexual orientation are the same as were once faced when developmental researchers began to investigate the psychosocial experience of puberty. Brooks-Gunn (1990) indicated that she worked with the Girl Scouts and private girls' schools in her early studies specifically because these organizations were willing to accept the discussion of pubertal development at a time when public schools were not. In order to work with public schools, Petersen and colleagues (1988) created a noninvasive measure of puberty that has subsequently been used extensively in large school-based studies of early adolescence (see Graber, Petersen, & Brooks-Gunn, 1996, for a review of measurement issues). Presently, many researchers who may not consider puberty a primary interest or area of expertise have become aware of its importance and now include at least some simple measures of this construct in their protocols. Thus, creative individuals have successfully dealt with barriers in the goal of having a better, more comprehensive understanding of adolescent development and experiences.

Barriers are not insurmountable for developmental scientists who have become aware that they are overlooking the experiences of a subset of their samples, but research innovations need be commensurate with initiatives that decrease homophobia (among youths, parents, and schools). In order for meaningful progress to occur a broader group of researchers needs to test the water to explore different contexts in which relevant questions can be integrated into a study design. At the same time, those with an expertise in the development of sexual orientation need to develop an array of measures that can be used under different circumstances. For example, we have often been asked to recommend a "good but quick" measure of puberty. Although we may not personally conduct research with such minimalistic approaches, we have often provided a list of measures and under what circumstances each is best, as well as a recommendation for the minimum questions that should be included to make it worthwhile. Recommendations made by Gonsiorek, Sell, and Weinrich (1995) regarding the use of the Sell Scale of Sexual Orientation fit this model of collegial advice; it should be noted that their "minimal" assessment is still seven questions long. Another approach is to form collaborative efforts across studies to answer questions relevant to both types of investigations. For example, protocol commonalities in studies of lesbian, gay, and bisexual youths and school-based sample studies can be created or may already exist; such commonalities would be the basis for collaborative analyses.

These and other approaches for research also speak to the barriers to prevention or health promotion programming alluded to previously. Achieving a better understanding of youth and sexuality in general can promote healthier adolescent development for all youths. As such, this goal need not be only the concern of a small group who focus solely on lesbian, gay, and bisexual youths, but of the larger group of developmental scientists.

References

American Association of University Women Educational Foundation (1993). *Hostile hallways: The AAUW survey on sexual harassment in America's schools.* Washington, DC: American Association of University Women.

Baumeister, R. F. (1998). The self. In D. Gilber, S. Fiske, & G. Lindzey (Eds.), *Handbook of social psychology* (4th ed., pp. 680–740). New York: McGraw-Hill.

Bell, A., Weinberg, M., & Hammersmith, S. (1981). *Sexual preference: Its development in men and women.* Bloomington, IN: Indiana University Press.

Bem, D. J. (1996). Exotic becomes erotic: A developmental theory of sexual orientation. *Psychological Review, 103,* 320–335.

Boxer, A. M., Cook, J. A., & Herdt, G. (1991). Double jeopardy: Identity transitions and parent-child relations among gay and lesbian youth. In K. Pillemer & K. McCartney (Eds.), *Parent-child relations throughout life* (pp. 59–92). Hillsdale, NJ: Erlbaum.

Brooks-Gunn, J. (1984). The psychological significance of different pubertal events to young girls. *Journal of Early Adolescence, 4,* 315–327.

Brooks-Gunn, J. (1988). Antecedents and consequences of variations in girls' maturational timing. *Journal of Adolescent Health Care, 9*(5), 365–373.

Brooks-Gunn, J. (1990). Overcoming barriers to adolescent research on pubertal and reproductive development. *Journal of Youth and Adolescence, 19*(5), 425–440.

Brooks-Gunn, J., & Furstenberg, F. F., Jr. (1989). Adolescent sexual behavior. *American Psychologist, 44*(2), 249–257.

Brooks-Gunn, J., & Graber, J. A. (1994). Puberty as a biological and social event: Implications for research on pharmacology. *Journal of Adolescent Health, 15*(8), 663–671.

Brooks-Gunn, J., & Graber, J. A. (1999). What's sex got to do with it? The development of health and sexual identities during adolescence. In R. J. Contrada & R. D. Ashmore (Eds.), *Self, social identity, and physical health: Interdisciplinary explorations* (pp. 155–182). New York: Oxford University Press.

Brooks-Gunn, J., Graber, J. A., & Paikoff, R. L. (1994). Studying links between hormones and negative affect: Models and measures. *Journal of Research on Adolescence, 4*(4), 469–486.

Brooks-Gunn, J., & Paikoff, R. L. (1997). Sexuality and developmental transitions during adolescence. In J. Schulenberg, J. Maggs, & K. Hurrelmann (Eds.), *Health risks and developmental transitions during adolescence* (pp. 190–219). New York: Cambridge University Press.

Brooks-Gunn, J., & Reiter, E. O. (1990). The role of pubertal processes. In S. Feldman & G. Elliot (Eds.), *At the threshold: The developing adolescent* (pp. 16–53). Cambridge, MA: Harvard University Press.

Brooks-Gunn, J., & Zahaykevich, M. (1989). Parent-daughter relationships in early adolescence: A developmental perspective. In K. Kreppner & R. M. Lerner (Eds.), *Family systems and life-span development* (pp. 223–246). Hillsdale, NJ: Erlbaum.

Burton, L. M., Allison, K. W., & Obeidallah, D. (1995). Social context and adolescence: Perspectives on development among inner-city African-American teens. In L. J. Crockett & A. C. Crouter (Eds.), *Pathways through adolescence: Individual development in relation to social contexts* (pp. 119–138). Mahwah, NJ: Erlbaum.

Buzwell, S., & Rosenthal, D. (1996). Constructing a sexual self: Adolescents' sexual self-perceptions and sexual risk-taking. *Journal of Research on Adolescence*, 6(4), 489–513.

Byne, W., & Parsons, B. (1993). Human sexual orientation: The biologic theories reappraised. *Archives of General Psychiatry*, 50, 228–239.

Camarena, P. M., Sarigiani, P. A., & Petersen, A. C. (1990). Gender specific pathways to intimacy in early-adolescence. *Journal of Youth and Adolescence*, 19, 19–32.

Colten, M. E., & Gore, S. (Eds.). (1991). *Adolescent stress: Causes and consequences.* New York: Aldine de Gruyter.

Connolly, J., & Goldberg, A. (1999). Romantic relationships in adolescence: The role of peers in their emergence and development. In W. Furman, B. B. Brown, & C. Feiring (Eds.), *Contemporary perspectives on adolescent relationships* (pp. 266–290). New York: Cambridge University Press.

Cramer, D. W., & Roach, A. J. (1988). Coming out to Mom and Dad: A study of gay males and their relationships with their parents. *Journal of Homosexuality*, 15, 79–92.

D'Augelli, A. R. (1991). Gay men in college: Identity processes and adaptations. *Journal of College Student Development*, 32, 140–146.

D'Augelli, A. R. (1998). Enhancing the development of lesbian, gay, and bisexual youths. In E. D. Rothblum and L. A. Bond (Eds.), *Preventing heterosexism and homophobia* (pp. 124–150). Thousand Oaks, CA: Sage.

D'Augelli, A. R., & Hershberger, S. L. (1993). Lesbian, gay, and bisexual youth in community settings: Personal challenges and mental health problems. *American Journal of Community Psychology*, 21, 421–448.

De Cecco, J. P., & Elia, J. P. (Eds.). (1993). *If you seduce a straight person, can you make them gay? Issues in biological essentialism versus social constructionism in gay and lesbian identities.* New York: Harrington Park Press.

Deisher, R. W. (1989). Adolescent homosexuality: Preface. In G. Herdt (Ed.), *Gay and lesbian youth* (pp. xiii–xv). New York: Haworth.

Devaney, B. L., & Hubley, K. S. (1981). *The determinants of adolescent pregnancy and childbearing.* Final report to the National Institute of Child Health and Human Development. Washington, DC: Mathemetica Policy Research.

Diamond, L. M. (1998). Development of sexual orientation among adolescent and young adult women. *Developmental Psychology*, 14, 1085–1095.

Downey, G., Rincon, C., & Bonica, C. (1999). Rejection sensitivity and adolescent romantic relationships. In W. Furman, B. B. Brown, & C. Feiring (Eds.), *Contemporary perspectives on adolescent relationships* (pp. 148–174). New York: Cambridge University Press.

Erikson, E. H. (1968). *Identity youth and crisis.* New York: W. W. Norton.

Feiring, C. (1996). Concepts of romance in 15-year-old adolescents. *Journal of Research on Adolescence*, 6, 181–200.

Gaddis, A., & Brooks-Gunn, J. (1985). The male experience of pubertal change. *Journal of Youth and Adolescence*, 14, 61–69.

Gibson, P. (1989). *Gay male and lesbian youth suicide.* United States Department of Health and Human Services Report to the Secretary's Task Force on Youth Suicide. Washington, DC: Department of Health and Human Services.

Gonsiorek, J. C., Sell, R. L., & Weinrich, J. D. (1995). Definition and measurement of sexual orientation. *Suicide and Life-Threatening Behavior*, 25, 40–51.

Graber, J. A., Britto, P. R., & Brooks-Gunn, J. (1999). What's love got to do with it? Adolescents' and young adults' beliefs about intimate relationships. In W. Furman, B. B. Brown, & C. Feiring (Eds.), *Contemporary perspectives on adolescent relationships* (pp. 364–395). New York: Cambridge University Press.

Graber, J. A., & Brooks-Gunn, J. (1995). Models of development: Understanding risk in adolescence. *Suicide and Life-Threatening Behavior, 25*, 18–25.

Graber, J. A., & Brooks-Gunn, J. (1996). Transitions and turning points: Navigating the passage from childhood through adolescence. *Developmental Psychology, 32*(4), 768–776.

Graber, J. A., Brooks-Gunn, J., & Galen, B. R. (1998). Betwixt and between: Sexuality in the context of adolescent transitions. In R. Jessor (Ed.), *New perspectives on adolescent risk behavior* (pp. 270–316). New York: Cambridge University Press.

Graber, J. A., Petersen, A. C., & Brooks-Gunn, J. (1996). Pubertal processes: Methods, measures and models. In J. A. Graber, J. Brooks-Gunn, & A. C. Petersen (Eds.), *Transitions through adolescence: Interpersonal domains and context* (pp. 23–53). Hillsdale, NJ: Erlbaum.

Gross, L., Aurand, S., & Addessa, R. (1988). *Violence and discrimination against lesbian, and gay people in Philadelphia and the Commonwealth of Philadelphia*. Philadelphia: Philadelphia Lesbian and Gay Task Force.

Grumbach, M. M., & Styne, D. M. (1998). Puberty: Ontogeny, neuroendocrinology, physiology, and disorders. In J. D. Wilson, D. W. Fostor, & H. M. Kronenberg (Eds.), *Williams textbook of endocrinology* (pp. 1509–1625). Philadelphia: W. B. Saunders.

Hamer, D. H., Hu, S., Magnuson, V. L., Hu, N., & Pattatucci, A. M. L. (1993). A linkage between DNA markers on the X chromosome and male sexual orientation. *Science, 261*, 321–327.

Hammen, C. (2000). Interpersonal factors in an emerging developmental model of depression. In S. L. Johnson, A. M. Hayes, T. M. Field, N. Schneiderman, & P. M. McCabe (Eds.), *Stress, coping, and depression* (pp. 71–88). Mahwah, NJ: Erlbaum.

Herdt, G., & Boxer, A. M. (1993). *Children of Horizons: How gay and lesbian teens are leading a new way out of the closet*. Boston: Beacon.

Herman-Giddens, M. E., Slora, E. J., Wasserman, R. C., Bourdony, C. J., Bhapkar, M. V., Koch, G. G., & Hasemeier, C. M. (1997). Secondary sexual characteristics and menses in young girls seen in office practice: A study from the Pediatric Research in Office Settings Network. *Pediatrics, 99*(4), 505–511.

Hofferth, S. L., & Hayes, C. D. (1987) *Risking the future: Adolescent sexuality, pregnancy, and childbearing*. Washington, DC: National Academy Press.

Kagan, J. (1984). *The nature of the child*. New York: Basic Books.

Katchadourian, H. (1990). Sexuality. In S. Feldman & G. Elliot (Eds.), *At the threshold: The developing adolescent* (pp. 330–351). Cambridge, MA: Harvard University Press.

Krystal, G. J. (1987). A very silent gay minority. *The School Counselor, 34*, 304–307.

Levay, S. (1991). A difference in the hypothalamic structure between heterosexual and homosexual men. *Science, 253*, 1034–1037.

Lewin, K. (1939). The field theory approach to adolescence. *American Journal of Sociology, 44*, 868–897.

Markus, H., & Cross, S. (1990). The interpersonal self. In L. A. Previn (Ed.), *Handbook of personality: Theory and research* (pp. 576–608). New York: Guilford Press.

Marshall, W. A., & Tanner, J. M. (1986). Puberty. In F. Falkner & J. M. Tanner (Eds.), *Human growth: Postnatal growth neurobiology* (Vol. 2, pp. 171–209). New York: Plenum.

McClintock, M., & Herdt, G. (1996). Rethinking puberty: The development of sexual attraction. *Current Directions in Psychological Science, 5,* 178–183.

Moore, K. A., Nord, C. W., & Peterson, J. L. (1989). Nonvoluntary sexual activity among adolescents. *Family Planning Perspectives, 21,* 110–114.

Moore, S., & Rosenthal, D. (1993). *Sexuality in adolescence.* New York: Routledge.

National Survey of Family Growth (1997). Fertility, family planning, and women's health: New data from the 1995 national survey of family growth. *Vital and Health Statistics, Series 23.* Hyattsville, MD: Department of Health and Human Services.

Orenstein, P. (1994). *School girls: Young women, self-esteem, and the confidence gap.* New York: Doubleday.

O'Sullivan, L. F., Meyer-Bahlburg, H. F. L., & Watkins, B. X. (in press, a). A qualitative study of mother-daughter communication about sex among urban, low-income, African-American and Latina families. *Journal of Adolescent Research.*

O'Sullivan, L. F., Meyer-Bahlburg, H. F. L., & Watkins, B. X. (in press, b). Social cognitions associated with pubertal development in a sample of urban, low-income, African-American and Latina girls. *Journal of Adolescent Health.*

Paikoff, R. L. (1995). Early heterosexual debut: Situations of sexual possibility during the transition to adolescence. *American Journal of Orthopsychiatry, 65*(3), 389–401.

Paikoff, R. L., & Brooks-Gunn, J. (1991). Do parent-child relationships change during puberty? *Psychological Bulletin, 110,* 47–66.

Paikoff, R. L., & Brooks-Gunn, J. (1994). Psychosexual development across the lifespan. In M. Rutter, & D. Hay (Eds.), *Development through life: A handbook for clinicians* (pp. 558–582). Oxford: Blackwell.

Petersen, A. C. (1983). Menarche: Meaning of measures and measuring meaning. In S. Golub (Ed.), *Menarche: The transition from girl to woman* (pp. 63–76). Lexington, MA: Lexington Books.

Petersen, A. C., Crockett, L., Richards, M., & Boxer, A. (1988). A self-report measure of pubertal status: Reliability, validity, and initial norms. *Journal of Youth and Adolescence, 17,* 117–133.

Petersen, A. C., Leffert, N., & Graham, B. L. (1995). Adolescent development and the emergence of sexuality. *Suicide and Life-Threatening Behavior, 25,* 4–17.

Pilkington, N. W., & D'Augelli, A. R. (1995). Victimization of lesbian, gay, and bisexual youth in community settings. *Journal of Community Psychology, 23,* 33–56.

Reiter, E. O., & Grumbach, M. M. (1982). Neuroendocrine control mechanisms and the onset of puberty. *Annual Review of Physiology, 44,* 595–613.

Remafedi, G. (1987). Homosexual youth: A challenge to contemporary society. *Journal of the American Medical Association, 258,* 222–225.

Remafedi, G., Resnick, M., Blum, R., & Harris, L. (1992). Demography of sexual orientation in adolescents. *Pediatrics, 89,* 714–721.

Rierdan, J., & Koff, E. (1985). Timing of menarche and initial menstrual experience. *Journal of Youth and Adolescence, 14,* 237–244.

Rodgers, J. L. (1996). Sexual transitions in adolescence. In J. A. Graber, J. Brooks-Gunn, & A. C. Petersen (Eds.), *Transitions through adolescence: Interpersonal domains and context* (pp. 85–110). Mahwah, NJ: Erlbaum.

Rotheram-Borus, M. J., Hunter, J., & Rosario, M. (1994). Suicidal behavior and gay-related stress among gay and bisexual male adolescents. *Journal of Adolescent Research, 9,* 498– 508.

Ruble, D. N., & Brooks-Gunn, J. (1982). Psychological correlates of tampon use in adolescents. *Annals of Internal Medicine, 96,* 962–965.

Rutter, M. (1994). Continuities, transitions and turning points in development. In M. Rutter & D. F. Hay (Eds.), *Development through life: A handbook for clinicians* (pp. 1–25). London: Blackwell Scientific Publications.

Savin-Williams, R. C. (1990). *Gay and lesbian youth: Expressions of identity.* Washington, DC: Hemisphere.

Savin-Williams, R. C. (1994a). Dating those you can't love, and loving those you can't date. In R. Montemayor, G. R. Adams, & T. P. Gullotta (Eds.), *Personal relationships during adolescence* (pp. 196–215). Thousand Oaks, CA: Sage.

Savin-Williams, R. C. (1994b). Verbal and physical abuse as stressors in the lives of lesbian, gay male and bisexual youths: Associations with school problems, running away, substance abuse, prostitution, and suicide. *Journal of Consulting and Clinical Psychology, 62,* 261–269.

Savin-Williams, R. C. (1995). An exploratory study of pubertal maturation timing and self-esteem among gay and bisexual male youths. *Developmental Psychology, 31,* 56–64.

Savin-Williams, R. C. (1998, Fall). Forgotten youth: Gay, lesbian, and bisexual teens. *Society for Research on Adolescence Newsletter,* 1–2.

Simon, R., Eder, D., & Evans, C. (1992). The development of feeling norms underlying romantic love among adolescent females. *Social Psychology Quarterly, 55,* 29–46.

Steinberg, L. D. (1987). The impact of puberty on family relations: Effects of pubertal status and pubertal timing. *Developmental Psychology, 23,* 451–460.

Strommen, E. F. (1989). Hidden branches and growing pains: Homosexuality and the family tree. *Marriage and Family Review, 14,* 9–34.

Troiden, R. R. (1988). Homosexual identity development. *Journal of Adolescent Health Care, 9,* 105–113.

Udry, J. R., Billy, J. O., Morris, N. M., Groff, T. R., & Raj, M. S. (1985). Serum androgenic hormones motivate sexual behavior in adolescent boys. *Fertility and Sterility, 43*(1), 90–94.

Udry, J. R., & Campbell, B. C. (1994). Getting started on sexual behavior. In A. S. Rossi (Ed.), *Sexuality across the life course* (pp. 187–207). Chicago: University of Chicago Press.

Udry, J. R., Talbert, L., & Morris, N. M. (1986). Biosocial foundations of adolescent female sexuality. *Demography, 23,* 217–230.

Youniss, J. (1980). *Parents and peers in social development: A Sullivan-Piaget perspective.* Chicago: University of Chicago Press.

2

Biological Factors in the Development of Sexual Orientation

Scott L. Hershberger

The purpose of this chapter is to review evidence on the role of biological factors in the development of sexual orientation from sources as diverse as studies of lateral preference, cognitive abilities, and anthropometry.

Homosexuality is a sexual attraction to someone of the same anatomical sex; heterosexuality is a sexual attraction to someone of the opposite sex. Closely allied to sexual attraction is fantasy. If someone has sexual fantasies about others of the same sex, then the fantasies are homosexual; if someone has sexual fantasies about others of the opposite sex, then the fantasies are heterosexual. If a person's sexual attractions and fantasies are primarily homosexual, then that person may be labeled "lesbian" or "gay." Conversely, if a person's sexual attractions and fantasies are primarily heterosexual, then that person may be labeled "heterosexual." When attraction and fantasy are directed to members of both sexes, a person may be labeled "bisexual." Attraction and fantasy are not the only dimensions that could be used to define a person as lesbian, gay, bisexual, or heterosexual, but they are typically the most reliable. Physiological responses to erotic stimuli are one alternative, but men and women respond differently to stimuli of different sensory modalities (Laan & Everaerd, 1995), thereby rendering difficult unambiguous comparisons between men and women. Same-sex sexual behavior or opposite-sex sexual behavior could serve as another criterion for sexual orientation, but personal and environmental constraints on sexual activity restrict its usefulness. Asking individuals whether they would self-identify lesbian, gay, or bisexual is another possibility, but this has the limitation that responses to this question are often based on social and political aspects of homosexuality and not sexual desire. Nonetheless, attraction/fantasy, physiological responses, behavior, and self-identity are significantly, but not perfectly, positively correlated.

Many often ask where bisexuality falls in the lesbian/gay–heterosexual dichotomy. Given that bisexuality exists, does it make sense to define sexual orientation dichotomously? Operationally, bisexual people are frequently categorized with lesbians and gay men for three reasons. First, the population incidence of both homosexuality and bisexuality is so small (e.g., most population-based surveys find fewer than 5% of the population endorsing a lesbian, gay, or bisexual orientation, e.g., Billy, Tanfer, Grady, & Klepinger, 1993; Laumann, Gagnon, Michael, & Michaels, 1994), that combining lesbians, gay men, and bisexual people into one category increases analytic power. Second, when lesbians/gay men, bisexual people, and heterosexual people are analyzed as three separate categories, conclusions rarely differ from analyzing lesbians, gay men, and bisexual people together (e.g., Hershberger, 1997). Third, combining lesbians, gay men, and bisexual people into one category, and contrasting that category with heterosexual people, is consistent with the most basic question many of the biological studies address: Is there evidence for biological influence on the expression of homosexual behavior? Certainly, most bisexual men and women would admit to some homosexual inclinations. In addition, the existence of bisexuality does not invalidate claims concerning the biological etiology of sexual orientation (Firestein, 1996). Nor does bisexuality render biological explanations of sexual orientation invalid, although it would complicate the explanations required (see Pattatucci, 1998). Finally, most traits studied by psychologists are multicategoried or dimensional; examining the extremes of a dimension (whether it be lesbian/gay or heterosexual, schizophrenic or nonschizophrenic) often serves to clarify the analysis.

Biological Etiology

Two approaches are most often taken to the biological causes of same-sex sexual orientation: neurohormonal and genetic. The neurohormonal approach is based upon the hypothesis that sexual orientation depends on the early sexual differentiation of hypothalamic brain structures (Ellis & Ames, 1987). According to this view, gay men and heterosexual women have neural sexual orientation centers that are similar to each other and different from those of heterosexual men and lesbians. Furthermore, the differentiation of these structures depends on prenatal androgen action. More generally, the neurohormonal approach suggests that male homosexuality may best be understood from the perspective of somatic feminization, and female homosexuality, from the perspective of somatic masculinization. Masculinization of brain structures in heterosexual men and lesbians occurs because of relatively high levels of androgens, whereas feminization of brain structures occurs in the absence of sufficient levels of androgen. Androgens influence the development of the organizational structure of the nervous system. Thus, the neurohormonal view does not predict that homosexuals and heterosexuals will have different levels of circulating hormones during adulthood. Rather, the theory predicts that comparable levels of the same hormones will have different activational effects based on different prenatally organized neural structures. The second, genetic approach has primarily involved the application of techniques from human behavioral genetics (a branch of population genetics), such as family, twin and adoption studies, to investigate the degree of genetic influence on individual differences in sexual orientation (Bailey, 1995). Recently, techniques from molecular genetics have supplemented the behavioral genetic approach to the study of sexual orientation.

Neurohormonal-based Theories

Evidence consistent with the neurohormonal theory of sexual orientation has been obtained from nine areas of research: (1) the experimental manipulation of the sexual behavior of nonhuman animals; (2) the examination of humans exposed to atypical patterns of prenatal hormones; (3) the detection of neuroanatomical differences in the neural structures of lesbian, gay, and heterosexual people; (4) the identification of cognitive, and (5) anthropometric traits that differentiate lesbian and gay people from heterosexual people that are also thought to be sexually dimorphic; (6) differences in lateral preference between lesbian, gay, and bisexual people and heterosexual people; (7) differences in birth order between gay and heterosexual males; (8) gender identity atypicality of lesbian and gay people in childhood; and (9) sibling sex ratio differences.

Sexual Behavior of Nonhuman Animals

Numerous studies exist examining the effects of prenatal patterns of sex steroid secretion on the development of sexually dimorphic behaviors in nonhuman animals (see Breedlove, 1994, for a review). Nearly all of these studies support the idea that the prenatal hormonal environment influences predispositions toward certain sexually dimorphic behaviors. The basic paradigm of most of these animal studies is to manipulate the prenatal hormonal environment so that it is more consistent with the hormonal environment of the other sex. Animals exposed to such hormonal changes frequently exhibit postnatal behaviors of the opposite sex. For example, male rats that have experienced prenatal androgen deficient hormonal environments exhibit lordosis, unusual levels of nonaggressiveness, and atypical play behavior. On the other hand, female rats that have experienced unusually high levels of androgens exhibit mounting behavior, increased levels of aggressiveness, and an avoidance of maternal rearing behaviors.

The use of animal sexual behavior as a model of human sexual orientation is not without its critics (Adkins-Regan, 1988; Byne & Parsons, 1993; Meyer-Bahlburg, 1984). Three primary criticisms have been made concerning the use of animal models in this area. First, the hormonal mechanisms responsible for the display of male-typical and female-typical behaviors are not identical across all mammalian species (Whalen & Edwards, 1967). All mammalian species exhibit behavioral masculinization, which refers to the increased likelihood of male-typical behavior (e.g., mounting behavior), whereas many fewer mammalian species exhibit behavioral defeminization, which refers to the decreased likelihood of female-typical behavior (e.g., lordosis). In rats, behavioral masculinization and defeminization are both present, but in many higher mammals, such as nonhuman primates, behavioral defeminization is largely absent. Most would agree that nonhuman primate behavior would serve as a better model of human sexual behavior than rat behavior. Yet an important part of the evidence for prenatal hormonal effects on human sexual behavior rests on generalization from rats. A second criticism is that human behavior has evolved beyond the instinctual processes that occur in nonhuman animals. Traits that are under the control of hormones in animals may be more likely to be the result of learning in humans (Feder, 1984). A third criticism is that mounting, lordosis, and other behaviors of nonhuman animals have little to do with human sexual orientation. As Feder (1984) pointed out, using nonhuman animal behavior as a model of human sexual behavior confuses the question, "Who is a person sexually attracted to?" with the question, "What role does a person take when he or she has sex?" Male rats that exhibit lordosis are supposed to represent human gay males, but in contradiction, males who mount these other male rats are not similarly labeled.

On the other hand, some of the best evidence for psychosocial influences on sexually dimorphic behavior comes from studies of nonhuman primates. For example, Harlow and Harlow (1965) noted that biologically normal monkeys reared under conditions of harsh deprivation during infancy avoided sexual interaction or were inept at it. Summarizing the results from many controlled laboratory experiments, Lovejoy and Wallen (1988) concluded that sexually dimorphic behavior in nonhuman primates is the result of the interaction between a specific rearing environment and the animal's prenatal hormonal environment. Some sexually dimorphic behaviors such as mounting and lordosis may be influenced more by the prenatal hormonal environment, whereas others, such as aggressiveness, are the result of the rearing environment. It seems reasonable to assume that the complexity of the determinants of sexually dimorphic behaviors in nonhumans is true for humans as well.

Humans Exposed to Atypical Patterns of Prenatal Hormone Exposure

The importance of prenatal sex hormones in nonhuman animals has encouraged researchers to examine their effects in humans. In contrast to the experimental manipulation of prenatal conditions for animals, the prenatal hormonal environments of humans cannot be ethically manipulated.

As an approximation to the study of the effects of the prenatal hormonal environment in humans, researchers rely on individuals whose prenatal sex steroid environment is atypical due to some disorder. Congenital adrenal hyperplasia (CAH) has undoubtedly been the most studied. CAH is an inherited, autosomal recessive disorder of adrenal steroidogenesis, and effects 1 in every 5,000 to 15,000 births (White, New, & Dupont, 1987). CAH causes an excessive production of adrenal androgens; in females, this results in full or partially masculinized external genitalia at birth. It is possible to treat CAH so that the excessive androgen production ceases and genitalia are surgically repaired. The question remains, though, whether CAH females exhibit masculinized postnatal behavior due to the prenatal effects of atypical androgen levels. The consensus of a number of studies is that some behavioral masculinization occurs. This includes "masculine" toy preferences (e.g., Berenbaum & Hines, 1992); high rates of a masculine gender identity (e.g., Ehrhardt & Baker, 1974); elevated rates of homosexual fantasy and behavior (e.g., Dittmann, Kappes, & Kappes, 1992); and low rates of heterosexual cohabitation and marriage (e.g., Zucker et al., 1992).

Some CAH female studies have been subject to methodological criticisms (reviewed by Berenbaum, 1990), including a reliance on interview measures and raters' prior knowledge of the participants' CAH status, vague explanations as to how sexual orientation was determined, the absence of control or comparison groups, the use of different types of CAH-affected females (e.g., salt-wasters and simple virilizers) and the use of late-treated subjects. This last criticism is especially serious, since late-treated subjects experience considerable postnatal virilization. It might be expected that postnatally virilized CAH females would evoke different reactions from the environment than non-CAH or treated CAH subjects. The most recent studies of CAH-affected women are not subject to these criticisms, and have found essentially the same results as past studies (e.g., Berenbaum & Snyder, 1995; Zucker et al., 1992).

Neuroanatomical Differences

Neuroanatomical differences between men and women in the hypothalamic region (Allen, Hines, Shryne, & Gorski, 1989; Swaab & Fliers, 1985) have suggested the possibility that such differences could exist between lesbian and gay people and heterosexual people. LeVay's (1991) study generalized a sex difference found in one region of the hypothalamus studied by Allen et al. (1989) to gay males and heterosexual males: interstitial nuclei area three of the anterior hypothalamus (INAH-3) was significantly larger in heterosexual men than in gay men or in heterosexual women. It should be noted that a sex difference found in INAH-2 by Allen et al. was not found to differ between gay men and heterosexual men. No replications of LeVay's study have been reported to date.

Several critics have commented on methodological flaws in LeVay's (1991) study (e.g., Byne & Parsons, 1993; Friedman & Downey, 1993). Unlike Allen et al. (1989), who had three individuals independently trace the INAH regions, LeVay traced them alone. In addition, there was little or no sexual biographical information on the deceased subjects autopsied by LeVay. Further, all of the gay male subjects examined by LeVay (and six—approximately 38%—of the heterosexual males) died of AIDS, raising the question as to whether the disease itself may have affected the INAH size. However, LeVay has reported that AIDS status did not affect the results.

Cognitive Ability Differences

The existence of sex differences for certain cognitive abilities is well established (Hyde, 1981; Hyde & Linn, 1988; Maccoby & Jacklin, 1974; Voyer, Voyer, & Bryden, 1995). The most dramatic differences are found on measures of spatial ability, in particular measures of mental rotation, with males typically outperforming females (Linn & Peterson, 1985; Voyer et al., 1995). Prenatal organizational effects of the androgen environment on the nervous system have been implicated for spatial ability differences in both nonhumans (Williams & Meck, 1991) and humans (Resnick, Berenbaum, Gottesman, & Bouchard, 1986). Knowledge of the effects of androgen in humans has come largely from studies of women with congenital adrenal hyperplasia, who perform better on average on spatial tasks than other women. In contrast to spatial abilities, some evidence exists for female superiority in verbal fluency (Hyde & Linn, 1988), although the sex difference here is much smaller. Vocabulary itself does not differ between the sexes (Hyde & Linn, 1988). If reliable sex differences exist on cognitive abilities, their origins may again be traced to the early prenatal environment. In addition to the left hemisphere of the brain where specialized language functions exist, females have language abilities in the visuo-spatial right hemisphere (McGlone, 1980). The presence of language functions in the right hemisphere may interfere with the process of spatial information in females (thus accounting for their poorer performance), but at the same time may improve women's processing of linguistic information. Women can call upon either their right or left hemisphere for interpreting linguistic information.

The effects of prenatal hormones on the organizational structure of the nervous system have also been proposed to explain the origin of within-sex sexual orientation differences in cognitive abilities (Halpern & Crothers, 1997). A number of studies have found differences on cognitive tasks between heterosexual and gay men, and between lesbians and heterosexual women. Further, in general, the cognitive ability profile of gay men parallels that of heterosexual women, and the cognitive ability profile of lesbians parallels that of heterosexual men. Reliable within-sex sexual orientation differences would support a neurohormonal view of sexual orientation. Zucker and Bradley (1995) recently reviewed the literature on within-sex sexual orientation cognitive abilities, but came to no firm conclusions other than to suggest that, similar to the between-sex difference in spatial abilities, gay men typically perform less well than heterosexual men.

The ambiguity in results communicated by Zucker and Bradley's (1995) review may be attributable to three factors. First, although a number of studies exist in this area examining differences between gay and heterosexual men, few exist examining differences between lesbians and heterosexual women. This is especially problematic. Unlike for males, few clear predictions or strong theoretical rationales have been proposed for the existence of female sexual orientation differences, or if they exist, what direction they would take. Consensus is emerging that the nature and development of female same-sex sexual orientation differs from that of male same-sex sexual orientation (Bailey & Bell, 1993; Pattatucci, 1998). Second, these studies have used different measures of the same construct, rendering conflicting results difficult to interpret. Third, there are limits to the conclusions that can be reached by even the most skillfully conducted literature review. Without the benefit of quantitatively combining results across studies, decisive conclusions cannot be made.

In view of this third difficulty, a meta-analysis was conducted of the world's literature comparing homosexual and heterosexual men, and comparing homosexual and heterosexual women (Hershberger & Pych, 1999). A brief discussion of the meta-analysis follows. In order to be useful in the analysis, a study had to meet two minimum requirements. First, participants must have been administered a measure of cognitive ability. Second, there must have been a group of participants who were identified as lesbian or gay, and in good health. Results were obtained from all adult age groups, but most came from ages 30–35. Of 35 studies, all included data on gay males, but only 10 included data on lesbians. Among the 35 studies, 6 included gay males but no heterosexual males, 14 included both gay and heterosexual males, and 10 included gay and heterosexual males, and lesbian and heterosexual females. Two more comments are in order with respect to the studies included in the meta-analysis. First, it is obvious that if a study included only gay men, there was no heterosexual male comparison group. This problem was overcome by locating the standardization (norm) data for the measure in question (usually in the test's manual) and using these data to represent the (largely) heterosexual male sample. Standardization data were used only if there was no more than a five-year age difference and a one-year education difference between the standardization sample and the individual study's sample. This was done for 6 studies of the total 35. Second, studies with only lesbians were not included. To my knowledge, there are no studies with only lesbian participants responding to cognitive measures. Once studies were located, the individual measures included in each study were categorized by the type. There were 17 categories (factors) of cognitive ability identified.

For men, the average effect size was significantly ($p < .05$) in favor of gay men for these factors: general intelligence, verbal intelligence, performance intelligence, vocabulary, logical reasoning, openness to experience, verbal fluency, and perceptual motor speed. Conversely, the average effect size was significantly in favor of heterosexual men for verbal memory, mental rotation, and psychomotor skill. Some of the results for men are consistent with known sex differences, whereas others are not. For example, openness to experience, although not a factor of cognitive ability, is moderately correlated with cognitive ability measures and assesses proclivity toward intellectual pursuits. It also shows a female advantage (Cattell, Eber, & Tatsuoka, 1970), consistent with the significant effect size found here. Although not predicted, a significant effect size for general intelligence in favor of gay men is probably attributable to the large amount of verbal content contained within these measures, relative to nonverbal content. Certainly, superior performance of gay men on verbal intelligence and verbal fluency are to be expected from a neurohormonal perspective. Superior gay male performance on perceptual motor speed is also to be expected, given the known female advantage in this area (Estes, 1974). There were no clear expectations for the psychomotor skill factor. This factor consisted of two tests: a throw task (in which men perform better than women; Watson & Kimura, 1991), and the Purdue Pegboard test (in which women outperform men; Yeudall, Fromm, Reddon, & Stefanyk, 1986). Not expected were significant effect sizes in favor of gay men for verbal memory, vocabulary, and logical reasoning; none of these factors is typically associated with sex differences. Counter to expectation, a significant effect size for performance intelligence in favor of gay men was found. Performance intelligence is characterized mostly by measures at least moderately related to spatial ability. A nonsignificant effect size for numerical ability was also surprising, given that the main test comprising this factor, the Arithmetic subtest of the Wechsler Adult Intelligence Scale-Revised, usually shows a sex difference in favor of males (Lezak, 1983). As expected, heterosexual men performed better on two factors of spatial ability, mental rotation, and spatial perception. As expected, there was no difference on a third factor of spatial ability, spatial visualization (cf., Voyer et al., 1995).

For women, significant average effect sizes were fewer, but all favored lesbians: general intelligence, verbal intelligence, performance intelligence, logical reasoning, judgment, and perceptual motor speed. Only one significant effect size, performance intelligence, showed a lesbian-heterosexual female difference consistent with a neurohormonal prediction: lesbians, like heterosexual men, performed better on spatial ability tasks. On the other two spatial ability factors expected to show large female differences in favor of lesbians, mental rotation and spatial perception, no differences were found. Contrary to prediction, perceptual motor speed and verbal intelligence were superior among lesbians.

Three primary limitations of this meta-analysis can be cited. In evaluating the results for both men and women, most of the significant effects were based on essentially conflicting results across studies. As confirmed by a chi-square test for homogeneity, a very different picture of within-sex sexual orientation differences may be obtained based on which particular study is examined. For example, for men, one study of judgment reveals an effect size of .67, and another study an effect size of –.14. Thus, the first study suggests that gay men are more than half a standard deviation better in judgment, whereas the second study suggests less than a quarter of a standard deviation difference in favor of heterosexual males. Another limitation of this meta-analysis concerns the necessity of having had to use test standardization data for heterosexual males when a study consisted of only gay males. Although care was taken to ensure that the standardization sample was well matched in education and age to the study sample, the two samples could have differed in many ways related to cognitive ability performance. Yet a third limitation is the relative paucity of information for women. Certainly, whatever confidence is placed in the results of this study, more confidence should be given to the results for men. Women have been severely under represented in within-sex cognitive ability studies. This is no doubt due to the limited theorizing that has taken place with respect to predicting how and why lesbians might differ from heterosexual women. Nonetheless, the results of this meta-analysis again reveal the mental rotation and spatial perception superiority of heterosexual men. Given the linkages that have been discovered between androgens and spatial ability, this is consistent with a neurohormonal explanation of sexual orientation.

Anthropometric and Related Physical Differences

Sexually dimorphic anthropometric and related physical differences are well established; these differences appear to generalize to sexual orientation status. In brief, the most consistent results for gay men, compared to heterosexual men, are their earlier pubertal status (e.g., Blanchard & Bogaert, 1996a; Bogaert & Blanchard, 1996; Manosevitz, 1970; Stephan, 1973); their greater lightness (e.g., Bogaert & Blanchard, 1996; Coppen, 1959; Evans, 1972; Herzog, Newman, & Warshaw, 1991; Siever, 1994; Silberstein, Mishkin, Striegel-Moore, Timko, & Rodin, 1989; Yager, Kurtzman, Landsverk, & Wiesmeier, 1988); their shorter stature (e.g., Blanchard & Bogaert, 1996a; Bogaert & Blanchard, 1996; Coppen, 1959); and their larger penises (e.g., Bogaert & Hershberger, 1999). Conversely, lesbians, compared to heterosexual women, are stronger (Perkins, 1981), heavier (Bogaert, 1998b; Gettelman & Thompson, 1993; Perkins, 1981), and taller (Bogaert, 1998b; Perkins, 1981). There have been other interesting data concerning physical differences among lesbian, gay, and heterosexual people. Whereas the physical attractiveness of prehomosexual boys diagnosed with gender identity disorder is rated higher than other boys (Zucker, Wild, Bradley, & Lowry, 1993), the physical attractiveness of prehomosexual girls diagnosed with gender identity disorder is rated lower than other girls (Fridell, Zucker, Bradley, & Maing, 1996).

Lateral Preference Differences

Lateral preference is another sexually dimorphic characteristic believed to be related to cerebral lateralization. In general, men are more lateralized and exhibit higher rates of left-handedness than women (McGlone, 1980). For example, Hahn (1987) reviewed 41 studies of cerebral asymmetry in children; of studies that showed sex differences, 83% found boys to be more lateralized than girls. In fact, the greater laterality of males has been used to explain the female disadvantage on some spatial ability tasks. Levy (1969) argued that male superiority on some spatial ability tasks resulted from the lateralization in men of verbal abilities in the left hemisphere and spatial abilities in the right hemisphere. As noted earlier, the presence of some verbal ability in the right hemisphere of women permits superior verbal processing but inferior spatial processing owing to decreased capacity in the right hemisphere.

The primary model used to explain brain lateralization was developed by Geschwind and Galaburda (1985; for a criticism of this theory, see Bryden, McManus, & Bulman-Fleming, 1994). In this model, high levels of prenatal testosterone slow the development of the normally dominant left hemisphere. This allows the right hemisphere to become predominant, thus causing left-handedness. This is why more men than women are left-handed. The model predicts that lesbians should also show elevated rates of left-handedness, based on the alleged prenatal presence of atypically high testosterone levels. On the other hand, the prediction for gay men is less straightforward. Elevated rates of left-handedness are also predicted for gay men owing to the timing and amount of testosterone production. It is hypothesized that gay men initially experience atypically high levels of testosterone (during the phase of fetal development in which cerebral lateralization occurs) and then later experience atypically low levels of testosterone (during the phase of fetal development in which sexual orientation is determined). Atypically high levels of prenatal testosterone are supposedly experienced because of maternal stress, a conjecture that has received mixed support (Bailey, 1995). However, the evidence suggests that left-handedness is elevated in both gay men and lesbians. For example, Zucker and Bradley (1995) noted 15 studies that compared handedness in gay men and heterosexual men, and 5 studies that compared handedness in lesbians and heterosexual women. Of the 15 male studies, 8 showed elevated rates of left-handedness in gay men, and 7 found no difference. Of the 5 female studies, 3 showed elevated rates of left-handedness in lesbians and 2 showed no difference.

Handedness is not the only measure of lateral preference or of cerebral asymmetry found to be related to sexual orientation. Hall and Kimura (1994) report a bias toward leftward asymmetry in dermal ridges (fingerprints) in gay men. McCormick and Witelson (1994) found, using a dichotic listening test, that heterosexual men and women were more lateralized than gay men and lesbians. Sanders and Ross-Field (1986) and Sanders and Wright (1997) found from a dot detection task that heterosexual men showed the male-typical left visual field advantage, whereas gay men and heterosexual women showed no such advantages. Reite, Sheeder, Richardson, and Teale (1995) report that electrophysiological brain measures indicative of interhemispheric activity differ between gay and heterosexual men, but not between gay men and lesbians. Gay men and lesbians show more symmetric interhemispheric activity than heterosexual men, whereas heterosexual men show more asymmetric hemispheric activity. Electroencephalographic (EEG) activity was recorded by Alexander and Sufka (1993) from gay men and heterosexual men and women. Different hemispheric patterns of activity were found between gay and heterosexual men, but not between gay men and heterosexual women during affective judgments of spatial and verbal stimuli.

Birth Order Differences

A birth order difference between gay and heterosexual men is among the most consistent research findings related to sexual orientation. In nearly every study on the issue, gay men more often report they were born later than other members of the general population. Early studies finding this effect include Slater (1958, 1962), Hare and Moran (1979), Hare and Price (1969, 1974), and Price and Hare (1969). Table 2.1 lists 10 of the most recent studies, along with the average value of the Slater index (1962) computed for the study. Slater's index is the number of a proband's older siblings divided by the number of all the proband's siblings. The index ranges from 0 for an eldest sibling to 1 for a youngest sibling, with an expected value of .5 if all birth orders are equally likely. As shown in table 2.1, gay males were born later than heterosexual males in every study. As a measure of effect size, each additional older brother increases the probability of male homosexuality by 33% (Blanchard & Bogaert, 1997a). The data also suggest that the later birth of gay men depends only on the number of older brothers and not sisters (Blanchard & Bogaert, 1996a,b), that the late birth order effect does not generalize to lesbians (Blanchard & Sheridan, 1992; Bogaert, 1997; Hare & Moran, 1979), and that it does generalize to nonwhite populations (Bogaert, 1998a). Blanchard and Bogaert (1997b) have also shown that birth intervals preceding heterosexual and gay males do not differ, a question of interest because longer birth intervals are commonly seen following a male child relative to a female child.

One hormonal explanation for the later birth of gay men in families with other children points to a maternal immune response to the H-Y antigen of male fetuses developed over the previous male pregnancies, modifying the sexual differentiation of the brain of later-born male fetuses (Blanchard & Klassen, 1997). Psychosocial explanations for the birth order effect could also be advanced. For example, fathers may have less time to spend with later-born male children when there are older male children present (Nash & Hayes, 1965); later-born sons may elicit more maternal attention (West, 1977); later-born sons may be inclined to feel inadequate in relation to older broth-

Table 2.1
Sibling Birth Order for Males

	BIRTH ORDER	
STUDY	HOMOSEXUAL PROBANDS	HETEROSEXUAL CONTROLS
Blanchard & Sheridan (1992)	.59	.40
Blanchard & Zucker (1994)	.49	.42
Zucker & Blanchard (1994)	.60	.50
Blanchard et al. (1995)	.58	.45
Blanchard & Bogaert (1996a)	.52	.46
Blanchard & Bogaert (1996b)	.51	.41
Blanchard et al. (1996)	.61	.37
Bogaert et al. (1997)[a]	.56	.42
Bogaert (1998a)[a]	.52	.49
Blanchard & Bogaert (1998b)[b, c]	.51	−.21

[a]This study used Berglin's (1982) birth order index.
[b]This study defined birth order as the number of siblings older than the proband minus the number of siblings younger than the proband.
[c]Results reported for offenders against adults only.

ers (van den Aardweg, 1986); and mothers may "feminize" later-born sons to satisfy emotional needs for a daughter (Nash & Hayes, 1965). Both the biological and psychosocial theories have some support, but one question that remains for the psychosocial theories to address is why these processes do not appear to be as relevant to the development of female homosexuality.

Gender Identity Atypicality during Childhood

Along with the birth order effect, the greater recalled gender identity atypicality of gay men during childhood is a robust finding in sexual orientation research (Bailey & Zucker, 1995). If hormones influence the development of sexually dimorphic behavior and sexual orientation, an atypical gender identity would be expected among gay males. Retrospective and prospective studies have shown that male same-sex sexual orientation is strongly associated with atypical childhood gender identity, including decreased aggression, decreased sports participation, the desire to be female, and being perceived as a "sissy" by others. Retrospective studies of lesbians produce similar results, with many lesbians being perceived as "tomboys" in childhood. However, the effect is significantly smaller for women. The effect becomes substantially smaller by adulthood for both males and females, probably due to the effects of socialization (Harry, 1983).

Sibling Sex Ratio

In the 1930s, before the availability of techniques for karotyping the sex chromosomes, it was mistakenly suggested that gay men were genetic females (Lang, 1940). A prediction that followed from this hypothesis was that gay men would have more brothers than heterosexual males. Given the slight imbalance in the birth of males compared to females (106 males to every 100 females), a "genetic female" would be more likely to have brothers than a genetic male. Thus, the sibling sex ratio among gay men should significantly exceed the 106:100 ratio. Early studies by Jensch (1941), Kallmann (1952a), and Lang (1960) using institutionalized gay men found sibling sex ratios that significantly exceeded the population norm, but later, more rigorously conducted studies using noninstitutionalized gay probands (Blanchard & Bogaert, 1996a,b; Blanchard & Zucker, 1994; Zucker & Blanchard, 1994), and institutionalized gay probands (Blanchard & Bogaert, 1998) failed to find a difference between the ratios of gay and heterosexual men. Three contemporary studies find an excess of brothers among extremely feminine gay men. Blanchard and Sheridan (1992), Blanchard, Zucker, and Hume (1995), and Blanchard, Zucker, Cohen-Kettenis, Gooren, and Bailey (1996) sampled gender-dysphoric gay men and boys. The finding of a sibling sex ratio effect only among extremely feminine gay men might suggest that the effect is not general to all gay men, and provides support to the notion that the strength of biological components of homosexuality might vary among men, and that biological contributions to male homosexuality are most likely in gender atypical men (Meyer-Bahlburg, 1993). One study has also found a significant sibling sex ratio effect for nonwhite homosexual males (Bogaert, 1998a).

Evidence for a sibling sex ratio effect for women, such that lesbians have an excess of sisters relative to heterosexual women, is weakly supported. Opposite to that predicted for gay men, the sibling sex ratio for lesbians should fall significantly below 1.00. Of the two studies that have studied females, one (Lang, 1960) found a significant sibling sex ratio, whereas the other (Blanchard & Sheridan, 1992) did not.

Genetic-based Theories

Genetic differences could also trigger differences in sexual orientation, perhaps by inducing differences in prenatal androgen levels or sensitivity to androgen, or through some other mechanism. The evidence for genetic influences on sexual orientation is reviewed from (1) twin studies, (2) family studies, and (3) molecular genetic studies.

Twin Studies

Table 2.2 summarizes the twin concordance rates for homosexuality found in large-sample male and female twin studies. In the case of males, with one exception (Hershberger, 1997), the MZ (monozygotic twin) concordances are higher than the DZ (dizygotic twin) concordances. One combined male and

Table 2.2
Concordances for Twin Studies of Male and Female Homosexuality

STUDY	MZ		DZ		ASCERTAINMENT METHOD
	N[a]	%	N	%	
Males					
Kallmann (1952a,b)	37/37	100	3/26	15	Word of mouth
Heston & Shields (1968)	3/5	60	1/7	14	Serial admission
Buhrich et al. (1991)	8/17	47	0/3	0	Twin registry
Bailey & Pillard (1991)	29/56	5	12/54	22	Advertisement
Bailey et al. (1996)	7/34	20	0/20	0	Twin registry
Hershberger (1997)	4/16	25	2/8	25	Twin registry
Females					
Bailey et al. (1993)	34/71	48	6/37	16	Advertisement
Bailey et al. (1996)	6/25	24	2/19	11	Twin registry
Hershberger (1997)	6/11	55	2/8	25	Twin registry
Combined					
King & McDonald (1992)	2/16	13	2/16	13	Advertisement
Whitam et al. (1993)	22/34	65	4/14	29	Advertisement

[a]The number of proband co-twins concordant for homosexuality/the number of probands.

female study, King and McDonald (1992), found no difference in the MZ and DZ concordance rates. The concordances and implied heritabilities vary dramatically among studies. For example, Kallmann's results imply a heritability exceeding 1.0, whereas King and McDonald's imply a heritability of 0.0. Thus, although the studies generally support a genetic contribution to male sexual orientation, the magnitude of the potential contribution varies widely. For females, all three studies imply significant heritability, but again of varying magnitude. One source of variation among these studies is the method for recruiting study participants. It has been argued, for instance, that advertising for twins will more likely result in the participation of twins who are more alike than twins who are sampled from a population-based twin registry. This hypothesis is borne out by the Bailey, Dunn, and Martin (1996) twin registry study in which the implied heritabilities are considerably lower than those found in the recruitment-by-advertisement studies of Bailey and Pillard (1991) and Bailey, Pillard, Neale, and Agyei (1993).

Twin studies have been subject to a number of criticisms. One criticism has been that twin studies are relatively uninformative, providing relatively little information beyond some global heritability estimate. This does not need to be true—twin studies can be extremely useful in answering a number of basic genetic questions. For example, the Hershberger (1997) study attempted to answer the question as to whether male and female homosexuality are influenced by the same genes or whether they are genes unique to one of the sexes. It could be the case, for instance, that the total genetic influence on males and females is the same, but that the genetic source of the influence differs. The answer to this question requires the presence of opposite-sex twins, who are necessarily dizygotic. This "fifth" twin group (in addition to the four twin groups of male and female monozygotics and same-sex dizygotics) permitted this question to be asked about not only the genes influencing self-identified sexual orientation but also the genes influencing attraction toward persons of the opposite and same sex, and the genes influencing the number of opposite-sex sex and same-sex sex partners. The study concluded that genetic influences were stronger in magnitude for women than for men, but that the set of genes influencing sexual orientation, attraction, and number of sex partners were the same (e.g., the genetic correlation between men and women is 1.00). Using the twin method, Bailey and Pillard (1991) studied whether gender atypicality in childhood was indicative of a different causal path for homosexuality. For example, it may be that more feminine male homosexuality is genetically induced, whereas more masculine male homosexuality is environmentally induced. If this were the case, then the expectation would be that more feminine gay males would be more likely to have a gay co-twin than more masculine homosexuals. Bailey and Pillard concluded that the probability of having a homosexual co-twin did not differ between those twins who during childhood were either masculine or feminine.

Another criticism of the twin method concerns the "equal environments assumption" that the trait-relevant environment is of equivalent for MZ and DZ twins. Some authors (e.g., Lewontin, Rose, & Kamin, 1984) argue that parents treat MZ twins more similarly than DZ twins, and that this similar treatment, rather a similar genotype, explains the greater similarity in MZ behavior. There is no doubt that, in many respects, MZ twins are treated more similarly: they are more likely to have been dressed alike, to have had the same friends, and to have shared the same room as children, among other things. The relevant question is, however, whether more similar treatment causes them to be more similar, and the evidence to date suggests that it does not (Plomin, DeFries, & McClearn, 1990). One of the most interesting studies addressing the equal environments assumption found that DZ twins who were mistakenly considered MZ twins by their parents were no more similar than other DZ twins, and less similar than MZ twins who were mistaken as DZ twins (Scarr & Carter-Saltzman, 1979).

Another serious criticism of the twin method was alluded to earlier with respect to the variability of heritabilities implied by the different studies. The method by which twins are sampled or obtained may dramatically influence the results. Ideally, one would recruit probands by interviewing every member of a well-defined population. On the other hand, relying on volunteers obtained through advertisements probably introduces a number of biases. For example, Kendler and Eaves (1989) have identified a "concordance-dependent ascertainment bias" in which twins who are more alike tend to volunteer. If gay or lesbian probands were more willing to volunteer if they had a same-sex oriented co-twin, this could spuriously inflate concordance rates, although if the effect were equal for both MZ and DZ twins, heritability estimates would not be affected. Lastly, it is well known that more MZ twins than DZ twins, and more females than males, volunteer to participate in twin studies (Lykken, McGue, & Tellegen, 1987). However, this is only of particular concern to twin studies of sexual orientation if the frequency of homosexuality differed between MZ and DZ twins; no evidence exists that this is so.

Family Studies

Although less conclusive concerning the role of genes than studying the concordance of twins, sibling studies at least confirm whether a trait runs in families. Two findings are readily apparent here. First, gay and lesbian probands tend to have more gay and lesbian siblings than heterosexual probands (e.g., Bailey & Benishay, 1993; Bailey et al., 1999; Hershberger, 1997; Pattatucci & Hamer, 1995; Pillard, 1990; Pillard, Poumadere, & Carretta, 1982; Pillard & Weinrich, 1986). Second, gay male probands are more likely to have gay male siblings than lesbian probands, and to a lesser extent, lesbian probands are more likely to have lesbian siblings than gay male probands (e.g., Bailey & Bell, 1993; Bailey & Benishay, 1993; Bailey & Pillard, 1991; Bailey et al., 1993; Henry, 1948; Hershberger, 1997; Pattatucci & Hamer, 1995; Pillard, 1990; Pillard et al., 1982; Pillard & Weinrich, 1986). In other words, male or female homosexuality may run in families, but usually not both.

Two other family studies have examined parental influences on offspring homosexuality. Bailey, Nothnagel, and Wolfe (1995) found that the heterosexual and homosexual adult sons of gay fathers did not differ in the length of time they had lived with their fathers, the amount of contact they had with their fathers, how much they accepted their fathers' homosexuality, and the quality of the relationship with their fathers. These results argue against a simplistic psychosocial explanation for the development of a same-sex sexual orientation. Golombok and Tasker (1996) examined longitudinally the development of children raised by lesbian and heterosexual mothers. No significant difference was found between the children of lesbian and heterosexual mothers in the proportion identifying as lesbian or gay as an adult.

Molecular Genetic Studies

The first molecular genetic study to address the location for specific genes for homosexuality was conducted by Hamer, Hu, Magnuson, Hu, and Pattatucci (1993). Using a sample of brothers concordant for homosexuality, a linkage between the distal portion of Xq28, the subtelomeric region of the long arm of the X chromosome, and a male same-sex sexual orientation was discovered. Hamer et al. were guided to look in this region based on the results of a pedigree analysis that showed an excess of homosexual maternal relatives of the probands. Subsequently, Hu et al. (1995) replicated the Hamer et al. results for men—but with a lower effect size—but failed to find an association between the Xq28 region and female homosexuality.

Both the Hamer et al. (1993) and Hu et al. (1995) studies are linkage studies, research that aims to map genes onto chromosomes by examining chromosomal segments from siblings who share a common trait (in this case, a homosexual orientation). In contrast, association studies explore the relation between genetic variation at a specific locus and variation in a trait. This strategy was used by Macke et al. (1993), who examined DNA sequence variation in the androgen receptor gene, assuming that some variants may affect the sexual differentiation of the brain, and hence sexual orientation. No significant differences in the distribution of variations to this gene were found between gay and heterosexual men. In addition, linkage analysis showed that siblings concordant for homosexuality were no more likely than chance to share this gene.

Obviously, a great many more molecular genetic studies of sexual orientation need to be done. The Hamer et al. (1993) and Hu et al. (1995) results need to be replicated by independent investigators, a critical requirement for the results of molecular genetic studies given the rate of nonreplicability for other psychologically relevant traits such as depression, schizophrenia, and alcoholism. One nonsuccessful attempt at independent replication has been reported (Eber, 1996), but methodological differences between that study and Hamer et al. and Hu et al. may account for this discrepancy. Also, some of the criticisms voiced by the critics of these studies (e.g., Risch, Squires-Wheeler, & Keats, 1993) need to be addressed. For one, Risch et al. speculate that Hamer's finding of an elevated rate of gay men's maternal relatives might be attributable to the often greater knowledge people have of their mother's side of the family.

Conclusion

The amount of evidence suggesting that biology plays an important role in the development of male and female sexual orientation is rapidly increasing. A number of characteristics, among them the lower spatial performance of gay males, the elevated rate of left-handedness among both gay males and lesbians, and many others, are not readily amenable to simple environmental explanation. This is not to say that the current evidence is without considerable ambiguity, or that many questions do not remain to be answered. One important unanswered question concerns the nature of genetic influences on sexual orientation in women. Hu et al.'s (1995) work identified a possible locus for homosexuality in men selected to meet very specific criteria (e.g., both brothers must have been concordant for homosexuality); this locus was not related to female homosexuality. Indeed, the degree to which sexual orientation is biologically influenced in women remains considerably less clear than it does for men. A consensus is forming that although biological influences are important for both men and women, they are probably more important in influencing male sexual orientation. However, further proof of this view awaits additional research.

Although many studies in the area of biological influences on sexual orientation offer conflicting results, the research does show at least five findings with respect to men that are almost always found and are of a significant effect size: (1) gay men weigh significantly less than heterosexual men; (2) *preadult* gay males are more gender atypical than heterosexual males; (3) the spatial ability of gay men is inferior to that of heterosexual men; (4) there is a genetic influence on male sexual orientation; and (5) gay men tend to be born later in families with multiple male siblings than heterosexual males. Further, if one examines the subgroup of gay males that identify themselves are transsexuals or transgendered individuals, these effects become intriguingly even stronger. Unfortunately, at the present time, compilation of such a list for females is not possible. Neither enough research nor consistency of results have accumulated to make such broad conclusions possible. Though certainly there are suggestive biological correlates of female sexual orientation that have been identified (e.g., greater height of lesbians), these results have not been replicated in enough studies to be conclusive. Future investigations into the biological determinants of *male* sexual orientation would do well to precede upon the basis of theory that acknowledges the known correlates of sexual orientation cited above. Until some theory does so, it is unlikely that the ultimate biological reasons why some men are gay and others are heterosexual will be found. To some extent, a neurohormonal theory of sexual orientation does this, but many details need to be filled in of the type proposed—for example, by Blanchard and Klassen (1997)—for a sibling birth order effect. It is all well and good to propose that hormones are responsible for sexual orientation development, but just how are they responsible? The answer to this question will undoubtedly be complex, and probably not applicable to all males. As for biological reasons for female sexual orientation development, the research is still in its infancy; both theory and empirical findings are sparse. Even knowledge of simple correlates of female sexual orientation differences of the type known for males is lacking. Much basic theoretical and empirical work remains to be done.

References

Adkins-Regan, E. (1988). Sex hormones and sexual orientation in animals. *Psychobiology, 16*, 335–347.

Alexander, J. E., & Sufka, K. J. (1993). Cerebral lateralization in homosexual males: A preliminary EEG investigation. *International Journal of Psychophysiology, 15*, 269–274.

Allen, L. S., Hines, M., Shryne, J. E., & Gorski, R. A. (1989). Two sexually dimorphic cell groups in the human brain. *Journal of Neuroscience, 9,* 497–506.

Bailey, J. M. (1995). Biological perspectives on sexual orientation. In A. R. D'Augelli & C. J. Patterson (Eds.), *Lesbian, gay, and bisexual identities over the lifespan* (pp. 102–135). New York: Oxford University Press.

Bailey, J. M., & Bell, A. P. (1993). Familiarity of female and male homosexuality. *Behavior Genetics, 23,* 313–322.

Bailey, J. M., & Benishay, D. S. (1993). Familial aggregation of female sexual orientation. *American Journal of Psychiatry, 150,* 272–277.

Bailey, J. M., Dunn, M., & Martin, N. G. (1996). *Sex differences in the distribution and determination of sexual orientation.* Unpublished manuscript.

Bailey, J. M., Nothnagel, J., & Wolfe, M. (1995). Retrospectively-measured individual differences in childhood sex-typed behavior among gay men: Correspondence between self- and maternal reports. *Archives of Sexual Behavior, 24,* 613–622.

Bailey, J. M., & Pillard, R. C. (1991). A genetic study of male sexual orientation. *Archives of General Psychiatry, 48,* 1089–1096.

Bailey, J. M., Pillard, R. C., Dawood, K., Miller, M. B., Farrer, L. A., Trivedi, S., & Murphy, R. (1999). A family history study of male sexual orientation using three independent samples. *Behavior Genetics, 29,* 79–86.

Bailey, J. M., Pillard, R. C., Neale, M. C., & Agyei, Y. (1993). Heritable factors influence female sexual orientation. *Archives of General Psychiatry, 50,* 217–223.

Bailey, J. M., & Zucker, K. J. (1995). Childhood sex-typed behavior and sexual orientation: A conceptual analysis and quantitative review. *Developmental Psychology, 31,* 43–55.

Berenbaum, S. A. (1990). Congenital adrenal hyperplasia: Intellectual and psychosexual functioning. In C. S. Homles (Ed.), *Psychoneuroendocrinology: Brain, behavior, and hormonal interactions* (pp. 227–260). New York: Springer-Verlag.

Berenbaum, S. A., & Hines, M. (1992). Early androgens are related to childhood sex-typed toy preferences. *Psychological Science, 3,* 203–206.

Berenbaum, S. A., & Snyder, E. (1995). Early hormonal influences on childhood sex-typed activity and playmate preferences: Implications for the development of sexual orientation. *Developmental Psychology, 31,* 31–42.

Berglin, L. G. (1982). Birth order as a quantitative expression of date of birth. *Journal of Epidemiology and Community Health, 36,* 298–302.

Billy, J., Tanfer, K., Grady, W., & Klepinger, D. (1993). The sexual behavior of men in the United States. *Family Planning Perspectives, 25,* 61–66.

Blanchard, R., & Bogaert, A. F. (1996a). Biodemographic comparisons of homosexual and heterosexual men in the Kinsey interview data. *Archives of Sexual Behavior, 25,* 551–579.

Blanchard, R., & Bogaert, A. F. (1996b). Homosexuality in men and number of older brothers. *American Journal of Psychiatry, 153,* 27–31.

Blanchard, R., & Bogaert, A. F. (1997a). Additive effects of older brothers and homosexual brothers in the prediction of marriage and cohabitation. *Behavior Genetics, 27,* 45–54.

Blanchard, R., & Bogaert, A. F. (1997b). The relation of close birth intervals to the sex of the preceding child and the sexual orientation of the succeeding child. *Journal of Biosocial Science, 29,* 111–118.

Blanchard, R., & Bogaert, A. F. (1998). Birth order in homosexual versus heterosexual sex offenders against children, pubescents, and adults. *Archives of Sexual Behavior, 27*, 595–603.

Blanchard, R., & Klassen, P. (1997). H-Y antigen and homosexuality in men. *Journal of Theoretical Biology, 185*, 373–378.

Blanchard, R., & Sheridan, P. M. (1992). Sibship size, sibling sex ratio, birth order, and parental age in homosexual and nonhomosexual gender dysphorics. *Journal of Nervous and Mental Disease, 180*, 40–47.

Blanchard, R., & Zucker, K. J. (1994). Reanalysis of Bell, Weinberg, and Hammersmith's data on birth order, sibling sex ratio, and parental age in homosexual men. *American Journal of Psychiatry, 151*, 1375–1376.

Blanchard, R., Zucker, K. J., Cohen-Kettenis, P. T., Gooren, L. J. G., & Bailey, J. M. (1996). Birth order and sibling sex ratio in two samples of Dutch gender-dysphoric homosexual males. *Archives of Sexual Behavior, 25*, 495–514.

Blanchard, R., Zucker, K. J., & Hume, C. S. (1995). Birth order and sibling sex ratio in homosexual male adolescents and probably prehomosexual feminine boys. *Developmental Psychology, 31*, 22–30.

Bogaert, A. F. (1997). Birth order and sexual orientation in women. *Behavioral Neuroscience, 111*, 1395–1397.

Bogaert, A. F. (1998a). Birth order and sibling sex ratio in homosexual and heterosexual non-White men. *Archives of Sexual Behavior, 27*, 467–473.

Bogaert, A. F. (1998b). Physical development and sexual orientation in women: Height, weight, and age of puberty comparisons. *Personality and Individual Differences, 24*, 115–121.

Bogaert, A. F., Bezaeu, S., Kuban, M., & Blanchard, R. (1997). Pedophilia, sexual orientation, and birth order. *Journal of Abnormal Psychology, 106*, 331–335.

Bogaert, A. F., & Blanchard, R. (1996). Physical development and sexual orientation in men: Height, weight and age of puberty differences. *Personality and Individual Differences, 21*, 77–84.

Bogaert, A. F., & Hershberger, S. L. (1999). The relation between sexual orientation and penile size. *Archives of Sexual Behavior, 28*, 213–221.

Breedlove, S. M. (1994). Sexual differentiation of the human nervous system. *Annual Review of Psychology, 45*, 389–418.

Bryden, M. P., McManus, I. C., & Bulman-Fleming, M. B. (1994). Evaluating the empirical support for the Geschwind-Behan-Galaburda model of cerebral lateralization. *Brain and Cognition, 26*, 103–167.

Buhrich, N. J., Bailey, J. M., & Martin, N. G. (1991). Sexual orientation, sexual identity, and sex-dimorphic behaviors in male twins. *Behavior Genetics, 21*, 75–96.

Byne, W., & Parsons, B. (1993). Human sexual orientation: The biologic theories reappraised. *Archives of General Psychiatry, 50*, 228–239.

Cattell, R. B., Eber, H. W., & Tatsuoka, M. (1970). *Handbook for the 16 PFQ.* Champaign, IL: IPAT.

Coppen, A. J. (1959). Body-build of male homosexuals. *British Medical Journal, 200*, 1443–1445.

Dittmann, R. W., Kappes, M. E., & Kappes, M. H. (1992). Sexual behavior in adolescent and adult females with congenital adrenal hyperplasia. *Psychoneuroendocrinology, 17*, 153–170.

Eber, G. (1996, October). *Family and linkage studies of male homosexuality*. Paper presented at the meeting of the American Society of Human Genetics, San Francisco, CA.

Ehrhardt, A. A., & Baker, S. W. (1974). Fetal androgens, human central nervous system differentiation, and behavior sex differences. In R. C. Friedman, R. M. Richart, & R. L. Vande Wiele (Eds.), *Sex differences in behavior* (pp. 33–51). New York: Wiley.

Ellis, L., & Ames, M. A. (1987). Neurohormonal functioning and sexual orientation: A theory of homosexuality-heterosexuality. *Psychological Bulletin, 101*, 233–258.

Estes, W. K. (1974). Learning theory and intelligence. *American Psychologist, 29*, 740–749.

Evans, R. B. (1972). Physical and biochemical characteristics of homosexual men. *Journal of Consulting and Clinical Psychology, 39*, 140–147.

Feder, H. H. (1984). Hormones and sexual behavior. *Annual Review of Psychology, 35*, 165–200.

Firestein, B. A. (1996). Bisexuality as a paradigm shift: Transforming our disciplines. In B. A. Firestein (Ed.), *Bisexuality: The psychology and politics of an invisible minority* (pp. 263–291). Thousand Oaks, CA: Sage.

Friedman, R. C., & Downey, J. (1993). Neurobiology and sexual orientation: Current relationships. *Journal of Neuropsychiatry and Clinical Neurosciences, 5*, 131–153.

Fridell, S. A., Zucker, K. J., Bradley, S. J., & Maing, D. M. (1996). Physical attractiveness of girls with gender identity disorder. *Archives of Sexual Behavior, 25*, 17–31.

Geschwind, N., & Galabruda, A. M. (1985). Cerebral lateralization. Biological mechanisms, associations, and pathology: I. A hypothesis and a program for research. *Archives of Neurology, 42*, 428–459.

Gettelman, T. E., & Thompson, J. K. (1993). Actual differences and stereotypical perceptions in body image and eating disturbance: A comparison of male and female heterosexual and homosexual samples. *Sex Roles, 29*, 545–562.

Golombok, S., & Tasker, F. (1996). Do parents influence the sexual orientation of their children? Findings from a longitudinal study of lesbian families. *Developmental Psychology, 32*, 3–11.

Hahn, W. K. (1987). Cerebral lateralization of function: From infancy through childhood. *Psychological Bulletin, 101*, 376–392.

Hall, J. A., & Kimura, D. (1994). *Dermatogyphic asymmetry and sexual orientation in males*. (Research Bulletin #179). London, Canada, University of Western Ontario.

Halpern, D. F., & Crothers, M. (1997). *Sex, sexual orientation, and cognition*. In L. Ellis & L. Ebertz (Eds.), *Sexual orientation: Toward biological understanding* (pp. 181–198). Westport, CT: Praeger.

Hamer, D. H., Hu, S., Magnuson, V. L., Hu, N., & Pattatucci, A. M. L. (1993). A linkage between DNA markers on the X chromosome and male sexual orientation. *Science, 261*, 321–327.

Hare, E. H., & Moran, P. A. P (1979). Paternal age and birth order in homosexual patients: A replication of Slater's study. *British Journal of Psychiatry, 134*, 178–182.

Hare, E. H., & Price, J. S. (1969). Birth order and family size: Bias caused by changes in birth rate. *British Journal of Psychiatry, 15*, 647–657.

Hare, E. H., & Price, J. S. (1974). Birth order and birth rate bias: Findings in a representative sample of the adult population of Great Britain. *Journal of Biosocial Science, 6*, 139–150.

Harlow, H. F., & Harlow, M. K. (1965). The affectional systems. In A. M. Schrier, H. F. Harlow, & F. Stollnitz (Eds.), *Behavior of nonhuman primates: Modern research trends* (pp. 405–422). Cambridge: Cambridge University Press.

Harry, J. (1983). Parasuicide, gender, and gender deviance. *Journal of Health and Social Behavior, 24*, 350–361.

Henry, G. W. (1948). *Sex variants: A study of homosexual patterns.* New York: Hoeber.

Hershberger, S. L. (1997). A twin registry study of male and female sexual orientation. *Journal of Sex Research, 34*, 212–222.

Hershberger, S. L., & Pych, J. (1999). *Sexual orientation differences in cognitive abilities: A meta-analysis.* Unpublished manuscript.

Herzog, D. B., Newman, K. L., & Warshaw, M. (1991). Body image dissatisfaction in homosexual and heterosexual males. *Journal of Nervous and Mental Disease, 86*, 356–359.

Heston, L. L., & Shields, J. (1968). Homosexuality in twins: A family study and a registry study. *Archives of General Psychiatry, 18*, 149–160.

Hu, S., Pattatucci, A. M. L., Patterson, C., Li, L., Fulker, D. W., Cherny, S. S., Kruglyak, L., & Hamer, D. H. (1995). Linkage between sexual orientation and chromosome Xq28 in males but not in females. *Nature Genetics, 11*, 248–256.

Hyde, J. S. (1981). How large are cognitive gender differences? *American Psychologist, 36*, 892–901.

Hyde, J. S., & Linn, M. C. (1988). Gender differences in verbal ability: A meta-analysis. *Psychological Bulletin, 104*, 53–69.

Jensch, K. (1941). Weiterer beitrag zur genealogie der homosexualität [Further contributions to the genealogy of homosexuality]. *Archiv für Psychiatrie und Nervenkrankheiten, 112*, 679–696.

Kallmann, F. J. (1952a). Twin and sibship study of overt male homosexuality. *American Journal of Human Genetics, 4*, 136–146.

Kallmann, F. J. (1952b). Comparative twin study on the genetic aspects of male homosexuality. *Journal of Nervous and Mental Disease, 115*, 283–298.

Kendler, K. S., & Eaves. L. J. (1989). The estimation of probandwise concordance in twins: The effect of unequal ascertainment. *Acta Geneticae Medicae et Gemellologiae, Twin Research, 38*, 253–270.

King, M., & McDonald, E. (1992). Homosexuals who are twins: A study of 46 probands. *British Journal of Psychiatry, 160*, 407–409.

Laan, E., & Everaerd, W. (1995). Determinants of female sexual arousal: Psychophysiological theory and data. *Annual Review of Sex Research, 6*, 32–76.

Lang, T. (1940). Studies on the genetic determination of homosexuality. *Journal of Nervous and Mental Disease, 92*, 55–64.

Lang, T. (1960). Die homosexualität als genetisches problem [Homosexuality as a genetic problem]. *Acta Geneticae Medicae et Gemellologiae, 9*, 370–381.

Laumann, E. O., Gagnon, J. H., Michael, R. T., & Michaels, S. (1994). *The social organization of sexuality: Sexual practices in the United States.* Chicago: University of Chicago Press.

LeVay, S. (1991). A difference in hypothalamic structure between heterosexual and homosexual women. *Science, 253,* 1034–1037.

Levy, J. (1969). Possible basis for the evolution of lateral specialization of the human brain. *Nature, 224,* 612–615.

Lewontin, R. C., Rose, S., & Kamin, L. J. (1984). *Not in our genes.* New York: Pantheon.

Lezak, M. D. (1983). *Neuropsychological assessment* (2nd ed.) New York: Oxford University Press.

Linn, M. C., & Petersen, A. C. (1985). Emergence and characterization of gender differences in spatial abilities: A meta-analysis. *Child Development, 56,* 1479–1498.

Lovejoy, J., & Wallen, K. (1988). Sexually dimorphic behavior in group-housed rhesus monkeys (Macaca mulatta). *Psychobiology, 16,* 348–356.

Lykken, D. T., McGue, M., & Tellegen, A. (1987). Recruitment bias in twin research: The rule of two-thirds reconsidered. *Behavior Genetics, 17,* 343–362.

Maccoby, E. E., & Jacklin, C. N. (1974). *The psychology of sex differences.* Stanford, CA: Stanford University Press.

Macke, J. P., Bailey, J. M., King, V., Brown, T., Hamer, D., & Nathans, J. (1993). Sequence variation in the androgen receptor gene is not a common determinant of male sexual orientation. *American Journal of Human Genetics, 53,* 844–852.

Manosevitz, M. (1970). Early sexual behaviors in adult homosexual and heterosexual males. *Journal of Abnormal Psychology, 76,* 396–402.

McCormick, C. M., & Witelson, S. F. (1994). Functional cerebral asymmetry and sexual orientation in men and women. *Behavioral Neuroscience, 108,* 523–531.

McGlone, J. (1980). Sex differences in human brain asymmetry: A critical review. *Brain and Behavioral Sciences, 3,* 215–263.

Meyer-Bahlburg, H. F. L. (1984). Psychoendocrine research on sexual orientation: Current status and future options. *Progress in Brain Research, 61,* 375–398.

Meyer-Bahlburg, H. F. L. (1993). Psychobiologic research on homosexuality. *Child and Adolescent Psychiatric Clinics of North America, 2,* 489–500.

Nash, J., & Hayes, F. (1965). The parental relationships of male homosexuals: Some theoretical issues and a pilot study. *Australian Journal of Psychology, 17,* 35–43.

Pattatucci, A. M. (1998). Molecular investigations into complex behavior: Lessons from sexual orientation studies. *Human Biology, 70,* 367.

Pattatucci, A. M. L., & Hamer, D. H. (1995). Development and familiality of sexual orientation in females. *Behavior Genetics, 25,* 407–420.

Perkins, M. W. (1981). Female homosexuality and body build. *Archives of Sexual Behavior, 10,* 337–345.

Pillard, R. C. (1990). The Kinsey scale: Is it familial? In D. P. McWhirter, S. A. Sanders, & J. M. Reinsch (Eds.), *Homosexuality/heterosexuality: Concepts of sexual orientation* (pp. 88–100). New York: Oxford University Press.

Pillard, R. C., Poumadere, J., & Carretta, R. A. (1982). A family study of sexual orientation. *Archives of Sexual Behavior, 11,* 511–520.

Pillard, R. C., & Weinrich, J. D. (1986). Evidence of familial nature of male homosexuality. *Archives of General Psychiatry, 43,* 808–812.

Plomin, R., DeFries, J. C., & McClearn, G. E. (1990). *Behavioral genetics: A primer* (2nd ed.). New York: W. H. Freeman.

Price, J. S., & Hare, E. H. (1969). Birth order studies: Some sources of bias. *British Journal of Psychiatry, 115,* 633–646.

Reite, M., Sheeder, J., Richardson, D., & Teale, P. (1995). Cerebral laterality in homosexual males: Preliminary communication using magnetoencephalography. *Archives of Sexual Behavior, 24,* 585–593.

Resnick, S. M., Berenbaum, S. A., Gottesman, I. I., & Bouchard, T. J. (1986). Early hormonal influences on cognitive functioning in congenital adrenal hyperplasia. *Developmental Psychology, 22,* 191–198.

Risch, N., Squires-Wheeler, E., & Keats, B. J. B. (1993). Male sexual orientation and genetic evidence. *Science, 262,* 2063–2065.

Sanders, G., & Ross-Field, L. (1986). Sexual orientation and visuo-spatial ability. *Brain and Cognition, 5,* 280–290.

Sanders, G., & Wright, M. (1997). Sexual orientation differences in cerebral asymmetry and in the performance of sexually dimorphic cognitive and motor tasks. *Archives of Sexual Behavior, 26,* 463–480.

Scarr, S., & Carter-Saltzman, L. (1979). Twin method: Defense of a critical assumption. *Behavior Genetics, 9,* 527–542.

Siever, M. D. (1994). Sexual orientation and gender as factors in socioculturally acquired vulnerability to body dissatisfaction and eating disorders. *Journal of Consulting and Clinical Psychology, 62,* 252–260.

Silberstein, L. R., Mishkind, M. E., Striegel-Moore, R. H., Timko, C., & Rodin, J. (1989). Men and their bodies: A comparison of homosexual and heterosexual men. *Psychosomatic Medicine, 51,* 337–346.

Slater, E. (1958). The sibs and children of homosexuals. In D. R. Smith & W. M. Davidson (Eds.), *Symposium on nuclear sex* (pp. 79–83). London: Heinemann Medical Books.

Slater, E. (1962). Birth order and maternal age of homosexuals. *Lancet, 1,* 69–71.

Stephan, W. G. (1973). Parental relationships and early social experiences of activist male homosexuals and male heterosexuals. *Journal of Abnormal Psychology, 82,* 340–353.

Swaab, D. F., & Fliers, E. (1985). A sexually dimorphic nucleus in the human brain. *Science, 228,* 1112–1115.

van den Aardweg, G. J. M. (1986). *On the origins and treatment of homosexuality: A psychoanalytic interpretation.* New York: Praeger.

Voyer, D., Voyer, S., & Bryden, M. P. (1995). Magnitude of sex differences in spatial abilities: A meta-analysis and consideration of critical variables. *Psychological Bulletin, 117,* 250–270.

Watson, N. V., & Kimura, D. (1991). Nontrivial sex differences in throwing and intercepting: Relation to psychometrically-defined spatial functions. *Personality and Individual, 12,* 375–385.

West, D. J. (1977). *Homosexuality re-examined.* Minneapolis: University of Minnesota Press.

Whalen, R. E., & Edwards, D. A. (1967). Hormonal determinants of the development of masculine and feminine behavior in male and female rats. *Anatomic Record, 157,* 173–180.

Whitam, F. L., Diamond, M., & Martin, J. (1993). Homosexual orientation in twins: A report on 61 pairs and three triplet sets. *Archives of Sexual Behavior, 22,* 187–206.

White, P. C., New, M. I., & Dupont, B. (1987). Congenital adrenal hyperplasia. *New England Journal of Medicine, 316,* 1519–1524, 1580–1586.

Williams, C. L., & Meck, W. H. (1991). The organizational effects of gonadal steroids on sexually dimorphic spatial ability. *Psychoneuroendocrinology, 16*, 155–176.

Yager, J., Kurtzman, F., Landsverk, J., & Wiesmeier, E. (1988). Behaviors and attitudes related to eating disorders in homosexual male college students. *American Journal of Psychiatry, 145*, 495–497.

Yeudall, L. T., Fromm, D., Reddon, J. R., & Stefanyk, W. O. (1986). Normative data stratified by age and sex for 12 neuropsychological tests. *Journal of Clinical Psychology, 42*, 918–946.

Zucker, K. J., & Blanchard, R. (1994). Re-analysis of Bieber et al.'s 1962 data on sibling sex ratio and birth order in male homosexuals. *Journal of Nervous and Mental Disease, 182*, 528–530.

Zucker, K. J., & Bradley, S. J. (1995). *Gender identity disorder and psychosexual problems in children and adolescents*. New York: Guilford Press.

Zucker, K. J., Bradley, S. J., Oliver, G., Hood, J. E., Blake, J., & Fleming, S. (1992, July). *Psychosexual assessment of women with congenital adrenal hyperplasia: Preliminary analyses*. Poster presented at the meeting of the International Academy of Sex Research, Prague.

Zucker, K. J., Wild, J., Bradley, S. J., & Lowry, C. B. (1993). Physical attractiveness of boys with gender identity disorder. *Archives of Sexual Behavior, 22*, 23–34.

3

Exotic Becomes Erotic

Integrating Biological and Experiential Antecedents of Sexual Orientation

Daryl J. Bem

The common question "What causes homosexuality?" is scientifically misconceived because it presumes that heterosexuality is so well understood—so obviously the "natural" evolutionary consequence of reproductive advantage—that only deviations from it are theoretically problematic. Freud himself did not so presume: "[Heterosexuality] is also a problem that needs elucidation and is not a self-evident fact based upon an attraction that is ultimately of a chemical nature" (1905/1962, pp. 11–12).

I agree with Freud. In fact, I would go further and assert that even the use of gender as the basis for choosing a sexual partner is a problem that needs elucidation. Accordingly, my Exotic-Becomes-Erotic (EBE) theory of sexual orientation (D. J. Bem, 1996) seeks to account for three major observations: First, most men and women in our culture have an exclusive and enduring erotic preference for either male or female persons; gender is, in fact, the overriding criterion for most people's erotic choices. Second, most men and women in our culture have an exclusive and enduring erotic preference for opposite-sex persons. And third, a substantial minority of men and women have an exclusive and enduring erotic preference for same-sex persons.

In seeking to account for these observations, EBE theory provides a single unitary explanation for both opposite-sex and same-sex desire—and for both men and women. In addition, the theory seeks to account for sex differences in sexual orientation and departures from the modal patterns, such as bisexual orientations, orientations that are not enduring but fluid and changeable, and sexual orientations that are not even based on the gender of potential partners.

The academic discourse on sexual orientation is currently dominated by biological essentialists—who can point to evidence linking sexual orientation to biological factors, and social constructionists—who can point to evidence that sexual orientation is itself a socially constructed, culture-bound notion (De Cecco & Elia, 1993; Stein, 1992). The personality, clinical, and developmental theorists who once dominated the discourse on this topic have fallen conspicuously silent. Some have probably become closet converts to biology because they cannot point to a coherent body of evidence that supports a developmental, experience-based account of sexual orientation. This would be understandable; such theories have not fared well empirically.

The most telling data come from an intensive, large-scale interview study conducted in the San Francisco Bay Area by the Kinsey Institute for Sex Research (Bell, Weinberg, & Hammersmith, 1981a). Using retrospective reports from adult respondents, the investigators compared approximately 1,000 gay men and lesbians with 500 heterosexual men and women to test several hypotheses about the development of sexual orientation. The study (hereinafter, the "San Francisco study") yielded virtually no support for current experience-based theories of sexual orientation, including those based on processes of learning or conditioning or on family psychodynamics. In fact, family variables were not strongly implicated in the development of sexual orientation for either men or women.

But before we all become geneticists, biopsychologists, or neuroanatomists, it seemed to me worth another try. In particular, I believed that the theoretical and empirical building blocks for a coherent developmental, experience-based theory of sexual orientation were already scattered about in the literature. Accordingly, the development of EBE theory was an exercise in synthesis and construction.

Overview of the Theory

The central proposition of EBE theory is that individuals can become erotically attracted to a class of individuals about whom they felt different during childhood. Figure 3.1 shows how this phenomenon is embedded into the overall sequence of events that lead to an individual's erotic attractions—the component of sexual orientation addressed by the theory. The sequence begins at the top of the figure with Biological Variables (labeled A) and ends at the bottom with Erotic Attraction (F).

- A→B. According to the theory, biological variables such as genes or prenatal hormones do not code for sexual orientation per se but for childhood temperaments, such as aggression and activity level.
- B→C. A child's temperaments predispose him or her to enjoy some activities more than others. One child will enjoy rough-and-tumble play

Overview of the Theory

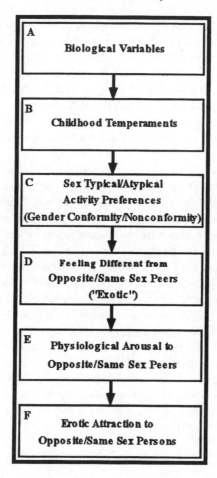

Figure 3.1. The temporal sequence of
events leading to sexual orientation
for most men and women in a gender-
polarizing culture.

and competitive team sports (male-typical activities); another will prefer to socialize quietly or play jacks or hopscotch (female-typical activities). Children will also prefer to play with peers who share their
activity preferences; for example, the child who enjoys baseball or football will selectively seek out boys as playmates. Children who prefer
sex-typical activities and same-sex playmates are referred to as gender conforming; children who prefer sex-atypical activities and opposite-sex playmates are referred to as gender nonconforming.

• C→D. Gender-conforming children will feel different from opposite-sex peers, and gender-nonconforming children will feel different from same-sex peers.

- D→E. These feelings of being different produce heightened physiological arousal. For the male-typical child, it may be felt as antipathy or contempt in the presence of girls ("girls are yucky"); for the female-typical child, it may be felt as timidity or apprehension in the presence of boys. A particularly clear example is provided by the "sissy" boy who is taunted by male peers for his gender nonconformity and, as a result, is likely to experience the strong physiological arousal of fear and anger in their presence. The theory claims, however, that every child—conforming or nonconforming—experiences heightened, nonspecific physiological arousal in the presence of peers from whom he or she feels different. For most children, this arousal in neither affectively toned nor consciously experienced.
- E→F. Regardless of the specific source or affective tone of the childhood arousal, it is subsequently transformed into erotic attraction. Steps D→E and E→F thus encompass specific psychological mechanisms that transform exotic into erotic (D→F).

It is important to emphasize that figure 3.1 is not intended to describe an inevitable, universal path to sexual orientation but the modal path followed by most men and women in a gender-polarizing culture like ours, a culture that emphasizes the differences between the sexes by pervasively organizing both the perceptions and realities of communal life around the male-female dichotomy (S. L. Bem, 1993).

Evidence for the Theory

Exotic Becomes Erotic (D→F)

The central proposition that individuals can become erotically attracted to a class of individuals from whom they felt different during childhood is very general and transcends erotic orientations that are based on gender. For example, a light-skinned person could come to eroticize dark-skinned persons through one or more of the processes described by the theory. To produce a differential erotic attraction to one sex or the other, however, requires that the basis for feeling different must itself differentiate between the sexes; that is, to arrive at a sex-based erotic orientation, an individual must feel different for sex-based or gender-related reasons. Simply being lighter-skinned, poorer, more intelligent, or more introverted than one's childhood peers does not produce the kind of feeling different that produces differential homoerotic or heteroerotic attraction.

Data consistent with this analysis come from the San Francisco study, in which 71% of the gay men and 70% of the lesbians in the sample reported that they had felt different from their same-sex peers during childhood, a feeling that for most respondents was sustained throughout childhood and adolescence. When asked in what ways they had felt different, they over-whelmingly cited gender-related reasons. Gay men were most likely to say that they had not liked boys' sports; lesbians were most likely to say that had been more masculine than other girls and had been more interested in sports than other girls. In contrast, fewer than 8% of heterosexual men or women said that they had felt different from same-sex childhood peers for gender-related reasons. Those who had felt different from their peers tended to cite such reasons as having been poorer, more intelligent, or more intro-verted. (All statistical comparisons between gay and heterosexual respon-dents were significant at $p < .0005$.)

In addition to the San Francisco study, several other studies have reported that gay men and lesbians recall having felt different from same-sex peers on gender-related characteristics during childhood (e.g., Newman & Muzzonigro, 1993; Savin-Williams, 1998; Telljohann & Price, 1993; Troiden, 1979). The major weakness of all these studies, including the San Francisco study, is that they rely on adults' retrospective reports of childhood feelings. It is true that the respondents in some of the studies were relatively close in time to their child-hood years; in one study, for example, 88% of gay male youths as young as 14 years reported having felt different from other boys on gender-related characteristics during their childhood years (Savin-Williams, 1998) . More-over, the link between childhood gender nonconformity and sexual orien-tation—described in the next section—has been confirmed in over 40 stud-ies, including 7 prospective ones (Bailey & Zucker, 1995). Nevertheless, there are no studies that explicitly identified children who felt different from same- or opposite-sex peers and then followed them up into adulthood to assess their sexual orientations.

Gender Conformity and Nonconformity: The Antecedents of Feeling Different (C→D)

Feeling different from one's childhood peers can have any of several ante-cedents, some common, some idiosyncratic. The most common antecedent is gender polarization. Virtually all human societies polarize the sexes to some extent, setting up a sex-based division of labor and power, emphasiz-ing or exaggerating sex differences, and, in general, superimposing the male-female dichotomy on virtually every aspect of communal life (S. L. Bem, 1993). These practices ensure that most boys and girls will grow up feeling different from opposite-sex peers and, hence, will come to be erotically at-tracted to them later in life. This, according to the theory, is why gender becomes the most salient category and, hence, the most common criterion for selecting sexual partners in the first place and why heteroeroticism is the modal preference across time and culture.

A less common occurrence is the child who comes to feel different from same-sex peers and who, according to the theory, will develop same-sex erotic attractions. As noted above, the most common reasons given by gay men and lesbians in the San Francisco study for having felt different from same-sex peers in childhood were sex-atypical preferences and behaviors in childhood—gender nonconformity. In fact, childhood gender conformity or nonconformity was not only the strongest but the only significant childhood predictor of later sexual orientation for both men and women in the study (Bell et al., 1981a). As table 3.1 shows, the effects are large and significant. For example, compared with heterosexual men, gay men were significantly less likely to have enjoyed boys' activities (e.g., baseball and football) during childhood, more likely to have enjoyed girls' activities (e.g., hopscotch, playing house, and jacks), and less likely to rate themselves as having been masculine. These were the three variables that defined gender nonconformity in the study. Additionally, gay men were more likely than heterosexual men to have had girls as childhood friends. The corresponding comparisons between lesbian and heterosexual women are also large and significant.

It is also clear from the table that relatively more women than men reported enjoying sex-atypical activities and having opposite-sex friends during childhood. As these data confirm, enjoying male-typical activities is common for a girl in our society, implying that it is not sufficient by itself to cause her to feel different from other girls. In fact, we see in the table that the difference between the percentages of lesbians and heterosexual women who report having enjoyed boys' activities during childhood (81% vs. 61%, respectively) is less than half the size of the difference between them in their aversion to girls' activities (63% vs. 15%). Moreover, this latter difference is virtually identical to that between gay men and heterosexual men in their reported childhood aversions to boys' activities (63% vs. 10%).

Table 3.1
Percentage of Respondents Reporting Gender-Nonconforming Preferences and Behaviors During Childhood

| | MEN | | WOMEN | |
RESPONSE	GAY (N = 686)	HETEROSEXUAL (N = 337)	LESBIAN (N = 293)	HETEROSEXUAL (N = 140)
Had not enjoyed sex-typical activities	63	10	63	15
Had enjoyed sex-atypical activities	48	11	81	61
Atypically sex-typed (masculinity/femininity)	56	8	80	24
Most childhood friends were opposite sex	42	13	60	40

Note. Percentages have been calculated from the data given in Bell, Weinberg, and Hammersmith (1981b, pp. 74–75, 77). All chi-square comparisons between gay and heterosexual subgroups are significant at $p < .0001$.

As noted in the previous section, the San Francisco study does not stand alone. A meta-analysis of 41 studies confirmed that gay men and lesbians are more likely than heterosexual men and women to recall gender-nonconforming behaviors and interests in childhood (Bailey & Zucker, 1995). As the authors observed, "these are among the largest effect sizes ever reported in the realm of sex-dimorphic behaviors" (p. 49). Prospective longitudinal studies come to the same conclusion. In the largest of these, 75% of gender-nonconforming boys became bisexual or homosexual in later years compared to only 4% of gender-conforming boys (Green, 1987). In six other prospective studies, 63% of gender-nonconforming boys later had homosexual orientations (Zucker, 1990). One must generalize from these prospective studies with caution, however, because most of the boys studied were more sex-atypical than most gay men would have been during their childhood years; many would have met the *Diagnostic and Statistical Manual of Mental Disorders* (4th. ed; DSM-IV) diagnostic criteria for gender identity disorder (American Psychiatric Association, 1994). Also, there are currently no prospective studies of gender-nonconforming girls.

How Does Exotic Become Erotic? (D→E→F)

EBE theory proposes that exotic becomes erotic because feeling different from a class of peers in childhood produces heightened nonspecific physiological arousal (D→E) that is subsequently transformed into erotic attraction (E→F). To my knowledge, there is no direct evidence for the first step in this sequence beyond the well-documented observation that "exotic" stimuli produce heightened physiological arousal in many species, including our own (Mook, 1987); filling in this empirical gap in EBE theory must await future research. In contrast, there are at least three mechanisms that can potentially effect the second step: transforming generalized arousal into erotic attraction (D. J. Bem, 1996). Only one of these, the extrinsic arousal effect, is discussed here.

In his first-century Roman handbook, *The Art of Love,* Ovid advised any man who was interested in sexual seduction to take the woman in whom he was interested to a gladiatorial tournament, where she would more easily be aroused to passion. He did not say why this should be so, however. A contemporary version of Ovid's claim was introduced by Walster (Berscheid & Walster, 1974; Walster, 1971), who suggested that it constitutes a special case of Schachter and Singer's (1962) two-factor theory of emotion. That theory states that the physiological arousal of our autonomic nervous system provides the cues that we feel emotional but that the more subtle judgment of *which* emotion we are feeling often depends on our cognitive appraisal of the surrounding circumstances. According to Walster, then, the experience of erotic desire results from the conjunction of physiological arousal and the cognitive causal attribution (or misattribution) that the arousal is elicited by a potential sexual partner.

Although not all investigators agree that it arises from a cognitive attribution process, there is now extensive experimental evidence that an individual who has been physiologically aroused will show heightened sexual responsiveness to an appropriate target person. In one set of studies, male participants were physiologically aroused by running in place, by hearing an audio tape of a comedy routine, or by hearing an audio tape of a grisly killing (White, Fishbein, & Rutstein, 1981). No matter how they had been aroused, these men reported more erotic interest in a physically attractive woman than did men who had not been aroused. This effect has also been observed physiologically. In two studies, preexposure to a disturbing (non-sexual) videotape subsequently produced greater penile tumescence in men and greater vaginal blood volume increases in women when they watched an erotic videotape than did preexposure to a non-disturbing videotape (Hoon, Wincze, & Hoon, 1977; Wolchik et al., 1980).

In other words, generalized physiological arousal, regardless of its source or affective tone, can subsequently be experienced as erotic desire. At that point, it *is* erotic desire. My proposal, then, is that an individual's protracted and sustained experience of feeling different from same- or opposite-sex peers throughout childhood and adolescence produces a correspondingly sustained physiological arousal that gets eroticized when the maturational, cognitive, and situational factors coalesce to provide the critical defining moment.

Just when that moment arrives, however, is influenced by many factors, including actual sexual experience with opposite- and same-sex peers. A recent review suggests that, in general, men and women recall their first sexual attractions—whether same-sex or opposite-sex—as occurring when they were between 10 and 10.5 years of age (McClintock & Herdt, 1996). Nevertheless, social norms and expectations inevitably influence an individual's awareness and interpretation of early arousal. Most individuals in our culture are primed to anticipate, recognize, and interpret opposite-sex arousal as erotic or romantic attraction and to ignore, repress, or differently interpret comparable same-sex arousal. We should also expect to see cohort effects. For example, the heightened visibility of gay men and lesbians in our society is now prompting individuals who experience same-sex arousal to recognize it, label it, and act on it at earlier ages than in previous years (Dubé, 1997; Fox, 1995; Savin-Williams, 1995, 1998).

The Biological Connection $(A \rightarrow F)$ vs. $(A \rightarrow B)$

In recent years, many sexuality researchers, the public, and segments of the lesbian/gay/bisexual community have been quick to embrace the thesis that a homosexual orientation is coded in the genes or is directly influenced by prenatal hormones and brain neuroanatomy. Even the authors of the San Francisco study—whose findings failed to support most experience-based theories of sexual orientation—appeared ready to concede the ball game to biology. Public opinion has also changed. In 1983, only 16% of Americans believed that "homosexuality is something that people are born with"; by 1993, that figure had nearly doubled to 31% (Moore, 1993). Many members of the lesbian/gay/bisexual community welcome this trend. For example, *The Advocate*, a national gay and lesbian newsmagazine, reported that 61% of its readers believed that "it would mostly help gay and lesbian rights if homosexuality were found to be biologically determined" (1996). (There has been increasing awareness, however, that biological explanations of group differences have historically been anything but politically benign [e.g., D. J. Bem, 1998a; LeVay, 1993]).

In contrast to the increasingly prevailing view that sexual orientation is directly influenced by prenatal biological factors, EBE theory proposes that such factors influence sexual orientation only indirectly, by intervening earlier in the chain of events to influence a child's temperaments and subsequent activity preferences. Only the genetic findings are discussed here.

GENES AND HOMOSEXUALITY

There have now been several studies showing a correlation between an individual's genotype and his or her sexual orientation. In one, a sample of 115 gay men who had male twins, 52% of identical twin brothers were also gay compared with only 22% of fraternal twin brothers and 11% of adopted brothers (Bailey & Pillard, 1991). In a comparable sample of 115 lesbians, 48% of identical twin sisters were also lesbians compared with only 16% of fraternal twin sisters and 6% of adopted sisters (Bailey, Pillard, Neale, & Agyei, 1993). A subsequent study of nearly 5,000 twins who had been systematically drawn from a twin registry confirmed the significant heritability of sexual orientation for men but not for women (Bailey & Martin, 1995). Finally, an analysis of families in which there were two gay brothers suggested a correlation between a homosexual orientation and the inheritance of genetic markers on the X chromosome (Hamer & Copeland, 1994; Hamer, Hu, Magnuson, Hu, & Pattatucci, 1993).

But these same studies also provided evidence for the link proposed by EBE theory between an individual's genotype and his or her childhood gender nonconformity. For example, in the 1991 study of male twins, the correlation on gender nonconformity between gay identical twins was .76 ($p < .0001$), compared to a nonsignificant correlation of only .43 between gay fraternal twins (Bailey & Pillard, 1991). This implies that even when sexual orientation is held constant, there is a significant correlation between the genotype and gender nonconformity. Similarly, the 1993 family study found that gay brothers who shared the same genetic markers on the X chromosome were more alike on gender nonconformity than were gay brothers who did not (Hamer & Copeland, 1994; Hamer et al., 1993). Finally, childhood gender nonconformity was significantly heritable for both men and women in the large twin registry study—even though sexual orientation itself was not heritable for the women (Bailey & Martin, 1995).

EBE theory further specifies that this link between the genotype and gender nonconformity (A→C) is composed of two parts: a link between the genotype and childhood temperaments (A→B) and a link between those temperaments and gender nonconformity (B→C). This implies that the mediating temperaments should possess three characteristics: First, they should be plausibly related to those childhood activities that define gender conformity and nonconformity. Second, because they manifest themselves in sex-typed preferences, they should show sex differences. And third, because they are hypothesized to derive from the genotype, they should have significant heritabilities. (For general discussions and reviews of childhood temperaments, see Goldsmith et al., 1987; Kohnstamm, Bates, & Rothbart, 1989).

One likely candidate is aggression and its benign cousin, rough-and-tumble play. In one study, gay men scored lower than heterosexual men on a measure of childhood aggression (Blanchard, McConkey, Roper, & Steiner, 1983), and parents of gender-nonconforming boys specifically rate them as having less interest in rough-and-tumble play than do parents of gender-conforming boys (Green, 1976). Second, the sex difference in aggression during childhood is one of the largest psychological sex differences known (Hyde, 1984). Rough-and-tumble play in particular is more common in boys than in girls (DiPietro, 1981; Fry, 1990; Moller, Hymel, & Rubin, 1992). And third, individual differences in aggression have a large heritable component (Rushton, Fulker, Neale, Nias, & Eysenck, 1986).

Another likely candidate is activity level, considered to be one of the basic childhood temperaments (Buss & Plomin, 1975; 1984). Like aggression, differences in activity level would seem to characterize the differences between male-typical and female-typical play activities in childhood. Moreover, gender-nonconforming boys and girls are lower and higher on activity level, respectively, than are control children of the same sex (Bates, Bentler, & Thompson, 1973, 1979; Zucker & Green, 1993). Second, the sex difference in activity level is as large as it is for aggression. Even before birth, boys in utero are more active than girls (Eaton & Enns, 1986). And third, individual differences in activity level have a large heritable component (Plomin, 1986; Rowe, 1997).

GENES AND HETEROSEXUALITY

As noted earlier, EBE theory suggests that heterosexuality is the modal outcome across time and culture because virtually all human societies polarize the sexes to some extent, setting up a sex-based division of labor and power, emphasizing or exaggerating sex differences, and, in general, superimposing the male-female dichotomy on virtually every aspect of communal life. These gender-polarizing practices ensure that most boys and girls will grow up seeing the other sex as exotic and, hence, erotic. Thus, the theory provides a culturally based alternative to the assumption that evolution must necessarily have programmed heterosexuality into the species for reasons of reproductive advantage.

I am certainly willing to concede that heterosexual behavior is reproductively advantageous, but it does not follow that it must therefore be sustained through genetic transmission. As long as prevailing environments support or promote a reproductively successful behavior sufficiently often, it will not necessarily get programmed into the genes by evolution. This is true even in species whose sexual choices are far more "hardwired" than our own. For example, it is presumably reproductively advantageous for ducks to mate with other ducks, but as long as most baby ducklings encounter other ducks before they encounter a member of some other species (including ethologists), evolution can simply implant the imprinting process itself into the species rather than the specific content of what, reproductively speaking, needs to be imprinted (Hess & Petrovich, 1977). Analogously, because most cultures ensure that boys and girls will see each other as exotic, it would be sufficient for evolution to implant an exotic-becomes-erotic process into our species rather than heterosexuality per se. In fact, in some species an exotic-becomes-erotic process is actually a built-in component of sexual imprinting. For example, Japanese quail reared with their siblings later preferred their slightly different-appearing cousins to their own siblings (Bateson, 1978). This has been interpreted as a mechanism that prevents inbreeding—a biologically promoted incest taboo.

Other Biological Correlates

In addition to the genotype, prenatal hormones and brain neuroanatomy have been correlated with sexual orientation in some studies (for summaries, reviews, and critiques see Bailey, 1995; D. J. Bem, 1996; Byne & Parsons, 1993; Zucker & Bradley, 1995). But these correlations—even if they turn out to be replicable and not artifactual—do not necessarily controvert the EBE account. Any biological factor that correlates with one or more of the intervening processes proposed by EBE theory could also emerge as a correlate of sexual orientation. For example, any neuroanatomical feature of the brain that correlates with childhood aggression or activity level is likely to emerge as a difference between gay men and heterosexual men, between women and men, and between heterosexual women and lesbians. Even if EBE theory turns out to be wrong, the more general point—that a mediating personality variable could account for observed correlations between biological variables and sexual orientation—still holds.

Individual Differences

As noted earlier, figure 3.1 is not intended to describe an inevitable, universal path to sexual orientation but only the modal path followed by most men and women in a gender-polarizing culture like ours. Individual differences, including apparent exceptions to the theory, can arise in a number of ways. First, of course, the theory could simply be wrong or incomplete in fundamental ways. But some of the apparent exceptions to the sequence of events laid out in figure 3.1 are arguably theory-consistent variations.

One such possibility is that some individuals enter the EBE path in the middle of the sequence rather than at the beginning. For example, some children may come to feel different from same-sex peers not because of a temperamentally induced preference for sex-atypical activities but because of more idiosyncratic factors, such as a physical disability, an illness, or an atypical lack of contact with same-sex peers. Some of the gay men and lesbians in the San Francisco study reported that although they had been sex typical in childhood, they still felt different from their same-sex peers. Moreover, sex-typical lesbians in the study were more likely than heterosexual women to report that most of their friends in grade school had been boys. And, consistent with the subsequent steps in the EBE path, this was the strongest predictor of homosexual involvements in adolescence and their homosexual orientation in adulthood.

Cultural factors can also enter to create individual differences that appear to be exceptions to the EBE model. For example, some children might have an activity preference that is gender neutral or even sex typical in the wider culture but gender deviant in their own peer subculture. A contemporary example is the boy who is a clever computer hacker: He would be considered a "regular guy" or even a hero in some male subcultures but a gender-deviant "nerd" in others. Similarly, a child can be permissibly gender nonconforming in some ways—and hence not feel different from same-sex peers—if he or she is gender conforming in other ways that are more gender defining in his or her subculture. And finally, changes in the wider culture can produce cohort effects; behaviors that are gender nonconforming in one cohort can become more or less so in a later cohort.

For some individuals, the erotic attractions predicted by EBE theory might be supplemented or even superseded by erotic attractions acquired after adolescence. For example, the same-sex eroticism of most of the bisexual men and women in the San Francisco study appeared to be a socially learned, post-adolescent "add-on" to an already established heterosexual orientation. Correspondingly, the bisexual respondents differed from their exclusively homosexual counterparts on some of the major antecedent variables. For example, the path correlation between gender nonconformity and same-sex eroticism was only .18 for the bisexual women, but it was .62 for the exclusively homosexual women. In fact, 80% of the bisexual women and 75% of the bisexual men in the study reported that as children they had been sex-typically feminine or masculine, respectively.

Finally, some women who would otherwise be predicted by the EBE model to have a heterosexual orientation might choose for social or political reasons to center their lives around other women. This could lead them to avoid seeking out men for sexual or romantic relationships, to develop affectional and erotic ties to other women, and to self-identify as lesbians or bisexuals (Kitzinger, 1987).

This last observation points to an important sex difference: women's sexual orientations appear to be more fluid than men's. Many studies, including the San Francisco study and a national random survey of Americans (Laumann, Gagnon, Michael, & Michaels, 1994), have found that women are more likely to be bisexual than exclusively homosexual, whereas the reverse is true for men. Nonheterosexual women are also more likely to see their sexual orientations as flexible, even "chosen," whereas men are more likely to view their sexual orientations in essentialist terms, as inborn and unchangeable (Whisman, 1996). For example, men who come out as gay after leaving heterosexual marriages or relationships often describe themselves as having "finally realized" their "true" sexual orientations. Similarly situated lesbians, however, are more likely to reject the implication that their previous heterosexual relationships were inauthentic or at odds with who they really were: "That's who I was then, and this is who I am now."

The greater fluidity of women's sexual orientations is consistent with EBE theory. As noted earlier, figure 3.1 describes the path to sexual orientation *in a gender-polarizing culture*. But in our society women grow up in a (phenomenologically) less gender-polarized culture than do men. Compared with boys, girls are punished less for being gender nonconforming, and, as the data in table 3.1 reveal, they are more likely than boys to engage in both sex-typical and sex-atypical activities and are more likely to have childhood friends of both sexes. This implies that girls are less likely than boys to feel *differentially* different from opposite-sex and same-sex peers and, hence, are less likely to develop exclusively heteroerotic or homoerotic orientations.

Accordingly, many of today's nonheterosexual women may be giving us a preview of what sexual orientations might look like in a less gender-polarized future. It is possible that we might even begin to see more men and women who, instead of using gender as the overriding criterion for selecting their partners, might base their erotic and romantic choices on a more diverse and idiosyncratic variety of attributes. As I have remarked elsewhere, "Gentlemen might still prefer blonds, but some of those gentlemen (and some ladies) might prefer blonds of any sex" (D. J. Bem, 1996, p. 332).

Future Research

I noted in the introduction that the development of EBE theory has been an exercise in synthesis and construction; it has been assembled from findings scattered across several literatures. This means that there are several causal links and psychological events proposed in the theory that have not been directly or adequately tested. For example, the theory implies that gender nonconforming children should show more autonomic arousal in the presence of same-sex peers than in the presence of opposite-sex peers (and vice versa for gender conforming children). As noted earlier, this has not yet been tested.

Although it is unlikely that we will soon have prospective longitudinal studies that assess whether children who feel different from same-sex peers for gender reasons are more likely than other children to emerge as adults with homosexual orientations, it is still possible to ask children who are (or are not) gender nonconforming how different they feel from same- and opposite-sex peers. Because the link between childhood gender nonconformity and adult sexual orientation is fairly well established, such data, if confirming, would strengthen the EBE claim that feeling different from childhood peers is also an antecedent of adult sexual orientation. It is particularly important to study children who are only moderately sex-atypical rather than those likely to be diagnosed as having a gender identity disorder.

I have asserted, and subsequently defended, the claim that the EBE account of erotic attraction is as valid for women as it is for men (D. J. Bem, 1998b), but not everyone is convinced (Peplau, Garnets, Spalding, Conley, & Veniegas, 1998). There appears to be agreement that there are real differences between men and women in the salience of their sexual interests and in their willingness to engage in sexual activity in the absence of intimacy or romantic involvement, but there is disagreement over the relevance of these differences for the nature of men's and women's sexual orientations. Whether this disagreement can be resolved empirically remains to be seen, but the issue certainly warrants further conceptual clarification—if only to decide whether it can, in fact, be resolved empirically.

Finally, there is the major issue of whether any of the biological variables (e.g., genes, prenatal hormones, brain neuroanatomy) directly code for sexual orientation per se or operate only indirectly through some set of mediating processes, such as those in EBE theory. Existing data appear to be consistent with both possibilities, and this is likely to remain so until a link between a biological variable and sexual orientation can be demonstrated that cannot plausibly be attributed to a mediating variable.

On the other hand, it may be possible to test the competing models in an indirect way by performing path analyses on data from existing twin studies (Bailey & Martin, 1995; Bailey & Pillard, 1991; Bailey et al., 1993). All of these studies gathered information from monozygotic and dizygotic twin pairs about their sexual orientation and their childhood gender nonconformity. The EBE model predicts that the correlation between the genotype and sexual orientation reported in these studies is mediated by gender nonconformity and, hence, should vanish when gender nonconformity is entered into the path model. In contrast, the competing "direct" model appears to assume that the genotype is independently linked to both gender nonconformity and sexual orientation; hence, the correlation between the genotype and sexual orientation should remain unchanged when gender nonconformity is entered into the path model. I have performed a very preliminary path analysis on unpublished data from the Bailey and Martin study (1995), an analysis which appears to support the EBE model. But nothing definitive can be said until there is agreement that this is a valid test of the competing models and, if it is, that the details of the path analysis are in order and that the results can be replicated in all three sets of data.

References

The Advocate (Eds.). (1996). *Advocate Poll Results*. p. 8

American Psychiatric Association (1994). *Diagnostic and statistical manual of mental disorders* (4th ed.). Washington, DC: Author.

Bailey, J. M. (1995). Biological perspectives on sexual orientation. In A. R. D'Augelli & C. J. Patterson (Eds.), *Lesbian, gay and bisexual identities over the lifespan* (pp. 102–135). New York: Oxford University Press.

Bailey, J. M., & Martin, N. G. (1995, September). *A twin registry study of sexual orientation*. Paper presented at the twenty-first annual meeting of the International Academy of Sex Research, Provincetown, MA.

Bailey, J. M., & Pillard, R. C. (1991). A genetic study of male sexual orientation. *Archives of General Psychiatry, 48*, 1089–1096.

Bailey, J. M., Pillard, R. C., Neale, M. C., & Agyei, Y. (1993). Heritable factors influence sexual orientation in women. *Archives of General Psychiatry, 50*, 217–223.

Bailey, J. M., & Zucker, K. J. (1995). Childhood sex-typed behavior and sexual orientation: A conceptual analysis and quantitative review. *Developmental Psychology, 31*, 43–55.

Bates, J. E., Bentler, P. M., & Thompson, S. K. (1973). Measurement of deviant gender development in boys. *Child Development, 44*, 591–598.

Bates, J. E., Bentler, P. M., & Thompson, S. K. (1979). Gender-deviant boys compared with normal and clinical control boys. *Journal of Abnormal Child Psychology, 7*, 243–259.

Bateson, P. P. G. (1978). Sexual imprinting and optimal outbreeding. *Nature, 273*, 659–660.

Bell, A. P., Weinberg, M. S., & Hammersmith, S. K. (1981a). *Sexual preference: Its development in men and women*. Bloomington: Indiana University Press.

Bell, A. P., Weinberg, M. S., & Hammersmith, S. K. (1981b). *Sexual preference: Its development in men and women. Statistical appendix*. Bloomington: Indiana University Press.

Bem, D. J. (1996). Exotic becomes erotic: A developmental theory of sexual orientation. *Psychological Review, 103*, 320–335.

Bem, D. J. (1998a). The exotic-becomes-erotic theory of sexual orientation. In J. Corvino (Ed.), *Same sex: Debating the ethics, science, and culture of homosexuality* (pp. 121–134). New York: Rowman & Littlefield.

Bem, D. J. (1998b). Is EBE theory supported by the evidence? Is it androcentric? A reply to Peplau et al. *Psychological Review, 105*, 395–398.

Bem, S. L. (1993). *The lenses of gender: Transforming the debate on sexual inequality*. New Haven, CT: Yale University Press.

Berscheid, E., & Walster, E. (1974). A little bit about love. In T. Huston (Ed.), *Foundations of interpersonal attraction* (pp. 355–381). New York: Academic Press.

Blanchard, R., McConkey, J. G., Roper, V., & Steiner, B. W. (1983). Measuring physical aggressiveness in heterosexual, homosexual, and transsexual males. *Archives of Sexual Behavior, 12,* 511–524.

Buss, A. H., & Plomin, R. (1975). *A temperament theory of personality development.* New York: Wiley.

Buss, A. H., & Plomin, R. (1984). *Temperament: Early developing personality traits.* Hillsdale, NJ: Erlbaum.

Byne, W., & Parsons, B. (1993). Human sexual orientation: The biologic theories reappraised. *Archives of General Psychiatry, 50,* 228–239.

De Cecco, J. P., & Elia, J. P. (1993). *If you seduce a straight person, can you make them gay? Issues in biological essentialism versus social constructionism in gay and lesbian identities.* Binghamton, NY: Harrington Park Press.

DiPietro, J. A. (1981). Rough and tumble play: A function of gender. *Developmental Psychology, 17,* 50–58.

Dubé, E. M. (1997). *Sexual identity and intimacy: Development among two cohorts of gay and bisexual men.* Unpublished masters thesis, Cornell University, Ithaca, NY.

Eaton, W. O., & Enns, L. R. (1986). Sex differences in human motor activity level. *Psychological Bulletin, 100,* 19–28.

Fox, R. C. (1995). Bisexual identities. In A. R. D'Augelli & C. J. Patterson (Eds.), *Lesbian, gay and bisexual identities over the lifespan* (pp. 48–86). New York: Oxford University Press.

Freud, S. (1905/1962). *Three essays on the theory of sexuality.* New York: Basic Books.

Fry, D. P. (1990). Play aggression among Zapotec children: Implications for the practice hypothesis. *Aggressive Behavior, 17,* 321–340.

Goldsmith, H. H., Buss, A. H., Plomin, R., Rothbart, M. K., Thomas, A., Chess, S., Hinde, R. A., & McCall, R. B. (1987). Roundtable: What is temperament? Four approaches. *Child Development, 58,* 505–529.

Green, R. (1976). One-hundred ten feminine and masculine boys: Behavioral contrasts and demographic similarities. *Archives of Sexual Behavior, 5,* 425–426.

Green, R. (1987). *The "sissy boy syndrome" and the development of homosexuality.* New Haven, CT: Yale University Press.

Hamer, D., & Copeland, P. (1994). *The science of desire: The search for the gay gene and the biology of behavior.* New York: Simon & Schuster.

Hamer, D. H., Hu, S., Magnuson, V. L., Hu, N., & Pattatucci, A. M. L. (1993). A linkage between DNA markers on the X chromosome and male sexual orientation. *Science, 261,* 321–327.

Hess, E. H., & Petrovich, S. B. (1977). *Imprinting.* Stroudsburg, PA: Dowden, Hutchinson & Ross.

Hoon, P. W., Wincze, J. P., & Hoon, E. F. (1977). A test of reciprocal inhibition: Are anxiety and sexual arousal in women mutually inhibitory? *Journal of Abnormal Psychology, 86,* 65–74.

Hyde, J. S. (1984). How large are gender differences in aggression? A developmental meta-analysis. *Developmental Psychology, 20,* 722–736.

Kitzinger, C. (1987). *The social construction of lesbianism.* London: Sage.

Kohnstamm, G. A., Bates, J. E., & Rothbart, M. K. (1989). *Temperament in childhood.* New York: Wiley.

Laumann, E. O., Gagnon, J. H., Michael, R. T., & Michaels, S. (1994). *The social organization of sexuality: Sexual practices in the United States.* Chicago: University of Chicago Press.

LeVay, S. (1993). *The sexual brain.* Cambridge, MA: MIT Press.

McClintock, M. K., & Herdt, G. (1996). Rethinking puberty: The development of sexual attraction. *Current Directions in Psychological Science, 5,* 178–183.

Moller, L. C., Hymel, S., & Rubin, K. H. (1992). Sex typing in play and popularity in middle childhood. *Sex Roles, 26,* 331–353.

Mook, D. B. (1987). *Motivation: The organization of action.* New York: Norton.

Moore, D. W. (1993). Public polarized on gay issue. *The Gallup Poll Monthly,* 30–34.

Newman, B. S., & Muzzonigro, P. G. (1993). The effects of traditional family values on the coming out process of gay male adolescents. *Adolescence, 28,* 213–226.

Peplau, L. A., Garnets, L. D., Spalding, L. R., Conley, T. D., & Veniegas, R. C. (1998). A critique of Bem's "Exotic Becomes Erotic" theory of sexual orientation. *Psychological Review, 105,* 387–394.

Plomin, R. (1986). *Development, genetics, and psychology.* Hillsdale, NJ: Erlbaum.

Rowe, D. C. (1997). Genetics, temperament, and personality. In R. Hogan, J. Johnson, & S. Briggs (Ed.), *Handbook of personality psychology* (pp. 367–386). San Diego, CA: Academic Press.

Rushton, J. P., Fulker, D. W., Neale, M. C., Nias, D. K. B., & Eysenck, H. J. (1986). Altruism and aggression: The heritability of individual differences. *Journal of Personality and Social Psychology, 50,* 1192–1198.

Savin-Williams, R. C. (1995). Lesbian, gay male, and bisexual adolescents. In A. R. D'Augelli & C. J. Patterson (Eds.), *Lesbian, gay, and bisexual identities over the lifespan* (pp. 165–189). New York: Oxford University Press.

Savin-Williams, R. C. (1998). *". . . and then I became gay: Young men's stories."* New York: Routledge.

Schachter, S., & Singer, J. E. (1962). Cognitive, social, and physiological determinants of emotional state. *Psychological Review, 69,* 379–399.

Stein, E. (Ed.). (1992). *Forms of desire: Sexual orientation and the social constructionist controversy.* New York: Routledge.

Telljohann, S. K., & Price, J. P. (1993). A qualitative examination of adolescent homosexuals' life experiences: Ramifications for secondary school personnel. *Journal of Homosexuality, 26,* 41–56.

Troiden, R. R. (1979). Becoming homosexual: A model of gay identity formation. *Psychiatry, 42,* 362–373.

Walster, E. (1971). Passionate love. In B. I. Murstein (Ed.), *Theories of attraction and love* (pp. 85–99). New York: Springer.

Whisman, V. (1996). *Queer by choice.* New York: Routledge.

White, G. L., Fishbein, S., & Rutstein, J. (1981). Passionate love and the misattribution of arousal. *Journal of Personality and Social Psychology, 41,* 56—62.

Wolchik, S. A., Beggs, V. E., Wincze, J. P., Sakheim, D. K., Barlow, D. H., & Mavissakalian, M. (1980). The effect of emotional arousal on subsequent sexual arousal in men. *Journal of Abnormal Psychology, 89,* 595–598.

Zucker, K. J. (Ed.). (1990). *Gender identity disorders in children: Clinical descriptions and natural history.* Washington, DC: American Psychiatric Press.

Zucker, K. J., & Bradley, S. J. (1995). *Gender identity disorder and psychosexual problems in children and adolescents.* New York: Guilford Press.

Zucker, K. J., & Green, R. (1993). Psychological and familial aspects of gender identity disorder. *Child and Adolescent Psychiatric Clinics of North America, 2,* 513–542.

II

PSYCHOLOGICAL CHALLENGES

4

Toward a Reconceptualization
of the Coming-Out Process
for Adolescent Females

Margaret S. Schneider

The modern wave of psychological research on sexual orientation began with Evelyn Hooker's study comparing a nonclinical sample of gay men with a nonclinical sample of heterosexual men on a variety of psychological characteristics (Hooker, 1957). It provided the impetus for a line of research comparing gay men and lesbians to heterosexual men and women on a variety of psychological characteristics. These studies demonstrated that homosexuality was not a mental illness and, in and of itself, posed no barrier to the ability of an individual to be a productive and healthy member of society (see Gonsiorek, 1982). This resulting line of research eventually formed the basis for removing homosexuality from the *DSM-II* (Bayer, 1981). It provided the scientific foundation for viewing a gay or lesbian sexual orientation as a normal variant of psychosexual development. While there had been considerable theorizing about the etiology of homosexuality using a disease model, this new perspective invited the question of how a same-sex sexual orientation develops in a social context in which same-sex desire is stigmatized and everyone is assumed to be heterosexual.

The 1970s saw a profusion of proposed models of the coming-out process (see Gonsiorek & Rudolph, 1991). Currently, Cass's (1979) model is the one that is most often cited. Although this line of inquiry has tapered off, some researchers continue to refine their original work (for example, Troiden, 1989). There continues to be interest in the psychosocial consequences of coming out, and there has been some revived interest in the development of a lesbian identity in particular (Kahn, 1991; Kitzinger & Wilkinson, 1995; Levine, 1997; Rust, 1993; Weille, 1993).

The numerous models of the coming-out process have been useful in identifying some of the commonalities, the milestones, and the barriers to coming out; they have highlighted significant events that are an integral part of the process and have captured the emotional component—the confusion, the distress, and the ultimate relief and joy at arriving at a positive lesbian or gay identity. They have been an impetus for further research. However, both individually and collectively, these models have limitations aside from the confusion that results when trying to reconcile one with the others (Cass, 1984; Shively, Jones, & De Cecco, 1984), not the least of which is the degree to which they disregard the lesbian experience.

The primary purpose of this chapter is to examine some theoretical issues in the development of a lesbian identity and discuss the implications for young women—not just for those who come out as teenagers but also for those young women who do so first in young adulthood or later. I will use as a point of departure some general comments about current models of the coming-out process. The critique and analysis that I present in this chapter is based on existing commentary and research, as well as on my own interview data collected from lesbians between the ages of 15 and 37. These data are from two different studies. The first data were collected in the early 1980s from 30 lesbians between the ages of 19 and 37 (Eisner, 1982). Twelve women in this sample came out as teenagers; the remainder came-out during young or later adulthood. The second set of data was collected from teenage lesbians between the ages of 15 and 20 as part of an ongoing project conducted between 1983 and 1988, some of which is reported elsewhere (Schneider, 1989, 1991; Tremble, Schneider, & Appathurai, 1989). Although the changing social context has altered some aspects of the coming-out process for young lesbians—for example, teens seem to be coming out at an increasingly early age (Savin-Williams & Rodriguez, 1993; Savin-Williams, 1998)—the particular issues that I wish to raise are as applicable today as they were in the 1980s.

All the data were collected using an existential-phenomenological approach (Valle & King, 1978). The purpose was to understand the experience of coming out by exploring the meaning of the events for each individual. The method was designed in order to identify common themes in the process and to understand the meaning of milestones and how they contributed to the process. Participants were interviewed using a semi-structured, open-ended format. The interview started with the statement, "Begin wherever you want and tell me how you realized or decided that you were a lesbian." Participants were asked to describe the meaning of the events they discussed and how these events contributed to their awareness of their same-sex attraction, their identification as lesbian, or their positive evaluation of being a lesbian. At the end participants were asked to identify events that stood out as milestones for them. The open-ended nature of the interviews resulted in rich descriptions of the many influences in the lives of women who eventually came to a lesbian self-identification.

Stage-Sequential Models of the Coming-Out Process

There is general agreement that coming out is a developmental process. However, each model of the coming-out process uses different markers of development. For example, Lee (1977) focuses on behavior and significant events such as sexual activity and, particularly, self-disclosure; Cass (1979) focuses on cognitive congruency; and, Troiden (1989) presents a sociological analysis of how individuals come to understand themselves as belonging to a social category through the meaning of their sexuality. These approaches are neither incompatible nor mutually exclusive, but they operate on different levels. Consequently, not only is there little consensus about what constitutes the essence of the process, but there is also little accord as to what constitutes closure of the process. I will come back to the issue of reconciling these models later in the chapter, but first I will examine a number of assumptions upon which all these models are based—assumptions that do not seem to pertain to many lesbians.

The first assumption is that a positive gay or lesbian identity emerges in fairly orderly, sequential stages and that the milestone events that mark progression through the process, such as first same-sex sexual experience, first long-term relationship, and first contact with the gay/lesbian community, usually take place in a particular order. This continues to be an integral part of these models in spite of the general acknowledgement of the heterogeneity of the process, owing to cultural, individual, and sex differences. For example, in the introduction to *Psychological Perspectives on Lesbian and Gay Male Experiences*, Garnets and Kimmel (1993) review the numerous stage-sequential models of coming out, and then essentially sabotage the concept of stage-sequential models of the coming-out process. They write:

> Although generally a stage-sequential linear progression is assumed in lesbian and gay male identity development, the data indicate that the process might be better conceptualized as a repeating spiral pattern. . . . One may traverse the same psychological territory again and again. . . . Moreover, some events do not happen to everyone and, if they do occur, they happen in different ways. (p. 15)

In my own samples of lesbians, there was considerable variation in the ordering of events. For example, some participants decided that they were lesbians prior to their first same-sex experience while others decided after their first same-sex experience. Some decided they were lesbians before coming in contact with a lesbian community or friendship network, while others decided after their first contact. Other studies have also found variations in the order of events. Among these are Savin-Williams' and Rodriguez' (1993) study in which some gay and lesbian youths identified themselves as homosexual prior to experiencing any same-sex sexual activity while others self-identified afterward. Rust (1993) provides flowcharts to illustrate the variation in her sample of lesbians.

Why, then, in spite of evidence to the contrary, do we persist in thinking about the coming-out process as a linear, stage-sequential process involving a specific ordering of events? First, it is not irrelevant that this is the way social scientists in general, and psychologists in particular, have been trained to think about maturation in spite of the critiques of stage theory of human development (Burman, 1994). Second, information about average ages (for example, average age of first same-sex experience or first contact with a lesbian/gay community), which is the focus of many studies, obscures individual differences and gives a misleading sense of uniformity to the process (Rust, 1996). Levine (1997), for example, uses average ages to validate the order of events proposed in Cass's (1979) model without discussing variations in the order of events. In this way order becomes reified and prescriptive. But more important, I believe, the stage-sequential model stems from specific underlying assumptions related to the development of homosexuality.

Essentialism of Same-Sex Attraction

In the coming-out discourse, there is a fundamental and unspoken assumption that a homosexual orientation is acquired, if not in the womb, then at or soon after birth. This discourse, according to Kitzinger and Wilkinson (1995), involves "identifying oneself as homosexual. . . . [It] is merely a process of learning to recognize and accept what one was all along: Indeed, the very expression *coming-out* suggests that the lesbian has always been inside, awaiting debut" (p. 95). In other words, if same-sex attractions were acknowledged and viewed as legitimate just as other-sex attractions are, then gay and lesbian development would unfold just as heterosexuality does, becoming unmistakably evident, for most people, around puberty.

There is sufficient evidence to suggest that there is some biological involvement in the development of sexual orientation (Byne, 1996; Pillard, 1996) and, as a corollary, that sexual orientation may be established around birth at least in males, who have been the focus of the preponderance of the research on the biological basis of sexual orientation (see, for example, Bailey & Zucker, 1995; Blanchard, 1997). Thus, there is some support for arguing the essentialism of males' sexual orientation. However, the nature of the biological involvement is unclear (Byne, 1996), and some research could be interpreted to suggest that whatever biological mechanisms are operating may be different for males and for females. For example, gay males in comparison to heterosexual males are more likely to have gay brothers but not lesbian sisters (Pillard, Poumadere, & Carretta, 1982; Pillard & Weinrich, 1986). Lesbians, in comparison to heterosexual women, are more likely to have more lesbian sisters but not more gay brothers (Bailey & Benishey, 1993;

Pillard, 1988). Other studies have found birth order and sibling sex ratio effects for gay males but not for lesbians (Blanchard, 1997). Retrospective studies of gender-atypical childhood behavior and sexual orientation show significantly larger effect sizes for men than for women (Bailey & Zucker, 1995).

The biologically based research alone suggests that, at this point, it would be unwise to generalize from the male to the female situation. Thus, even if there were evidence that sexual orientation in males has some biological determinants, the same could not yet be claimed for females. What is most telling, however, is the consistency in the narratives of the gay male experience in comparison to the variability of lesbian narratives. Notwithstanding the above-noted individual variations in the coming-out process, there is considerable uniformity in gay males' experience of the emergence of their same-sex sexual desire. Most gay males, in retrospect, say that they were always gay and feel as if they were born gay; they experienced coming out as a process of recognizing and accepting their same-sex feelings. These experiences are consistent with an essentialist view of sexual orientation (which, I would caution, does not ipso facto mean that the essentialist position is factually correct). However, lesbian experiences appear much more varied, and some are clearly incompatible with an essentialist assumption.

While it is true that some lesbians feel that they were always lesbians from the time that their first attractions became apparent, other lesbians describe a much more fluid sexuality (Bart, 1993; Brown, 1995; Gonsiorek, 1993). In my own research, there were four discernable patterns of the coming-out process. First, there were women who described themselves as always having been lesbian—that is, that their developing sexual awareness was consistently toward the same sex. Women in this group described themselves as having been born homosexual. Young women who definitely identified themselves as lesbians during adolescence tended to be in this group. Some of the women who came out in adulthood were also in this group and described themselves as having denied their true lesbian identity throughout their life.

Second, there were women who described themselves as having been heterosexual for the first part of their lives and then in mid-life, after falling in love with a woman, became lesbian. This is a pattern that has been noted by others (Bart, 1993; Burch, 1993; Golden, 1987; Kitzinger & Wilkinson, 1995) and is unique to lesbians. Women in this group are variously referred to as "elective lesbians" (Golden, 1987) or "bisexual lesbians" (Burch, 1993). While it may be tempting to characterize these women as repressed lesbians who only discovered their authentic selves in mid-life, that simply does not reflect their experience, and to insist on doing so reduces a very genuine and satisfying part of their lives to a charade. Not surprisingly, women in this group tend to state that they chose to be lesbians. If there is any vestige left of "the love that dares not speak its name," this group of lesbians represents it. There is remarkably little research about them, despite the fact that they appear to comprise a sizable portion of the lesbian population. (In my re-search, this group constituted 16% of the first set of participants.) Not only is their experience inconsistent with traditional models of coming out but these women also create ideological and political difficulties among lesbi-ans and in the lesbian and gay subculture in general, which has substantial investment in the concept that sexual orientation does not change over the life course.

A third group of women described more nebulous experiences. During adolescence they experienced periods of confusion, turmoil, and vacillation between same-sex and other-sex attractions. Some were trying to understand their compelling same-sex attraction in the context of the heterosexual as-sumption or, alternately, trying to deny their same-sex attractions altogether with, for some, the added difficulty of attempting to reconcile their strong lesbian attractions with their experience of some heterosexual attractions as well. Others may have been having a sexual relationship with another girl, without labeling the relationship as "lesbian." This group was most likely to label themselves "bisexual" for a period of time.

A fourth group of lesbians described their adolescence as "being on hold." They may have felt that they did not fit in, they may have dated boys with varying degrees of enthusiasm, or they may have not been very aware of any sexual feelings in particular throughout most of their adolescence. As one person commented in retrospect, "I was just floating." Some of them describe their adolescence as a time in which they denied or repressed their same-sex feelings while others remember it as a time of "deferring" their sexuality.

With same-sex attraction as a given, there is an implicit concomitant view that any detour or slow-down in the coming-out process represents a de-velopmental delay, and that coming out after adolescence is a failure of sorts. This is evident in the negative terms, such as "confusion," "suppression," "denial," "avoidance," and the like (for example, see Troiden, 1989), which are used to characterize the phases of the process that precede the acknowl-edgment of one's same-sex feelings and labeling oneself as gay or lesbian. There is no doubt that for many gay and lesbian people, regardless of when they come out, adolescence is a time of turmoil, fear, and pain as their same-sex attractions emerge and become increasingly compelling; but for oth-ers, adolescence is a time when, rather than wrestling their sexuality to the ground, teenagers who will eventually identify as gay or lesbian simply put their sexuality "on the back burner." To reduce this strategy to "de-nial" or "repression" is not giving credit to the judgment or instincts of youths themselves and devalues the experience of those who come out in young adulthood or later, or those who genuinely identify as heterosexual during adolescence. In terms of the psychodynamics involved, there is phe-nomenologically and psychologically a vast difference between deferral and denial.

When individual lesbians come out after adolescence, they may, indeed, be deferring, delaying, or denying. However, these are individualistic explanations. Any theory of lesbian identity development must account for the finding that lesbians, in general, tend to come out at a later age than their gay male counterparts (Chapman & Brannock, 1987; Herdt & Boxer, 1993; Savin-Williams, 1995; Weinberg, Williams, & Prior, 1994). Is there something unique about the sexual and psychological development of females, about the social context in which women become aware of their sexuality, or about the development of a lesbian identity as distinct from the development of a gay identity in males that results in the later development of a lesbian identity? In short, the answer is yes, and I will return to a discussion of the unique characteristics of female development and lesbian development that contribute to this pattern. The point I want to emphasize is that both my findings and those of others (e.g., Diamond, 1998) suggest that there are multiple trajectories for the development of a lesbian identity, and that rather than being a developmental process that necessarily starts at birth, the development of a lesbian identity may be more accurately conceptualized as, as Diamond (1998) puts it, an emergent phenomenon that can be activated at any phase of a woman's life given a particular set of conditions that have yet to be identified. What may appear to be delay may actually be a question of timing and context.

This discussion has illustrated that existing models of the coming-out process do not represent the full range of lesbian experiences. Not all lesbians come out during adolescence and, furthermore, even if there were no stigma attached to being homosexual, some lesbians would still come out later in life. Thus, in any cross-section of adolescent girls there will be females who are at various places on a trajectory toward developing a lesbian identity. Some will clearly identify as lesbians during adolescence; others may be in a lesbian relationship but not identifying it as such; some may be in turmoil, trying to deny their same-sex attractions, while others may have placed a moratorium on the issue; and, a final group may identify themselves as heterosexual and come out as lesbians later in life. These findings are consistent with Diamond's (1998) study of nonheterosexual college women. Diamond reported considerable variation in antecedent events and in the ages at which first awareness of same-sex attraction occurred. She also found that nearly half of the young women she studied reported undergoing changes in their sexual attractions over time. Studies by Pattatucci and Hamer (1995) and Weinberg, Williams, and Prior (1994) have also shown that sexual and emotional attractions in women may change over the life span.

To represent coming out as a developmental process, any conceptualization must incorporate the idea of developmental plasticity—that is, the idea that human functioning is not fixed, but changeable over time (D'Augelli, 1994). D'Augelli observes:

> The development of sexual orientation is a life-long process. This concept strikes at the heart of a view of sexual orientation as fixed early in life. . . . That sexual and affectional feelings can change in varying degrees over the course of one's life must be assumed; efforts to suggest otherwise are disguised social constructions. (p. 320)

I would take issue with this position only in that it does appear, phenomenologically at least, that some people's sexual orientation is fixed and does not change over the life span. Perhaps, sexual orientation is fixed in some individuals, or it is fixed in everyone, early in life, but with a greater or lesser degree of flexibility that varies from person to person. The important point that D'Augelli makes, however, is that it is misleading to assume that any one person's sexual and affectional orientation will remain static over her lifetime, or to assume, when there are shifts in sexual orientation, that one orientation is necessarily more authentic than the other. What this means is that any comprehensive examination of adolescent issues for lesbians and any comprehensive theory of the development of a lesbian identity must not only take into account the experiences of those who do come out during adolescence but also seek to understand the adolescent experiences of those who come out later in their lives.

Alternatives to Stage-Sequential Models

In the previous section, I argued that the existing stage-sequential models of the coming-out process have limited utility in describing the coming-out process in general, and for lesbians in particular. In fact, I propose that the critical research endeavor is not to develop a model per se but rather, as Brown (1995) suggests, to delineate a "set of necessary and sufficient conditions for the development of a lesbian self" (p. 11). Stating the problem in this way allows for both variability and commonalities in the process.

The first step is to find a way to identify and integrate the different levels of functioning involved in coming out and the various factors that come into play. For example, Fassinger and Miller (1996) provide empirical evidence that coming out involves two independent processes: developing an individual sexual identity and developing a group membership identity. D'Augelli (1994) identifies three sets of factors: "subjectivities and actions," which I conceptualize as psychological factors and internal processes (both cognitive and emotional); "interactive intimacies," which comprise interpersonal factors; and "sociohistorical connections," which constitute social context. D'Augelli (1994) also identifies six processes involved in the development of a lesbian or gay identity: exiting a heterosexual identity; developing a lesbian or gay identity (i.e., an individual sexual identity); developing a lesbian or gay social identity (i.e., a group membership identity); becoming a lesbian or gay offspring; developing a lesbian or gay intimacy status; and entering a lesbian or gay community. In short, the coming-out process involves multiple levels and multiple processes. Going one step further, each level and process involves a set of events (e.g., meeting other people who are gay or lesbian for the first time), cognitions (e.g., the first awareness of same-sex attraction), behaviors (e.g., the first same-sex sexual experience), and emotions (e.g., feeling positive or negative about one's gay or lesbian identity) that, combined, constitute the "necessary and sufficient conditions" to which Brown (1995) alludes.

A variety of both events, cognitions, behaviors, and emotions represent milestones in the coming-out process. For example, some young lesbians in my studies identified their first awareness of same-sex feelings (cognition) as a milestone because it motivated them to seek out a lesbian community. Others identified meeting other lesbians (an event) as a milestone because it made it easier for them to recognize their same-sex feelings and to consider the possibility that they, too, were lesbians. In other words, milestones are consequential and significant because they propel the development of a lesbian identity. Some milestones not only move the coming-out process forward but are also life-altering; they constitute what Savin-Williams (1998) refers to as turning points. For example, one young woman said that when a school psychologist told her that she could not change her sexual orientation she decided to stop trying to suppress her lesbian identity and to start seeking social support.

Whether or not the elements within each process occur in a relatively orderly fashion is subject to empirical testing. However, what is clear from my own work is that in order to understand the evolution of a gay or lesbian identity, it is critical to understand the individual meanings attributed to the events, behaviors, cognitions, and emotions involved in coming out, particularly those that are identified as milestones. Herein lies the value of a phenomenological, qualitative approach to studying the coming-out process and particularly in understanding both the individual differences in the process and the systematic differences associated with culture, ethnicity, class, and gender.

Models of coming out incorporate the idea that particular milestones move the process forward. In fact, research participants can readily identify their own personal milestones when asked to do so. They recognize particular cognitions, events, and so on, as milestones when these are a priori identified as such by the researcher; however, when research participants are asked about the importance of these milestones, it becomes evident that the meanings are not uniform. Furthermore when participants identify their own milestones, they name a variety of events and cognitions that have far more variation than is reflected in existing models and the meaning ascribed to some of the milestones runs counter to conventional wisdom. I will discuss the implications of this finding in the following section, but first I will illustrate what I mean by the differences in meanings.

By way of example, nearly three-quarters of the first set of participants recalled having childhood "crushes" on other females, often adults such as teachers, camp counselors, and Girl Scout leaders. Of these women, nearly two-thirds felt that their crushes were early portents of their later lesbian identity. Yet, in spite of the legendary gym-teacher stories that abound in lesbian coming-out stories, more than one-third did not believe that these crushes were related to their development as lesbians. They believed that their experiences were no more than the crushes on mentors and role models that are typical among girls. Much the same pattern was evident with regard to atypical gender roles. Nearly half the women reported that they were "tomboys" as children, but of those, only half construed this as being related to their development as a lesbian. In other words, experiences such as childhood "crushes" and gender-atypical behavior, which have been considered by researchers to be precursors of the emergence of a lesbian identity (Bailey & Zucker, 1995), do not necessarily hold the same meaning for individual lesbians.

Both lesbian and gay male adults often report that they felt different from other children even prior to adolescence. This may be the result of gender-atypical temperament or behavior or may be experienced as a generalized existential feeling of being apart (Savin-Williams & Rodriguez, 1993). Among the participants in my first study, over three-quarters of the lesbians reported feeling different as they were growing up, but only a little more than half believed that feeling different was related to their developing lesbian identity.

Taken together, these findings raise some very important theoretical and methodological issues. Are childhood experiences such as "crushes," gender-atypicality, and feeling different an integral part of the development of a lesbian or gay sexual orientation? Do these experiences take on particular significance, and are they more likely to be remembered, by adults who ultimately identify as gay or lesbian; or, as Harry (1982) suggests, do these experiences serve to "unglue" these individuals from prevailing norms and make it more likely that they will recognize their same-sex orientation and act upon it by coming out? While there is considerable evidence that gender atypicality in childhood, for example, is associated with the development of a homosexual orientation (Bailey & Zucker, 1995), the reasons for this association are not clear and the correlation is far from perfect. These kinds of questions and issues should alert researchers to the importance of exploring and understanding the individual experiences and meanings that have tended to be lost in the percentages and statistics.

Among the participants in my research, there was considerable variation in the circumstances that constituted milestones. A relationship or emotional attachment was the most commonly cited event leading the respondents to adopt a lesbian identity. Others included contact with a lesbian community, their first same-sex experience, and a variety of idiosyncratic events. Respondents adopted a lesbian identity as the result of being in therapy, after spontaneously blurting it out to friends, after experiencing transformative life events, or after accomplishments that boosted their self-esteem. (I will return to a further examination of these last two categories of events later in the chapter.) There was similar variation in the events that contributed to feeling positive about being a lesbian, and how respondents felt about being a lesbian, once they had labeled themselves.

The variation in the meaning of events is understandable from a developmental perspective. Coming out is a unique developmental process because it is not as necessarily or as strongly age related as some other aspects of development. This means that coming out will pose unique challenges, have different repercussions, and therefore have different meanings depending upon the individual's age. A 12-year-old who realizes that she is a lesbian is going to face different tasks and understand her sexual orientation in a way that is different from that of a 17-year-old who comes out during her first year at a university, or a 30-year-old who falls in love with another woman and leaves her marriage and an established lifestyle.

The variation in the meaning of events is also understandable from a phenomenological perspective and may well account for the diversity in the coming-out process. The order of events may vary because of the diversity of meanings associated with particular events. For example, an individual who has a same-sex sexual encounter may believe the experience to be an anomaly and therefore not consider herself to be lesbian until some time later when she meets other lesbians by chance and begins to feels an affinity for them. Alternately, she may have a same-sex sexual encounter, on that basis immediately label herself lesbian, and then be motivated to seek out a community. In short, in order to understand the coming-out process it is critical to appreciate the meanings ascribed to the various events, as well as the range of events that individuals consider to be part of the process.

The Psychological and Social Context of Coming Out

When lesbians tell their coming-out stories, their narratives almost invariably reflect the way that the process is embedded in and connected to other developmental processes and life events. It becomes evident that many lesbians view the development of their lesbian identity as integral to their development as individuals. Furthermore, they often set their stories in a social context of roles, relationships and expectations that serves as a backdrop to the narratives.

Psychological Development

DeMonteflores and Schultz (1978) define the coming-out process as the developmental process through which people who are gay or lesbian come to recognize their sexual orientation and integrate this knowledge and its meaning into their lives. Although there is tacit acknowledgment, as reflected in this definition, of the importance of integrating one's gay or lesbian identity with the other aspects of one's identity, very little attention has been paid to this in research or in commentary. Much research has been pragmatically driven—with a focus on outcomes and a primary purpose of identifying mental health issues for gay and lesbian adolescents and adults (for a review of this research, see Rivers, 1997; Travers & Schneider, 1997). However, in order to understand gay and lesbian individuals holistically, a broad developmental perspective is critical, particularly because so many lesbians, at least the ones with whom I have talked, understand the development of their lesbian identity as integral to their development as a whole person. As Savin-Williams (1998) points out, we need to understand "how sexual minorities lead their lives" (p. 10).

A case in point is the identification of milestones. In addition to the usual and predictable ones such as the first same-sex sexual experience or the first contact with a lesbian community, my research participants often named other milestones that had no immediately obvious connection to sexual orientation issues. These milestones illustrate the way in which the coming-out process is embedded in other developmental processes. For example, participants frequently made a connection between coming out and the development of self-esteem. Self-esteem was a critical factor in being able to come out, and having the wherewithal to come out was tremendously empowering in a way that contributed to self-esteem.

> In dealing with being gay, I was trying to become comfortable with myself as a person and identify why I didn't like myself. . . . Just a whole lot of soul-searching and thinking about why did I not feel good as a person and then asking myself if that was reasonable. . . . and it was really nice to be able to go through the whole process and it wasn't until I felt comfortable with myself as a person that I started coming out.

> I enrolled at the university in a Humanities course. And I got an 'A' and I was just delighted. That was a really big step for me. Then I didn't seem so afraid of myself. After then I went back to Ottawa and joined a lesbian coming-out group.

> I feel that being gay was one of the major factors in my being the fabulous person that I am right now. I made the decision when I was very young. . . . Once you've made that decision, it's so big, about what you are and who you are, that there's no obstacle after that. If I could do that then I could do anything.

Previous studies of self-esteem and coming out have yielded mixed results. Higher levels of self-esteem have been associated with coming out at an earlier age among gay men in one study (Harry & DeVall, 1978), and among lesbians in another (Savin-Williams, 1990). However, these findings are not consistent and the nature of the relationship between self-esteem and coming out is not clear (Savin-Williams & Rodriguez, 1993). The narratives that I collected provide some insight into the reciprocal, interactive relationship between coming out and self-esteem.

Emerging from many of these accounts is a portrait of women who bring their own strengths, limitations, and life-long patterns to the coming-out process. For example, life experiences that had an impact on an individual's ability to establish and maintain relationships tended to "muddy the water" as women tried to reach clarity about their lesbian identity. The following comment is from a woman who had been sexually abused as a child.

> In therapy I did a lot of work on why I avoided men and then it was okay to *choose* not to be with men as opposed to keeping on thinking that I was avoiding men. I can remember dating a man that I didn't particularly like, thinking that if I dumped him it would be one more case of avoiding getting close to a man. Instead of choosing that this person wasn't anybody that I really cared for, I would be down on myself for not enjoying myself.

A second woman who had also been sexually abused described her difficulty defining appropriate boundaries with other women. Because she tended to sexualize relationships inappropriately, friendships with women became even more complex as she tried to determine the limits of the different kinds of relationships that she could have with women.

> I didn't know how to approach women if I was interested. I didn't know how to talk to women without them thinking I was picking them up. Like everybody in the world becomes a potential lover. You can get as friendly as you want with women . . . that used to be the case, you get as friendly as you want but sex never entered it. Well now it does. I didn't know how to approach women without being intrusive, without coming on to them. Or even how to come on to them if I wanted to. What sort of ways to come on to them that weren't really icky.

Histories of abuse or unstable family environments tended to complicate the coming-out process because the same chaos that might have characterized some women's early relationships in their families was carried over into their intimate, romantic relationships. They tended to not be able to recognize exploitive situations, and sometimes did not have the interpersonal skills needed to nurture and maintain relationships. This is particularly significant for lesbians because of the importance of relationships as milestones in the development of a lesbian identity. To the extent that they were unable to maintain relationships, they were deprived of the clarity that functioning relationships could lend to the coming-out process.

These examples illustrate the need to conceptualize the development of a lesbian identity in the context of an individual's overall psychological development. It is along the same lines as other research that has demonstrated the importance of understanding the development of multiple social identities, as in the case of minority group members for whom coming-out conflicts with their minority group membership (Gonsiorek & Rudolph, 1991; McCarn & Fassinger, 1996). The point here is that coming out is one of many psychological and social processes and must be understood in that context.

The Social Context of Coming Out

The coming-out process takes place in a social context of heterosexism and homophobia. Homophobia creates the negativity that makes coming out so difficult while heterosexism creates a set of roles, expectations, and social pressures that must be discarded in order to recognize same-sex desire and to identify as gay or lesbian. The effects of the stigmatization of homophobia have been studied extensively, particularly in terms of risk factors for adolescents; however, less attention has been paid to the "exit" from the heterosexual assumption (to borrow and adapt a phrase from D'Augelli, 1994) that is required in order to recognize and act upon same-sex desire.

What emerged from my research was a sense of the ways in which individuals found it necessary to "decontextualize" themselves in order to be free of the pressure to be heterosexual and to be able to come out. For example, nearly one-quarter of the women in the first sample said that a trip or a move was an event that led to them to label themselves lesbian. It appears that getting away from familiar surroundings or familial influences freed individuals to explore who they really were. These two women left home in their late teens specifically to escape the expectations of family and friends.

> I had to break away from my mother to really call myself a lesbian. I knew she could accept it and I wanted to talk to her about it, but I wasn't sure enough in myself. I was sure she would make some statement like, "It's just a phase." That wouldn't change me but it would throw me off. . . . So I went away for six months to the West Coast

> I decided it was time to deal with it. It seemed easier to deal with it away from home, away from all the influences of people's expectations and friends. I didn't know a soul in Vancouver.

In a third instance, the feeling of isolation while traveling one summer between high school and university allowed a strong same-sex attraction to finally rise to the surface of awareness.

> It was very intimate. [My best friend and I] traveled in a van for six weeks to countries where you couldn't speak English to any other person except each other. And I was finding myself very strongly attracted to her. And that really raised the whole lesbianism to a level of consciousness for me. That I really was a lesbian.

The need to extricate oneself from the expectations of others is a theme that was conspicuous in the narratives of some of the women who came out during adulthood as well. They described their adult development as a process of freeing themselves from the expectations of others that was necessary before they were able to explore their lesbian identity. As a whole, these comments suggest some explanation for the consistent finding that females come out at a later age than gay males in the same age cohort—namely, that it is necessary for women to separate themselves from their social context, to "unstick" themselves from roles, expectations, and wishes of others, in order to reach some clarity about their own identity, including their sexual orientation. So, rather than undoing denial, the task for lesbians can be viewed as clearing away the "noise" in order to consolidate who they are and to whom they are attracted.

The social context of a lesbian community or friendship network is generally recognized as a critical component of developing a positive lesbian identity. Although some lesbians come out first in isolated same-sex relationships, it is contact with other lesbians that gives them a sense that they are not alone and that they have a future to look forward to. However, what is unique in the lesbian experience is that some lesbians are drawn to the idea of being a lesbian at a time when they are identifying as heterosexual and have experienced no same-sex attraction. They may wonder whether it might make more sense to be a lesbian because so much of their emotional life is focused on their female friends. They may begin to question their gender roles and feel that they would have more freedom if they were lesbians. Ultimately they find within themselves the capacity to be erotically attracted to other females and are able to adopt a lesbian identity.

In other words, what some lesbians express is that being a lesbian feels congruent with who they are emotionally; in terms of their gender-role, being a lesbian seems to fulfill a social imperative as much as, eventually, a sexual one. Once again, this underscores the need to view lesbian identity development as taking place within multiple social and psychological contexts.

The Lesbian Experience and the Role of Relationships

This chapter began with a general critique of models of the coming-out process, particularly as they relate to the lesbian experience. The data that I discussed highlight some important aspects of the coming-out process for lesbians. In this section I will discuss a final critical issue distinguishing the development of a lesbian identity: the role of relationships.

Although significant differences between the gay male and lesbian experience have been noted (Garnets & Kimmel, 1993; Gonsiorek, 1993), they have been largely relegated to a figurative footnote in the research and commentary on coming out. Most models of coming out are based on the male experience from which the lesbian experience is extrapolated. These models revolve around the emergence of same-sex sexual attraction while the importance of relationships is downplayed and they are generally depicted as taking place later in the process. For example, Lee (1977), who bases his article on data from both gay males and lesbians, highlights sexual fantasies, first sexual experiences, and anonymous sex as significant milestones. Not only does he give short shrift to relationships in general but also dismisses isolated relationships that occur early in the process as "rare" although admittedly "more common among lesbians." Coleman (1981/1982) places the development of relationships well after sexual experimentation. Troiden (1989) places commitment, "the taking of a lover—that is, the fusion of gay sexuality and emotionality into a meaningful whole (p. 370)," at a late stage of the coming-out process. The available average age data do suggest that relationships come late in the coming-out process. McDonald (1982), Dank (1971), and Troiden (1989) all state that, on average, the age for the first same-sex relationship is several years after the age for same-sex sexual experiences.

This trend can be attributed, in part, to the fact that much of the available information was collected from males and reflects males' ability to separate the recreational from the emotional components of sexuality. It may also be a function of the times in which these models were developed—times in which the prevailing zeitgeist was unsupportive of gay and lesbian relationships and when the opportunities for meeting others who were gay or lesbian were often limited to venues associated with casual sex such as bars and (in the case of males) bathhouses. There is, too, the possibility that narratives from gay males minimize the role of relationships in reaction to the expectations imposed by the masculine role—in other words that gay males socially construct the role of sex and relationships in their own process to conform to traditional views of masculinity.

Studies of lesbians are no less immune to focusing on sexual activity as the organizing theme in the coming-out process. For example, in a survey by Chapman and Brannock (1987), a significant portion of lesbian participants indicated that emotional attraction to women was an important factor in identifying themselves as lesbians. Yet the survey itself places an inordinate emphasis on sexual practices. Of 25 items, 10 focus specifically on sexual behavior, and of these, 8 pertain to sexual activity with males.

The ubiquitous and unexamined centrality of the sexual act in descriptions of the coming-out process, combined with the relative disregard for the role of relationships, stands in direct contrast to much of what is known about female sexuality in general and about the coming-out process among lesbians, in which same-sex feelings typically emerge in the context of a relationship or emotional attachment to a particular person (reviewed by Garnets & Kimmel, 1993; Gonsiorek, 1993; Gonsiorek & Rudolph, 1991). Elsewhere I have illustrated how attention to relationships in the lives of young lesbians can be a critical component in counseling young lesbians (Schneider, 1997). For any model of the coming-out process to be relevant to lesbians, it must bring relationships to the fore. The other pitfall of this seeming fixation on sexual activity as the defining characteristic of sexual orientation is that it obscures the real experiences of gay or lesbian people who have had other-sex experiences or who will, in the course of their lifetime, have some sexual relations with the other sex (Bell & Weinberg, 1978; Saghir & Robins, 1973). For example, Rust (1992) found that almost all the lesbian women in her sample had heterosexual relationships at some time in their lives, and that 43% had had heterosexual relationships after coming out as a lesbian. Two-thirds reported some other-sex attraction at the time of the research.

A variety of relationships play important roles in the development of a lesbian identity. Their nature depends upon the age of the individual at the time—falling in love with one's best friend at age 15 is qualitatively different, and has different consequences, from falling in love with one's best friend and leaving one's husband to live with each other at age 35—but both can be called relationships. In addition, the relationships do not necessarily have an erotic component. They can include close friendships, mentorships, or other emotional attachments, but the hallmark of these relationships is the intense feeling that persists over an extended period of time.

All my research participants identified at least one relationship as a significant part of her coming-out process. Almost half became sexually involved for six months or more with the first female they were attracted to, often a female they knew first as a friend. Another third became aware of their sexual feelings after developing an unreciprocated attachment, including falling in love, with a female. Regardless of whether or not the feelings were mutual, however, the awareness of sexual feelings emerged in the context of an existing friendship or emotional attachment to a particular individual, rather than as a generalized attraction to the same sex. These results are consistent with other studies, cited by Dubé, Savin-Williams, and Diamond (this volume), which found that the first same-sex sexual contact for many lesbians was with a close friend, and that many lesbians reported having intense friendships with females accompanied by unreciprocated sexual feelings.

The events that led to adopting the label "lesbian" were varied. While some participants cited a single event and others cited a series of events, the most common event, by itself or in combination with others, was the establishment of an intimate long-term relationship. Furthermore, when asked to identify the milestones in the coming-out process, nearly half cited a long-term relationship. Again, what constituted long term was age related. For older lesbians it frequently meant living together in a committed monogamous relationship. In adolescent terms it often meant a romantic friendship during the school year that ended at the beginning of summer vacation when the two girls went their separate ways. But, in either context, it is not a misnomer to call them relationships.

The following excerpts are reflections from those research participants who came out during their adolescence. In describing their own adolescence, they illustrate the connection between emotional closeness and the emergence of sexual feelings.

> I was just thinking how close we were, you know? Nothing sexual at all came into it. We were just very, very close. I was still at school at the time. . . . My

parents had moved so I went back home with her [during the school break]. . . . We were just staying in a trailer and we were sleeping in the same bed anyway, and it just happened.

Well, I was just attracted to women all the time. I always had crushes on them. . . . I wasn't really aware of any sexual attraction. When I was 12 or 13 I had a girlfriend, Anne. We were in Brownies together . . . and we would walk each other home once a week through the field where it was dark, we would kiss each other. That was my first [sexual] awareness.

She was a friend of mine from high school and we had probably been friends for two or three years at this point. . . . I had an attraction to her and she obviously had an attraction to me and there was one particular evening when we were at my parent's home, I was living at home at the time . . . and [the sexual relationship] started there. . . . I had always admired women, you know, my own friends and older women and I know that's quite common among 13- and 14-year-olds. But with me, it didn't go away. . . . And then when I was 17, I realized, well, this is it.

I had some very close relationships with girls when I was young. Not sexual. . . . When I was a teenager, from about 14 on until, well, probably 17, I had a very intense, yet nonsexual, relationship with this woman. . . . Helen and I, we had never sexually related, in terms of making love, but as close as you were going to get to it. . . . I was very attracted to her.

Even when the sexual aspect of the attraction is more apparent and pronounced at an earlier age than in the examples above, the emotional attachment is nonetheless critical to the emergence of a lesbian awareness.

Yes, well I guess there was both [the sexual and emotional component] for me. It was different, I agree. . . . But all my friends were always boys. And girls were separate things. Girls were something . . . well girls were sexual things for me. And girls were something to look at . . . [My first physical relationship] I guess when I was about 11. I had a close girlfriend and we slept together, but that wasn't so strange. I thought of it as being a lesbian. Even then. But my girlfriend didn't at all. And whenever I said something like that she would become very upset and say: "Oh no! We're just practising for being with boys" or something like that. . . .

I was about 8 years old, I guess. I didn't know the label that they put on people like me . . . that I was gay . . . All I knew was that I felt really strongly toward women. . . . I knew that I wanted to be touched by women. That I knew that I liked holding hands with girls. . . . I knew that I liked laying down with my sisters and them reading me a story; I just liked the whole comforting feeling of the [girls] that I was friends with, my sisters. . . . And when I was 9, I had a [sexual] experience with a girl. Then I knew that it was that, the sexual part also included how I felt.

The following excerpt is noteworthy because the interviewee not only describes the significance of a relationship but also states that it was the strength of her feelings toward the other young woman, not the sexual component of the relationship, that really told her that she was a lesbian. It is also significant that the woman resists openly admitting that she is a lesbian—not because of anticipated homophobia, but because she believes that to do so would destroy the relationship.

> As a young teenager, I felt attractions to women that I tried to identify. I thought that it was also part of that stage where you're growing and infatuation for a role model is acceptable and normal. I think it was as I started getting 16 and . . . feelings for women were still there, I started to wonder if I was gay or not. . . . I developed very close friendships with straight women and knew that I'd probably cared for them a little bit more than was probably 'normal'. . . . I still justified the same way, Oh you're just an excessively caring person, because you have that need for friendships. When I moved to Toronto and I lived with this woman. . . . She was straight but probably not totally considering [our sexual relationship]. . . . *I just knew, as my feelings for her grew and grew and grew, that I was gay* but I had to suppress it because I knew if I didn't, I would lose her. . . . I knew that would scare her away. To have sex with me if I wasn't gay was okay but to have sex with me if I was [gay] wasn't [okay]. . . . I couldn't quite understand . . . where she was coming from, but that's the way it was.

The following example further illustrates how the nature and quality of an intimate relationship can influence when and how a lesbian labels herself. In contrast to instances in which satisfying relationships help consolidate a sense of being a lesbian, unsuccessful relationships have the potential to confuse the issue.

> I had my first girlfriend at 16, and we lived together for eight years [but] I didn't consider myself gay. . . . we didn't have a very good relationship. So I went to a therapist . . . and I told her that I was lesbian and I didn't want to be any more and after a few months of therapy I broke up with Terry and discovered that I was a lesbian. Like I wanted to be a lesbian. But I just wanted to break up with her, so I thought going out with men was the answer. So I did. Well, when we broke up, I dated men. . . . See she couldn't compete with men. So she couldn't really stop me whereas if I said I was going to date women. . . . Then, when we broke up and I was going out with men, she said, 'You're the one who said we were lesbians and now you're telling that we're not.' And I was really confused. In the beginning I [had called myself a lesbian] to keep her, not that I believed it.

These reflections illustrate several salient aspects of lesbian identity development. First, lesbian identity development is both sexual and relational. This means that it is unlikely that a female will define herself as lesbian based on sexual attraction alone. More likely she will experience sexual feelings in the context of a same-sex friendship or intimate relationship. Second, these excerpts demonstrate that females are as likely to be as concerned about maintaining relationships as they are about arriving at some clarity about their sexual orientation; and in the same vein, the quality of a particular relationship may have an influence on the readiness of a young woman to identify herself as a lesbian. In short, relationships constitute a significant part of the process; they have the potential to move the process along or to impede it, depending on their nature.

Relationships and a Theory of Lesbian Identity Development

The previous section highlighted the importance of relationships in the coming-out process for lesbians. At this point I would go one step further to propose that relationships are central to the coming-out process and that any theory of lesbian identity development must revolve around the development, establishment, and maintenance of relationships. That is not to say that relationships are, or should be, the only focus of the theory, but that they must be the organizing theme. This proposal emerges from the empirical data that I have presented and from the general commentary on lesbian identity development in the current literature on differences in the lesbian and gay male experience, and is consistent with theorists such as De Cecco and Shively (1984) and Weeks (1991), who suggest that sexual identity only has meaning in the context of relationships over time and across situations. In terms of the psychology of women and the role of relationships in the lives of lesbians, there are two relevant areas of thought. The first is self-in-relation theory; the second is Adrienne Rich's (1980) notion of the lesbian continuum, both of which I will describe below.

Self-in-Relation Theory

Self-in-relation theory posits that a woman's growth and development takes place in the context of interactive relationships; that the basic goal of women's psychological development is the "deepening capacity for relationship and relational competence" (Surrey, 1991, p. 53); and that feeling related to others is, for females, self-enhancing. Self-in-relation theorists propose to "trace the development of identity through specific relationship and relational networks" (Surrey, 1991, p. 38). Furthermore—and this is particularly refreshing—rather than pathologizing females as overly dependent, they propose that female development is the psychological norm from which males deviate because of an inordinate emphasis on agency, independence, and autonomy (Jordan, Kaplan, Miller, Stiver, & Surrey, 1991). When viewed through the lens of self-in-relation theory, the development of a lesbian identity can be understood as a characteristically female process. In the context of self-in-relation theory, the importance of relationships to lesbian identity development is both understandable and obvious. So, too, is the finding that lesbians come out at a later age, on average, than their male counterparts. This bears some explanation.

At puberty both boys and girls are becoming more independent; they begin to become aware of their sexuality and will begin to experiment. Thus, adolescence, at least in Western culture, is inherently a time of rebellion. However, the rebellion holds different meaning for boys and girls. As Marcia points out:

> Adolescent boys are encouraged to make life decisions that will often lead to increased interpersonal conflict with both authorities and families. The experience of such conflict can be an identity-confirming event. However, if an adolescent girl, who is expected to become proficient in interpersonal relationships, creates such tension and conflict by her decisions, she may take this as a *disconfirmation* of the success of her identity formation. (Marcia, 1980, p. 179)

In other words, girls experience a double bind when they exercise their independence in a meaningful way. Furthermore, developing independence and maintaining boundaries within a relational context is a highly complex task—far more complex than simply developing independence, as boys are expected to do. In short, the developmental tasks for adolescent females are not only more complex but also engender conflicts that tend to undermine their self-esteem and general well-being. The evidence for this is in, among other things, the higher incidence of symptoms such as depression and eating disorders in adolescent girls in general (Pipher, 1994).

Young women who become aware of same-sex attraction during puberty will be coming out during a period in their lives that is developmentally difficult at the best of times, when they are contending with complex developmental tasks, and when conflict undermines the very sense of themselves (and coming out would certainly place them in conflict with their family and peers). Furthermore, coming out is a more complex process for females because it involves not just sexual feelings but sexual feelings interpreted within the context of a relationship. Lastly, adolescent lesbians are likely to be slower at having a same-sex sexual experience because, like their heterosexual counterparts, they are not socialized to take the lead in sexual encounters. Thus, insofar as a sexual experience does constitute a milestone event, it is not likely to be initiated quickly even within a relationship.

It is important to consider, from a relational perspective, the nature of the visible gay and lesbian community that is available to young lesbians coming out in large urban centers. Aside from the obvious issue of the adult-focused nature of the community, which is problematic for gay and lesbian adolescents, the most visible components of the community tend to reflect the male inclination to value the ability to separate the recreational from the affiliative aspects of sex and sexuality. These components include overt cruising in streets and parks, sexually explicit advertisements and articles in community newspapers, and an abundance of bars. While these elements pose no concrete threat in the way females may feel threatened when being harassed by heterosexual males, they nonetheless reify the male objectification of sexual partners that has so often victimized women. They also underscore the male privilege that bestows on men the economic power to—at least in visible ways—dominate the landscape. It is important to consider the consequences for young lesbians of being relational in a relatively nonrelational community that they are told they are part of which nonetheless does not reflect their lives.

In summary, there is a theoretical foundation for focusing on relationships as an organizing feature of the development of a lesbian identity that is useful in explicating some of the aspects of lesbian identity development, particularly the differences in coming out between males and females.

The Lesbian Continuum

The second idea that is critical in understanding the coming-out process is Rich's notion of the lesbian continuum. In a groundbreaking article, "Compulsory Heterosexuality and Lesbian Existence," Rich (1980, p. 650) wrote that the lesbian experience is "a profoundly female experience." In the article she locates the lesbian relationship on a continuum of relationships among women, both erotic and platonic, characterized by support, sharing, and bonding. The concept of a lesbian continuum could only emerge from the reality of the intensity with which women relate to each other. By conceptualizing women's relationships with each other on a continuum, the development of a lesbian identity then becomes a question of movement along the continuum. While not everyone necessarily begins at the same place on the continuum, I hypothesize that there are conditions or combination of conditions that lead to movement along the continuum toward, or indeed away from, a lesbian identity. Identifying these conditions is precisely the research question that I posed earlier. One of the strengths of this conceptualization is that it can encompass those experiences of lesbians that have been treated, for the most part, as anomalous—political and ideological lesbians—and it provides a framework for how an attraction for a lesbian "lifestyle" in the absence of any erotic feelings can constitute the first step in a trajectory toward a lesbian identity.

Conclusion

In spite of the mounting evidence for the importance of relationships in the lives of young lesbians, researchers have been largely remiss in addressing the pivotal role that relationships have for young lesbians. When examined from the perspective of relationships, the lives of young lesbians become more clearly illuminated. The sex differences that have been noted between gay males and lesbians become more than interesting footnotes; rather, they become understandable manifestations of the lesbian experience.

The challenge for researchers and theorists at this time is to conceptualize a theory of lesbian identity development that authentically represents the female experience of coming out, is grounded in developmental theory, and is contextualized. In view of the relational nature of females' sexual development, as well as lesbian identity development, the organizing factor in such a theory must be the development of relationships in the holistic context of what is known about the lives of girls and women.

References

Bailey, J. M. & Benishey, D. (1993). Familial aggregation of female sexual orientation. *American Journal of Psychiatry, 150*, 272–277.

Bailey, J. M., & Zucker, K. J. (1995). Childhood sex-typed behavior and sexual orientation: A conceptual analysis and quantitative review. *Developmental Psychology, 31*, 43–55.

Bart, P. B. (1993). Protean women: The liquidity of female sexuality and the tenaciousness of lesbian identity. In S. Wilkinson & C. Kitzinger (Eds.), *Heterosexuality: A Feminism & Psychology reader* (pp. 246–252). London: Sage.

Bayer, R. (1981). *Homosexuality and American psychiatry.* New York: Basic.

Bell, A., & Weinberg, M. (1978). *Homosexualities.* New York: Simon and Schuster.

Blanchard, R. (1997). Birth order and sibling sex ratio in homosexual versus heterosexual males and females. *Annual Review of Sex Research, 8*, 27–67.

Brown, L. (1995). Lesbian identities: Concepts and issues. In A. R. D'Augelli & C. J. Patterson (Eds.), *Lesbian, gay and bisexual identities over the lifespun: Psychological perspectives* (pp. 3–23). New York: Oxford University Press.

Burch, B. (1993). *On intimate terms: The psychology of difference in lesbian relationships.* Chicago: University of Illinois Press.

Burman, E. (1994). *Deconstructing developmental psychology.* New York: Routledge.

Byne, W. (1996). Biology and homosexuality: Implications of neuroendocrinological and neuroanatomical studies. In R. P. Cabaj & T. S. Stein (Eds.), *Textbook of homosexuality and mental health* (pp. 129–146). Washington, DC: American Psychiatric Press.

Cass, V. (1979). Homosexual identity formation: A theoretical model. *Journal of Homosexuality, 4*, 219–235.

Cass, V. (1984). Homosexual identity: A concept in need of definition. *Journal of Homosexuality, 9*(2/3), 105–125.

Chapman, B. E., & Brannock, J. C. (1987). Proposed models of lesbian identity development: An empirical examination. *Journal of Homosexuality, 14*, 69–80.

Coleman, E. (1981/1982). Developmental stages of the coming-out process. *Journal of Homosexuality, 11*(1/2), 189–207.

Dank, B. M. (1971). Coming out in the gay world. *Psychiatry, 34*, 180–197.

D'Augelli, A. R. (1994). Identity development and sexual orientation: Toward a model of lesbian, gay, and bisexual development. In E. J. Trickett, R. J. Watts & D. Birman (Eds.), *Human diversity: Perspectives on people in context* (pp. 312–333). San Francisco: Jossey-Bass.

De Cecco, J. P., & Shively, M. G. (1984). From sexual identity to sexual relationships: A contextual shift. *Journal of Homosexuality, 9*(2/3), 1–26.

DeMonteflores, C., & Schultz, S. J. (1978). Coming out: Similarities and differences for lesbians and gay men. *Journal of Homosexuality, 34*, 59–72.

Diamond, L. M. (1998). Development of sexual orientation among adolescent and young adult women. *Developmental Psychology, 38*(5), 1085–1095.

Eisner, M. (nee Schneider) (1982). *An investigation of the coming-out process, lifestyle, and sex-role orientation of lesbians.* Unpublished doctoral thesis, York University, Toronto, ON.

Fassinger, R. E., & Miller , B. A. (1996). Validation of an inclusive model of sexual minority identity formation on a sample of gay men. *Journal of Homosexuality, 32*(2), 53–78.

Garnets, L. D., & Kimmel, D. C. (1993). Introduction: Lesbian and gay male dimensions in the psychological study of human diversity. In L. D. Garnets & D. C. Kimmel (Eds.), *Psychological perspectives on lesbian and gay male experiences* (pp. 1–51). New York: Columbia University Press.

Golden, C. (1987). Diversity and variability in women's sexual identities. In Boston Lesbian Psychologies Collective (Eds.), *Lesbian psychologies: Explorations and challenges* (pp. 18–34). Urbana, IL: University of Illinois Press.

Gonsiorek, J. C. (1982). Results of psychological testing on homosexual populations. In W. Paul, J. Weinrich, J. Gonsiorek, & M. Hotvedt (Eds.), *Homosexuality: Social, psychological, and biological issues* (pp. 71–80). Beverly Hills: Sage.

Gonsiorek, J. (1993). Mental health issues of gay and lesbian adolescents. In L. D. Garnets & D. C. Kimmel (Eds.), *Psychological perspectives on lesbian and gay male experiences* (pp. 469–485). New York: Columbia University Press.

Gonsiorek, J. C., & Rudolph, J. R. (1991). Homosexual identity: Coming out and other developmental events. In J. C. Gonsiorek & J. D. Weinrich (Eds.), *Homosexuality: Research implications for public policy* (pp. 161–176). Newbury Park CA: Sage.

Harry, J. (1982). *Gay children grown up.* New York: Praeger.

Harry, J., & DeVall, W. B. (1978). *The social organization of gay males.* New York: Praeger.

Herdt, G., & Boxer, A. M. (1993). *Children of Horizons: How gay and lesbian teens are leading a new way out of the closet.* Boston: Beacon Press.

Hooker, E. (1957). The adjustment of the male overt homosexual. *Journal of Projective Techniques, 21,* 17–31.

Jordan, J., Kaplan, A., Baker Miller, J., Stiver, I., & Surrey, J. (1991). *Women's growth in connection: Writings from the Stone Center.* New York: Guilford.

Kahn, M. J. (1991). Factors affecting the coming out process for lesbians. *Journal of Homosexuality, 21*(3), 47–70.

Kitzinger, C., & Wilkinson, S. (1995). Transitions from heterosexuality to lesbianism: The discursive production of lesbian identities. *Developmental Psychology, 31*(1), 95–104.

Lee, J. A. (1977). Going public: A study in the sociology of homosexual liberation. *Journal of Homosexuality, 3,* 49–78.

Levine, H. (1977). A further exploration of the lesbian identity development process and its measurement. *Journal of Homosexuality, 34*(2), 67–77.

Marcia, J. (1980). Identity in adolescence. In Adelson, J. (Ed.), *Handbook of adolescent psychology* (pp. 159–187). Toronto: John Wiley & Sons.

McCarn, S. R., & Fassinger, R. E. (1996). Revisioning sexual minority identity formation: A new model of lesbian identity and its implications for counseling and research. *The Counseling Psychologist, 24*(3), 508–534.

McDonald, G. J. (1982). Individual differences in the coming out process for gay men: Implications for theoretical models. *Journal of Homosexuality, 6,* 47–60.

Pattatucci, A. M. L., & Hamer, D. H. (1995). Development and familiality of sexual orientation in females. *Behavior Genetics, 25,* 407–420.

Pillard, R. C. (1988). Sexual orientation and mental disorders. *Psychiatric Annals*, *18*, 52– 56.

Pillard, R. C. (1996). Homosexuality from a familial and genetic perspective. In R. P. Cabaj & T. S. Stein (Eds.), *Textbook of homosexuality and mental health* (pp. 115–128). Washington, DC: American Psychiatric Press.

Pillard, R. C., Poumadere, J. I., & Carretta, R. A. (1982). A family study of sexual orientation. *Archives of Sexual Behavior*, *11*, 511–520.

Pillard, R. C., & Weinrich, J. D. (1986). Evidence of familial nature of male homosexuality. *Archives of General Psychiatry*, *43*, 808–812.

Pipher, M. (1994). *Reviving Ophelia: Saving the selves of adolescent girls*. New York: Ballantine.

Rich, A. (1980). Compulsory heterosexuality and lesbian existence. *Signs: Journal of Women in Culture and Society*, *5*, 631–660.

Rivers, I. (1997). Violence against lesbian and gay youth and its impact. In M. Schneider (Ed.), *Pride and prejudice: Working with lesbian, gay and bisexual youth* (pp. 31–48). Toronto: Central Toronto Youth Services.

Rust, P. (1992). The politics of sexual identity: Sexual attraction and behavior among lesbian and bisexual women. *Social Problems*, *39*(4), 366–386.

Rust, P. (1993). "Coming out" in the age of social constructionism: Sexual identity formation among lesbian and bisexual women. *Gender & Society*, *7*(1), 50–77.

Rust, P. (1996). Finding a sexual identity and community: Therapeutic implications and cultural assumptions in scientific models of coming out. In E. D. Rothblum & L. A. Bond (Eds.), *Preventing heterosexism and homophobia* (pp. 87–123). Thousand Oaks, CA: Sage.

Saghir, M., & Robins, E. (1973). *Male and female homosexuality*. Baltimore: Williams and Wilkins.

Savin-Williams, R. C. (1990). *Gay and lesbian youth: Expressions of identity*. Washington DC: Hemisphere.

Savin-Williams, R. C. (1995). Lesbian, gay male, and bisexual adolescents. In A. R. D'Augelli & C. J. Patterson (Eds.), *Lesbian, gay, and bisexual identities over the lifespan: Psychological perspectives* (pp. 165–189). New York: Oxford University Press.

Savin-Williams, R. C. (1998). *". . . and then I became gay": Young men's stories*. New York: Routledge.

Savin-Williams, R. C., & Rodriguez, R. G. (1993). A developmental, clinical perspective on lesbian, gay male, and bisexual youths. In T. Gullotta, G. Adams, & R. Montemayor (Eds.), *Adolescent sexuality: Advances in adolescent development, Volume 5*, (pp. 77–101) Newbury Park, CA.: Sage.

Schneider, M. (1989). Sappho was a right-on adolescent: Growing up lesbian. *Journal of Homosexuality*, *17*(1/2), 111–130.

Schneider, M. (1991). Developing services for gay and lesbian adolescents. *Canadian Journal of Community Mental Health*, *10*(1), 133–150.

Schneider, M. (1997). The significance of relationships in the lives of young lesbians. In M. Schneider (Ed.), *Pride and prejudice: Working with lesbian, gay and bisexual youth* (pp. 97–115). Toronto: Central Toronto Youth Services.

Shively, M. G., Jones, C., & De Cecco, J. P. (1984). Research on sexual orientation: Definitions and methods. *Journal of Homosexuality*, *9*, 127–136.

Surrey, J. (1991). The "self-in-relation": A theory of women's development. In

J. Jordan, A. Kaplan, J. Baker Miller, I. Stiver, & J. Surrey (Eds.), *Women's growth in connection: Writings from the Stone Center* (pp. 51–66). New York: Guilford.

Travers, R., & Schneider, M. (1997). A multi-faceted approach to reduce risk factors for lesbian, gay and bisexual youth. In M. Schneider (Ed.), *Pride and prejudice: Working with lesbian, gay and bisexual youth* (pp. 49–67). Toronto: Central Toronto Youth Services.

Tremble, B., Schneider, M., & Appathurai, C. (1989). Growing up gay or lesbian in a multicultural context. *Journal of Homosexuality, 17*(3/4), 253–268.

Troiden, R. R. (1989). The formation of homosexual identities. *Journal of Homosexuality, 17*(1/2), 43–73.

Valle, R. S., & King, M. (1978). *Existential-phenomenological alternatives for psychology*. New York: Oxford.

Weeks, J. (1991). *Against nature: Essays on history, sexuality and identity*. London: Rivers Oram Press.

Weille, K. L. H. (1993). Reworking developmental theory: The case of lesbian identity formation. *Clinical Social Work Journal, 21*(2), 151–159.

Weinberg, M. S., Williams, C. J., & Pryor, D. W. (1994). *Dual attraction: Understanding bisexuality*. New York: Oxford University Press.

5

Developmental Trajectories of Gay, Lesbian, and Bisexual Youths

Mary Jane Rotheram-Borus and Kris A. Langabeer

Most societies anticipate that their citizens are heterosexual; social rituals and customs such as marriage, definitions of family, organization of health benefits, job roles, and vocations are structured to anticipate gender differences and heterosexual attraction and mating (Asher, 1990; Baruch, Barnett, & Rivers, 1985; Howes, 1988; Loevinger, 1976). Expected developmental trajectories are also highly linked to gender and an anticipation of heterosexual pairing. Attractiveness to the opposite gender is an organizing principle of peer groups, social cliques, and status during adolescence (Bem, 1987). Thus, the sequence of developmental tasks and indices of personal adjustment are similarly gender-linked and associated with heterosexual gender roles (Maccoby & Jacklin, 1978). This chapter will examine the developmental trajectories of youths whose lives are not consistent with these expectations: gay, lesbian, and bisexual youths.

A primary developmental task of adolescence is establishing a personal identity. Adolescents search and commit to their personal and social identities in at least five domains: gender roles, vocational choices, religious and political beliefs, and ethnicity (Erikson, 1968; Marcia, 1989; Phinney, Lochner, & Murphy, 1990; Phinney & Rotheram-Borus, 1987). These processes are not generally associated with significant psychological problems: most youths are able to maintain close family and peer relationships and form a healthy sense of their personal identity by early adulthood (Leffert & Petersen, 1996; Petersen, 1988; Petersen, et al. 1993; Rutter, Graham, Chadwick, Yule, 1976; Weiner & Del Gaudio, 1976). Youths who experience a high degree of distress that persists over time are a small subgroup who generally demonstrate a cluster of problem behaviors: early initiation of sexual behavior with multiple partners, excessive substance use, contact with the criminal justice system, problems at school, and emotional distress (Dryfoos, 1997; Ensminger, 1987). It is anticipated that youths who demonstrate these problem behaviors go on to adulthood to experience substantial problems in meeting society's traditional expectations for stable employment and relationships (Baruch et al., 1985; Levenson, 1978).

This chapter examines whether adolescents who self-identify as gay, lesbian, or bisexual experience similar developmental trajectories as heterosexual-identified youths. That is, do most gay, bisexual, and lesbian youths search and commit to a personal identity as their dominant developmental task during adolescence as opposed to dealing with being gay? Is this developmental period relatively calm, with most youths maintaining positive relationships with peers and families throughout adolescence? What is the frequency of multiple problem behavior syndrome among gay, lesbian, and bisexual youths? Is it similar to heterosexual youths? This chapter examines the developmental trajectories observed among gay, lesbian, and bisexual youths to determine if their trajectories are distinctive from those of their heterosexual peers.

Developmental Exploration of Sexual Orientation

There is a fundamental problem in estimating the prevalence of a social status that has negative social sanctions (Rotheram-Borus, Rosario, & Koopman, 1991). Youths who are gay, lesbian, or bisexual recognize that homosexuality is considered an undesirable status by many: family, friends, teachers, members of their close social network, and the broader culture may disapprove of their homosexual orientation (Gemelli, 1996; Remafedi, Farrow, & Deisher, 1991). Therefore, many adolescents who suspect they are gay, bisexual, or lesbian, or actually identify as such, may hide their status, particularly on any school-based or home-linked survey. Therefore, we can speculate on youths' developmental trajectories, but there are no representative samples from which to generalize.

Four criteria are used to determine if a youth is gay, lesbian, or bisexual: behavior, attraction patterns, erotica preferences, and self-labels (Kinsey, Pomeroy, & Martin, 1948). Because of the difficulties in sampling youths who are likely to be hiding, have not yet recognized their own patterns of attraction, or are unwilling to disclose their sexual orientation, estimates of the number of gay, lesbian, and bisexual youths to date have been based on two sources: self-labels and reports of behavior with same-gender and cross-gender partners.

A minority of youths self-identify as gay, lesbian, or bisexual. While early estimates suggested that as many as 10% of the male population was more or less exclusively homosexual for at least three years between the ages of 16 and 55 (Kinsey et al., 1948), more current estimates suggest that only 2%–

3% of adult males report sexual contact with another man in the previous year (Binson et al., 1995; Catania et al., 1992; Fay, Turner, Klassen, & Gagnon, 1989; Rogers & Turner, 1991). Laumann, Michael, and Gagnon (1994) estimated that 2.4% of the men and 1.3% of the women they studied self-identified as homosexual or bisexual. There are few data estimating the number of youths (i.e., under age 21 years) who self-identify as gay, lesbian, or bisexual. In a survey of 34,196 high school students, French and colleagues (1996) found that 275 (.8%) identified as bisexual and 119 (.34%) as homosexual. In a study of 4,159 Massachusetts high school students, 104 (2.5%) self-identified as gay, lesbian, or bisexual (Garofalo, Wolf, Kessel, Palfrey, & DuRant, 1998). During adolescence, many young people experiment sexually with same-gender partners, but do not see themselves as lesbian or gay and do not later develop same-gender sexual patterns as adults (Savin-Williams, 1990). One study reports that 17% of boys and 6% of girls aged 16 to 19 had at least one homosexual experience (Sorensen, 1973). Most lesbian, gay, or bisexual adults indicate that they were not aware or did not disclose to others regarding their sexual orientation until early adulthood (Sullivan & Schneider, 1987). Some theorists argue that development of a gay identity begins prior to puberty (Troiden, 1988), while others believe sexual orientation is not stable until adulthood (Sullivan & Schneider, 1987). And, there seem to be gender differences in this area. Recognizing and disclosing one's sexual orientation appears to be more common among male adolescents. Lesbian adolescents are likely to self-identify as lesbian at a later age than males who self-identify as gay (Hunter & Schaecher, 1995), and fewer adolescent females self-identify as lesbian compared to males who self-identify as gay (Rosario, Meyer-Bahlburg, et al., 1996).

There have been at least five theorists who have devised developmental models of sexual orientation, all of them consistent with Erikson's (1959) life span model of development: Cass (1979); Coleman (1981–82); Sophie (1985–86); Troiden (1988); and Rotheram-Borus and Fernandez (1995). The theories are compared and summarized in table 5.1. Their theories are similar in that each acknowledges a period of awareness, identification, or discovery of one's sexual orientation. Each references a period of comparison, exploration, confusion, or search. Finally, each results in an integration, achievement, or commitment to a sexual orientation. The theories vary in whether acceptance or pride are necessary for successful achievement of one's identity.

These theories do not stand alone, but draw directly from other developmental theories that focus on heterosexual youths. Marcia's (1989) operationalization of Erikson's theory on the stages of the identity search (1968) may apply to sexual orientation. For example, becoming comfortable with one's sexual orientation is a process quite similar to the search and commitment for a personal identity (Rotheram-Borus & Fernandez, 1995). Sexual orientation theorists are not alone in drawing on the developmental tasks of searching and committing; theorists of other identity-related pro-

Table 5.1

Theories of Identity Development for Gay Male Youths

STAGE	CASS, 1979	COLEMAN, 1981–82	SOPHIE, 1985–6	TROIDEN, 1988	ROTHERAM-BORUS & FERNANDEZ, 1995
1	Identity confusion (first awareness)	Pre coming out	First awareness	Sensitization	Diffused (no exploration, no commitment)
2			Identity acceptance	Identity assumption	Foreclosed (commitment, no exploration)
3	Identity comparison	Exploration	Testing and exploration	Confusion	Moratorium (exploration, no commitment)
4	Identity pride; identity synthesis	Identity integration	Identity integration	Commitment	Achieved (exploration and commitment)

cesses also utilize these concepts. For example, models of the development of ethnic identity (Cross, 1978; Rosenthal, 1987) are similar to developmental theories of personal identity in their focus on a process of recognition of prejudice, search and examination of alternative roles in relating to their own ethnic group and their role in relation to those who are members of the dominant cultural group, and commitment to a social identity in relation to their ethnicity. In the theories of ethnic identity development, pride in one's own group is consistently included as a component of a healthy identity.

Among adolescents, the current data on the personal identity search examine the areas of vocation, religious and political beliefs, gender roles, and ethnicity (Marcia, 1989). Youths in the process of developing a sexual orientation identity can be classified in at least four different statuses: (1) diffuse (sexual orientation is not considered or salient for the youth, there is a lack of focus or awareness of one's sexual orientation; at best gay, lesbian, or bisexual youths may have a vague and unarticulated feeling of being different); (2) foreclosed (a sexual orientation is assumed without reflection on one's sexual orientation); (3) moratorium (the active process of exploring one's sexual orientation is initiated but not resolved); and (4) achieved (youths have explored, committed, and are sharing their identities with others) (see Archer, 1989, for a review). Initiating a search for one's identity in a particular domain can vary based on youths' social characteristics. For example, the search for ethnic identity among White, Anglo-Saxon Protestants in the United States is often not initiated (Phinney & Tarver, 1988). When youths' ethnic identity is similar to the dominant cultural norm, ethnic identity has low salience for them; youths are foreclosed with respect to their ethnic identity (Phinney & Tarver, 1988; Rotheram-Borus & Wyche, 1994). Similarly, most youths do not engage in the process of exploring their sexual orientation. Owing to a cultural norm of presumed heterosexuality, most youths are "foreclosed" with respect to their sexual orientation. There is little consideration of exploring alternative sexual orientations. Everyday social routines, customs, media, values, attributional sets, and cues presume a heterosexual orientation and no other alternatives are considered. Only when youths' social attractions, preferred erotica, strong emotional commitments, and sexual partners are not solely heterosexual do youths begin searching for information, identifying the narrowness of existing societal norms, beliefs, and attitudes; and exploring their beliefs, attitudes, and behaviors. It has been argued that gay, lesbian, and bisexual youths experience an additional developmental period of conflict over their sexual orientation (Paroski, 1987; Remafedi, 1987a; Rotheram- Borus, & Fernandez, 1995; Rosario, Rotheram-Borus, & Reid, 1996). Gay, lesbian, and bisexual youths experience a diffuse sense of their difference from their peers and the broader culture. When the diffuse feeling is recognized or labeled by the youth for him or herself as attraction and interest for same-gender partners, a state of moratorium may occur. Youths who are actively engaged in a search for information, acceptance of themselves, and making decisions about who, when, and how to disclose information about their sexual orientation may be labeled as being in a state of moratorium, and they may experience greater distress (Rotheram-Borus, 1989).

The exploration of one's sexual orientation is generally referred to as "coming out" (Gonsiorek & Rudolph, 1991; Kohn, 1991). Coming out is characterized by a set of processes: recognizing oneself as different from others (i.e., not heterosexual); defining what it means to be to be lesbian, gay, or bisexual; and exploring the meaning of being lesbian, gay, or bisexual. Youths often choose a reference group within the gay, lesbian, and bisexual culture—that is, a subgroup whose beliefs, attitudes, values, and behavior patterns most resemble those of the adolescent. Over time, youths engage in behaviors that are generally consistent with their sexual orientation and disclose their sexual orientation to others. The coming-out process is not a discrete event or a stage-defined trajectory, but a process that occurs and evolves throughout the life span.

Developmental processes that parallel the exploration of sexual orientation occur in other domains of functioning. Vocational plans, religious beliefs, and sex role behaviors similarly evolve; however, it was previously presumed by adolescent researchers (Marcia, 1989; Archer, 1993) that basic decisions are made regarding these issues during adolescence, and then there are only fine-tunings that occur over time. The emerging empirical data on adult development, which finds development continuing throughout the life span, do not support this theory (Fiske & Chiriboga, 1990; Levenson, 1978). Choices in one's religious, political, vocational, and gender roles evolve over the life span and sometimes shift in fundamental ways over time; the evolution of one's sexual orientation is only just beginning to be studied.

Adolescent researchers recognize that adolescents often create "false selves" in order to avoid criticism from parents, siblings, friends, and so on (Harter, Marold, Whitesell, & Cobbs, 1996). Heterosexual youths create false selves in order to experiment with roles, to test their parents' support, or to generate social support from others. "Passing" or generating a social image as a heterosexual by gay, lesbian, and bisexual youths has been extensively documented. However, in contrast to many of the false selves generated by heterosexual youths, passing by gay, lesbian, and bisexual youths is often a way to avoid serious negative sanctions. Youths are justified in fearing disclosure of their sexual orientation to family, friends, and peers (Boxer, Cook, & Herdt, 1991; D'Augelli & Hershberger, 1993; Rotheram-Borus, et al., 1991), for they are often rejected, punished, and abandoned after doing so (Savin-Williams, 1994; Uribe & Harbeck, 1992). Parents and family members, the people adolescents generally expect to receive unconditional love and acceptance from, may be the hardest people to come out to; families are capable of withdrawing emotional support and resources (food, shelter, clothing, schooling, money) from the adolescent.

As shown in table 5.2, the sexual orientation of a substantial proportion of gay and lesbian youth is "discovered," as opposed to disclosed by choice.

Table 5.2
Information Available on the Coming Out and Victimization of Young Gay, Bisexual, and Lesbian Youths

Study (Timeframe)	N	Disclosure			Ridiculed	Physically Assaulted
		Discovered	Told Parents	Told Friends		
Males						
Rosario, Rotheram-Borus, & Reid, 1996 (3 months)	136	33%	38%	50%	50%	
Remafedi, 1987b (Lifetime)	29		39%	93%	55%	30%
Remafedi, Farrow, & Deisher, 1991 (Lifetime)	137	70% (discovered/told parents)				39%
Males and Females						
Pilkington & D'Augelli, 1995 (Lifetime)	194				80%	17% hit, kicked, beaten 33% objects thrown at 10% assaulted with weapon 22% sexually assaulted
D'Augelli, 1992b (Lifetime)	121				77%	8% objects thrown at 3% punched, hit, beaten 1% assaulted with weapon
Garofalo, Wolf, Kessel, Palfrey, & DuRant, 1998	104					32.7% threatened with weapon at school

Rosario, Rotheram-Borus, and Reid (1996) found that about 33% of the youths they studied had been discovered to be gay by their parents and another 38% chose to disclose to their parents. Remafedi (1987b) found a very similar rate of those who had disclosed to their parents (39%). In combining discovered and disclosure rates, Remafedi et al. (1993) found 70% of youths were "out." A review of studies on youths' disclosure to parents shows that a higher percentage of youths disclosed their same-sex attraction to parents in the 1990s than did youths in the 1980s, and 60%–80% had disclosed to their mothers, whereas one-third to two-thirds had told their fathers (Savin-Williams, 1998). Because youths often have the choice to hide their sexual orientation, many youths do not seek information regarding homosexuality, do not seek social support regarding their sexual orientation, nor experiment behaviorally during adolescence (Sullivan & Schneider, 1987). Youths may lead a self-protective double life, but they then face the challenge of keeping their two lives separate and the possible mental and emotional conflict brought on by the subsequent self-doubt, -monitoring, -denial, or -hatred, and isolation from family and peers (Uribe & Harbeck, 1992). While there are no empirical data on the impact of hiding one's orientation, it has often been hypothesized that those who hide lose self-esteem and a sense of connection to others, and lag in their developmental progression to a healthy adulthood. There are some theories that low self-image and depressed affect are associated with increased risk for multiple problem behaviors, particularly substance use (Rotheram-Borus, Rosario, Van Rossem, Reid, & Gillis, 1995). Those who cannot hide because of their mannerisms, dress, or intense desires for bonding with same-gender peers often face the full force of harassment and discrimination (Remafedi et al., 1991).

When young people tell their parents, they may face anything from a dismissal of their feelings to an actual dismissal from the household. In one study, 8 of 13 lesbians disclosed to their parents and in each case, their parents called it a passing phase (Uribe & Harbeck, 1992). Of 120 lesbians and gay men (aged 14 to 21) surveyed by Telljohann and Price (1993), 42% of the females and 30% of the males reported that their families responded negatively to the news of their sexual orientation. Boxer et al. (1991) found that 10% of the young people they studied were evicted from their home when they told their fathers they were gay or lesbian. Remafedi (1987b) reports that 26% of his sample were forced to leave their homes owing to conflicts with their families over their sexual identity, and that only 21% of mothers and 10% of fathers were seen as being supportive after their sons came out to them.

Besides strong messages of disapproval from many societal institutions and parents, lesbian, gay, and bisexual youths often face verbal and physical abuse in school or on the streets, especially in urban areas (D'Augelli, 1992b; Dean, Wu, & Martin, 1992; Hunter, 1990; Martin & Hetrick, 1988; Pilkington & D'Augelli, 1995; Remafedi, 1987a; Rosario, Rotheram-Borus, et al., 1996; Savin-Williams, 1994). Gay youths report being ridiculed for their sexual orientation, with rates ranging from 50% (Rosario, Rotheram-Borus et al., 1996) to 80% (D'Augelli & Hershberger, 1993). On a school yard youths may hear the term "faggot" or "dyke" as the ultimate put-down of themselves or others (Ness, 1996; Uribe & Harbeck, 1992). In one study of gay male youths, more than half had been verbally abused and almost one-third physically attacked (Remafedi, 1987b). In another, 40% of the gay male youths reported being physically attacked (Remafedi et al., 1991). Besides actual attacks, there is the fear that is generated by the pervasive threat of verbal or physical attacks created by living in a culture that denigrates homosexuality. D'Augelli and Hershberger (1993) found that 31% feared verbal harassment, 26% feared physical abuse at school, and 17% had been physically assaulted.

Even though coming out may elicit negative reactions at any age, adolescents have additional challenges facing such abuse because they are in the midst of developing personal and social identities, have fewer coping mechanisms, and lack the independent resources and educational status that adults generally have. Therefore, adolescents are more vulnerable to the continuing negative sanctions against homosexuality. The anticipated and received punishment for having same-gender partners is also likely to be associated with more depressed affect (Rotheram-Borus, Rosario, Van Rossem, et al., 1995) and lower self-esteem for lesbian, gay, and bisexual youths (Hetrick & Martin, 1987).

While for many heterosexuals, emerging romantic and sexual feelings are exciting and positive, gay, lesbian, and bisexual youths may fear romantic feelings because they link the youths with a stigmatized group. And, youths may feel they cannot seek support from their parents, friends, teachers, physicians, or religious leaders in their identity search (Besner & Spungin, 1995; Uribe & Harbeck, 1992). Young males have described the process of coming out with no support systems as extremely painful (Uribe & Harbeck, 1992). Young women have also described feelings of not fitting in, with some thinking there was no one else like them, and fear over losing friends (Uribe & Harbeck, 1992).

The negative social sanctions experienced by gay, lesbian, and bisexual youths may be less destructive if there are positive models for youths to help guide an identity search and commitment process. However, there are few positive models to help gay, lesbian, and bisexual youths manage their identity search (Boxall & Perry, 1994; Drummond & Boxall, 1994). There are only a handful of political figures, sports heros, musicians, motion picture and television stars, academic leaders, and business leaders who have publicly identified themselves as gay. There is not a genre of easily accessible literature that allows youths to read about how others successfully identified and met the challenges associated with identifying as gay, bisexual, or lesbian. Most youths may not know an adult with whom to identify as a role model or turn to for help or guidance. Many gay and lesbian teachers and administrators fear the negative consequences (harassment, job loss) of revealing their sexual orientation (Lyons & Atwood, 1994; Sanford, 1989; Uribe & Harbeck, 1992). Even if a teacher has a desire to act as a role model for teens, he or she may fear being accused of sexual exploitation or of "promoting" homosexuality. Therefore, teachers are unlikely to be available or supportive to youths.

Multiple Problem Behaviors

Despite the pressures created by the threat of rejection and abuse, most lesbian, gay, and bisexual youths cope with the increased stress and excel (Savin-Williams, 1990; Uribe & Harbeck, 1992). However, it has also been argued that multiple problem behaviors characterize the lives of lesbian, gay, and bisexual youths (Gonsiorek, 1988; Price & Telljohann, 1991; Remafedi et al., 1991; Uribe & Harbeck, 1992). To examine this question, we will first examine the evidence of the prevalence of each of the problem behaviors reported among gay, lesbian, and bisexual youths.

Sexual Behavior

Romantic relationships are often more challenging for adolescents who are sexually or affectionately attracted to members of their same gender. If only 2%–3% of youths are lesbian, gay, or bisexual, and most are not aware or do not come out until early adulthood, youths who seek to initiate a romantic relationship with someone of the same gender have a small group of potential romantic partners. The negative social sanctions associated with homosexuality and the high anxiety accompanying romantic relationships in early adolescence further heighten the risk of rejection for seeking to initiate a romantic relationship among one's peers. Therefore, youths may seek partners in marginalized social settings in urban areas where there are many persons bartering sex and selling drugs. Youths may then become involved in a pattern of high-risk behaviors. For example, while youths in the Los Angeles area may be afraid to seek a romantic relationship among peers at school, they are generally aware that West Hollywood is a gay-identified area of the city. For young males especially, meeting romantic partners is more likely in West Hollywood than it is in school settings. Social service agencies attempting to serve the needs of gay and lesbian youths are typically situated in neighborhoods that are characterized by high rates of sex bartering and drug use. The agencies locate in these settings because there are many gay, lesbian, and bisexual youths in these settings; conversely, youths come to the neighborhood to get services at the gay-identified agencies. In Los Angeles there are numerous major agencies within miles of each other serving high-risk youths, particularly gay, lesbian, and bisexual youths.

Youths are attracted to the services offered at these agencies and the opportunities for social interactions. The risk of meeting seropositive sexual partners or partners who are substantially older than the youth and of being
offered substances or the opportunity to barter sex are substantially increased
when youths have little choice except for these settings. The concentration
of services in high-risk areas and the identification of specific neighborhoods
as gay-identified, though advantageous in many ways, may greatly increase
risk for youths.

The existing data on sexual behavior among gay, lesbian, and bisexual
youths, typically available from convenience samples of males, are summarized in table 5.3. These studies show a range in the age of initiation of sexual
behavior by bisexual and gay males (median 12.5–16 years; Remafedi, 1994;
Rotheram-Borus et al., 1992), and a higher number of sexual partners than
national norms for adolescents (e.g., median = 8 at age 15 years; Rotheram-
Borus et al., 1992). Many of the samples have been small, self-selected ones,
where the reports of risk acts are exceptionally high. For example, Remafedi
(1994) found that 63% of gay male youths in his sample from community
sites in Minnesota reported unprotected anal intercourse and/or intravenous substance use. There have been several samples of young gay men and
lesbians whose risk acts have been studied. Among them are a sample of
131 minority male adolescents in New York City (Rotheram-Borus, Rosario,
et al., 1994); 154 minority gay, lesbian, and bisexual youths in New York City
(Rosario, Hunter, & Gwadz, 1997); 216 young gay and lesbian youths from
New York City, San Francisco, and Los Angeles (Rotheram-Borus, Marelich,
& Srinivasan, 1999); 149 New York City gay males (Meyer & Dean, 1995);
61 gay male university students (D'Augelli, 1992a); 194 lesbian, gay, and
bisexual youths from community-based organizations in 14 metropolitan
areas (D'Augelli & Hershberger, 1993); 394 high school students in Minnesota who self-identified as gay or bisexual (French et al., 1996); and 239
(Remafedi, 1994) and 29 (Remafedi, 1987a,b) gay and bisexual male youths
in Minnesota responding to newspaper advertisements, direct appeals at
groups and events, and referrals.

Across these samples, gay male and lesbian youths engage in substantial
numbers of sexual risk acts. When heterosexual, bisexual, and homosexual
males are recruited from similar settings (e.g., social service settings, homeless shelters), the number of risk acts is similar across youths of different sexual orientations. For example, Rotheram-Borus and colleagues (1999), using
samples drawn from community-based agencies, found that both heterosexual
and gay males engaged in about 20 sexual acts over a 3-month period. While
same-gender partners engage in different types of sexual risk acts from cross-
gender partners, the overall frequency of sexual acts is similar. While the
number of sexual risk acts were similar, condom use was significantly different for each gender and sexual orientation grouping. The patterns of condom
use paralleled the actual risk of HIV transmission; the groups at highest risk

Table 5.3
A Summary of Sexual Behaviors Reported by Gay, Bisexual, and Lesbian Youths in a Series of Studies

STUDY (TIMEFRAME)	N	PARTNERS		VAGINAL	ANAL		COMMERCIAL SEX
		MALE	FEMALE		RECEPTIVE	INSERTIVE	
Males							
Remafedi, 1987a,b	29	M 7 (1 year)	M 5.6 (1 year)	~51% (Lifetime)			17% (Lifetime)
Remafedi, 1994 (Lifetime)	239	M 70	M 6	42%	67%	68%	11%
Rotheram-Borus, Rosario, Meyer-Bahlburg et al., 1994 (Lifetime)	131	Median 7	Median 2	48%	73%	66%	22%
Males and Females							
Rosario, Meyer-Bahlburg, et al., 1996, & Rosario, Hunter, & Gwadz, 1995 (Lifetime)	80 Males 76 Females	Median 3 Median 3	Median 1 Median 3	46% 61%	69%	74%	
Rotheram-Borus, Marelich, & Srinivasan, 1999 (3 months)	160 Males 53 Females	M 5 M 1.4		13% 43%	56% 4.3%		

within each gender were most likely to use condoms: gay males in homosexual activity and bisexual females in heterosexual intercourse.

Sexual behavior typically varies significantly by ethnicity and age. Researchers have demonstrated that there tend to be few ethnic differences in sexual behavior among samples of white, African-American, and Latino gay male youths (Remafedi, 1987a,b; Rotheram-Borus et al., 1992). Because gay and bisexual youths are typically confronting negative social sanctions for being gay, ethnicity may not be as salient to these youths during this developmental period (Rotheram-Borus & Fernandez, 1995). Increasing age is consistently associated with risk. Similar to other adolescents, the sexual behavior of gay males increases with age, as does their risk for contracting sexually transmitted diseases, including HIV.

Sexual behaviors among male gay or bisexual youths are particularly problematic because of the high seroprevalence rate of HIV among the partners of young gay male youths. Youths have reported preferring older adult gay men (Harry & DeVall, 1978) who are more likely to be living with HIV (CDC, 1995; Lemp et al., 1994). Seroprevalence rates have ranged from 4%–12% among young gay men (Dean & Meyer, 1995; Lemp et al., 1994; Osmond et al., 1994; Silvestre et al., 1993). For young gay men attending sexually transmitted disease clinics or runaway shelters, rates are as high as 32% (see table 5.4). In addition to its threat to physical health, HIV infection is the most serious threat to the long-term adjustment of gay and bisexual male youths. Lesbian youths are generally assumed to be at relatively low risk of HIV infection; however, lesbian adolescents are more likely than gay males to have cross-gender sex (Rosario et al., 1995). These reports are consistent with self-reports from lesbian women who say that they have or have had heterosexual sex (Lemp et al., 1995; Norman, Perry, Stevenson, Kelly, & Roffman, 1996; Reinisch, Sanders, & Ziemba-Davis, 1995) Often the male partners of young lesbians are young gay or bisexual males (32%; Rosario et al., 1995). Lesbian adolescents attend the same social service agencies and programs as gay male adolescents, and clinic staff at gay-identified agencies report that lesbian adolescents' cross-gender friendships with gay male youths sometimes evolve into sexual experimentation. Although the sexual orientation of their female partners is unknown, about half of the gay male adolescents in our recent study reported engaging in heterosexual intercourse after self-identifying as gay, and they were far less likely to use condoms with their female partners than with their male partners (Rotheram-Borus, Rosario, et al., 1994). These data support clinicians' impressions that many lesbian adolescents engage in heterosexual behavior, sometimes with multiple partners and with infrequent condom use, at times with the intention to become pregnant (Hunter, 1995). Lesbian partners of gay males are at high risk for HIV infection. Future monitoring of young lesbians must be conducted to reassess their risk of HIV.

Table 5.4
HIV Seroprevalence Rates Among Young Gay/Bisexual Men

STUDY	N	LOCATION	YEAR(S) OF STUDY	SITES(S)	AGE	% HIV+	RANGE HIV+
Dean & Meyer, 1995	87	NYC	1990–91	Snowball	18–24	9%	
Wendell et al., 1992	~760	14 cities	1988–89	STD clinics	20–24	30.1% (Median)	9.7%–55.6%
Lemp et al., 1994	122	San Francisco	1992–93	Snowball	17–19	4.1%	
	303	"	"	"	20–23	11.60%	
Osmond et al., 1994	84	San Francisco	1992–93	Household survey	18–23	4.80%	
Sweeney et al., 1995		24 cities	1990–92	Runaway shelters/ STD clinics	<20		13%–17%
Silvestre et al., 1993	121	Pittsburgh area	1984	Snowball	≤22	7.40%	
	61	"	1992	"		6.60%	
Stricof et al., 1991	109	NYC	1988–89	Runaway shelters	15–20	24.80%	
Allen et al., 1994		cities	1989–92	Runaway shelters	15–24	32.30%	25.3%–37.5%
Kaslow et al., 1987		5 cities	1984–85	Snowball	18–24	29%	

Mental Health Issues

There has been a great deal of controversy about mental health problems among gay, lesbian, and bisexual youths. In a national sample of 1,925 lesbians, a higher percentage in the 17- to 24-year-old age group reported concerns about family than any other age group (Bradford, Ryan, & Rothblum, 1994), which could reflect not only the greater dependence on family of this age group but also the concerns of young lesbians regarding losing the support of their family. Thirty-one percent of the young women had experienced depression, 17% anxiety, and 10% other symptoms of emotional distress in the past, and 14% were currently experiencing depression, 9% anxiety, and 6% other symptoms. D'Augelli and Hershberger (1993) found that 60% of the 194 lesbian, gay, and bisexual youths they studied reported feeling overwhelmed in the previous year. However, it is difficult to compare this to a sample of heterosexual adolescents. It may be a common and developmentally appropriate response to feel overwhelmed in adolescence.

It has been argued that lesbian, gay, and bisexual youths are at increased risk for completed suicide (Gibson, 1989). A summary of studies reporting on the rates of attempted suicide, counseling, and psychiatric hospitalizations is presented in table 5.5 There are no data to support the concern about completed suicide (Shaffer, Fisher, Parides, & Gould, 1995). However, there is evidence that youths are at increased risk for suicide attempts. Evidence comes from clinicians' observations (Hunter & Schaecher, 1990), the frequency of youths' reports in each of the samples, retrospective reports of young gay men (Schneider, Farberow, & Kruks, 1989), and interviews with staff or psychiatrists working with gay youths (Kourany, 1987). Recent empirical data on predominantly white, middle-class, nonclinical samples of gay and bisexual male youths support these estimates. Remafedi (1987a) and Remafedi and colleagues (1991) found that 30%–34% of gay male youths recruited from newspaper advertisements and drop-in centers in Minneapolis or Seattle had attempted suicide and that nearly one-half (44%) had tried to kill themselves more than once. Among gay males who attempted suicide (Remafedi et al., 1991), exhibiting more feminine gender roles, sexual and drug abuse, arrests for criminal behavior and early awareness of their gay orientation were more common. Among older gay adolescents and young adults in Los Angeles, 20% had attempted suicide and 46% reattempted suicide at least once (Schneider et al., 1989). Suicide attempters were significantly younger than nonattempters when they became aware of their homosexual orientation and were more likely to come out in isolation and to be rejected by others for their homosexuality (Schneider et al., 1989).

In a study of 138 gay or bisexual males aged 14–19 (mainly low-income African-American or Hispanic) presenting at a social service agency for lesbian and gay adolescents in New York City (The Hetrick-Martin Institute), 39% had attempted suicide; and of those making an attempt, more than half

Table 5.5

Mental Health of Gay, Bisexual, and Lesbian Youths

Study	N	% Attempted Suicide	% Counseling	Psychiatric Hospitalization
Remafedi, 1987a	29	34%	72%	31%
D'Augelli & Hershberger, 1993	142 Males	42%		
	52 Females			
Remafedi, 1994	239	30%		15%
Rotheram-Borus, Hunter, & Rosario, 1994	138	39%		
Bradford, Ryan, & Rothblum, 1994	168 Females	24%	62%	
Garofalo, Wolf, Kessel, Palfrey, & DuRant, 1998	104 Males and Females	35% (1 year)		

made more than one attempt (Rotheram-Borus, Hunter, et al., 1994). Seventeen percent had a family member who had attempted suicide, and 12% had a family member who had completed suicide. About one-third said they had at least one friend who had attempted suicide, and 16% reported having at least one friend who had killed him- or herself. In a sample of 194 gays, lesbians, and bisexuals (D'Augelli & Hershberger, 1993), 42% had attempted suicide, with no difference between the rates for gay and lesbian youths. These youths had greater psychiatric symptomatology, were more "out" to others, had lost more friends due to their orientation, were more worried about excessive alcohol use, had lower self-esteem, and knew their orientation at a younger age.

In a national study of lesbian health, 24% of the 17- to 24-year-olds reported having attempted suicide, a higher percentage than any other age group in the sample (Bradford et al., 1994). Among all age groups in this study, more African-American (27%) and Latina (28%) women were likely to have attempted suicide than white women (16%). Each of these studies report rates of attempts higher than those reported nationally (7.5%; Garrison, McKeown, Valois, & Vincent, 1993) or for youths of similar age, gender, and ethnic groups (CDC, 1991). Therefore, self-identifying as gay, bisexual, or lesbian appears to be associated with increased risk for attempted suicide. Similar to patterns of attempts among nongay youths, the pool of suicide attempters appears quite different from those who complete. Only a very small percentage of attempters ever kill themselves. The severity and circumstances of the adolescents' attempts also appear to be quite diverse, indicating the range of motivations and contexts that have elicited the attempts.

Substance Abuse

From clinicians' reports about lesbians, alcohol and drug use is believed to be high, although there are few existing data to support this hypothesis (Rosario, Hunter, & Gwadz, 1997; Rotheram-Borus, et al., 1999). Studies focusing on the substance use of gay, lesbian, and bisexual adolescents can be seen in table 5.6. In the few samples of gay males, all based on convenience samples or involving participants recruited from social service agencies, at least 75% used alcohol; the rates of marijuana use ranged from 42%–76%, in each case substantially higher than the national average (Remafedi, 1987a; Rotheram-Borus, Rosario, et al., 1994; Rosario, Hunter, & Gwadz, 1997). Hard drug use, in particular, was high and of greater concern since use of these drugs (crack/cocaine and heroin) is associated with HIV infection. Among seropositive gay and bisexual youths, 24% injected drugs (Rotheram-Borus, Lee, et al., in press). Methamphetamine (Rotheram-Borus, Luna, Marotta, & Kelly, 1994) has been the drug of choice among youths on the West Coast for the last 10 years, and is directly associated with HIV infection in that it leads to a heightened interest in sexual activity that can last

Table 5.6
Percent of Gay, Bisexual, and Lesbian Youths who Have Ever Used Substances

STUDY (TIMEFRAME)	SITE	N	ALCOHOL	MARIJUANA	COCAINE/CRACK	HEROIN/INJECTING
Males						
Remafedi, 1987a (Current)	Minneapolis	29	79%	76%	21%	
Remafedi, 1994 (Lifetime)	Minnesota	239	44% ≥ 5 drinks, 1 or more occasions in last 2 weeks	66%	23% /8%	/5%
Rotheram-Borus, Rosario, Meyer-Bahlburg et al., 1994 (Lifetime)	NYC	131	76%	42%	25% /8%	0%
Males and Females						
Rosario, Hunter, & Gwadz, 1997 (Lifetime)	NYC	78 Males 76 Females	78% 88%	50% 62%	10% 18%	1% /3% 3% /1%
Rotheram-Borus, Reid, Marelich, & Srinivasan, 1998 (Lifetime)	NYC, San Francisco, LA	160 Males 53 Females	100% 92%	91% used drugs in lifetime 92% used drugs in lifetime		
Males and Females						
Garofalo, Wolf, Kessel, Palfrey, & DuRant, 1998	Massachusetts	104 Males and Females	86.8%	68.5%	33%	22.2%

for several days (Frosch, Shoptaw, Huber, Rawson, & Ling, 1996; Kipke, O'Connor, Palmer, & MacKenzie, 1995; Paul, Stall, & Davis, 1993). Prolonged use of the drug, however, is associated with sexual dysfunction, which also leads to increases in risky sexual practices to enhance sexual desire, which, in turn, escalates HIV risk.

School Problems

Lesbian, gay, and bisexual youths who face harassment by their peers may perform poorly in school, become truant, or drop out (Hunter & Schaecher, 1990; Martin & Hetrick, 1988; Price & Telljohann, 1991). In a study of gay and bisexual male youths, Rotheram-Borus et al. (1991) found that 60% had failed a grade, although this was normative for youths of similar socioeconomic status and ethnicities in New York City. Remafedi (1987a,b) reports that 40% of his sample of gay and bisexual male youths were truant and 28% had dropped out of school. More than 80% reported some problems in school.

The Relationship among Multiple Problem Behaviors

The high rates of risk behaviors warrant substantial concern about the long-term adjustment of lesbian, gay, and bisexual youths. However, as noted at several points in this review, the samples are unrepresentative and may be biased. Because youths are often approached in the context of a temporary crisis situation (e.g., in seeking services at a social service agency), the rates of problem behaviors may be exaggerated. The more traditional explanations or theories of multiple problem behaviors linking adolescent risk acts via an underlying trait of unconventionality (Jessor, Donovan, & Costa, 1996) may not be applicable for gay or lesbian youths. It is not a desire or a long-term behavior pattern toward being unconventional that motivates youths' patterns of sexual attraction and behaviors. The predictors, mediators, and motivations of these actions may need to be modified to more accurately reflect the behavior patterns of gay and lesbian youths. However, two samples have been followed longitudinally over one to two years, and it appears that the rates of problem behaviors are not heightened, except for sexual behavior (Rosario, Hunter, & Gwadz, 1997; Rotheram-Borus, Rosario, Van Rossem, et al., 1995).

Among 136 gay male youths who were followed over two years, most youths demonstrated low rates of problem behaviors consistently over time (39%; Rotheram-Borus, Rosario, Van Rossem, et al., 1995). For example, 43% of gay youths used alcohol only very infrequently; most (58%) reported low use of drugs over two years, and 63% had very few delinquent acts. Most youths did not use hard drugs or marijuana frequently. While rates of attempted suicide appear higher than among other adolescents, about three-fourths of gay/bisexual youths had never attempted suicide. More than half (52%) of the youths reported emotional distress in the normal range consistently over two years of repeated assessments. Overall, the most common profile of a consecutive series of youths recruited from a community-based agency (a site that may be expected to serve youths at higher risk than typical) was to report low rates of all problem behaviors, in contrast to stereotypes of gay and bisexual youths and the high rates of specific behaviors if behaviors are examined individually and cross-sectionally. Most youths (60%) also reported highly stable behavior patterns over two years. Only 1% of youths reported increasing problem behaviors overall; 4% of youths decreased their risk acts over two years. Youths who reported a higher rate on one problem behavior did not report a cluster of problem behaviors. While there were high rates of sexual risk acts, the other problem behaviors did not cluster in a manner similar to that reported for heterosexual youths. Youths who had mental health problems did not report higher rates of substance use or school problems. Similarly, youths with school problems were not abusing substances more often than those without school problems. This failure to cluster indicates that there may be different developmental processes for gay and lesbian youths. In contrast to heterosexual youths, the meaning and motivation of risk behaviors is likely to be different for gay, lesbian, and bisexual youths. Explanations other than a tendency toward unconventionality must be generated to assist us in understanding youths' behavior patterns over time.

Even more encouraging are data from intervention studies. At least three studies of HIV prevention activities with gay youths have been reported. Each found that youths initially had accurately perceived themselves at higher risk for HIV infection, and each reported substantial reductions in HIV risk acts after receiving an intervention (around 20%–30% reductions; Rotheram-Borus, Rosario, Reid, et al., 1995; Remafedi, 1994; Rotheram-Borus, Gwadz, Fernandez, & Srinivasan, 1998). Youths who changed their behaviors and sustained this change over 1 year, however, were youths with low emotional distress and low rates of substance use (Rotheram-Borus, Rosario, Reid, & Gillis, 1995). More than 40% of youths consistently protected themselves in all sexual encounters. Another 30% significantly improved their sexual self-protection and maintained these changes over two years. The most important mediators of positive responses to interventions among youths of unknown HIV serostatus appear to be: youths' difficulties in coping with coming out, their mental health status, whether or not they engage in commercial sex, and their substance use (not necessarily injecting drug use).

In addition to the positive results associated with HIV prevention activities, most gay and bisexual seropositive youths respond responsibly to learning about being seropositive: about 50% of injecting drug users who are young gay men stopped their substance use within two years after learning of their serostatus (Rotheram-Borus, Lee, et al., in press). Youths appear to reverse the developmental trajectory outlined by Kandel and Logan (1984; a progression from less serious drugs to more serious drugs) after learning they are infected with HIV. Rather than hard drugs being the dominant substance used, most youths are using alcohol and marijuana. While abstinence from substance use may remain the goal, there are dramatic and sustained changes in substance-use risk acts when gay and bisexual males learn that they are seropositive for HIV. In addition, most gay and bisexual seropositive youths disclose their serostatus to their sexual partners (69%; Lee & Rotheram-Borus, in press), and their reported condom use increases significantly compared to their use prior to learning that they were seropositive (66% of acts protected). About one-third of youths adopt a pattern of sexual abstinence over long periods of time. In response to an intervention, youths increased their health care utilization, reduced self-destructive coping patterns, and increased positive action coping. The number of physical health symptoms decreased significantly and was maintained for 15 months. Surprisingly, emotional distress was associated with a greater number of positive changes in risk behaviors over time, not increased risk acts. Even though substantial changes occurred in response to learning their serostatus, youths also responded to an intervention by increasing their health adherence and reducing transmission acts (Rotheram-Borus, Murphy, Lee, & the Teens Linked To Care Consortium, in press). There were decreases in physical symptoms and distress associated with health, sexual risk acts with seronegative partners, and substance use. These data again support a picture of gay and bisexual male youths as responsibly protecting themselves and their partners.

Summary

Prior to coping with their sexual orientation, most lesbian, gay, and bisexual youths are healthy, as most children are healthy. Prior to adolescence, gay, lesbian, and bisexual youths are likely to have been doing reasonably well in school, to have ongoing relationships with parents and peers, to have interests in hobbies, recreational activities, and goals, and to be members of religious communities. Youths' diverse social and personal identities do not disappear when they recognize that their sexual orientations are different from their heterosexual peers. The strengths that youths built from infancy through middle childhood are present to assist them as they cope with their sexual orientation.

The limited data that we have on lesbian, gay, and bisexual youths paint a paradoxical picture. When problem behaviors are assessed independently, each sample studied to date indicates that gay, lesbian, and bisexual youths engage in multiple behaviors placing the youths at high risk for multiple negative outcomes. However, when youths are monitored longitudinally over time, it appears that the majority of youths are at low risk for multiple problem behaviors. Only in the areas of sexual acts and suicide attempts do there appear to be high rates of behavior relative to peers of the same gender and socioeconomic status. Substance use, progress at school, feelings of anxiety and depression, conduct problems, and the rates of delinquency appear normative among gay, lesbian, and bisexual youths. These data point to the resiliency of youths with nonheterosexual orientations.

In addition, these data are similar to those observed for ethnic minorities (i.e., among African-American and Latino youths in the United States) and for women. It has been argued that being a member of an ethnic group that is historically both a minority in status and a minority in numbers places youths at increased risk for negative outcomes (Stiffman & Davis, 1990). These theories were subsequently revised and the advantages of coping with two cultures, one's own ethnic group and that of the dominant ethnic group, have been emphasized (Phinney, 1993; Ramirez, Castaneda, & Herold, 1974). Similarly, being female was historically perceived as a disadvantage that was overcome by a minority of women; in the last 20 years, the strengths and attributes associated with being female have been emphasized and celebrated (Gilligan, 1982; Leadbeater & Way, 1996). Youths may also receive benefits and build unique strengths associated with being gay, lesbian, or bisexual, despite the negative social sanctions regarding their sexual orientation.

In a different and more intensive manner than heterosexual youths, gay, lesbian, and bisexual youths must develop skills to judge and anticipate acceptance from peers and adults, seek information on their own regarding lesbian/gay culture, and examine their values, attitudes, and beliefs regarding sexuality and their sexual orientation. There are likely to be benefits, as well as costs, to youths who initiate this search process and who at an early age commit to a set of behaviors and relationships with respect to their sexual orientation. There has been little focus on whether there is a heightened or early self-awareness, increased maturity or independence, or increased self-esteem for being able to negotiate the norms in more than one social world simultaneously. Given the findings of benefits for those with ethnic and gender minority status, it is likely that in the next few years, a set of potential benefits to those who are gay, lesbian, or bisexual will be identified.

As we begin to gather data on the developmental trajectories of gay, lesbian, and bisexual youths, it is critical to consider the policy implications of any interventions that are recommended for gay, bisexual, and lesbian youths. Much of the prevailing literature has adopted a deficit model of development, perceiving gay, lesbian, and bisexual youths as predominantly stigmatized and rejected, and seeing a need for buffering this stress by providing significant and ongoing interventions. The perceived need for such intervention has been heightened by the real threat of HIV for gay and bisexual males, in particular. Federally funded initiatives and programs have been mounted across the nation, in conjunction with local communities, to provide education and support for self-identified gay, lesbian, and bisexual youths to help them cope with the threat of HIV (CDC, 1998; Health Resources and Services Administration, 1997). However, interventions often have unintended negative consequences. Being labeled as a person in need of intervention is itself stigmatizing. Interventions aimed at enhancing the self-esteem of gay, bisexual, and lesbian youths have the unintended consequence of communicating to youths that they have deficits because of their sexual orientation.

Not enough attention has been focused on changing the cultural context in which gay, lesbian, and bisexual youths experience their adolescence. The media have increasingly provided positive coverage for issues of gay, bisexual, and lesbian adults. For example, "Ellen," a popular television situation comedy, starred a lesbian who "came out" and coped with situations surrounding her sexual orientation (Marin & Miller, 1997). Gay men and women have commanded cover stories in national news magazines (Handy, 1997; Kantrowitz, 1996; Salholz, Beck, Kantrowitz, & Senna, 1993). Hundreds of businesses now offer domestic partner benefits to partners of their gay and lesbian employees (Ginsberg, 1997); polls show increasing acceptance of some aspects of homosexuality (Yang, 1997); and there are scattered incidents of growing approval (Blumenthal, 1993; Egan, 1996; Jefferson, 1993). Some communities have provided resources for gay and lesbian youths (Cano & Carvajal, 1994; Gevelinger & Zimmerman, 1997; Winerip, 1994; Yarber, 1993). Thus, there have been some positive shifts in the mainstream culture's attitudes and treatment of gay, lesbian, and bisexual persons.

However, some increase in positive coverage does not mean a supportive environment for gay, lesbian, or bisexual youths. When the media covers a gay-related issue (e.g., "Ellen"), considerable controversy often surrounds it. Many still consider gays, lesbians, and bisexuals to be, at best, tolerated but not allowed the full benefits of the culture (e.g., marriage rights; Moore, 1996) to, at worse, deviants who are a threat to society (Diamond, 1994). There continues to be a high and increasing number of hate crimes toward gay and lesbian persons (Herek, Gillis, Cogan, & Glunt, 1997). Some still fear that heterosexual youths will be solicited into homosexuality (Brooke, 1996; Drummond & Boxall, 1994; Shaw, 1995). The existing data consistently point to interpersonal conflict, stress, and high rates of verbal punishment and rejection from others being linked to disclosure of being gay, lesbian, and bisexual. Thus, while there are some small indications of increasing cultural acceptance of homosexuality in the United States, being gay, lesbian, or bisexual remains a stigmatizing status that often elicits punishment.

Rather than focusing on the adjustment of individual youths, it is critical to design interventions for the culture to increase the national level of acceptance of cultural diversity. National interventions to discourage smoking cigarettes, encourage seat belt use, and prevent HIV have been successfully launched in many countries. Modeling international models (e.g., Denmark, Finland, Iceland, The Netherlands) of greater acceptance of diverse sexual orientations and lifestyles is an alternative strategy to pursue when attempting to facilitate the adjustment of gay, lesbian, and bisexual youths.

Programs for destigmatizing gay, lesbian, and bisexual persons may be an important strategy to consider in helping to support young adults, and although these may be controversial now owing to the continuing stigmatization of gays, lesbians, and bisexuals, considering the progress made in other areas of civil rights in the last 30 years, they will be increasingly commonplace in the future.

References

Allen, D. M., Lehman, S., Green, T. A., Lindegren, M. L., Onorato, I. M., Forrester, W., & the Field Services Branch (1994). HIV infection among homeless adults and runaway youth, United States, 1989–1992. *AIDS, 8,* 1593–1598.

Archer, S. L. (1989). The status of identity: Reflections on the need for intervention. *Journal of Adolescence, 12,* 345–359.

Archer, S. L. (1993). Identity in relational contexts: A methodological proposal. In J. Kroger (Ed.), *Discussions on ego identity* (pp. 75–99). Hillsdale, NJ: Erlbaum.

Asher, S. R. (1990). Recent advances in the study of peer rejection. In S. R. Asher & J. D. Coie (Eds.), *Peer rejection in childhood* (pp. 3–14). Cambridge: Cambridge University Press.

Baruch, G., Barnett, R., & Rivers, C. (1985). *Lifeprints: New patterns of love and work for today's women.* New York: New American Library.

Bem, S. L. (1987). Gender schema theory and its implications for child development: Raising gender-aschematic children in a gender-schematic society. In R. M. Walsh (Ed.), *The psychology of women: Ongoing debates* (pp. 226–245). New Haven: Yale University Press.

Besner, H. F., & Spungin, C. I. (1995). *Gay and lesbian students: Understanding their needs.* Washington, DC: Taylor & Francis.

Binson, D., Michaels, S., Stall, R., Coates, T. J., Gagnon, J. H., & Catania, J. A. (1995). Prevalence and social distribution of men who have sex with men: United States and its urban centers. *Journal of Sex Research, 32,* 245–254.

Blumenthal, R. (1993, February 21). Gay officers find acceptance on New York's police force. *New York Times, 142,* pp. 1(N), 1(L).

Boxall, B., & Perry, T. (1994, April 1). Gay leaders condemn ruling in boy Scouts case. *Los Angeles Times, 113,* pp. B3.

Boxer, A. M., Cook, J. A., & Herdt, G. (1991). Double jeopardy: Identity transitions and parent-child relations among gay and lesbian youth. In K. Pillemer & K. McCartney (Eds.), *Parent-child relations throughout life* (pp. 59–92). Hillsdale, NJ: Erlbaum.

Bradford, J., Ryan, C., & Rothblum, E. D. (1994). National Lesbian Health Care Survey: Implications for mental health care. *Journal of Consulting and Clinical Psychology, 62,* 228–242.

Brooke, J. (1996, February 28). To be young, gay and going to a high school in Utah. *New York Times, 145,* pp. A1(N), B8(L).

Cano, D., & Carvajal, D. (1994, January 13). Gay support meetings on campus OKed. *Los Angeles Times, 113,* pp. A22.

Cass, V. C. (1979). Homosexual identity formation: A theoretical model. *Journal of Homosexuality, 4,* 219–235.

Catania, J. A., Coates, T. J., Stall, R., Turner, H., Peterson, J., Hearst, N., Dolcini, M. M., Hudes, E., Gagnon, J., Wiley, J., & Groves, R. (1992). Prevalence of AIDS-related risk factors and condom use in the United States. *Science, 258,* 1101–1106.

Centers for Disease Control and Prevention. (1991). Attempted suicide among high school students: United States, 1990. *Morbidity and Mortality Weekly Report, 40,* 633–635.

Centers for Disease Control and Prevention. (1995). *Information for HIV prevention community Planning Groups (#2): HIV/AIDS among young gay and bisexual men.* Atlanta, GA: Author.

Centers for Disease Control and Prevention. (1998). *Adolescent AIDS fact sheet.* Atlanta, GA: Author.

Coleman, E. (1981–82). Developmental stages of the coming out process. Homosexuality and Psychotherapy. *Journal of Homosexuality, 7,* 31–43.

Cross, W. E. (1978). The Thomas and Cross models of psychological nigrescence: A review. *Journal of Black Psychology, 5,* 13–31.

D'Augelli, A. R. (1992a). Sexual behavior patterns of gay university men: Implications for preventing HIV infection. *Journal of American College Health, 41,* 25–28.

D'Augelli, A. R. (1992b). Lesbian and gay male undergraduates' experiences of harassment and fear on campus. *Journal of Interpersonal Violence, 7,* 383–395.

D'Augelli, A. R., & Hershberger, S. L. (1993). Lesbian, gay, and bisexual youth in community settings: Personal challenges and mental health problems. *American Journal of Community Psychology, 21,* 421–448.

Dean, L., Wu, S., & Martin, J. L. (1992). Trends in violence and discrimination against gay men in New York City: 1984 to 1990. In G. M. Herek & K. T. Berrill (Eds.), *Hate crimes: Confronting violence against lesbians and gay men* (pp. 46–64). Newbury Park, CA: Sage.

Dean, L., & Meyer, I. (1995). HIV prevalence and sexual behavior in a cohort of New York City gay men (aged 18–24). *Journal of Acquired Immunodeficiency Syndrome, 8,* 208–211.

Diamond, S. (1994). The Christian right's anti-gay agenda. *Humanist, 54,* 32–34.

Drummond, T., & Boxall, B. (1994, January 10). Gay rights fight moves on campus; activists on both sides have targeted high schools in battles over curriculum and support groups. *Los Angeles Times, 113,* pp. A1.

Dryfoos, J. G. (1997). The prevalence of problem behaviors: Implications for programs. In R. P. Weissberg, T. P. Gullotta, R. L. Hampton, B. A. Ryan, & G. R. Adams (Eds.), *Healthy children 2010: Enhancing children's wellness, 8* (pp. 17–46). Newbury Park, CA: Sage.

Egan, T. (1996, September 12). What once was, isn't anymore (gay candidates enjoy unprecedented acceptance in Southern states). *New York Times,* A12(N), B8(L).

Ensminger, M. E. (1987). Implications of longitudinal studies of delinquency for prevention research. In J. A. Steinberg & M. M. Silverman (Eds.), *Preventing mental disorders: A research perspective* (NIMH ADM Publication No. 87–1492, pp. 140–148). Rockville, MD: U.S. Department of Health and Human Services.

Erikson, E. H. (1959). *Identity and the life cycle.* New York: International Universities Press.

Erikson, E. H. (1968). *Identity, youth, and crisis* (1st ed.). New York: W. W. Norton.

Fay, R. E., Turner, C. F., Klassen, A. D., & Gagnon, J. H. (1989). Prevalence and patterns of same-gender sexual contact among men. *Science, 243,* 338–348.

Fiske, M., & Chiriboga, D. A. (1990). *Change and continuity in adult life.* San Francisco: Jossey-Bass.

French, S. A., Story, M., Remafedi, G., Resnick, M. D., & Blum, R. W. (1996). Sexual orientation and prevalence of body dissatisfaction and eating disordered behaviors: A population-based study of adolescents. *International Journal of Eating Disorders, 19,* 119–126.

Frosch, D., Shoptaw, S., Huber, A., Rawson, R. A., & Ling, W. (1996). Sexual HIV risk among gay and bisexual male methamphetamine abusers. *Journal of Substance Abuse Treatment, 13,* 483–486.

Garofalo, R., Wolf, R. C., Kessel, S., Palfrey, J., & DuRant, R. H. (1998). The association between health risk behaviors and sexual orientation among a school-based sample of adolescents. *Pediatrics, 101,* 895–902.

Garrison, C. Z., McKeown, R. E., Valois, R. F., & Vincent, M. L. (1993). Aggression, substance use, and suicidal behaviors in high school students. *American Journal of Public Health, 83,* 179–184.

Gevelinger, M. E., & Zimmerman, L. (1997). How Catholic schools are creating a safe climate for gay and lesbian students. *Educational Leadership, 55,* 66–69.

Gemelli, R. (1996). *Normal child and adolescent development.* Washington, DC: American Psychiatric Press.

Gibson, P. (1989). Gay male and lesbian youth suicide. In U.S. Department of Health and Human Services (Ed.), *Report of the Secretary's Task Force on Youth Suicide* (pp. 110–142). Washington, DC: Author.

Gilligan, C. (1982). *In a different voice: Psychological theory and women's development.* Cambridge, MA: Harvard University Press.

Ginsberg, S. (1997, July 6). More companies reaching out with gay-friendly policies; domestic partner benefits gain momentum in tight labor market, despite risk of offending conservative customers. *Washington Post, 120,* H4.

Gonsiorek, J. C. (1988). Mental health issues of gay and lesbian adolescents. *Journal of Adolescent Health Care, 9,* 115–122.

Gonsiorek, J. C., & Rudolph, J. R. (1991). Homosexual identity: Coming out and other developmental events. In J. C. Gonsiorek & J. D. Weinrich (Eds.), *Homosexuality: Research implications for public policy* (pp. 161–176). Newbury Park, CA: Sage.

Handy, B. (1997, April 14). Roll over, Ward Cleaver. *Time, 149,* 78–84.

Harry, J., & DeVall, W. (1978). Age and sexual culture among homosexually oriented males. *Archives of Sexual Behavior, 7,* 199–209.

Harter, S., Marold, D. B., Whitesell, N. R., & Cobbs, G. (1996). A model of the effects of perceived parent and peer support on adolescent false self behavior. *Child Development, 67,* 360–374.

Health Resources and Services Administration. (1997). *Getting HIV-positive youth into care: Issues and opportunities.* U.S. Department of Health & Human Services, Rockville, MD: Author.

Herek, G. M., Gillis, J. R., Cogan, J. C., & Glunt, E. K. (1997). Hate crime victimization among lesbian, gay, and bisexual adults. *Journal of Interpersonal Violence, 12,* 195–215.

Hetrick, E. S., & Martin, A. D. (1987). Developmental issues and their resolution for gay and lesbian adolescents. *Journal of Homosexuality, 14,* 25–43.

Howes, C. (1988). Peer interaction of young children. *Monographs of the Society for Research in Child Development*, 53 (Serial No. 217).

Hunter, J. (1990). Violence against lesbian and gay male youth. *Journal of Interpersonal Violence*, 5, 295–300.

Hunter, J. (1995). At the crossroads: Lesbian youth. In K. Jay (Ed.), *Dyke life: From growing up to growing old. A celebration of the lesbian experience* (pp. 50–61). New York: Basic Books.

Hunter, J., & Schaecher, R. (1990). Lesbian and gay youth. In M. J. Rotheram-Borus, J. Bradley, & N. Obolensky, R. (Eds.), *Planning to live: Evaluating and treating suicidal teens in community settings* (pp. 297–316). Tulsa: University of Oklahoma Press.

Hunter, J., & Schaecher, R. (1995). Lesbian and gay adolescents: An overview of developmental and clinical issues. In R. L. Edwards (Ed.), *Encyclopedia of social work: Vol. 2* (19th ed., pp. 1055–1063). Washington, DC: National Association of Social Workers Press.

Jefferson, D. J. (1993, April 22). Businesses offering products for gays are thriving; rise in activism and public acceptance of lifestyles increase demand. *Wall Street Journal*, pp. B2(W), B2(E).

Jessor, R., Donovan, J. E., & Costa, F. (1996). Personality, perceived life chances, and adolescent behavior. In K. Hurrelmann & S. F. Hamilton (Eds.), *Social problems and social contexts in adolescence: Perspectives across boundaries* (pp. 219–233). New York: Aldine de Gruyter.

Kandel D. B., & Logan J. A. (1984). Patterns of drug use from adolescence to adulthood: I. Periods of risk for initiation, continued use, and discontinuation. *American Journal of Public Health*, 74, 660–667.

Kantrowitz, B. (1996, November 4). Gay families come out. *Newsweek*, 128, 50–57.

Kaslow, R. A., Ostrow, D. G., Detels, R., Phair, J. P., Polk, F., Rinaldo, C. R. (1987). The Multicenter AIDS Cohort Study: Rationale, organization, and selected characteristics of the participants. *American Journal of Epidemiology*, 126, 310–318.

Kinsey, A. C., Pomeroy, W. B., & Martin, C. E. (1948). *Sexual behavior in the human male*. Philadelphia: W. B. Saunders.

Kipke, M. D., O'Connor, S., Palmer, R., & MacKenzie, R. G. (1995). Street youth in Los Angeles. Profile of a group at high risk for Human Immunodeficiency Virus infection. *Archives of Pediatrics and Adolescent Medicine*, 149, 513–519.

Kohn, M. J. (1991). Factors affecting the coming out process for lesbians. *Journal of Homosexuality*, 21, 47–70.

Kourany, R. F. C. (1987). Suicide among homosexual adolescents. *Journal of Homosexuality*, 13, 111–117.

Laumann, E. O., Michael, R. T., & Gagnon, J. H. (1994). A political history of the National Sex Survey of Adults. *Family Planning Perspectives*, 26, 34–38.

Leadbeater, B. J. R., & Way, N. (Eds.). (1996). *Urban girls: Resisting stereotypes, creating identities*. New York: New York University Press.

Lee, M., & Rotheram-Borus, M. J. (in press). Disclosure of serostatus among youth living with HIV. *AIDS and Behavior*.

Leffert, N., & Petersen, A. C. (1996). Biology, challenge, and coping in adolescence: Effects on physical and mental health. In M. H. Bornstein & J. L. Genevro (Eds.), *Child development and behavioral pediatrics. Crosscurrents in contemporary psychology* (pp. 129–154). Hillsdale, NJ: Erlbaum.

Lemp, G. F., Hirozawa, A. M., Givertz, D., Nieri, G. N., Anderson, L., Lindegren, M. L., Janssen R. S., & Katz, M. (1994). Seroprevalence of HIV and risk behaviors among young homosexual and bisexual men: The San Francisco/ Berkeley Young Men's Survey. *Journal of the American Medical Association, 272,* 449–454.

Lemp, G. F., Jones, M., Kellogg, T. A., Nieri G. N., Anderson, L., Withum, D., & Katz M. (1995). HIV seroprevalence and risk behaviors among lesbians and bisexual women in San Francisco and Berkeley, California. *American Journal of Public Health, 85,* 1549–1552.

Levenson, D. (1978). *Seasons of a man's life.* New York: Knopf.

Loevinger, J. (1976). *The meaning and measure of ego development.* San Francisco: Jossey-Bass.

Lyons, A., & Atwood, J. A. (1994). Influence of sexual preference cues on rating applicants for a teaching position. *Psychological Reports, 74,* 337–338.

Maccoby, E. E., & Jacklin, C. N. (1978). *The psychology of sex differences.* Stanford, CA: Stanford University Press.

Marcia, J. E. (1989). Identity diffusion differentiated. In M. A. Luszcz & T. Nettelbeck (Eds.), *Psychological development: Perspectives across the life-span* (pp. 289–294). Amsterdam: North-Holland.

Marin, R., & Miller, S. (1997, April 14). Ellen steps out. *Newsweek, 129,* 64–68.

Martin, A. D., & Hetrick, E. S. (1988). The stigmatization of the gay and lesbian adolescent. *Journal of Homosexuality, 15,* 163–183.

Meyer, I. H., & Dean, L. (1995). Patterns of sexual behavior and risk taking among young New York City gay men. *AIDS Education & Prevention, 7* (Suppl.), 13–23.

Moore, D. W. (1996). Public opposes gay marriages. *Gallup Poll Monthly, 369,* 19–21.

Ness, C. (1996, June 30). Gay in America: 1996. *San Francisco Examiner,* p. A1.

Norman, A. D., Perry, M. J., Stevenson, L. Y., Kelly, J. A., & Roffman, R. A. (1996). Lesbian and bisexual women in small cities—at risk for HIV? *Public Health Reports, 111,* 347–352.

Osmond, D. H., Page, K., Wiley, J., Garrett, K., Sheppard, H. W., Moss, A. R., Scharager, L., & Winkelstein, W. (1994). HIV infection in homosexual and bisexual men 18 to 29 years of age: The San Francisco Young Men's Health Study. *American Journal of Public Health, 84,* 1933–1937.

Paroski, R. (1987). Health care delivery and the concerns of gay and lesbian adolescents. *Journal of Adolescent Health Care, 8,* 188–192.

Paul, J. P., Stall, R., & Davis, F. (1993). Sexual risk for HIV transmission among gay/ bisexual men in substance-abuse treatment. *AIDS Education and Prevention, 5,* 11–24.

Petersen, A. C. (1988). Adolescent development. *Annual Review of Psychology, 39,* 583–607.

Petersen, A. C., Compas, B. E., Brooks-Gunn, J., Stemmler, M., Ey, S., & Grant, K. E. (1993). Depression in adolescence. *American Psychologist, 48,* 169–182.

Phinney, J. S. (1993). Multiple group identities: Differentiation, conflict, and integration. In J. Kroger (Ed.), *Discussions on ego identity* (pp. 47–73). Hillsdale, NJ: Erlbaum.

Phinney, J. S., Lochner, B. T., & Murphy, R. (1990). Ethnic identity development and psychological adjustment in adolescence. In A. R. Stiffman & L. E. Davis

(Eds.), *Ethnic issues in adolescent mental health* (pp. 53–72). Newbury Park, CA: Sage.

Phinney, J., & Rotheram-Borus, M. J. (Eds.). (1987). *Children's ethnic socialization: Pluralism and development*. Newbury Park, CA: Sage.

Phinney, J., & Tarver, S. (1988). Ethnic identity search and commitment in Black and White eighth graders. *Journal of Early Adolescence, 8*, 265–277.

Pilkington, N. W., & D'Augelli, A. R. (1995). Victimization of lesbian, gay, and bisexual youth in community settings. *Journal of Community Psychology, 23*, 34–56.

Price, J. H., & Telljohann, S. K. (1991). School counselors' perceptions of adolescent homosexuals. *Journal of School Health, 61*, 433–438.

Ramirez, M., Castaneda, A., & Herold, P. L. (1974). The relationship of acculturation to cognitive style among Mexican Americans. *Journal of Cross-Cultural Psychology, 5*, 424–433.

Reinisch, J. M., Sanders, S. A., & Ziemba-Davis, M. (1995). Self-labeled sexual orientation and sexual behavior: Considerations for STD-related biomedical research and education. In M. Stein & A. Baum (Eds.), *Chronic diseases: Perspectives in behavioral medicine* (pp. 241–257). Mahwah, NJ: Erlbaum.

Remafedi, G. (1987a). Adolescent homosexuality: Psychosocial and medical implications. *Pediatrics, 79*, 331–337.

Remafedi, G. (1987b). Male homosexuality: The adolescent's perspective. *Pediatrics, 79*, 326–330.

Remafedi, G. (1994). Predictors of unprotected intercourse among gay and bisexual youth: Knowledge, beliefs, and behavior. *Pediatrics, 94*, 163–168.

Remafedi, G., Farrow, J. A., & Deisher, R. W. (1991). Risk factors for attempted suicide in gay and bisexual youth. *Pediatrics, 87*, 869–875.

Rogers, S. M., & Turner, C. F. (1991). Male-male sexual contact in the U.S.A.: Findings from five sample surveys, 1970–1990. *The Journal of Sex Research, 28*, 491–519.

Rosario, M., Hunter, J., & Gwadz, M. (1995, October). *The HIV-risk acts and coming-out process of lesbian and gay youth*. Abstracts of the American Public Health Association 123rd Annual Meeting & Exhibition (No. 3045). San Diego, CA.

Rosario, M., Hunter, J., & Gwadz, M. (1997). Exploration of substance use among lesbian, gay, and bisexual youth: Prevalence and correlates. *Journal of Adolescent Research, 12*, 454–476.

Rosario, M., Meyer-Bahlburg, H. F. L., Hunter, J., Exner, T. M., Gwadz, M., & Keller, A. M. (1996). The psychosexual development of urban lesbian, gay, and bisexual youth. *Journal of Sex Research, 33*, 113–126.

Rosario, M., Rotheram-Borus, M. J., & Reid, H. M. (1996). Gay-related stress and its correlates among gay and bisexual male adolescents of predominantly Black and Hispanic background. *Journal of Community Psychology, 24*, 136–159.

Rosenthal, D. (1987). Ethnic identity development in adolescents. In J. S. Phinney & M. J. Rotheram (Eds.), *Children's ethnic socialization: Pluralism and development* (pp. 156–179). Newbury Park, CA: Sage.

Rotheram-Borus, M. J. (1989). Ethnic differences in adolescents' identity status and associated behavior patterns. *Journal of Adolescence, 12*, 361–374.

Rotheram-Borus, M. J., & Fernandez, M. I. (1995). Sexual orientation and developmental challenges experienced by gay and lesbian youth. *Journal of Suicide and Life-Threatening Behavior, 25*, 1–10.

Rotheram-Borus, M. J., Gwadz, M., Fernandez, M. I., & Srinivasan, S. (1998). Timing of HIV interventions on reductions in sexual risk among adolescents. *American Journal of Community Psychology, 26*, 73–96.

Rotheram-Borus, M. J., Hunter, J., & Rosario, M. (1994). Suicidal behavior and gay-related stress among gay and bisexual male adolescents. *Journal of Adolescent Research, 9*, 498–508.

Rotheram-Borus, M. J., Lee, M., Zhou, S., O'Hara, P., Birnbaum, J. M., Swenderman, J. M., Wright, W., Pennbridge, J., Wight, R. G., & the Teens Linked to Care Consortium (in press). Variation in health and risk behavior among youth living with HIV. *AIDS Education and Prevention.*

Rotheram-Borus, M. J., Luna, G. C., Marotta, T., & Kelly, H. (1994). Going nowhere fast: Methamphetamine use and HIV infection. In R. Battjes, Z. Sloboda, & W. C. Grace (Eds.), *The context of HIV risk among drug users and their sexual partners* (pp. 155–182). Washington, DC: National Institute of Drug Abuse Monograph Series, No. 143.

Rotheram-Borus, M. J., Meyer-Bahlburg, H., Rosario, M., Koopman, C., Haignere, C., Exner, T., Matthieu, M., Henderson, R., & Gruen, R. (1992). Lifetime sexual behaviors among predominantly minority male runaways and gay/bisexual adolescents in New York City. *AIDS Education and Prevention, 4 (Suppl.)*, 34–42.

Rotheram-Borus, M. J., Murphy, D. A., Lee, M., and the Teens Linked To Care Consortium (in press). Seropositive youth make positive life changes. *American Journal of Public Health.*

Rotheram-Borus, M. J., Marelich, W. D., & Srinivasan, S. (1999). Risk for HIV among homosexual, bisexual, and heterosexual male and female youth. *Archives of Sexual Behavior, 28*, 159–177.

Rotheram-Borus, M. J., Rosario, M., & Koopman, C. (1991). Minority youth at high risk: Gay males and runaways. In S. Gore & M. E. Colten (Eds.), *Adolescent stress: Causes and consequences* (pp. 181–200). New York: Aldine de Gruyter.

Rotheram-Borus, M. J., Rosario, M., Meyer-Bahlburg, H., Koopman, C., Dopkins, S., & Davies, M. (1994). Sexual and substance use acts among gay and bisexual male adolescents in New York City. *Journal of Sex Research, 31*, 47–57.

Rotheram-Borus, M. J., Rosario, M., Reid, H., & Koopman, C. (1995). Predicting patterns of sexual acts among homosexual and bisexual youths. *American Journal of Psychiatry, 152*, 588–595.

Rotheram-Borus, M. J., Rosario, M., Van Rossem, R., Reid, H., & Gillis, J. R. (1995). Prevalence, course, and predictors of multiple problem behaviors among gay and bisexual male adolescents. *Developmental Psychology, 31*, 75–85.

Rotheram-Borus, M. J., & Wyche, K. (1994). Ethnic differences in identity development in the United States. In S. Archer (Ed.), *Interventions for adolescent identity development* (pp. 62–83). Newbury Park, CA: Sage.

Rutter, M., Graham, P., Chadwick, O. F., & Yule, W. (1976). Adolescent turmoil: Fact or fiction? *Journal of Child Psychology & Psychiatry & Allied Disciplines, 17*, 35–56.

Salholz, E., Beck, M., Kantrowitz, B., & Senna, D. (1993, June 21). The power and the pride. *Newsweek, 121*, 54–61.

Sanford, N. D. (1989). Providing sensitive health care to gay and lesbian youth. *Nurse Practitioner, 14*, 30–47.

Savin-Williams, R. C. (1990). *Gay and lesbian youth: Expressions of identity*. Washington, DC: Hemisphere.

Savin-Williams, R. C. (1994). Verbal and physical abuse as stressors in the lives of lesbian, gay male, and bisexual youth: Associations with school problems, running away, substance abuse, prostitution, and suicide. *Journal of Consulting and Clinical Psychology, 62*, 261–269.

Savin-Williams, R. C. (1998). The disclosure to families of same-sex attractions by lesbian, gay, and bisexual youths. *Journal of Research on Adolescence, 8*, 49–68.

Schneider, S. G., Farberow, N. L., & Kruks, G. N. (1989). Suicidal behavior in adolescent and young adult gay men. *Suicide and Life-Threatening Behavior, 19*, 381–394.

Shaffer, D., Fisher, P., Parides, M., & Gould, M. (1995). Sexual orientation in adolescents who commit suicide. *Suicide and Life-Threatening Behavior, 25* (Suppl), 64–71.

Shaw, M. (1995). Gay pride in high school. *Progressive, 59*, 13.

Silvestre, A. J., Kingsley, L. A., Wehman, P., Dappen, R., Ho, M., & Rinaldo, C. R. (1993). Changes in HIV rates and sexual behavior among homosexual men, 1984 to 1988/92. *American Journal of Public Health, 83*, 578–580.

Sophie, J. (1985–86). A critical examination of stage theories of lesbian identity development. *Journal of Homosexuality, 12*, 39–51.

Sorenson, R. (1973). *Adolescent sexuality in contemporary America*. New York: World.

Stiffman, A. R, & Davis, L. E. (Eds.) (1990). *Ethnic issues in adolescent mental health*. Newbury Park, CA: Sage.

Stonequist, E. V. (1965). *Race relations and the Great Society*. Saratoga Springs, NY: Skidmore College.

Stricof, R. L., Kennedy, J. T., Nattell, T. C., Weisfuse, I. B., & Novick, L. F. (1991). HIV seroprevalence in a facility for runaway and homeless adolescents. *American Journal of Public Health, 81*, 50–53.

Sullivan, T., & Schneider, M. (1987). Development and identity issues in adolescent homosexuality. *Child and Adolescent Social Work, 4*, 13–24.

Sweeney, P., Lindegren, M. L., Buehler, J. W., Onorato, I. M., & Janssen, R. S. (1995). Teenagers at risk of Human Immunodeficiency Virus Type I infection. *Archives of Pediatric Adolescent Medicine, 149*, 521–528.

Telljohann, S. K., & Price, J. H. (1993). A qualitative examination of adolescent homosexuals' life experiences: Ramifications for secondary school personnel. *Journal of Homosexuality, 26*, 41–56.

Troiden, R. R. (1988). Homosexual identity development. *Journal of Adolescent Health Care, 9*, 105–113.

Uribe, V., & Harbeck K. M. (1992). Addressing the needs of lesbian, gay, and bisexual youth: The origins of PROJECT 10 and school-based intervention. *Journal of Homosexuality, 22*, 9–28.

Wendell, D. A., Onorato, I. M., McCray, E., Allen, D. M., & Sweeney, P. A. (1992). Youth at risk: Sex, drugs, and Human Immunodeficiency Virus. *American Journal of Diseases of Children, 146*, 76–81.

Weiner, I. B., & Del Gaudio, A. C. (1976). Psychopathology in adolescence: An epidemiological study. *Archives of General Psychiatry, 33*, 187–193.

Winerip, M. (1994, February 23). A high school club for gay students has gained a foothold, though not everyone may feel secure. *New York Times*, pp. B12(N), B7(L).

Yang, A. S. (1997). The polls—Trends: Attitudes toward homosexuality. *Public Opinion Quarterly 61*, 477–508.

Yarber, M. L. (1993, January 14). Groups help gay students cope. *Los Angeles Times, 112*, pp. J5.

6

Intimacy Development, Gender, and Ethnicity among Sexual-Minority Youths

Eric M. Dubé,
Ritch C. Savin-Williams, and
Lisa M. Diamond

Developmental theories and supporting research emphasize that intimacy becomes most salient during adolescence (Erikson, 1963; Furman & Buhrmester, 1992; Praeger, 1995; Sullivan, 1953). To date, the literature on adolescent intimacy and interpersonal relationships is rich with data on interpersonal behaviors (Patterson, 1976), attachment relationships (Hazan & Shaver, 1987; Reis & Patrick, 1996), friendship networks (Buhrmester & Furman, 1987), and intimacy motivations (McAdams & Vaillant, 1982). While researchers have not reached a consensus on what intimacy is, for purposes of this paper intimacy is best understood as perceived closeness and mutual understanding on the part of relational partners. Consequently, intimacy can be achieved in romantic, sexual, and friendship relationships.

Theories and investigations on adolescent intimacy have evolved from a heterosexual default, either including presumably heterosexual youth or generalizing heterosexual processes to sexual-minority populations (Buhrmester & Furman, 1986; Fraley & Davis, 1997; Furman & Buhrmester, 1992; Monsour, 1992). As a result, the experiences of lesbian, gay, and bisexual youth are largely unknown or misunderstood. Only recently have psychologists theorized as to whether the relationship dynamics of sexual-minority youth differ in their characteristics, motivations, and functions (Savin-Williams & Diamond, 1999). For example, because opportunities for same-sex friendships and romantic relationships are not available to all sexual-minority youth, their pathways to intimacy development may be more variable than those among heterosexual youth. Indeed, research on sexual-minority populations has discovered that alternative types of relationships (i.e., same-sex sexual relationships, passionate friendships, roommates) may take on heightened importance within lesbian, gay, and bisexual populations (Berger, 1992; Blyth & Traeger, 1988; Diamond, 1998; Dubé, 1997; Nardi & Sherrod, 1994; Savin-Williams, 1998a; Telljohann & Price, 1993).

We take this historical inattention as our starting point. The basic premise that a youth's sexuality is an important context for understanding a life course trajectory is particularly significant for those classes of sexualities that are deemed nonnormative. We first present a theoretical perspective that forms the basis of our position on development among sexual-minority adolescents. We then describe not only how sexual orientation is a differential factor of adolescent intimacy development, but also how gender and ethnicity are implicated in the development of intimacy and relationships among sexual-minority youths. Our use of the term "sexual minority" is preferred over lesbian, gay, and bisexual primarily because the former term is more encompassing and appropriate when discussing youth populations, many of whom have not yet identified or labeled their sexual attractions.

Differential Developmental Trajectories

The possibility that sexual-minority youth have distinctive life courses becomes a reasonable expectation given that the expression of sexuality is the result of a complex mix of biological, psychological, social, and cultural factors. In some domains of sexuality a sexual-minority youth may share commonalities with other adolescents, with other sexual-minority youths, with subgroups of sexual-minority youths, and with no other adolescent. Thus, the premise that not all individuals have identical pathways in the development of their sexuality leads us to propose two corollaries:

1. Insofar as sexual-minority youths experience prototypical developmental milestones and needs during their second decade of life, they are similar to other adolescents. Thus, because of their species-specific biology and socialization experiences, sexual-minority youths proceed through developmental trajectories similar to their same-age peers, regardless of professed sexuality.
2. Insofar as they differ because of biological characteristics or social experiences that have predisposed their sexuality as "not heterosexual," and they have experienced the social and cultural consequences of that sexuality, sexual-minority youths display trajectories that differ from their heterosexual peers but are similar to those of other sexual minorities.

Developmental psychologists today would probably accept one but not both of these tenets. The first is assumed when the topic of sexual orientation is ignored in research designs and procedures. Typically, sexual orientation is seldom assessed, even when the study's focus is sexuality. The second is most evident, however subtly, in textbooks that may have positive comments regarding "homosexual behavior" and, increasingly, "homosexual adolescents," but relegate all discussion of such topics to separate chapter sections and restrict all pictures of them to those pages.

Many developmentalists would agree that sexual-minority youths necessarily experience growing up gay, lesbian, or bisexual as life altering because of the ways in which families, peers, teachers, religious leaders, and social institutions treat youths who are not heterosexual. Our goal is to move one step beyond the traditional gay versus heterosexual distinction to offer a third position, one we label *differential developmental trajectories* (for a more complete review see Savin-Williams, 1998a). "Differential" names the variability within and across individuals and "development" refers not only to specific events during particular moments of time but also to the full range of processes that occur throughout the life course. "Trajectories" highlights forward and multiple movements, and that future development will be influenced by past and current maturational episodes and their aftermath.

The disparate developmental trajectories that are experienced by lesbian, gay, and bisexual youths have been documented by our earlier research in regard to women's sexual identity (Diamond, 1998), men's sexual identity and sexual behavior (Dubé, 1997), and men's development from first memories of same-sex attractions to an integrated sexual identity (Savin-Williams, 1998a). Our research position is consonant with a contemporary emphasis on life-span developmental psychology, articulated by Compas, Hinden, and Gerhardt (1995): "The search for universal descriptions for all adolescents has been replaced by recognition of the wide variability that characterizes psychological development during the second decade of life" (p. 271).

Other developmental psychologists have proposed similar concepts (Crockett, 1995; Steinberg, 1995). Rutter (1989, 1992) referred to a "series of contingencies" that are compounded over time to ultimately form a trajectory unique to each individual or to subgroups of individuals. The perspectives of Steinberg and Crockett highlight the problem we find with most discussions of developmental trajectories—the failure to conceptualize *differential* developmental trajectories. Their conception of a developmental trajectory appears to apply only to individuals rather than to subgroups of individuals. A differential developmental trajectories perspective incorporates these views by proposing that the task of developmental research is to investigate general characteristics of sexual-minority individuals *and* intrapopulation similarities and differences throughout the life course.

In our research cited earlier we found support for the existence of *multiple* and *diverse* developmental trajectories. Thus, it is plausible to conceptualize that some trajectories apply to only some subgroups of individuals. We thus move one additional step beyond previous researchers who studied sexual identity development (Cass, 1984; D'Augelli, 1991; Savin-Williams, 1990; Troiden, 1979), proposing a third corollary:

3. Insofar as the causes of sexuality vary among sexual-minority individuals and the micro and macro culture in which they were reared and currently experience are diverse, the developmental trajectories must be in some regard unique within sexual-minority populations and common across subgroups of sexual minorities.

For example, lesbian adolescents, regardless of ethnicity, may share a trajectory that varies from gay male adolescents, but within lesbian adolescent populations, ethnicity may be a critical consideration that further differentiates lesbian youths. Other subgroups of sexual minorities may be defined by social or person variables, such as the degree to which a youth conforms with gender-typical sex roles, is shy or aggressive, or is reared in a gay-positive or gay-negative family.

Herein we discuss two of the most salient and widely researched differentiating factors among sexual-minority populations: gender and ethnicity. Our goal is to explore not only how gender and ethnicity influence intimacy and relationship development, but, more important, the mechanisms through which these differentiating factors exert their forces on sexual-minority adolescent development.

Gender

In discussing the influence of gender on intimacy development among sexual-minority youth, we must consider main effects of sexual orientation that operate across male and female adolescents, main effects of gender that operate across heterosexual and sexual-minority adolescents, and interaction effects producing unique pathways and outcomes among lesbian/bisexual youths, gay/bisexual youths, heterosexual males, and heterosexual females. In some cases, sexual orientation might accentuate existing gender differences. For example, a tendency for females to be highly disclosing in their intimate relationships might be heightened in a romantic relationship containing two women. In other cases, sexual orientation might counteract existing gender differences. For example, while heterosexual males are less likely than females to touch same-sex friends affectionately, gay/bisexual males may be more likely to do so because of their same-sex attractions or their experiences with same-sex sexual/romantic relationships. In this manner, gay male youths might be more similar to heterosexual adolescent females than males.

In order to explain such sexual orientation and gender effects, researchers must attend to the *mechanisms* through which they operate. This approach permits a systematic explanation of sexual-minority development that will prove more useful than a simple catalog of characteristics unique to sexual-minority males, sexual-minority females, heterosexual males, or heterosexual females. The first step in such a program is to pinpoint the features of gender and sexual orientation that are directly relevant to relational intimacy, and to consider how they might operate in concert to influence intimacy development among sexual-minority youth.

Gender Effects

Sullivan's seminal work (1953) continues to inform contemporary thinking on the importance of friends and romantic partners for adolescents (Buhrmester & Furman, 1986; Furman & Wehner, 1994). A critical feature of his model concerns the changing importance of cross-sex and same-sex friends during adolescence. Sullivan argued that the foundations for relational intimacy are laid in same-sex friendships, by which adolescents learn to develop and sustain a reciprocal, mutually validating peer relationship. As they mature and sexual interests become more salient, cross-sex friendships play a larger role, setting the stage for heterosexual romantic relationships.

Empirical research has largely confirmed this basic progression. While early and middle adolescents rely on same-sex friends for most of their intimacy and social support needs, cross-sex friendships become increasingly intimate and important from middle to late adolescence (Blyth, Hill & Theil, 1982; Buhrmester & Furman, 1986, 1987; Sharabany, Gershoni & Hofman, 1981). When serious romantic relationships appear in late adolescence, they typically become primary sources for intimacy and social support (Connolly & Johnson, 1996; Furman & Buhrmester, 1992; Hazan & Zeiffman, 1994). However, well-documented sex differences between the behavioral and interpersonal features of same-sex and cross-sex friendships must be taken into account when interpreting the developmental significance of youths' participation in these friendships.

Same-sex friendships among female youths involve higher levels of self-disclosure (Buhrmester & Prager, 1995; Caldwell & Peplau, 1982), greater mutual involvement and depth (Barth & Kinder, 1988), and more contact under times of stress than male youths' same-sex friendships (Buhrke & Fuqua, 1987). The interpersonal and behavioral intimacy of cross-sex friendships appears to occupy a middle position between that of female and male same-sex dyads (Buhrmester & Furman, 1986, 1987; Peplau, 1983; Reis, Senchak, & Solomon, 1985; Rose, 1985), suggesting that a critical factor differentiating the level of intimacy within an adolescent friendship is whether the dyad contains one, two, or no females. Beginning in early adolescence and extending throughout adulthood, females seek and achieve more intimacy in their friendships than males (Buhrmester & Furman, 1986, 1987; Sharabany et al., 1981), particularly through self-disclosure (for a review, see Buhrmester, 1996). Females rate higher than males on measures of caregiving within intimate relationships (Kunce & Shaver, 1994) and are more likely to express verbal and physical affection for their friends (Helgeson, Shaver, & Dyer, 1987; Monsour, 1992; Parks & Floyd, 1996). Studies have found females more effective, sensitive, and empathic in recognizing and responding to friends' distress (Belle, 1987; Burleson, 1982; Lang-Takac & Osterweil, 1992), and both sexes are more likely to seek out female friends when in need of support (Buhrke & Fuqua, 1987).

These findings have important developmental implications. Buhrmester (1996) emphasized that in addition to providing social support, intimate friendships foster social competence, helping adolescents to master the interpersonal skills necessary to sustain intimate ties with friends and romantic partners. Furthermore, he suggested that the pronounced sex differences in friendships might constitute a "learning effect." In other words, the greater interpersonal intimacy of female *adolescent* friendships may lead them to acquire a "taste" for highly intimate interactions over time, and these interactions further hone their interpersonal skills. Thus, if adolescent males had more opportunities to participate in affectionate, mutually disclosing friendships with other males, they might also develop a "taste" for such interactions and their pursuit of such relationships would foster greater social competence within intimate relationships. This argument suggests that adolescent males whose closest friends are females may develop more interpersonal skills regarding friendship intimacy than males with predominantly same-sex friends, and may be more likely to seek a higher level of behavioral or verbal intimacy in their friendships. Thus, studies of the effects of gender and sexual orientation on the development of relational intimacy might profit by examining how these factors influence participation in relationships with females and males, rather than focusing on participation in same-sex versus cross-sex friendships and romantic relationships.

Gender/Sexual Orientation Effects

With this in mind, how might we conceptualize the influence of interactions between gender and sexual orientation on adolescent intimacy development? As indicated above, the diversity of sexual-minority populations mitigates against gross generalizations. For example, some individuals recall experiencing same-sex attractions or engaging in gender-atypical behavior at an early age, while others traversed a childhood and early adolescence indistinguishable from their heterosexual peers (Savin-Williams, 1998a). How much do such differences matter? Can we expect their trajectories of intimacy development to converge or diverge as a function of gender and sexual orientation during late adolescence?

Perhaps the best theory-building strategy is to focus on those concomitants of sexual orientation common enough in middle to late adolescence to significantly shape this critical period of intimacy development. Two strong candidates are the presence of same-sex attractions and the perceived social meaning of these attractions. Regardless of whether a gay, lesbian, or bisexual adolescent *pursues* romantic or sexual relationships with either sex, the very presence of same-sex attractions can significantly alter the experience of same-sex and cross-sex friendships in ways that directly and indirectly affect intimacy development. Furthermore, the social stigma attached to same-sex sexuality may notably constrain an adolescent's opportunities and/or choices regarding the pursuit and management of reciprocal intimacy within platonic, sexual, and romantic relationships. These factors may redirect the traditional Sullivanian trajectory of intimacy development along gender specific lines.

Same-Sex Friendship and Sexual Attraction

For sexual-minority youth, same-sex friendships cannot be considered the safe haven from sexual interest that they represent for heterosexual youth because same-sex attractions may arise in these bonds. In his survey of friendships among adult sexual minorities, Nardi (1992) found that over three-fourths of his sample with a lesbian, gay, or bisexual best friend of the same sex had been attracted to their friend at one point and over half reported having been in love with this person. Approximately half of the men and a third of the women continued to harbor sexual or romantic feelings for their current best friend. Best friends play a significant role early in development as well. Savin-Williams (1998a) found that among gay and bisexual young adult men who engaged in same-sex sexual contact during childhood or early adolescence, the first such experience was nearly always with a best friend, neighborhood buddy, or cousin.

The complications inherent in managing sexual and romantic feelings for close platonic friends are difficult enough for adults and have long provided rich material for novels, television shows, and movies. Imagine their consequences, then, for adolescents simultaneously managing and often concealing a stigmatized sexual orientation. A young man or woman under these circumstances may perceive three basic options. First, he or she can attempt to initiate a sexual or romantic relationship out of the friendship, a route apparently more common among females than males. Many lesbian and bisexual women experience their first same-sex sexual contact or romantic relationship within a close friendship (Gramick, 1984; Schafer, 1977; Vetere, 1983). However, attempts at initiating a romantic relationship might bring shock and rejection from the desired friend, potentially gutting the adolescent's single most important source of intimacy and social support. In the face of this risk, an adolescent may pursue a second option—to suppress his or her romantic feelings and continue to enjoy the platonic intimacy of the bond. Alternatively, he or she might distance him or herself from the relationship in order to dampen the distracting sexual or romantic feelings and to avoid inadvertently revealing them.

These options may be differentially likely for female and male adolescents owing to the social meanings attached to same-sex intimacy. Young women are granted far more latitude than young men in expressing intense emotional and even physical affection for same-sex friends (Rands & Levinger, 1979; Stoneman, Brody, & MacKinnon, 1986), and thus an adolescent female may continue to pursue a rich, reciprocally intimate relationship with her best female friend without incurring suspicion of her sexual orientation. Among adolescent males, however, expressions of emotional intimacy are less normative and therefore more explicitly associated with same-sex sexuality (Kite, 1984; Nardi, 1992). In light of this gender difference, young gay and bisexual male adolescents may be more likely than lesbian and bisexual females to withdraw from close same-sex friends (Savin-Williams, 1996). Furthermore, some have suggested that sexual attractions constitute a more disruptive force in the platonic friendships of males than females (O'Meara, 1989), another factor that might propel gay/bisexual males into cross-sex friendships with greater frequency and at earlier ages than heterosexual male adolescents.

Implications for Intimacy Development and Outcomes

Same-sex attractions within same-sex friendships and the overall intimacy development of sexual-minority youth are highly sensitive to gender. Among boys, the key moderating variable may be participation in cross-sex friendships. These friendships frequently play a critical role for gay and bisexual male youth at an early age. As early as third and fourth grade, children who are unpopular with same-sex peers gravitate toward other-sex peers (Ladd, 1983). Gay and bisexual males who are stigmatized by other boys for gender atypicality may therefore seek female friends at a relatively early age. As Savin-Williams (1996) describes, "Girls became their saviors, offering sources of emotional sustenance as the male world of childhood became increasingly distasteful" (p. 101).

Relative preferences for other-sex and same-sex peers are fairly stable over childhood and early adolescence (Bukowski, Gauze, Hoza, & Newcomb, 1993), and therefore boys are likely to continue relying on female friends as they grow older. Indeed, Savin-Williams (1998a) found that the majority of gay and bisexual male adolescents first disclosed their sexual orientation to a same-age female peer. Because of the slightly advanced capacities for sensitivity and empathy among adolescent girls, gay/bisexual boys who invest considerable time and energy in cross-sex friendships may develop comparable skills at earlier ages than their male heterosexual counterparts. This may increase the overall level of intimacy that these males achieve in their adult same-sex friendships. Nardi suggested (1992) that among adult gay men, "Instrumental and expressive support, as well as self-disclosing feelings and emotions, comes from their friendships with other men, unlike what traditional male norms about friendship suggest" (p. 111). Thus, the capacity of gay and bisexual men to sustain intimate, non-sexual bonds with other men may actually be improved by their disproportionate involvement in cross-sex friendships during adolescence, providing an example of how gender and sexual orientation interact antagonistically to lessen the conventional gender gap regarding friendship intimacy.

Among lesbian and bisexual youths, gender and sexual orientation appear to have a synergistic effect on friendship intimacy, magnifying the intimacy of a young woman's same-sex friendships rather than propelling her into increased involvement with cross-sex friends. Many lesbian and bisexual women report having enjoyed unusually intense relationships with female friends during early adolescence (Butler, 1990; Diamond, 1997; National Lesbian and Gay Survey, 1992; Rothblum, 1993), some of which were accompanied by unambiguous, although concealed sexual attraction. Importantly, the best friends of lesbian and bisexual women may ably match this level of emotional investment and intensity in the *absence* of reciprocal sexual feelings. Both the historical and psychological literature document a long history of unusually intense friendship bonds between adult or adolescent women (Crumpacker & Vander Haegen, 1993; Faderman, 1981; Gouldner & Symons Strong, 1987; Hite, 1987; Rubin, 1985; Sahli, 1979; Smith-Rosenberg, 1975). In some cases, these bonds take on many of the characteristics of romantic relationships, including physical affection and cuddling, jealousy of other friends, mutual preoccupation, and separation distress (Diamond, 1997).

For the young lesbian or bisexual adolescent, such bonds may serve many of the functions traditionally associated with romantic relationships. If the risks of disclosing her sexual orientation by seeking a full-fledged romantic relationship with another lesbian or bisexual adolescent are too onerous, she may be content to enjoy the special intimacy she has carved out with her best friend. However, she may experience a unique sense of loss if and when her friend withdraws from the bond in order to pursue increasing amounts of time with cross-sex friends and male romantic partners.

With regard to long-term intimacy outcomes, it is notable that considerable fluidity between friendship and romantic love has been documented among adult lesbian and bisexual women (Weinstock & Rothblum, 1996). For example, many lesbians employ a "friendship script" in the process of courting future lovers (Peplau & Amaro, 1982; Rose, Zand & Cimi, 1993) in which a close emotional friendship provides the foundation for later sexual intimacy. This may prove responsible for the fact that lesbian and bisexual women are significantly more likely than gay and bisexual men to remain close friends, and often best friends, with former lovers (Becker, 1988; Hite, 1987; Nardi & Sherrod, 1994; Weinstock, 1997). While this may provide for especially strong romantic relationships among lesbians, it may also result in considerable ambiguity. Several women interviewed by Rose and her colleagues (1993) confessed that they had trouble distinguishing between friendships and romantic relationships. Overall, however, intimacy trajectories that magnify the role of same-sex friendships at the expense of cross-sex friendships and romantic relationships do not appear to hamper the development of relational intimacy skills among lesbian/bisexual adolescents or their abilities to meet needs for intimacy and social support during adolescence.

Implications for Romantic Relationships

Although contemporary sexual-minority youth have many more opportunities to meet and socialize with same-sex attracted peers during adolescence than previous cohorts, the unfortunate reality is that most youths find it exceedingly difficult to meet potential romantic partners. Even when they can be identified, the adolescent must weigh the benefits of the relationship against the possibility of disclosing his or her sexual orientation in a potentially hostile environment. As a result, many adolescents forgo participation in same-sex romantic relationships until early or mid-adulthood. Does this necessitate delays in the development of skills related to romantic pair bonds?

In actuality, sexual-minority adolescents typically continue to participate in cross-sex dating and romantic relationships, regardless of whether they experience attractions for the other sex (Savin-Williams, 1996). In some cases, these relationships may be pursued simply to hide a youth's sexual orientation and may therefore lack the intimacy of an authentic romantic bond. In other cases, however, youths may become romantically involved with close other-sex friends, developing intimacy skills within these bonds that will later apply to same-sex romantic relationships. Recall also that the same-sex friendships of some lesbian/bisexual adolescents may possess features of romantic relationships. These relationships may foster the development of mature relational intimacy skills in lesbian/bisexual adolescents regardless of whether they manage to forge a full-fledged romantic relationship from their friendship bond. Owing to the greater level of intimacy achieved in young women's same-sex friendships than in either cross-sex or male same-sex friendships, it is possible that participation in a romantic relationship plays a less significant role in the intimacy development of a young lesbian or bisexual woman than it does for a young gay or bisexual man. Such an effect is consistent with findings on heterosexual adolescents, but may be magnified by the interaction between gender and sexual orientation. In the final analysis, sexual-minority youths may be at serious risk for impaired intimacy outcomes in adulthood if they shy away from close same-sex bonds or do not supplement their social network with close cross-sex friendships. These youths are more likely to be gay or bisexual males than lesbian or bisexual females.

Many have noted the substantive and gender-differentiated role of friendship in the lives of adult sexual minorities (Nardi, 1992, Nardi & Sherrod, 1994; Weinstock, 1997; Weinstock & Rothblum, 1996). One of the respondents in Nardi's (1992) research reported, "When people ask if my best friend and I are lovers, I say 'No—we're much closer than that'" (p. 110). In a heterosexual context, such a statement would appear more typical of a woman than a man, owing to the lower levels of intimacy usually achieved in men's same-sex friendships and the high levels of intimacy typical of women's same-sex friendships. The adolescent pathways we described above provide a possible explanation for such unique outcomes. It is through changing the balance of emphasis and investment in platonic, sexual, and romantic relationships with females and males that sexual-minority adolescents create trajectories of intimacy development that violate conventional understanding of how young men and women learn to develop and sustain close, nurturing bonds with lovers and friends.

Ethnicity

Ethnicity as a context for development has recently received significant attention (Cross, 1991; Greene, 1997; Morales, 1990; Rotheram-Borus & Wyche, 1994; Tremble, Schneider & Appathurai, 1989). This research indicates that an adolescent's ethnic identity influences how he or she views the world and how the world reacts to the adolescent. However, research on sexual-minority populations all too often ignores these potentially strong ethnic influences, assuming that by predominantly sampling white men and women, findings can be generalized to ethnic minorities, also known as "double minorities." This bias may be waning because efforts to sample from sexual-minority populations of varying ethnicities have proved increasingly successful, in large part because lesbian, bisexual, and gay African Americans, Asian Americans, Latinos/as, and Native American Indians have created their own communities and because lesbian, gay, and bisexual white communities are becoming more accessible to ethnic sexual minorities. Despite this increase in sample diversity, few researchers have considered whether and how these subgroups differ among themselves and from their White counterparts.

While it is most parsimonious to hypothesize that sexual-minority youth are more similar to one another than different, regardless of culture or ethnicity, this perspective obscures crucial cultural differences among sexual minorities (Dubé, 1997). Given the diversity of lesbian, gay, and bisexual populations, understanding the role of ethnic identity in the formation of differential trajectories in intimacy development is imperative, especially in adolescence. In this section, we explore whether and how ethnicity influences intimacy development by examining specific components of ethnicity. This approach, consistent with a differential developmental trajectories perspective, affords an investigation of ethnicity without considering ethnic groups to be monolithic and allows for differences—familial, lingual, geographic, socioeconomic, religious, and cultural—between and among specific ethnic groups.

Components of Ethnicity

Ethnicity per se becomes a salient factor in understanding development when its operating mechanisms are conceptualized. Factors such as family structure and origin, religion, culture, language, and immigration status have been proposed as powerful socialization forces in the development of relationships and intimacy among ethnic sexual minorities (Dubé, 1998). These components also serve to further differentiate individuals within ethnic groups.

Rather than assume that all ethnic minorities who identify as lesbian, gay, or bisexual experience parallel developmental trajectories, we must keep in mind the specific factors that constitute ethnicity. For example, a Latina lesbian who emigrated to the United States and whose native language is Spanish may approach same-sex relationships differently from a third-generation Latina lesbian assimilated in the American 1990s culture. An African-American youth who identifies as gay and was raised by white parents may differ substantially from another African American who also identifies as gay but was raised by his family of origin. Are the experiences of these adolescents similar enough to warrant grouping them together for research purposes? While their ethnic and sexual identities are the same, their family structures, religions, and cultures may be sufficiently heterogeneous to exert differential forces on their development.

How, then, do these factors influence intimacy development among African-American, Asian-American, Native American Indian, and Latino/ a sexual-minority youth? Inchoate research on ethnic sexual minorities has either not been studied empirically or has been based on small, limited samples. Thus, it is essential to delineate the ways in which differentiating factors (e.g., religion, language) affect relationship and intimacy development among double minorities. Historically, research on ethnicity has typically taken one of two perspectives in elucidating how ethnic minorities differ in their development from their white counterparts. One view examines family and culture norms, including traditionality, religion, language, and acculturation; the other focuses on social obstacles, such as institutional and personal racism, discrimination, and absence of positive role models. We consider how family and cultural values and social obstacles become differentiating factors in the lives of ethnic minorities.

Family and Cultural Norms

Familial and cultural norms are perhaps the most salient components of ethnicity, evidenced by the fact that most research on ethnicity focuses on how family attitudes and practices and cultural values are the primary socializing agents in the lives of ethnic minorities (e.g., Morales, 1990; Tremble et al., 1989). The mechanisms through which family and culture exert their influence include language, acculturation, and religion.

Language spoken in the home, often taken as a measure of acculturation, has received little attention as to its influence on development of sexual-minority adolescents. Lingual differences, however, have the potential to modify how some individuals and their environments respond to one another. In a study of HIV risk among Asian-American gay and bisexual men,

Matteson (1997) found that acculturation and knowledge of English facilitated labeling and disclosure of a nonheterosexual identity. Furthermore, becoming fluent in English (i.e., higher levels of acculturation) led to lower risk of HIV infection and perhaps better skills developing intimate relationships, presumably because these men were able to negotiate and communicate their needs with sexual and relationship partners. Savin-Williams (1998a) suggested that knowledge of English facilitated an understanding and acceptance of a nonheterosexual identity among Asian-American adolescent and young adult males. These findings suggest that fluency in English (or the primary language of the lesbian and gay community) prepares ethnic sexual minorities for social interactions among other sexual minorities and, thus, for the development of intimate relationships. When lesbian, gay, and bisexual adolescents understand and label their sexual identity, they are more likely to initiate social interactions and relationships with other sexual minorities (Dubé, 1997). For instance, Espin (1987) studied dual-identity development among adult Latina lesbians and discovered that many women associated primarily with other lesbians, regardless of ethnicity. Reasons for doing so were twofold: they were concerned with developing emotionally intimate relationships, which were perceived to be more viable within sexual-minority populations than among Latino heterosexual men and women; and they considered being closeted and involved solely with heterosexual Latinos to be a more onerous task than risking disclosure and living as self-identified lesbians. Thus, identification as lesbian or bisexual may be met with a need to socializing with other sexual minorities.

The influence of acculturation may not, however, apply equally to all ethnic groups. Research on Native American Indian sexual minorities indicates that acculturation into mainstream American culture handicaps sexual identity development (Adams & Phillips, 1996; Williams, 1996). Native American Indian cultures have long accepted gender nonconforming individuals as well as fluidity in both gender and sexuality (Tafoya, 1997). In contrast to their Native religious beliefs, the adoption of mainstream Western religious values among some Native American Indian cultures may *decrease* tolerance for sexual minorities. For most ethnic groups, however, acculturation into mainstream American culture leads to increased identification and acceptance of a nonheterosexual identity that, as previously noted, is related to the development of intimate relationships with other sexual minorities.

In terms of family and personal religiosity, theoretical and anecdotal writings outline the importance of religion in the development and acceptance of sexual identity and same-sex intimacy. However, while religious commitments have been hypothesized by researchers to play an integral role among sexual-minority families, Wagner and colleagues found no relationship between religious beliefs and sexual identity development (Wagner, Serafini, Rabkin, Remien, & Williams, 1994). In their study of multicultural development among sexual-minority youths, Tremble and associates (1989) maintained that religion does not differentially influence ethnic sexual-minority life courses. Newman and Muzzonigro (1993), attempting to dis-entangle ethnicity and family traditionalism, found that high traditionality, not ethnicity, had a more powerful effect on youths' adjustment to a nonheterosexual identity. Smith (1997) warned that because cultural diversity exists within ethnic communities, religion may differentially influence how identities and relationships are established. Overall, the available empirical evidence does not support the view that the degree of family religiosity *differentially* influences the development of ethnic sexual minorities. Our understanding of these processes, however, relies on a limited number of studies.

Perhaps the most studied component of ethnicity has been cultural norms. Cultural norms include, but are not limited to, how a culture values gender roles, family ties, and sexuality in general. Latin cultures and their views on male sexuality have been most frequently understood by the concept of *machismo*, or the belief that men must act in traditionally masculine ways. Men who *prefer* sex with men, or are the receptive partners in anal sex, are not viewed as macho and are thus devalued (Carrier, 1995). Manalansan (1996) noted the tendency of many Latino men, regardless of sexual identity or sexual orientation, to engage in sexual behaviors with male and female partners. Sexual identity in Latin cultures is more contingent on gender roles than on sexual orientation or behaviors. That is, men who prefer the insertive role in sex with other men are considered masculine and heterosexual, whereas men who prefer the receptive role are deemed feminine and "homosexual." As a result, sex with other men may not include kissing or cuddling, nor does it generally evolve into a romantic relationship. Thus, fulfilling needs for emotional intimacy with men may be difficult for many Latino gay men, far more so than merely having sex with other men.

Of course, gender also influences women in Latin cultures. The cultural value placed on *machismo* equally suggests that women must not behave like men. Thus, Latina women who are attracted to and develop relationships with women may be seen as a threat. Further, Latina lesbians are not likely to propagate gender inequities that exist among Latin cultures, thus potentially causing further friction. Latina lesbians may, however, find more opportunity for same-sex intimacy given that their cultures afford considerable latitude to women in developing and expressing emotional and physical intimacy (Espin, 1987; Hidalgo, 1984).

The significance of these factors—language, religion, sex roles—elucidates the primary avenues through which cultural norms are transmitted within the family. For example, the centrality of the family among many Asian Americans may engender a sense of failure or shame when a family member identifies as lesbian, gay, or bisexual. Disclosing their sexual identity to family and friends in the Asian-American community may seem impossible and have detrimental effects on the acceptance of their same-sex attractions and participation in same-sex relationships (Chan, 1989). As a result, many Asian-American sexual minorities opt not to disclose to family and friends in the Asian-American community, or they choose to come out later in adulthood when the risk of family rejection is attenuated. For example, Savin-Williams (1998b) and Dubé (1997) reported that Asian-American young adult males disclosed their sexual identity to the first person and their family members at a later age than other youths, seldom socialized with other gays, and developed same-sex relationships at a late age. For many Asian Americans, a distinction emerged between their public persona and their actual feelings and activities, resulting in tension between their personally felt sexuality and how they were perceived by others (Chan, 1995; Matteson, 1997). Thus, Asian-American youths may be more likely to eschew identifying themselves as gay or lesbian, either because they fear it will overshadow their ethnic identity or because the practice of labeling sexuality is largely unknown. This pattern may be changing in large metropolitan areas such as New York, San Francisco, and Los Angeles, where sizable Asian-American lesbian, gay, and bisexual communities are forming support, social, and political groups.

Theoretical and clinical writings have also proposed that the families of ethnic-minority gays and lesbians are more homophobic than their white counterparts. Writers have based this argument on the notion that ethnic-minority families tend to be more religious and traditional in their views and practices. Newman and Muzzonigro (1993) found that perceived homophobia of family members among gay male youths was a function more of traditional values than of ethnicity. Gay and bisexual males from more traditional families not only expected higher levels of rejection from their families after disclosure of same-sex attractions but also were more likely to experience disapproval from their families. Among a group of Latino male youths, many believed that it was the Catholic Church and not their ethnicity per se that imposed traditional values, rigid gender roles, and internalized homophobia on them (Savin-Williams, 1998a). Similar findings were expressed by African-American youth regarding Black Protestant churches. Although these two samples consist of a relatively small number of self-selected male youths, they nevertheless point to some crucial issues related to the influences on intimacy development among sexual minorities.

One widely researched area of sexual identity is a youth's perceptions of how family members will react to the disclosure of same-sex attractions. Findings concur that perceived rejection is likely to deter disclosure of same-sex attractions (Savin-Williams, 1998b). Because ethnic sexual minorities are more likely than white lesbian, gay, and bisexual youths to fear rejection from their families (Hetrick & Martin, 1987; Icard, 1986), it is reasonable to hypothesize that they would be less likely to disclose to members of their family or ethnic community. Dubé (1997) found that compared to white gay and bisexual male youths, ethnic-minority males were less likely to disclose to significant others in their lives.

Research has also discerned that not disclosing, especially to parents and significant others, can lead to poor relationship quality (Berger, 1990). Dubé (1997) found that among gay and bisexual male youths, the extent of disclosure to others was indirectly related to the types of relationships they developed with male partners: men who disclosed to few individuals reported a high ratio of sexual to romantic relationships. If the same pattern governs the relationship functioning of ethnic sexual minorities, then a lack of disclosure could lead to low levels of sexual identity development and relationship quality. Thus, an indirect mechanism likely exists between ethnicity and intimacy development. Additional research is needed, however, to conclude whether the links between disclosure and relationship development are generalizable across gender and ethnicity.

From the limited research examining double minority development and the dynamics between sexual identity and intimacy, it is most parsimonious to conclude that the mechanisms through which ethnicity influences intimacy among sexual minorities are indirect ones. That is, being an ethnic minority may not directly affect the types of relationships pursued or levels of intimacy achieved; rather, norms among ethnic-minority families, such as homophobia and rigid gender roles, are most closely related to intimacy development to the extent that these family norms impede disclosure of sexual identity and thus the likelihood of developing intimate relationships with other sexual-minority youths.

Social Obstacles

Perhaps the second most common way of conceptualizing how ethnicity shapes adolescent development is through the obstacles faced by ethnic minorities. Not only may ethnic sexual minorities encounter homophobia from their families of origin, but they also may encounter racism from mainstream sexual-minority organizations, communities, and individuals. Consequently, these youths may not find a niche of lesbian and gay friends or even the support from organizations needed for making the adjustment to being comfortable with having same-sex attractions.

A large, national survey found that most gay and bisexual men reported primary attractions to white men, while only 13% rated any attraction to Latino men and 4% found either Asian-American or African-American men attractive (Kraft, 1996). Peplau, Cochran, and Mays (1997) found similar rates of differential attractions in the dating behaviors among African-American gay and bisexual males, but not among females. Savin-Williams (1998a) and Matteson (1997) reported that the majority of Asian-American males sampled preferred white males for sexual and romantic partners, primarily because they were either more attracted to the white beauty ideal or they associated dating white men with power and prestige. If, in fact, Asian-American males are preferentially attracted to white men and white men have the same pattern of attractions, then Asian-American gay youths may have difficulty fulfilling their needs for romantic relationships—of finding a suitable white male partner. Comparable data do not exist for lesbian and bisexual women. Thus, ethnic-minority youths who seek intimate relationships with other sexual minorities may experience fewer opportunities to do so.

Dubé (1997) noted that ethnic-minority male youths are equally likely as white male youths to meet their needs for same-sex intimacy despite racism and/or preferential attractions from gay and lesbian communities. Differences arise in the types of relationships these youths develop to meet intimacy needs. White male youths reported a higher ratio of sexual to romantic relationships compared to ethnic-minority male youths, suggesting that either white males more often seek intimacy through sexual relationships or they have more opportunity to develop them.

Findings about ethnic sexual minorities' experiences have been derived from a small number of studies. Projects that sample from general sexual-minority adolescent populations report difficulties in recruiting ethnic minorities, in part because such individuals are less likely to be "out" to others (including researchers). Studies that succeed at sampling ethnic sexual-minority youths often have major research limitations, either recruiting from segregated, ethnic-minority support groups (Hunter, 1990), or working from risk models of development that examine family rejection, HIV risk, and suicide attempts within mostly male, support group settings (Boyer, 1989; Coleman & Remafedi, 1989; Feldman, 1989; Hershberger & D'Augelli, 1995; Matteson, 1997).

Conclusions

Many of the findings on intimacy and relationships reported in this chapter are based on research that is not longitudinal in nature; on theories that describe maturation and change in a linear, stage-like progression; and on nonrepresentative samples. The net effect is that rigorous scientific evidence about the nature of development among subgroups of sexual minorities is not available. To build models that accommodate diversity in developmental trajectories, one of two theoretical positions can be taken. The first is to construct multiple models that explain the progression of intimacy and lifetime relationship involvement of subgroups of individuals. For example, one model could predict change over time among specific subpopulations of sexual minorities, such as Asian-American bisexual males, while another model attempts to delineate experiences of Latina lesbians. This position, however, is problematic because it necessitates the development of numerous, and perhaps an unwieldy number of, models. Proposing multiple models does not lead to the identification of developmental universals—a goal considered by some to be equally important as discovering developmental differences.

The second approach, a differential developmental trajectories position, necessitates an understanding of how sexual minorities are similar to other adolescents regardless of sexual orientation, to other sexual minorities, and to subgroups of sexual minorities. A differential developmental trajectories perspective advocates that future research concurrently investigate common development trajectories among sexual minorities and differential factors that influence how intimacy is achieved. From these data models can be established to describe not only diversity among sexual minorities in their lifetime relationship involvement but also how subgroups of individuals share some aspects of these experiences, such as meeting intimacy needs primarily through same-sex or mixed-sex friendships.

Researchers studying factors that differentially influence development should keep in mind that group differences are inadequate if the mechanisms through which these differences become manifested are not elucidated. While categorical coding of gender and ethnicity (e.g., female versus male and white versus African American) has historically been considered a suitable way to explore group differences, researchers must ask themselves what exactly being a female or a member of an ethnic group means. For example, what is it about being female that enhances the desire of a gay male youth to establish intimate cross-sex friendships, or how does being a Latina lesbian influence intimacy and relationship development? Future research should thus aim to disentangle the impact of factors such as sexual orientation, gender, and ethnicity.

Furthermore, research agendas should involve examination of how multiple factors simultaneously influence lifetime growth and change. As developmentalists, we argue that *multiple* factors exert their influences *concurrently* on an individual. Considering all these factors simultaneously complicates the research agendas of future investigators. Because of this, there is no dearth of research possibilities for investigating developmental trajectories of sexual-minority adolescents.

References

Adams, H., & Phillips, L. (1996, March). *Ethnic identity and sexual orientation in Native American Indians: An examination of self, community, and development.* Paper presented at the Society for Research on Adolescence, Boston, MA.

Barth, R. J., & Kinder, B. N. (1988). A theoretical analysis of sex differences in same-sex friendships. *Sex Roles, 19,* 349–363.

Becker, C. (1988). *Lesbian ex-lovers.* Boston: Alyson.

Belle, D. (1987). Gender differences in the moderators of stress. In R. C. Barnett, L. Beiner, & G. K. Baruch (Eds.), *Gender and stress* (pp. 257–277). New York: Free Press.

Berger, R. M. (1990). Passing: Impact on the quality of same-sex couple relationships. *Social Work, 35,* 328–332.

Berger, R. M. (1992). Passing and social support among gay men. *Journal of Homosexuality*, 23, 85–97.

Blyth, D. A., Hill, J. P., & Theil, K. S. (1982). Early adolescents' significant others: Grade and gender differences in perceived relationships with familiar and non-familiar adults and young people. *Journal of Youth and Adolescence*, 11, 425–449.

Blyth, D. A., & Traeger, C. (1988). Adolescent self-esteem and perceived relationships with parents and peers. In S. Salzinger, J. Antrobers, & M. Hammer (Eds.), *Social networks of children, adolescents, and college students* (pp. 171–194). Hillsdale, NJ: Erlbaum.

Boyer, D. (1989). Male prostitution and homosexual identity. In G. Herdt (Ed.), *Gay and lesbian youth* (pp. 151–184). New York: Harrington Park Press.

Buhrke, R. A., & Fuqua, D. R. (1987). Sex differences in same- and cross-sex supportive relationships. *Sex Roles*, 17, 339–352.

Buhrmester, D. (1996). Need fulfillment, interpersonal competence, and the developmental contexts of early adolescent friendship. In W. M. Bukowski, A. F. Newcomb, & W. W. Hartup (Eds.), *The company they keep: Friendship in childhood and adolescence* (pp. 158–185). New York: Cambridge University Press.

Buhrmester, D., & Furman, W. (1986). The changing functions of friends in childhood. In V. J. Derlega & B. A. Winstead (Eds.), *Friendship and social interaction* (pp. 41–62). New York: Springer-Verlag.

Buhrmester, D., & Furman, W. (1987). The development of companionship and intimacy. *Child Development*, 58, 1101–1113.

Buhrmester, D., & Prager, K. (1995). Patterns and functions of self-disclosure during childhood and adolescence. In K. J. Rotenberg (Ed.), *Disclosure processes in children and adolescents* (pp. 10–56). New York: Cambridge University Press.

Bukowski, W. M., Gauze, C., Hoza, B., & Newcomb, A. F. (1993). Differences and consistency between same-sex and other-sex peer relationships during early adolescence. *Developmental Psychology*, 67, 56–68.

Burleson, B. R. (1982). The development of comforting communication skills in childhood and adolescence. *Child Development*, 53, 1578–1588.

Butler, B. (Ed.). (1990). *Ceremonies of the heart: Celebrating lesbian unions*. Seattle: Seal Press.

Caldwell, M. A., & Peplau, L. A. (1982). Sex differences in same-sex friendship. *Sex Roles*, 8, 721–732.

Carrier, J. (1995). *De los otros: Intimacy and homosexuality among Mexican men*. New York: Columbia University Press.

Cass, V. (1984). Homosexual identity: A concept in need of a definition. *Journal of Homosexuality*, 9, 105–126.

Chan, C. S. (1989). Issues of identity development among Asian American lesbians and gay men. *Journal of Counseling and Development*, 68, 16–20.

Chan, C. S. (1995). Issues of sexual identity in an ethnic minority: The case of Chinese American lesbians, gay men, and bisexual people. In A. R. D'Augelli & C. J. Patterson (Eds.), *Lesbian, gay, and bisexual identities over the lifespan: Psychological perspectives* (pp. 87–101). New York: Oxford University Press.

Coleman, E., & Remafedi, G. (1989). Gay, lesbian, and bisexual adolescents: A critical challenge to counselors. *Journal of Counseling and Development*, 68, 36–40.

Compas, B. E., Hinden, B. R., Gerhardt, C. A. (1995). Adolescent development:

Pathways and processes of risk and resilience. *Annual Review of Psychology*, 46, 265–293.

Connolly, J. A., & Johnson, A. M. (1996). Adolescents' romantic relationships and the structure and quality of their close interpersonal ties. *Personal Relationships*, 3, 185–195.

Crockett, L. J. (1995). Developmental paths in adolescence: Commentary. In L. J. Crockett & A. C. Crouter (Eds.), *Pathways through adolescence: Individual development in relation to social contexts* (pp. 75–84). Mahwah, NJ: Erlbaum.

Cross, W. E. (1991). *Shades of black: Diversity in African-American identity*. Philadelphia: Temple University Press.

Crumpacker, L., & Vander Haegen, E. M. (1993). Pedagogy and prejudice: Strategies for confronting homophobia in the classroom. *Women's Studies Quarterly*, 21, 94–106.

D'Augelli, A. R. (1991). Gay men in college: Identity processes and adaptations. *Journal of College Student Development*, 32, 140–146.

Diamond, L. M. (1997, March). *Passionate friendships: Love and attachment among young lesbian, bisexual, and questioning women*. Paper presented at the Association for Women in Psychology, Pittsburgh, PA.

Diamond, L. M. (1998). Development of sexual orientation among adolescent and young adult women. *Developmental Psychology*, 34, 1085–1095.

Dubé, E. M. (1997). *Sexual identity and intimacy development among two cohorts of gay and bisexual men*. Unpublished master's thesis, Cornell University, Ithaca, NY.

Dubé, E. M. (1998, March). Sexual identity development among ethnic/sexual minority males. Paper presented at the society for Research on Adolescence, San Diego, CA.

Erikson, E. (1963). *Childhood and society*. (2nd ed.). New York: W. W. Norton.

Espin, O. M. (1987). Issues of identity in the psychology of Latina lesbians. In Boston Lesbian Psychologies Collective (Eds.), *Lesbian psychologies: Explorations and challenges* (pp. 35–51). Urbana: University of Illinois Press.

Faderman, L. (1981). *Surpassing the love of men*. New York: William Morrow.

Feldman, D. A. (1989). Gay youth and AIDS. In G. Herdt (Ed.), *Gay and lesbian youth* (pp. 185–194). New York: Harrington Park Press.

Fraley, R. C., & Davis, K. E. (1997). Attachment formation and transfer in young adults' close friendships and romantic relationships. *Personal Relationships*, 4, 131–144.

Furman, W., & Buhrmester, D. (1992). Age and sex differences in perceptions of networks of personal relationships. *Child Development*, 63, 103–115.

Furman, W. W., & Wehner, E. A. (1994). Romantic views: Toward a theory of adolescent romantic relationships. In R. Montemayor, G. R. Adams, & T. P. Gullotta (Eds.), *Personal relationships during adolescence* (pp. 168–195). Thousand Oaks, CA: Sage.

Gouldner, M., & Symons Strong, M. (1987). *Speaking of friendship: Middle-class women and their friends*. New York: Greenwood Press.

Gramick, J. (1984). Developing a lesbian identity. In T. Darty & S. Potter (Eds.), *Women-identified-women* (pp. 31–44). Palo Alto, CA: Mayfield.

Greene, B. (Ed.). (1997). *Ethnic and cultural diversity among lesbians and gay men*. Thousand Oaks, CA: Sage.

Hazan, C., & Shaver, P. (1987). Romantic love conceptualized as an attachment process. *Journal of Personality and Social Psychology*, 52, 511–524.

Hazan, C., & Zeiffman, D. (1994). Sex and the psychological tether. In D. Perlman & K. Bartholomew (Eds.), *Advances in personal relationships: A research annual* (Volume 5, pp. 151–177). London: Jessica Kingsley.

Helgeson, V. S., Shaver, P. R., & Dyer, M. (1987). Prototypes of intimacy and distance in same-sex and opposite-sex relationships. *Journal of Social and Personal Relationships, 4,* 195–233.

Hershberger, S. L., & D'Augelli, A. R. (1995). The impact of victimization on the mental health and suicidality of lesbian, gay, and bisexual youths. *Developmental Psychology, 31,* 65–74.

Hetrick, E. S., & Martin, A. D. (1987). Developmental issues and their resolution for gay and lesbian adolescents. *Journal of Homosexuality, 14,* 25–43.

Hidalgo, H. (1984). The Puerto Rican lesbian in the United States. In T. Darty & S. Potter (Eds.), *Women-identified-women.* Palo Alto, CA: Mayfield.

Hite, S. (1987). *Women and love.* London: Penguin.

Hunter, J. (1990). Violence against lesbian and gay male youths. *Journal of Interpersonal Violence, 5,* 295–300.

Icard, L. (1986). Black gay men and conflicting social identities: Sexual orientation versus racial identity. *Journal of Social Work and Human Sexuality, 4,* 83–93.

Kite, M. (1984). Sex differences in attitudes toward homosexuals: A meta-analytic review. *Journal of Homosexuality, 10,* 69–81.

Kraft, R. M. (1996, October). Carnal knowledge. *Genre,* 43–46.

Kunce, L. J., & Shaver, P. R. (1994). An attachment-theoretical approach to caregiving in romantic relationships. In D. Perlman & K. Bartholomew (Eds.), *Advances in personal relationships: A research annual* (Volume 5, pp. 205–237). London: Jessica Kingsley.

Ladd, G. W. (1983). Social networks of popular, average, and rejected children in school settings. *Merrill Palmer Quarterly, 29,* 283–307.

Lang-Takac, E., & Osterweil, Z. (1992). Separateness and connectedness: Differences between the genders. *Sex Roles, 27,* 277–289.

Manalansan, M. F. (1996). Double minorities: Latino, Black, and Asian men who have sex with men. In R. C. Savin-Williams & K. M. Cohen (Eds.), *The lives of lesbians, gays, and bisexuals: Children to adults* (pp. 393–415). Fort Worth, TX: Harcourt Brace.

Matteson, D. R. (1997). Bisexual and homosexual behavior and HIV risk among Chinese-, Filipino-, and Korean-American men. *Journal of Sex Research, 34,* 93–104.

McAdams, D. P., & Vaillant, G. E. (1982). Intimacy motivation and psychological adjustment: A longitudinal study. *Journal of Personality Assessment, 46,* 586–593.

Minton, H. L., & McDonald, G. J. (1983). Homosexual identity formation as a developmental process. *Journal of Homosexuality, 9,* 91–104.

Monsour, M. (1992). Meanings of intimacy in cross- and same-sex friendships. *Journal of Social and Personal Relationships, 9,* 277–295.

Morales, E. S. (1990). Ethnic minority families and minority gays and lesbians. *Marriage and Family Review, 14,* 217–239.

Nardi, P. M. (1992). That's what friends are for: Friends as family in the gay and lesbian community. In K. Plummer (Ed.), *Modern homosexualities* (pp. 108–120). London: Routledge.

Nardi, P. M., & Sherrod, D. (1994). Friendships in the lives of gay men and lesbians. *Journal of Social and Personal Relationships, 11,* 185–199.

National Lesbian and Gay Survey. (1992). *What a lesbian looks like*. London: Routledge.

Newman, B. S., & Muzzonigro, P. G. (1993). The effects of traditional family values on the coming out process of gay male adolescents. *Adolescence, 28*, 213–226.

O'Meara, D. (1989). Cross-sex friendship: Four basic challenges of an ignored relationship. *Sex Roles, 21*, 525–543.

Parks, M. R., & Floyd, K. (1996). Meaning for closeness and intimacy in friendship. *Journal of Social and Personal Relationships, 13*, 85–107.

Patterson, M. L. (1976). An arousal model of interpersonal intimacy. *Psychological Review, 89*, 235–245.

Peplau, L. A. (1983). Roles and gender. In H. Kelley, E. Berscheid, A. Christensen, J. H. Harvey, T. L. Huston, G. Levinger, E. McClintock, L. A. Peplau, & D. R. Peterson (Eds.), *Close relationships* (pp. 220–264). New York: W. H. Freeman.

Peplau, L. A., & Amaro, H. (1982). Understanding lesbian relationships. In W. Paul, J. D. Weinrich, J. C. Gonsiorek, & M. E. Hotvedt (Eds.), *Homosexuality: Social, psychological, and biological issues* (pp. 233–248). Beverly Hills, CA: Sage.

Peplau, L. A., Cochran, S. D., & Mays, V. M. (1997). A national survey of the intimate relationships of African American lesbians and gay men: A look at commitment, satisfaction, sexual behavior, and HIV disease. In B. Greene (Ed.), *Ethnic and cultural diversity among lesbians and gay men* (pp. 11–38). Thousand Oaks, CA: Sage.

Praeger, K. J. (1995). *The psychology of intimacy*. New York: Guilford Press.

Rands, M., & Levinger, G. (1979). Implicit theories of relationship: An intergenerational study. *Journal of Personal and Social Psychology, 37*, 645–661.

Reis, H. T., & Patrick, B. C. (1996). Attachment and intimacy: Component processes. In E. T. Higgins & A. W. Kruglanski (Eds.), *Social psychology: Handbook of basic principles* (pp. 523–563). New York: Guilford Press.

Reis, H. T., Senchak, M., & Solomon, B. (1985). Sex differences in intimacy of social interaction: Further examination of potential explanations. *Journal of Personality and Social Psychology, 48*, 1204–1217.

Rose, S., Zand, D., & Cimi, M. A. (1993). Lesbian courtship scripts. In E. D. Rothblum & K. A. Brehony (Eds.), *Boston marriages* (pp. 70–85). Amherst, MA: University of Massachusetts Press.

Rose, S. M. (1985). Same- and cross-sex friendships and the psychology of homosociality. *Sex Roles, 12*, 63–74.

Rothblum, E. D. (1993). Early memories, current realities. In E. D. Rothblum & K. A. Brehony (Eds.), *Boston marriages* (pp. 14–18). Amherst, MA: University of Massachusetts Press.

Rotheram-Borus, M. J., & Wyche, K. F. (1994). Ethnic differences in identity development in the United States. In S. L. Archer (Ed.), *Interventions for adolescent identity development* (pp. 62–83). Thousand Oaks, CA: Sage.

Rubin, Z. (1985). *Just friends: The role of friendship in our lives*. New York: Harper & Row.

Rutter, M. (1989). Pathways from childhood to adult life. *Journal of Child Psychology, 30*, 23–51.

Rutter, M. (1992). Adolescence as a transition period: Continuities and discontinuities in conduct disorder. *Journal of Adolescent Health, 13*, 451–460.

Sahli, N. (1979). Smashing: Women's relationships before the fall. *Chrysalis, 8*, 17–27.

Savin-Williams, R. C. (1990). *Gay and lesbian youth: Expressions of identity*. Washington, DC: Hemisphere.

Savin-Williams, R. C. (1996). Dating and romantic relationships among gay, lesbian, and bisexual youths. In R. C. Savin-Williams & K. M. Cohen (Eds.), *The lives of lesbians, gays, and bisexauls: Children to adults* (pp. 166–180). Fort Worth, TX: Harcourt Brace.

Savin-Williams, R. C. (1998a). *". . . and then I became gay:" Young men's stories*. New York: Routledge.

Savin-Williams, R. C. (1998b). The disclosure of same-sex attractions by lesbian, gay, and bisexual youths to their families. *Journal of Research on Adolescence, 8*, 49–68.

Savin-Williams, R. C., & Diamond, L. M. (1999). Sexual orientation as a developmental context for lesbian, gay, and bisexual children and adolescents. In W. K. Silverman & T. H. Ollendick (Eds.), *Developmental issues in the clinical treatment of children and adolescents* (pp. 241–258). Boston: Allyn & Bacon.

Schafer, S. (1977). Sociosexual behavior in male and female homosexuals. *Archives of Sexual Behavior, 6*, 355–364.

Sharabany, R., Gershoni, R., & Hofman, J. (1981). Girlfriend, boyfriend: Age and sex differences in intimate friendships. *Developmental Psychology, 17,* 800–808.

Smith, A. (1997). Cultural diversity and the coming out process: Implications for clinical practice. In B. Greene (Ed.), *Ethnic and cultural diversity among lesbians and gay men* (pp. 279–300). Thousand Oaks, CA: Sage.

Smith-Rosenberg, C. (1975). The female world of love and ritual: Relations between women in nineteenth century America. *Signs, 1*, 1–29.

Steinberg, L. (1995). Commentary: On developmental pathways and social contexts in adolescence. In L. J. Crockett & A. C. Crouter (Eds.), *Pathways through adolescence: Individual development in relation to social contexts* (pp. 245–253). Mahwah, NJ: Erlbaum.

Stoneman, Z., Brody, G. H., & MacKinnon, C. E. (1986). Same-sex and cross-sex siblings: Activity choices, roles, behaviors, and gender stereotypes. *Sex Roles, 9/10*, 495–511.

Sullivan, H. S. (1953). *The interpersonal theory of psychiatry*. New York: Norton.

Tafoya, T. (1997). Native gay and lesbian issues: The two-spirited. In B. Greene (Ed.), *Ethnic and cultural diversity among lesbians and gay men* (pp. 1–10). Thousand Oaks, CA: Sage.

Telljohann, S. K., & Price, J. P. (1993). A qualitative examination of adolescent homosexuals' life experiences: Ramifications for secondary school personnel. *Journal of Homosexuality, 26*, 41–56.

Tremble, B., Schneider, M., & Appathurai, C. (1989). Growing up gay or lesbian in a multicultural context. *Journal of Homosexuality, 17*, 253–267.

Troiden, R. (1979). Becoming homosexual: A model of gay identity acquisition. *Psychiatry, 42*, 362–373.

Vetere, V. A. (1983). The role of friendship in the development and maintenance of lesbian love relationships. *Journal of Homosexuality, 8*, 51–65.

Wagner, G., Serafini, J., Rabkin, J., Remien, R., & Williams, J. (1994). Integration of one's religion and homosexuality: A weapon against internalized homophobia? *Journal of Homosexuality, 26*, 91–110.

Walters, K., & Simoni, J. (1993). Lesbian and gay male group identity attitudes and self-esteem: Implications for counseling. *Journal of Counseling Psychology, 40,* 94–99.

Weinstock, J. S. (1997, March). *Lesbian friendships: Simply an alternative or is this a revolution?* Paper presented at the Association for Women in Psychology, Pittsburgh, PA.

Weinstock, J. S., & Rothblum, E. D. (1996). What we can be together: Contemplating lesbians' friendships. In J. S. Weinstock & E. D. Rothblum (Eds.), *Lesbian friendships: For ourselves and for each other* (pp. 3–30). New York: New York University Press.

Williams, W. L. (1996). Two-spirited persons: Gender non-conformity among Native American and Native Hawaiian youths. In R. C. Savin-Williams & K. M. Cohen (Eds.), *The lives of lesbians, gays, and bisexuals: Children to adults* (pp. 416–435). Fort Worth, TX: Harcourt Brace.

Wright, P. H., & Scanlon, M. B. (1991). Gender role orientations and friendship: Some attenuation, but gender differences abound. *Sex Roles, 24,* 551–566.

III

ISSUES FOR INTERVENTION AND SOCIAL CHANGE

7

Avoiding HIV/AIDS and the Challenge of Growing Up Gay, Lesbian, and Bisexual

Arnold H. Grossman

The realities of HIV/AIDS can be approached from a variety of perspectives. For many gay, lesbian, and bisexual youths and adults, these realities are linked to moral differentiations that society has based on modes of HIV transmission. Those termed "medical victims" (i.e., blood transfusion recipients, men with hemophilia, and infants infected perinatally) are seen as deserving compassion, while those who acquire the disease through sexual transmission are stigmatized and are associated with homosexuality and other "condemned lifestyles" (Manning, 1997; Novick, 1997). For many gay, lesbian, and bisexual youths, these perspectives frequently connect HIV/AIDS to several disquieting concerns: being a member of the social group blamed for starting the "gay plague," seeing portraits of gay men and lesbians with physically frightening manifestations, observing death and dying, witnessing increased anti-gay violence, viewing prevention messages that do not affirm "immoral" (i.e., homosexual) behaviors, engaging in same-sex behaviors that are labeled "taboo," and experiencing homophobic behaviors that underlie social attitudes toward sexuality, including sexual pleasure outside of marriage (Public Media Center, 1995). Gay, lesbian, and bisexual youths have to face these HIV/AIDS-related stigmatized portrayals while developing their personal, social, and sexual identities. Gay, lesbian, and bisexual youths must also meet the special challenge of avoiding HIV infection.

Heterosexuality Needs No Explanation

The biological sex of people with whom one is sexually intimate determines whether one is labeled as heterosexual, homosexual, or bisexual. However,

155

sexual orientation encompasses more than the gender of the people with whom one engages in sexual activities; it includes sexual attractions, fantasies, feelings, and self-identification, as well as sexual behaviors. Adolescents who grow to realize that they have sexual attractions to and fantasies about people of the opposite gender and who engage in sexual behaviors with them are not required to give any explanations about those behaviors. In fact, heterosexually identified adolescents are provided with opportunities to pursue social activities, learn dating skills, and explore relationships. Many cultures strongly encourage males to engage in sexual activities, training them to be dominant and independent in relationships with women. On the other hand, the mores of most communities present a double message to their young female members: enjoy the pleasures of sexuality (as portrayed in the mass media and advertising) and abstain from sexual activities until marriage (as proselytized by the family and religious institutions). Heterosexually identified adolescents have the support of their families, schools, and churches in their attempts to learn about their gender identities, gender roles, and sexual behaviors. They are provided with after-school athletic activities, youth clubs, parks, and recreational centers. In these spaces, youths learn the expectations and norms of heterosocial society (Grossman, 1998). As part of these lessons, most adolescents are provided with heterosexually based HIV/AIDS prevention education programs. Concurrently, homosexual attractions are either ignored or portrayed as shameful and abnormal. In relation to the latter, myths and stereotypes about gay, lesbian, and bisexual people are taught. In a society that embraces heterosexuality as normative behavior (D'Augelli, 1998), these messages lead to a heterosexual orientation being accepted as the "default" category. If individuals do not label themselves otherwise, they are assumed to be heterosexual in their orientation and behaviors. Consequently, those youths who are gay, lesbian, or bisexual and who decide not to disclose their sexual orientations are assumed to be heterosexual and are provided with HIV/AIDS education programs designed for heterosexual youths. These programs are not developmentally appropriate for gay, lesbian, and bisexual youth, do not address their unique concerns, and are not effective in helping them to avoid HIV infection. For example, these curricula frequently lack opportunities for gay, lesbian, and bisexual youths to acquire social skills appropriate to their adolescent development or to create peer support systems that enhance their identity formation (Cranston, 1991). These youths are also not given chances to learn the implications of general adolescent risk-taking characteristics such as living in the present or seeing themselves as invulnerable (Grossman, 1995); and this includes their not feeling susceptible to HIV infection as a result of their unsafe sexual behaviors. For instance, although a substantial number of urban African-American and Hispanic youths (of various sexual orientations) in one study worried about contracting AIDS, the majority believed it would not happen to them (Ford & Norris, 1993).

Giving Up the Privileges of Heterosexuality

Gay, lesbian, and bisexual youths tend to become aware of their same-sex feelings at about the age of 10 years, and they label these feelings at about 14. On average, they first disclose their sexual orientation to another person at 16 years of age, which begins the "coming out" process (D'Augelli, Hershberger, & Pilkington, 1998). In disclosing their sexual orientation, these youth frequently give up many heterosexual privileges. They lose opportunities to date, to develop intimate relationships, to learn socialization skills, to share feelings with peers, to experiment sexually in physically safe environments, and to achieve a sense of independence and competence. They are deprived of support networks and a sense of community, often leading to feelings of isolation and loneliness, and to barriers that prevent the construction of personal and social identities. Those resilient gay, lesbian, and bisexual youths grow into adulthood relatively unscathed, while others become emotionally scarred (DeCrescenzo, 1994). The disclosure of their sexual orientation often transforms them from adolescents with difficult information to manage into individuals with difficult circumstances to get through (Grossman, 1998). They have to learn how to meet others with similar sexual orientations, to gauge who will and who will not respond favorably to knowing about their same-sex orientation, and to escape from becoming a victim of those who stigmatize homosexuals (Rotheram-Borus, Hunter, & Rosario, 1995). Society's homophobia not only marginalizes these gay, lesbian, and bisexual youths and creates impediments to their developing authentic identities, but it increases the probability that they will be at risk for HIV infection. For example, Rosario and Rotheram-Borus (1992) found that gay adolescents' inability to predict others' reactions to the disclosure of their sexual orientation was correlated with risky sexual behaviors, substance use, and stress in other areas of their lives.

Before continuing with the discussion of risks for HIV infection among gay, lesbian, and bisexual youths, it is important to recognize that there is much variability among them. The diversity among gay, lesbians, and bisexual youths reflects differences with respect to their sexual behaviors and relationships based on their feelings from childhood, personal histories of attachments, and opportunities to meet potential partners. Many of the youths are sexually experienced by the time they are in high school, some by choice and some not. Some are sexually active only with members of their own sex, but many experiment with friends of both sexes over time. Some practice celibacy or monogamy, but many are involved with multiple partners or experience serial monogamy (i.e., many short-lived relationships with one partner at a time). If gay, lesbian, and bisexuals youths are sexually active, their need for approval and acceptance (especially if they are being victimized at home or at school) may be driving their risk-taking behaviors, including sexual and drug-using activities. Limited also by their levels of cognitive and social development, these youths may not be able to make a rational calculation about their HIV risk-taking behaviors. Though less often, other youths who engage in HIV-risky behaviors with same- and opposite-sex partners are facing hormonal challenges that are affecting their sexual behaviors or they are seeking to develop a personal identity as a transgender person.

Homophobia and HIV-Risk Behaviors

Having to cope with a disparaging and oppressive society creates unique stresses and developmental variations in identity development for gay, lesbian, and bisexual youths, especially in adolescence and young adulthood (Gonsiorek & Rudolph, 1991). As most gay, lesbian and bisexual youths do not want to be rejected by their families, friends, and teachers or experience verbal and physical abuse from their peers (D'Augelli et al., 1998), they hide their sexual orientation (Martin, 1982). Hiding often leads to feelings of marginality, deviance, and emotional and social isolation (Hetrick & Martin, 1987), and the youths' psychological energy becomes focused on avoiding situations in which their sexual orientation may be discovered. Additionally, it is important to note that the incidence of cancer and moderately serious infectious diseases has been found to increase in gay and bisexual men (over the age of 18) to the degree to which they conceal their homosexual identity (Cole, Kemeny, Taylor, & Visscher, 1996). According to Cole et al., these findings conceptually replicated the results of a previous study that documented accelerated HIV progression among gay men who concealed their homosexual identity. Similar studies need to be conducted among gay, lesbian, and bisexual youths to determine if the degree to which they conceal the expression of their homosexuality impacts their health, including the progression of HIV infection.

Those youths who do not totally conceal their homosexual or bisexual orientation either disclose their sexual identity or remain publicly hidden and find sexual activity as their primary source of social and emotional contact (Grossman, 1994). "Coming out of the closet" frequently leads to victimization (D'Augelli et al., 1998) and the use and abuse of alcohol and illicit drugs (Grossman & Kerner, 1998; Hunter, Rosario, & Rotheram-Borus, 1993; Rosario, Hunter & Gwadz, 1997). Gay, lesbian, and bisexual youths who self-identify during high school (grades 9–12) are more likely than their peers to report a variety of health risks and problem behaviors, including suicide, victimization, sexual risk behaviors, and multiple substance use (Garofalo, Wolf, Kessel, Palfrey, & DuRant, 1998).

Alcohol and drugs are frequently consumed as a way of coping with the stresses associated with prejudice and discrimination linked to homosexuality (Rosario & Rotheram-Borus, 1992). Becoming dependent on alcohol and drugs often leads to poor judgment and high-risk sexual behaviors for HIV infection (Remafedi, 1994b; Rotheram-Borus et al., 1995). For those who remain hidden, "the most troublesome conflict occurs at the intersection of HIV risk and the expression of homoeroticism through sexual behavior" (D'Augelli, 1998, p. 195). These conflicts may be more distressing for gay, lesbian, and bisexual youths who are also members of ethnic minority communities (Hunter & Haymes, 1997). Members of these communities frequently possess strong attachments to their ethnic cultures (Peterson, 1995), with some developing strong feelings of pride. They tend to define homosexuality in differing ways from the "white" majority because of their experiences with homophobia and racism (Kuszelewicz & Lloyd, 1995) and their devotions to three different communities: their family and ethnic/racial community, the lesbian and gay community, and society in general (Hunter & Schaecher, 1994). Additionally, HIV transmission through male-to-male sexual contact among adolescents has been found to vary by ethnicity, with transmission being much higher for African Americans than for Hispanics or Whites (Manloff, Gayle, Mays, & Rogers, 1989). As Diaz (1998) reminds us in his discussion of Latino gay men and HIV, it is important to acknowledge that many self-identified respondents in such studies do not publicly disclose their sexual orientation to family, co-workers, or even friends.

Gay and bisexual male youths who remain hidden often seek sexual contact with other males in places where prostitution occurs (e.g., selected streets and parks) and where they may be frequently exposed to HIV and other sexually transmitted infections. Often unable to feel worthy of romantic love, of being cherished, or of becoming a life companion, these gay and bisexual males view themselves as sexual commodities to be used by more "perfect" men (Novick, 1997). Lesbian and female bisexual youths who remain hidden may seek heterosexual relationships as protection against the discovery of their sexual orientation. Often occurring simultaneously with a lesbian relationship, females' heterosocial sexual activities place them at risk for HIV infection. This risk increases if the partner is a gay or bisexual male who engages in unprotected sex with other males (Hunter & Haymes, 1997; Rotheram-Borus et al., 1995). Findings of a study examining the sexual behaviors of 111 young (<21) gay and bisexual men in England and Wales indicated that 45% had had a female sexual partner, and 34% reported having had vaginal intercourse (Davies et al., 1992). Although the sexual orientation of the females was not reported, the investigators noted that youth is a time for sexual experimentation and that a proportion of young men (i.e., under 21 years) had sex with both a man and a woman in the month and year preceding the interview. The proportion was greater for the young men than it was for the older men in the larger cohort of the study.

Gay, lesbian, and bisexual youths have also been found to be at increased risk for suicidal ideation and attempts (Grossman & Kerner, 1998; Hershberger, Pilkington, & D'Augelli, 1997; Remafedi, Farrow, & Deisher, 1991; Remafedi, French, Story, Resnick, & Blum, 1998). In their study of 221 self-identified gay, lesbian, and bisexual youths (72% male and 28% female, with an average age of 18.5 years), Proctor and Groze (1994) found that 40% attempted suicide and 26% had a serious thought about it at least once. Hershberger et al. reported that 39% of their sample of 194 gay, lesbian, and bisexual youths engaged in suicidal thinking in the week prior to data collection, and that 42% reported at least one suicide attempt, with the number of past attempts ranging from 1 through 15. The investigators found that the strongest correlations with past suicide attempts were low self-esteem and the loss of friends owing to the disclosure of sexual orientation. In a sample of 36,254 public junior and senior high school enrollees in Minnesota, Remafedi and his colleagues (1998) found that suicide attempts were reported by 28% of the gay/bisexual males and 21% of the lesbian/bisexual females, 15% of the heterosexual females, and 4% of the heterosexual males. Sexual orientation was found to be associated with suicidal intent and attempts of only the gay/bisexual males. While drug overdose has been reported as the most common method of attempting suicide (used by 70% of the attempters in the Hershberger et al. [1997] study), no studies have investigated whether those gay, lesbian, and bisexual youths who consistently engage in high-risk sexual behaviors or other self-destructive behaviors are employing other methods of attempting suicide.

HIV/AIDS and Gay, Lesbian, and Bisexual Youths

Adolescent sexual orientation is conflated with teenage sexual behavior by most of American society. According to Ehrhardt (1996), social attitudes are polarized concerning the suppression of teenage sexual behavior and acceptance of the fact that youth will become sexually active during their teens. This frame of mind has led to ambivalent and insufficient approaches to sex education, focusing on biological reproduction versus healthy sexual relationships. As well as leaving adolescents uninformed and untaught about reaching responsible decisions regarding intimate relationships with same- or opposite-sex partners, the denial of teenage sexual activities has also led to a scarcity of studies that include adolescent sexual feelings or behaviors as normal aspects of human development. Those studies on adolescent sexuality that have been conducted tend to be "solely or predominantly conceptualized, assessed, and discussed within the context of risk behavior: risk for pregnancy, risk for STDs, and for HIV infection" (Ehrhardt, 1996, p. 11). This bias toward the negative consequences of teenage sexual behaviors has certainly been true of those studies examining HIV/AIDS among gay, lesbian, and bisexual youths.

Many adolescents in the United States are engaging in behaviors that increase their risks for HIV infection and AIDS (Centers for Disease Control and Prevention, 1995). While a small number of teenagers (ages 13–19 years) has been diagnosed with AIDS (i.e., 3,130 of 641,086 cumulative cases of AIDS through December 1997), 17% of all male and 22% of all female cases of AIDS reported through December 1997 were among young adults between the ages of 20 and 29 years. With the long time between HIV infection and diagnosis of AIDS, it appears liikely that many of these 111,368 people were infected during their adolescent years. Of the 30 states that reported HIV infection cases in 1997 (which does not include those who have developed AIDS), 4% of the cumulative total of 92,107 reported through December 1997 were between 13 and 19 years, while 14% were between 20 and 24, and 22% were between 25 and 29 (Centers for Disease Control and Prevention, 1997a). Among these are gay, lesbian, and bisexual youths.

Most of the studies concerning HIV/AIDS among sexual minority youths have focused on gay and bisexual male youths, their risks for HIV infection, and HIV seroprevalence rates among them. Kegeles, Hays, and Coates (1996) summarized the findings of some recent studies among gay and bisexual men. One study found that 18% of the young gay men (ages 18–29 years) in San Francisco were HIV positive, while a second study of gay and bisexual men (ages 17–22 years) in the San Francisco Bay Area reported a 9.4% seroprevalence rate. A surveillance study of 13 clinics for sexually transmitted diseases around the United States found the median rate of HIV infection among young homosexual/bisexual males (ages 20–24 years) to be 30%. Based on the findings of several studies, Kegeles and her colleagues calculated that 33% to 43% of young gay (and bisexual) men engaged in unprotected anal intercourse in the past two to six months. These findings are consistent with those revealed by Lemp et al. (1994) and the results reported by Dean and Meyer (1995). Lemp et al. found that one-third of youths in their study of 17- to 22-year-old homosexual and bisexual men in San Francisco had engaged in unprotected anal intercourse during the past six months. Unsafe sexual contact was associated with the lack of peer support for safe sex, as well as a history of forced sex. They also found that 4% of the 17- to 19-year-olds and 12% of the 20- to 22-year-olds were HIV positive. In their study, Dean and Meyer found that 37% of 18- to 24-year-old gay men had engaged in unprotected receptive anal intercourse over a two-year period. The findings of Lemp and his colleagues indicated that there were significant correlations between unprotected anal intercourse, the use of nitrites, a history of "forced sex" or sexual abuse, and perceived decreased peer support for safer-sex practices.

Summarizing findings of previous studies, Rotheram-Borus, Reid, and Rosario (1994) indicated that adolescent and young gay males (ages 14–22 years) have been found to have multiple sexual partners, use condoms infrequently, exchange sex for money or drugs, and engage in more sexual risk acts than older gay men. Additionally, they reported that many gay male adolescents have sexual relations with adult gay men and engage in noninjection drug use. In structured interviews with gay males aged 15 to 21 years, Gold and Skinner (1992) found that the two primary factors of self-justification related to "unsafe" sexual encounters were: (1) responding to a negative mood state, and (2) inferring that the partner was unlikely to be HIV-infected based on perceptible characteristics. Another situational factor facilitating the occurrence of unsafe sex, reported by the young gay men in the Gold and Skinner study, was the failure to communicate their desires concerning safe sex. In a study of 239 gay and bisexual male adolescents between the ages of 13 and 21 years, Remafedi (1994b) found that 63% were at "extreme risk" for HIV exposure based on histories of unprotected anal intercourse and/or intravenous drug use. Risky sexual behavior was not associated with sociodemographic characteristics, reported psychosocial problems, or HIV antibody testing. The young men often engaged in high-risk sex even when they were knowledgeable about HIV, were acquainted with HIV-infected persons, and were aware of their susceptibility. Persons in steady relationships were more likely than others to have unprotected intercourse; and inconsistent use of condoms was associated with non-communication with partners about risk reduction, substance use in sexual situations, and frequent anal intercourse. Although Remafedi found no relationship between knowing people with HIV disease and adherence to safer sex practices, Morris, Zavisca, and Dean (1995) found weak support between this variable and adherence to safer-sex practices in a sample of 563 young gay men. However, Morris et al. found that younger gay men with older partners were on the leading edge of the epidemic in their cohort—that is, they were more likely to be HIV-infected. Contrary to the Remafedi findings, in a study about sexual behavior and AIDS knowledge in a sample of young male prostitutes in Manhattan, of which 50% were homosexual and 26% were bisexual, Pleak and Meyer-Bahlburg (1990) reported that AIDS knowledge was high and positively correlated with the sexual-risk avoidance. Additionally, they found that the prostitutes were safest in sex with their male customers, less safe with the male partners they selected for pleasure, and least safe with their female partners. Although drug and alcohol abuse and dependence were frequent, they were not significantly associated with the degree of safety in sex.

In the study of 111 young (<21) gay and bisexual men in England and Wales cited above, Davies et al. (1992) found that condom use varied with relationship status. "Of those in a monogamous relationship, 50% *always* used a condom for receptive anal intercourse, 30% of those in a non-monogamous regular relationship, and 63% of those not in a regular relationship. The corresponding figures for the insertive mode are 33%, 43%, and 60%" (p. 267, italics in original). They also found that a higher proportion of the younger than the older men (from a larger cohort) were in non-monogamous regular relationships, which the investigators concluded were a major predictor of unsafe sexual behavior. Davies et al. also pointed out, however, that these young men were making reasoned and rational decisions about risk reduction by choosing to have regular anal intercourse within their relationships rather than with casual partners. Rightly, they judged that the efficacy of this response in limiting the spread of HIV is questionable. While Davies et al. found that condom use was slightly more consistent among the young gay men than older men, Ridge, Plummer, and Minichiello (1994) found that there was no difference in the level of recent unprotected anal intercourse among young gay men (<25 years) of different ages in Melbourne, Australia. They discovered, however, that those young men sampled from a gay commercial venue and those who reported no affiliation with a gay organization had a significantly higher level of recent unprotected anal sex than did other young gay men. According to the investigators, the results suggest that the commercial gay scene may not provide the same "safe-sex culture" for younger men as it may for older gay men (who usually have more power in such situations), while being part of a gay organization does seem to provide access to that culture for younger men. The findings also suggest that sexual HIV risk for young gay men is not socially uniform, and it may be more appropriate to define HIV risk within specific historical and culture cohorts than to work with the universally defined categories of "youth" and "adolescence." Studies are also needed to assess the efficacy of HIV risk-reduction intervention programs targeted to groups of young gay men in various communities of a geographical location and to those who use different "spaces" within those communities.

Cases of female-to-female transmission of HIV are extremely rare; however, research on adult lesbians have indicated that most have been sexually active with men. This sexual activity with men places them at risk for a range of sexually transmitted diseases (STDs), including HIV (Einhorn & Polgar, 1994; Ryan & Futterman, 1998). Two studies of women considered at high risk for HIV due to their sexual behavior, drug use, or place of residence found that 16% to 24% of these women self-identified as lesbian or bisexual. Additionally, the findings indicated that those women who reported at least one female sexual partner (regardless of self-identified sexual identity) were more likely to have engaged in anal sex with men, more likely to have injected drugs, and had higher HIV seroprevalence rates than do the exclusively heterosexual women (Gomez, 1995). Cochran and Mays (1996) found that over one-quarter of their sample of 18- to 24-year-old lesbian and bisexual women had heterosexual intercourse in the previous year. Of the bisexually identified women, 10% had sex with a gay male partner in the past year. Respondents who reported sex with a gay man were younger than other women, many in their adolescent years.

Consistent with adolescent sexual behaviors, lesbian teenagers often experiment sexually or have ongoing sexual contacts with friends in their social networks, including gay and bisexual male adolescents they meet at social and recreation programs or through same- and cross-gender friendships (Hunter & Schaecher, 1994). Consequently, their risk for HIV infection may be higher than expected as their male partners may be HIV-positive, or may be enaging in sex with other males who are. Additionally, both female and male youths tend not to employ safer-sex practices with friends, often falsely assuming that lesbians cannot contract HIV/AIDS. There are few HIV prevention messages addressed to lesbian and bisexual teenagers and to those questioning their identity (Hunter, 1996). In addition, the meaning of "safer sex" has been found to be particularly confusing between women, and definitions of it have been found to be highly variable (Einhorn & Polgar, 1994).

Some lesbian adolescents may try to hide their homosexuality by having sex with males or by becoming pregnant, placing themselves at risk for HIV and other sexually transmitted infections (Nelson, 1997). In a qualitative study of 20 young lesbians (mean age of 19 years) conducted in New York City, Hunter et al. (1993) found that 75% of them engaged in heterosexual vaginal intercourse, which was initiated a year before oral sex with females (means of 14 and 15.4 years, respectively). These findings were confirmed in a larger study of lesbian and gay adolescents (n = 164, ages 14–21 years). Four out of five young lesbian and bisexual female youths (n = 81) reported being sexually active with male partners in one study, and they had initiated sexual contact with males at an earlier age than with females. Findings of this study also indicated that these lesbian and bisexual females engaged in manual sex more than in any other sexual practice. An additional finding indicated that more of them engaged in oral, penile-vaginal, and vaginal-digital sex than in anal-penile sex (Rosario et al., 1996). In another study, 26% of the young women (ages 13–21 years) reported engaging in anal intercourse; however, only 15% of the lesbian-identified youth reported having engaged in this sexual activity (Ryan & Futterman, 1998).

In a study of 136 self-identified gay and bisexual male adolescents (ages 14–19 years), Rotheram-Borus et al. (1994) found that significant reductions occurred in the number of unprotected same-sex anal and oral acts as a result of an HIV-preventive intervention over a one-year period. However, those youth who were most likely to attend the HIV-intervention sessions increased their risk acts the most over two years (Rotheram-Borus et al., 1995). For both anal and oral sex, the best predictors of unsafe acts were high levels of anxiety and depression, and frequent alcohol use.

In a recent study of lesbian, gay, and bisexual urban youths (ages 14–21) in New York City, Hunter (1996) discovered that those who self-identified as gay/lesbian, versus those who labeled themselves as bisexual, had higher numbers of same-sex and lower numbers of opposite-sex contacts. Males having same-sex contacts were not as likely as females to be in relationships. Regardless of sexual identity status, however, both the young males and females were found to be at high risk for HIV infection because of unsafe sexual behaviors; both males and females reported high levels of unprotected same- and opposite-sex activities. Hunter also found no significant relationship between coming out and unprotected same-sex acts for either males or females; and a negative attitude toward their own homosexuality or bisexuality was not significantly related to unprotected sexual behaviors. Therefore, while choice of the gender of their sexual partners and the number of same-sex contacts were related to identity status, condom use was not. Hunter speculated that other issues may have been operating with regard to unprotected sexual acts, including a desire for exploration, substance use, and intimacy (e.g., wanting to be close, having sex without barriers), and that HIV-prevention approaches effective in reaching different communities of the gay, lesbian, and bisexual youths in the study may not have been employed.

HIV Prevention Education

Although the term "youth" does not have the associations normally attributed to the term "adolescents," it is important to acknowledge that for many people it carries implications regarding behavior and attitudes of individuals of certain ages, including the content thought to be appropriate for HIV prevention education programs. Additionally, differences of gender, ethnicity, and socioeconomic status have to be recognized. This chapter assumes a focus on young people who range in age from their mid-teens to their mid-twenties.

Novick (1997) described three layers of damage to be associated with HIV/AIDS stigma. First, individuals associated with AIDS are members of groups (including gay and bisexual men) whose fundamental human rights had been truncated before the appearance of HIV. Second, long-term stigmatization has profound effects on the lives of the disdained. With regard to gay and bisexual men, this branding and shame led to fostering short-term, and often anonymous, relationships that guaranteed HIV transmission. Finally, the stigmas intrude on creating or supporting HIV/AIDS prevention programs that are humane and sensitive to the needs of vulnerable people, including those specifically designed for gay, lesbian, and bisexual youths.

In discussing programs effective in reducing HIV risk behaviors for lesbian and gay youths, Rotheram-Borus and her colleagues (1995) concluded that it is important to help gay and bisexual youths feel positive about themselves and their life situations and to provide supportive programs to help youth confront coming-out issues. Other effective HIV intervention programs have recognized that behavior is not changed by knowledge alone. While knowledge about HIV/AIDS transmission is necessary, Bandura (1992) indicated that is not sufficient in changing behavioral practices. He pointed out that perceived self-efficacy is required for one to reduce the likelihood of engaging in risk behaviors. Studies focusing on the best ways to enhance perceived self-efficacy among various groups of gay, lesbian, and bisexual youths need to be conducted.

One important component for HIV-prevention education targeted to lesbian, gay, and bisexual youths is communicating an accepting environment to the youths and the significant adults in their lives. Homophobia drives many lesbian, gay, and bisexual youths away from needed information and care. A prevention program also has to be a reliable source of accurate information about lesbian, gay, and bisexual health issues, as well as HIV/ AIDS. Research has indicated that the education provided must be developmentally, language, culturally, and social-class relevant (National Institute of Health, 1997), and it should not be moralistic, prohibitive, or sex negative in its messages. Additionally, HIV/AIDS education programs face added challenges when they target groups such as African Americans and people with lower socioeconomic status, as research findings suggest that distrust is more prevalent among these groups and other individuals from relatively powerless sectors of the population (Herek & Capitanio, 1994).

According to the Centers for Disease Control and Prevention, approximately three-quarters of high school students have had sexual intercourse by the time they complete the 12th grade (Office of National AIDS Policy, 1996). Interventions should target the reduction of HIV-risk behaviors among these diverse groups of youth. Additionally, the results of studies should be used to dispel widely held myths that sex education programs result in the earlier onset of sexual behaviors or that condom availability fosters sexual and risky behaviors (NIH, 1997). In fact, Guttmacher et al. (1997) found the contrary among 7,119 students from 12 randomly selected New York City public schools. Other myths that have to be addressed are related to injection drug use. Results from studies do not support the assertions that needle-exchange programs lead to increased needle-injecting behavior among current users or that they increase the number of users (NIH, 1997).

Effective HIV prevention interventions are not single programs or single events; studies demonstrate that numerous intervention points over extended periods of time are more efficacious than once-only approaches (NIH, 1997). The interventions should be community based, sustained, and integrated with other prevention programs, such as programs on sexually transmitted diseases, unwanted pregnancies, and substance abuse. Prevention messages for lesbian, gay, and bisexual youths should facilitate their developing to their full potential and provide them with safe environments (e.g., schools, community centers, athletic leagues) in which to do so. Unfortunately, the policies of some school districts preclude the discussion of subjects such as sexual orientation, intercourse, and condom use (Office of National AIDS Policy, 1996).

Lesbian, gay, and bisexual youths should be involved in the design, development, and implementation of HIV prevention programs (NIH, 1997). Peer education has been demonstrated to be effective in helping youths to establish community norms regarding safer-sex and drug-using behaviors. Youths often find that peers make HIV/AIDS more relevant to their lives and that prevention messages are more realistic when delivered by their peers (DiClemente, 1993; Office of National AIDS Policy, 1996). Additionally, findings from research studies with gay men and heterosexual adolescents have indicated that perceptions of peer norms concerning sexual risk behavior are strongly associated with one's own sexual behavior (Kegeles et al., 1996). According to results of a study of 2,515 tenth-grade students in

Dade County (greater Miami, FL) public high schools, conducted by Langer, Zimmerman, Warheit, and Duncan (1993), peer interventions concerning AIDS-related knowledge, beliefs, attitudes, and skills are more effective with some groups than others. These researchers found that boys were significantly more likely to be peer-directed than girls, and girls were significantly more likely to be self-directed than boys. (Roughly, one-third of each gender group was defined as parent-directed.) Additionally, nearly half of the white, non-Hispanic students identified themselves as peer-directed, whereas only 19% of black, non-Hispanic students identified in the peer-directed group. Consequently, it is important that HIV prevention programs be designed to accommodate those who are peer-directed and those who are self-directed, and recognize that these characteristics may vary by gender and ethnicity. In a study of gay men, Kelly, St. Lawrence, Hood, and Brasfield (1989) found that perceived peer norms concerning the acceptability of safer-sex practices and AIDS health locus-of-control scores were associated with change in risk-reduction behaviors. Peer pressure is crucial among adolescents too, and it has been found to be the major reason for first sexual experiences among young people (Ingham, Woodcock, & Stenner, 1991).

HIV prevention interventions for lesbian, gay, and bisexual youths (as for other youths) should be embedded in a broad context of health, social, and recreational affairs. Experience and research have indicated that fears and cultural messages associated with AIDS do not make HIV education an appealing issue by itself, and social matters are highly important to young people (Kegeles et al., 1996). HIV interventions should be linked to other issues that gay, lesbian, and bisexual youths find important, such as coming out, finding and meeting potential partners, learning social skills, dating, relationships, intimacy, and sexual activities.

Providing HIV intervention to gay, lesbian, and bisexual youths requires addressing human sexuality, including the topic of sexual orientation. Talking about sexual matters is often difficult for professionals working with youths, as well as the youths'parents. Youths often find the lessons to be of little value, too biological, too vague, or conducted by teachers perceived to be embarrassed by the whole area (Woodcock, Stenner, & Ingham, 1992b). Researchers need to investigate the terminology and messages that effectively communicate HIV-prevention information to youths. For example, are messages that use such terms "know your partner" or "use protection to probhit the transmission of bodily fluids" effective or do they contain words that are open to interpretation? Ingham et al. (1991) found that advice containing ambiguous terminology leads youths to believe that they are following the advice when they are not doing so; however, this research has not been replicated.

As with other young people, HIV prevention designed with lesbian, gay, and bisexual youths needs to address issues related to their feelings of perceived immortality and personal invulnerability. Youths, especially those in their early teens, tend to be short-term thinkers, with the present

being important and the future perceived in vague terms. Others feel invulnerable to harm and make decisions to meet their immediate desires
rather than considering the long-term consequences. Woodcock, Stenner, and
Ingham (1992a) asked young people to justify, where appropriate, their
perceptions of invulnerability to HIV infection. The investigators were able
to categorize the responses into three groupings: (1) those young people who
did not take the threat of HIV infection more seriously than other risks in
life; (2) those who had their own ways of assessing risks related to perceived
(often irrelevant) properties of sexual partners, e.g., occupation, where they
lived, parent's occupation; and (3) those who thought their personal identity was not similar to those in "risk groups," and therefore they were safe.

Stresses in the lives of many lesbian, gay, and bisexual youths that are
not related to their sexual orientation must also be taken into consideration.
Problems arising from chaotic family environments, parental addictions, and
family violence, as well as from youths' ethnic, racial, gender, and economic
status, may create challenges related to living and survival that relegate HIV
prevention to a low status of relative importance. On the other hand, there
are lesbian, gay, and bisexual youths who become vulnerable to HIV infection because of feelings of shame, isolation, and worthlessness that result
from stigmatization and discrimination based on their sexual orientation.
Responding to opportunities to explore sexual and personal identities, as
well as meeting their needs for acceptance and intimacy, some lesbian, gay,
and bisexual youths place themselves in circumstances beyond their control—for example, agreeing to be involved in sexual or romantic relationships in which they become powerless (Hunter, 1996; Miller, Hunter, &
Rotheram-Borus, 1992). They become victims of sexual abuse and violence,
and are susceptible to HIV infection from their sexual partners, as well as
the negative consequences of victimization. These stressful experiences are
cumulative and increase the risk for infection. Therefore, HIV prevention
education interventions must be based on the premise that safer sex requires
reducing gay-related stresses (Rosario & Rotheram-Borus, 1992) and attaining a high level of sexual self-confidence. To assist youths in achieving these
goals, prevention education activities should focus on skill building (e.g.,
problem solving, decision making, and negotiation) and provide opportunities for youths to engage in role plays that allow them to practice those
skills (Remafedi, 1994a). Additionally, the programs need to provide opportunities for youths to learn the importance of exerting responsibility for protecting themselves and others from HIV infection (Miller et al., 1992; Office
of National AIDS Policy, 1996).

Effective HIV prevention education efforts have recognized the need to
confront myths about sexuality and HIV/AIDS. Myths that only gay men
engage in oral and anal sex, that homosexuality is a disturbed behavior or a
transient phase, and that lesbians are not at risk for HIV infection must be
explored. Other myths that need to be addressed are: that once people start
using condoms or dental dams, they will use them forever; that women can

readily protect themselves with condoms, as many women may not have control over male partners' use of condoms; and that individuals do not engage in sexual activities with same-sex as well as opposite-sex partners over time. Interventions also need to differentiate between those who are HIV-infected and uninfected and to provide primary prevention for the uninfected, without implying that there is something "wrong" with the lives of those who are infected (Odets, 1997). Research on effective interventions to combat these myths among gay, lesbian, and bisexual youths needs to be conducted.

Although directing his thinking to HIV prevention among gay men, Odets (1997) pointed to other realities that need to be acknowledged in primary prevention among gay, lesbian and bisexual youths; however, studies related to the outcomes of these messages have still not been undertaken. The messages are: (1) safer sex does not mean using protection every time one engages in sexual activity, but is *any* sex that does not transmit HIV; (2) HIV cannot be transmitted between two uninfected youth, therefore knowing one's HIV status is important; (3) gay, lesbian, and bisexual youths cannot live their lives in fear of being infected by their partners—it is not conducive to healthy relationships; and (4) uninfected gay, lesbian, and bisexual youths (who are hoping to stay uninfected) *are* hoping for futures that most infected youth cannot have, and ways must be found to help them remain uninfected.

Voluntary HIV counseling and testing programs provide opportunities for risk assessment, prevention education, early intervention, and research about the effectiveness of each of these processess among various age and ethnic groups of gay, lesbian, and bisxual youths. The main objective of counseling and testing with adolescents is to identify HIV-positive youth and to initiate appropriate medical care and support services. HIV counseling and testing also provide opportunities to relieve the anxiety of youth who are HIV-negative, to talk about sexual orientation and same-sex activities, to identify high-risk behaviors that may not have been previously discussed, and to link lesbian, gay, and bisexual adolescents with other services (Ryan & Futterman, 1998). For runaway or homeless youth, housing, food, education, job-training, help in obtaining health insurance, and other support services also become critical (Office of National AIDS Policy, 1996). Evaluation research about the relationships of effectiveness of counseling services appropriate for the youths' sexual orientation, language, culture, and age and social and emotional development levels needs to be conducted. Additionally, studies related to the sensitivity of services to lesbian, gay, and bisexual youths' fears and anxiety about HIV testing need to be undertaken.

For those youth who receive negative test results, posttest counseling not only provides them with opportunities to examine their own behaviors and develop individual HIV risk-reduction plans but also creates teachable moments in which providers can counteract untruths about the outcomes of HIV/AIDS treatments—for example, combination therapies are efficacious for everyone, and an undetectable viral load level means a person is noninfectious. For those youths who learn that they are HIV-positive, effective posttest counseling sessions become important first steps in understanding the meaning of their HIV status and in designing a plan of care. The plan should include a harm-reduction component, especially for those who engage in compulsive sexual activities, trade sex for food and shelter, or use injection drugs. Although access to a needle-exchange program among a group of youths (ages 16–24 years) who injected an illicit drug was found to be effective in reducing the sharing of needles, sharing other injection equipment, and use of unsterile needles (Kipke, Unger, Palmer, & Edgington, 1997), this research needs to be replicated with gay, lesbian, and bisexual youths. The efficacy of harm-reduction programs related to HIV-risk behaviors resulting from compulsive sexual activities, trading sex, and feelings of powerlessness in romantic relationships also need to be investigated.

Research on adolescent decision making has found that youth (particularly those aged 14 and over) have the capacity to make their own health-care decisions; however, because HIV testing is so anxiety provoking and a positive result has an enormous impact, Ryan and Futterman (1998) have recommended that youths identify a supportive adult who can be involved in the testing process. This person can also assist in explaining any limits relating to confidentiality and the potential negative impact of disclosing an HIV-positive status. Barriers to implementing effective counseling and testing services, and treatment programs for HIV-positive lesbian, gay, and bisexual adolescents include legal issues and parental rights. Most states in the United States consider youth aged 18 and over to be adults for legal purposes, which means that they can consent to treatment. Those under 18 years of age are minors, and parental consent is generally required for health care. Although all states have laws that allow minors to give consent with regard to the diagnosis and treatment of STDs, not every state classifies HIV as an STD. However, some states have laws that allow minors to consent to HIV testing and treatment, as well as treatment related to other health concerns—for example, alcohol and other substance abuse, rape, sexual assault and pregnancy (Ryan & Futterman, 1998). Researchers and providers need to investigate laws that authorize consent by minors and protect confidentiality in their respective localities.

HIV Prevention Intervention Studies with Gay/Bisexual Male Youths

Three significant research studies have tested the efficacy of HIV prevention education programs for gay and bisexual male youths. In an intervention conducted over a one-year period (1988–89), Rotheram-Borus et al. (1994) examined factors mediating changes in sexual behaviors that increased the risk of HIV infection among 136 gay and bisexual male adolescents ages 14 to 19. The youths were recruited from a gay-identified agency and were predominantly Hispanic (51%) and African American (31%). A 20-session intervention, with sessions rotated over a three-week sequence, allowed youths to join the intervention at various points. Small group sessions were held two or three days a week, with the content of the sessions varying by the day of the week. The intervention contained five components: (1) information about HIV communicated through video and art activities, (2) coping skills training to help youth manage risky situations, (3) access to health care and other resources, (4) addressing individual barriers to safer sex through private counseling, and (5) examining how prejudice against gays and positive feelings toward coming out might influence safer-sex attitudes. Sexual risk assessments were completed at 3, 6, and 12 months after the baseline interview. The researchers found that significant reductions occurred in the number of unprotected same-sex anal and oral acts among those youths who had less risk in their previous sexual history, who had been abstinent before enrollment, who did not engage in commercial sex, and who attended more sessions. The impact of the sessions varied significantly by race/ethnicity, with African-American youths most significantly reducing their risks over one year (e.g., the proportion of protected anal sex acts was 36% at baseline, 80% at 3 months, 67% at 6 months, and 84% at 12 months). Additionally, the youths in the study significantly reduced the number of sexual partners following the interventions, and this reduction was maintained through the 12-month follow-up. The cutback in the number of sexual partners was greatest among those youths who were not involved in commercial sexual activity. The investigators point to some limitations of the study: not having a control group and not randomly assigning participants to intervention and control conditions, not measuring the contributions of specific components of the intervention, and not basing the findings on a representative sample.

The second study involved 139 predominantly Caucasian (75%) gay and bisexual male youths, ages 13–22 (Remafedi, 1994a). Results demonstrated significant improvements in HIV-risk reduction over an average five-month period (with a range of three to six months). The program was part of an ongoing study of youth who were enrolled in 1989–1991, and it employed repeated contact with clients and diverse prevention strategies. The project included individualized HIV/AIDS risk assessments and risk-reduction counseling, peer education, and referrals to needed services. Compared to the initial HIV risk assessment, 60% fewer subjects reported unprotected anal intercourse with recent partners three to four months later. The participants also described less frequent anal intercourse and more consistent use of condoms during follow-up. Additionally, substance abuse severity scores and use of amphetamines and amyl nitrite declined. However, one-quarter of the subjects reported ongoing high-risk behaviors, which were associated with having more gay friends, multiple sexual partners, and frequent anal intercourse. Although he concluded that HIV-risk reduction improved over time, Remafedi acknowledged that the study was not designed to test the effect of the intervention and that other sources of knowledge and experience could have contributed to the reduction in HIV-risk behaviors. Further research is needed to determine which of the interventions is most efficacious and whether ongoing risk-taking behavior may reflect underlying psychosocial problems. Remafedi states that bold initiatives are necesssary to spare another generation of young gay and biseuxal men from HIV disease: HIV prevention interventions coupled with opportunities for positive adult role models, and health socialization with peers in safe environments. These projects need to be implemented and their outcomes evaluated.

The research by Rotheram-Borus et al. (1994) and Remafedi (1994a) were based in cognitive-behavioral frameworks of prevention. The results of their studies indicated that while high-risk gay and bisexual male youths (who were African American, Caucasian, and Latino) were accessible and amenable to HIV prevention interventions, they were not a homogenous group in their exposure to risks related to HIV, nor were they uniform in their responses to prevention programs. Moreover, there are no research reports of specific interventions directed to either young lesbians or to Asian-Pacific Islander and Native American gay and bisexual males. The two research studies also reinforced the importance of recognizing the unique dilemmas that gay, bisexual (and lesbian) youth must confront in establishing long-term relationships with same-gender partners.The findings demonstrated that: (1) gay and bisexual male youths engage in sexual activities with many partners in order to assess and affirm their personal and sexual identities; and (2) that effective HIV prevention approaches determine the youths' safer-sex knowledge and behaviors in these sexual relationships, which makes the relationships an important basis for designing interventions. Using harm-reduction strategies to minimize risky behaviors in ongoing sexual activities appears to be effective, except for those involved in commercial sexual activities who may need to learn other skills for negotiating safer sex in circumstances where there is an imbalance of power. Rotheram-Borus et al. (1994) conveyed the importance of designing innovative HIV-prevention strategies for youths who are already practicing safer sex to ensure consistency of those behaviors. Based on his findings, Remafedi (1994a) noted that some young gay and bisexual youths may initiate, continue, or return to high-risk behaviors, despite education and assistance from health professionals; consequently, other approaches may be required. Remafedi states that the youth may "benefit from social skills training, general educational development, and recognition and treatment of underlying psychosocial problems" (pp. 147–148). It is important that other investigators confirm his findings and determine the effectiveness of various prevention strategies.

Kegeles et al. (1996), the investigators of a third research study, developed and evaluated a community-level HIV risk-reduction intervention program in the early 1990s. The program was peer-led and implemented in a mid-size Oregon community for a period of eight months. It contained three components: peer outreach (used to disseminate safer-sex messages), small groups (focused on meeting men, clearing up misconceptions about safer sex, eroticizing safer sex, promoting condom use, and orchestrating safer sex strategies with partners), and a publicity campaign within the gay community (used articles and advertisements in the gay newspaper and word-of-mouth messages to spread awareness of the project, establish its legitimacy, invite young men to participate and provide a reminder of the norm of safer sex within the community). Longitudinal cohorts of young gay men (aged 18–29) were recruited in two communities, the second serving as a comparison community. The program was run by a "Core Group" of 12 to 15 young gay men and a community advisory board, with the Core Group choosing "The Mpowerment Project" as the intervention's name. The mean age of the men in the cohorts was 23 years, with 86% identifying as gay and 14% as bisexual; and 81% white, 6% Latino, 4% African American, 7% Asian or Pacific Islander, and 2% "other." In the intervention community, 65% (n = 103) of those who completed preintervention assessment answered postintervention surveys. Results of the study indicated that the proportion of men engaging in any unprotected anal intercourse decreased from 41% to 30%, decreasing from 20% to 11% with nonprimary partners and from 59% to 48% with boyfriends. No significant changes occurred in the comparison community over the same time period. The investigators concluded that the prevention approach effectively led to HIV-risk reduction and that HIV-prevention activities should be embedded in social and community programs.

It is important to note that the effective HIV prevention interventions, described in the Rotheram-Borus et al. (1994), Remafedi (1994a), and Kegeles et al. (1996) studies, were developed before the recent adoption of HIV-treatment guidelines endorsing antiviral drug treatments with "cocktail" therapies that include a protease inhibitor. Additional drugs that treat opportunistic infections have also been discovered. Both of these advances have contributed to a dramatic decrease in deaths associated with AIDS (Centers for Disease Control and Prevention, 1997b) . Future studies of HIV prevention interventions among lesbian, gay, and bisexual (as well has heterosexual) youths need to assess whether the advances in drug treatments have any effect on maintaining or reducing risky behaviors. Misconceptions about the safety and efficacy of these therapies and treatments, as well as the consequences of resistance and nonadherence to drug regimens, need to be investigated in future research. Examining factors such as locus of control, self-esteem, social support, substance use and abuse (concurrent with therapies), internalized homophobia, current and cumulative stress factors in relation to HIV, and mental health problems is important in determining the effect of long-term antiviral drug therapy with lesbian, gay, and bisexual youths.

In conducting a recent study, Rotheram-Borus and her colleagues (1997) found that a low number of HIV+ youths were linked to medical care, despite the availability of prophylactic treatment and an emphasis on early intervention among youths. Although this was not a study that focused on prevention interventions, its results provide information that is relevant to HIV prevention programs. Although the large majority of 102 youth were identified as HIV+ about 32 months prior to recruitment, significant percentages of them (75% identified as male, and 87% as "gay" or "bisexual") continued to engage in unprotected sexual activities and used considerable amounts of alcohol and other drugs. When their current risk behaviors were assessed over two consecutive 3-month periods, almost one-third had been sexually abstinent; however, among the youths who were sexually active, most had multiple sex partners, (M = 6, Time 1 and 5, Time 2) and used condoms (72–77% sexual acts protected). Most of them always used condoms (63–64%). The use of alcohol (63%), marijuana (41%), hard drugs (36%), and injection drugs (12%) was also substantial. The youths were found to be relatively healthy (i.e., not having disease symptoms), which may explain why they attended only about one-third of medical appointments related to their HIV infections. The investigators concluded that while all youths were linked to adolescent HIV programs, unhealthy behavior and risk acts remained common.

Conclusions

The challenges of HIV/AIDS prevention with gay, lesbian, and bisexual youths do not only involve protecting and advocating for them but also embrace processes that center on empowering them and their communities. Empowerment not only provides these youths with opportunities to become agents of their own desires but also develops into a decisive factor in helping gay, lesbian, and bisexual youths to confront homophobia, street violence, harassment, and the risks involved with sexual encounters. Youths who feel empowered are more secure in their identities, and they are less willing to take risks and engage in "reckless acts" that may lead to HIV infection. On the other hand, those who lack feelings of empowerment may face greater difficulties and are often unable to protect themselves (Herdt & Boxer, 1993).

Eradicating HIV and curing individuals with HIV disease are probably unattainable with the currently available classes of antivirals (Roland, 1998). HIV's ability to generate drug-resistant variants is a major factor that limits the effectiveness of antiretroviral therapies in reversing the natural history of AIDS (Centers for Disease Control and Prevention, 1998). Providing opportunities and training for lesbian, gay, and bisexual youths to develop self-esteem, interpersonal skills, supportive networks, and access to HIV risk-reduction materials and services is required (Cranston, 1991). Effective intervention programs are those that: (1) publicize occasions for meeting other young lesbian, gay, or bisexual people; (2) provide a variety of approaches that engage youths in determining ways to protect themselves from HIV infection; (3) assist youths in creating safer-sex strategies and peer norms; (4) help youths in coping with psychosocial problems arising from victimization based on their sexual orientation; (5) target specific subgroups of the lesbian, gay, and bisexual youth community, taking their particular needs and experiences into consideration (e.g., being and not being HIV infected); and (6) integrate HIV/AIDS prevention and care programs with other community services.

A review of research on the behavioral impact of HIV/AIDS and sexual health education on young people, commissioned by the Joint United Nations Programme on HIV/AIDS (UNAIDS), reported findings that provide evidence of the viability and effectiveness of education programs. The results also provide the rationale for establishing programs that can be communicated to policy makers, program planners, and educators; and they give future directions of HIV/AIDS prevention activities, including those directed to gay, lesbian, and bisexual youths. The major conclusions of the review were as follows: (1) education about sexual health and/or HIV does not encourage increased sexual activity; (2) 22 studies indicated that HIV and/or sexual health education delayed the onset of sexual activity, reduced the number of sex partners, or curtailed unplanned pregnancy and sexually transmitted disease (STD) rates; (3) responsible and safe behavior can be learned; and (4) sexual health education is best started before the onset of sexual activity. Further results indicated that only high-quality educational activities had an impact on behavior. Effective programs included the following elements: (1) a focused curriculum with clear statements about behavioral aims, including the delineation of the risks of unprotected sex and methods to avoid it; (2) a focus on learning activities that addressed social and media influences; (3) teaching and providing for practice in communication and negotiation skills; (4) encouraging openness in talking about sex; and (5) education activities that were grounded in theories which stress the social nature of learning (Centers for Disease Control and Prevention, 1998). HIV/AIDS prevention education programs incorporating these elements should be designed and implemented for all gay, lesbian, and bisexual youths so as to prevent their devastation by this disease. In addition, these educational efforts can change the tragedy of AIDS into opportunities for gay, lesbian, and bisexual youths to learn about themselves, to develop support systems, to become empowered, and to enhance their physical and mental health.

Many of the studies of gay, lesbian, and bisexual youths cited in this chapter (particularly those focused on HIV prevention intervention) were conducted in urban settings. There is a need for research to be conducted among youths living in suburban and rural communities. Additionally, many of the findings were based on studies of young people from self-selected populations (e.g., persons presenting at community-based agencies for gay, lesbian, and bisexual youths; HIV/AIDS prevention programs; and sexually transmitted disease clinics). Some of these community-based services tend to attract youths of particular socioeconomic statuses and racial/ethnic backgrounds, thereby limiting the generalizability of the research findings. Lacking representative samples from the population of gay, lesbian, and bisexual youths, and hampered by societal stigmas about homosexuality (e.g., students participating in anonymous studies in school settings may fear self-identifying as gay, lesbian, or bisexual), the studies may represent only HIV high-risk youths and may not provide an accurate portrayal of the population as a whole.

References

Bandura, A. (1992). A social cognitive approach to the exercise of control over AIDS infection. In R. J. DiClemente (Ed.), *Adolescents and AIDS: A generation in jeopardy* (pp. 89–116). Newbury Park, CA: Sage.

Centers for Disease Control and Prevention. (1995). Youth risk behavior surveillance—United States, 1993. *Morbidity And Mortality Weekly Report, 44* (no. SS-1).

Centers for Disease Control and Prevention. (1997a). *HIV/AIDS Surveillance Report, 9*(2), 1–43.

Centers for Disease Control and Prevention (1997b). Update: Trends in AIDS incidence—United States, 1996, *Morbidity And Mortality Weekly Report, 46*(37).

Centers for Disease Control and Prevention (1998, March). *HIV/AIDS prevention,* 1–19.

Cochran, S. D., & Mays, V. M. (1996). Prevalence of HIV-related sexual risk behaviors among 18 to 24 year-old lesbian and bisexual women. *Women's Health,* 2(1/2), 75–89.

Cole, S. W., Kemeny, M. E., Taylor, S. E., & Visscher, B. R. (1996). Elevated physical health risk among gay men who conceal their homosexual identity. *Health Pyschology, 15,* 243–251.

Cranston, K. (1991). HIV education for gay, lesbian, and bisexual youth: Personal risk, personal power, and the community of conscience. *Journal of Homosexuality, 22*(3/4), 247–259.

Davies, P. M., Weatherburn, P., Hunt, A. J., Hickson, F. C. I., McManus, T. J., & Coxon, A. P. M. (1992). The sexual behavior of young gay men in England and Wales. *AIDS Care, 4*(3), 259–272.

D'Augelli, A. R. (1998). Developmental implications of victimization of lesbian, gay, and bisexual youths. In G. Herek (Ed.), *Stigma and sexual orientation: Understanding prejudice against lesbians, gay men, and bisexuals* (pp. 187–210). Thousand Oaks, CA: Sage.

D'Augelli, A. R., Hershberger, S. L., & Pilkington, N. W. (1998). Lesbian, gay, and bisexual youths and their families: Disclosure of sexual orientation and its consequences. *American Journal of Orthopsychiatry, 68,* 361–371.

Dean, L., & Meyer, I. (1995). HIV prevalence and sexual behavior in a cohort of New York City gay men (aged 18–24). *Journal of Acquired Immune Deficiency Syndrome, 8,* 208–211.

DeCrescenzo. T. (Ed.). (1994). Helping gay and lesbian youth: New policies, new programs, new practice. *Journal of Gay & Lesbian Social Services, 1*(3/4), xix–xxiv.

Diaz, R. M. (1998). *Latino gay men and HIV: Culture, sexuality, and risk behavior.* New York: Routledge.

DiClemente, R. J. (1993). Preventing HIV/AIDS among adolescents: Schools as agents of behavior change. *Journal of the American Medical Association, 270,* 760–762.

Ehrhardt, A. A. (1996). Editorial: Our view of adolescent sexuality—A focus on risk behavior without developmental context. *American Journal of Public Health, 86,* 1523–1525.

Einhorn, L., & Polgar, M. (1994). HIV-risk behavior among lesbians and bisexual women. *AIDS Education and Prevention, 6,* 514–523.

Ford, K., & Norris, A. E. (1993). Knowledge of AIDS transmission, risk behavior, and perceptions of risk among urban, low-income, African-American and Hispanic youth. *American Journal of Preventive Medicine, 9,* 297–306.

Garofalo, R., Wolf, R. C., Kessel, S., Palfrey, J., & DuRant, R. H. (1998). The association between health risk behaviors and sexual orientation among a school-based sample of adolescents. *Pediatrics, 101,* 895–902.

Gold, R. S., & Skinner, M. J. (1992). Situational factors and thought processes associated with unprotected intercourse in young gay men. *AIDS, 6,* 1021–1030.

Gomez, C. (1995). Lesbians at risk for HIV: The unresolved debate. In G. M. Herek and B. Greene (Eds.), *AIDS, identity, and community: The HIV epidemic and lesbians and gay men* (pp. 19–31). Thousand Oaks, CA: Sage.

Gonsiorek, J., & Rudolph, J. (1991). Homosexual identity: Coming out and other developmental events. In J. Gonsiorek & J. Weinrich (Eds.), *Homosexuality: Research implications for public policy* (pp. 161–176). Newbury Park, CA: Sage.

Grossman, A. H. (1994). Homophobia: A cofactor of HIV disease in gay and lesbian youth. *Journal of the Association of Nurses in AIDS Care, 5*(1), 39–43.

Grossman, A. H. (1995). HIV/AIDS and adolescents: Lessons for the second decade. In *AIDS—Law and Humanity: Proceedings of an Interdisciplinary International Conference* (pp. 41–53). New Delhi, India: The Indian Law Institute.

Grossman, A. H. (1998). Queer youth and urban space: The case for a place of their own. In C. Aitchison & F. Smith (Eds.), *Gender, space and identity: Leisure, culture and commerce* (pp. 127–136). Eastbourne, UK: Leisure Studies Association.

Grossman, A. H., & Kerner, M. S. (1998). Self-esteem and supportiveness as predictors of emotional distress in gay male and lesbian youths. *Journal of Homosexuality, 35*(2), 25–39.

Guttmacher, S., Lieberman, L., Ward, D., Freudenberg, N., Aradosh, A., & DesJarlais, A. (1997). Condom availability in New York City public high schools: Relationships to condom use and sexual behavior. *American Journal of Public Health, 87,* 1427–1433.

Herdt, G., & Boxer, A. (1993). *Children of Horizons: How gay and lesbian teens are leading a new way out of the closet.* Boston: Beacon Press.

Herek, G. M., & Capitano, J. P. (1994). Conspiracies, contagion, and compassion: Trust and public reaction to AIDS. *AIDS Education and Prevention, 6,* 365–375.

Hershberger, S. L., Pilkington, N. W., & D'Augelli, A. R. (1997). Predictors of suicide attempts among gay, lesbian, and bisexual youth. *Journal of Adolescent Research, 12,* 477–497.

Hetrick, E., & Martin, A. (1987). Developmental issues and their resolution for gay and lesbian adolescents. *Journal of Homosexuality, 14*(1/2), 25–43.

Hunter, J. (1996). *Emerging from the shadows: Lesbian, gay, and bisexual adolescents.* Unpublished doctoral dissertation, The City University of New York.

Hunter, J., & Haymes, R. (1997). It's beginning to rain: Gay/lesbian/bisexual adolescents and AIDS. In M. S. Schneider (Ed.), *Pride and prejudice: Working with lesbian, gay and bisexual youth* (pp. 137–163). Toronto: Central Toronto Youth Services.

Hunter, J., Rosario, M., & Rotheram-Borus, M. J. (1993). *Sexual and substance abuse acts that place adolescent lesbians at risk for HIV.* Paper presented at the IX International Conference on AIDS/4th STD World Congress, Berlin, Germany.

Hunter, J., & Schaecher (1994). AIDS prevention for lesbian, gay, and bisexual adolescents. *Families in Society: The Journal of Contemporary Human Services* (Special Issue), 346–356.

Ingham, R., Woodcock, A., & Stenner, K. (1991). Getting to know you . . . young people's knowledge of partners at first intercourse. *Journal of Community and Applied Social Psychology, 1,* 117–132.

Kegeles, S. M., Hays, R. B., & Coates, T. J. (1996). The Mpowerment project: A community-level HIV prevention intervention for young gay men. *American Journal of Public Health, 86,* 1129–1136.

Kelly, J. A., St. Lawrence, J. S., Hood, H. V., & Brasfield, T. L. (1989). Behavioral intervention to reduce AIDS risk activities. *Journal of Consulting and Clinical Psychology, 57,* 60–67.

Kipke, M. D., Unger, J. B., Palmer, R., & Edgington, R. (1997). Drug-injecting street youth: A comparison of HIV-risk injection behaviors between needle exchange users and nonusers. *AIDS and Behavior, 1,* 225–232.

Kuszelewicz, M. A., & Lloyd, G. A. (1995). Lesbians and gays of color and HIV/AIDS: A literature review, 1988–1993. *Journal of Gay & Lesbian Social Services, 2*(3/4), 107–119.

Langer, L. M., Zimmerman, R. S., Warheit, G. J., & Duncan, R. C. (1993). Decision-making orientation and AIDS-related knowledge, attitudes and behaviors of Hispanic, African-American, and White adolescents. *Health Psychology, 12*(3), 227–234.

Lemp, G. F., Hirozawa, A. M., Givertz, D., Nieri, G. N., Anderson, L., Lindegren, M. L., Janssen, R. S., & Katz, M. (1994). Seroprevalence of HIV and risk behaviors among homosexual and bisexual men: The San Francisco/Berkeley Young Men's Survey. *Journal of the American Medical Association, 272,* 449–454.

Manloff, S. B., Gayle, H. D., Mays, M. A., & Rogers, M. F. (1989). Acquired immunodeficiency syndrome in adolescents: Epidemiology, prevention and public health issues. *Pediatric Infectious Disease Journal, 8,* 309–314.

Manning, P. K. (1997). Foreword. *Journal of Homosexuality, 32*(3/4), xxi–xxviii.

Martin, A. D. (1982). Learning to hide: The socialization of the gay adolescent. In S. Feinstein, J. Looney, A. Schwartzberg, & J. Sorotsky (Eds.), *Adolescent psychiatry: Developmental and clinical studies* (Vol. X, pp. 52–65). Chicago: University of Chicago Press.

Miller, S., Hunter, J., & Rotheram-Borus, J. (1992). *Adolescents living safely: AIDS awareness, attitudes, and actions for gay, lesbian and bisexual youths* (HIV Center for Clinical and Behavioral Studies). Unpublished report, New York State Psychiatric Institute.

Morris, M., Zavisca, J., & Dean, L. (1995). Social and sexual networks: Their role in the spread of HIV/AIDS among young gay men. *AIDS Education and Prevention, 7* (Supplement), 24–35.

National Institutes of Health. (1997, February 11–13). *Interventions to Prevent HIV Risk Behaviors: NIH consensus statement, 15*(2), 1–41. Bethesda, MD: Author.

Nelson, J. A. (1997). Gay, lesbian, and bisexual adolescents: Providing esteem-enhancing care to a battered population. *The Nurse Practitioner, 22*(2), 94–109.

Novick. A. (1997). Stigma and AIDS: Three layers of damage. *Journal of the Gay and Lesbian Medical Association, 1*, 53–60.

Odets, W. (1997). Why we do not do primary prevention for gay men. In J. Oppenheimer & H. Reckitt (Eds.), *Acting on AIDS: Sex, drugs & politics*. London: Serpent's Tail.

Office of National AIDS Policy (1996, March). *Youth & HIV/AIDS: An American agenda: A report to the President*. Washington, DC: Author.

Peterson, J. (1995). AIDS-related risks and same-sex behaviors among African-American men. In G. M. Herek and B. Greene (Eds.), *AIDS, identity, and community: The HIV epidemic and lesbians and gay men* (pp. 85–104). Thousand Oaks, CA: Sage.

Pleak, R. R., & Meyer-Bahlburg, H. F. L. (1990). Sexual behavior and AIDS knowledge of young male prostitutes in Manhattan. *Journal of Sex Research, 27*(4), 557–587.

Proctor, C. D., & Groze, V. K. (1994). Risk factors for suicide among gay, lesbian, and bisexual youths. *Social Work, 39*(5), 504–513.

Public Media Center. (1995). *The impact of homophobia and other social biases on AIDS*. San Francisco, CA: Author.

Remafedi, G. (1994a). Cognitive and behavioral adaptations to HIV/AIDS among gay and bisexual adolescents. *Journal of Adolescent Health, 15*, 142–148.

Remafedi, G. (1994b). Predictors of unprotected intercourse among gay male and bisexual youth: Knowledge, beliefs, and behavior. *Pediatrics, 9*(2), 163–168.

Remafedi, G., Farrow, J. A., & Deisher, R. W. (1991). Risk factors for attempted suicide in gay and bisexual youth. *Pediatrics, 87*(6), 869–875.

Remafedi, G., French, S., Story, M., Resnick, M., & Blum, R. (1998). The relationship between suicide risk and sexual orientation: Results of a population-based study. *American Journal of Public Health, 88*(1), 57–60.

Ridge, D. T., Plummer, D. C., & Minichiello, V. (1994). Young gay men and HIV: Running the risk? *AIDS Care, 6*(4), 371–377.

Roland, M. E. (1998). Antiviral adherence dilemmas. *Focus: A guide to AIDS research and counseling, 13*(3), 1–4.

Rosario, M., Hunter, J., & Gwadz, M. (1997). Exploration of substance use among lesbian, gay, and bisexual youth: Prevalence and correlates. *Journal of Adolescent Research, 12*, 454–476.

Rosario, M., Meyer-Bahlburg, H. F. L., Hunter, J., Exner, T. M., Gwadz, M., & Keller, A. M. (1996). The psychosexual development of urban lesbian, gay, and bisexual youths. *Journal of Sex Research, 33*(2), 113–126.

Rosario, M., & Rotheram-Borus, M. J. (1992). *HIV risk acts and gay male youth: The mediating role of stress*. Paper presented at the 8th International Conference on AIDS/3rd STD World Congress, Amsterdam, The Netherlands.

Rotheram-Borus, M. J., Hunter, J., & Rosario, M. (1995). Coming out as lesbian or gay in the era of AIDS. In G. M. Herek & B. Greene (Eds.), *AIDS, identity, and community: The HIV epidemic and lesbians and gay men* (pp. 151–168). Thousand Oaks, CA: Sage.

Rotheram-Borus, M. J., Murphy, D. A., Coleman, C. L., Kennedy, M., Reid, H. M., Cline, T. R., Birnbaum, J. M., Futterman, D., Levin, L., Schneir, A., Chabon, B., O'Keefe, Z., & Kipke, M. (1997). Risk acts, health care, and medical adherence among HIV+ youths in care over time. *AIDS and Behavior, 1*(1), 43–52.

Rotheram-Borus, M. J., Reid, H., & Rosario, M. (1994). Factors mediating changes in sexual HIV risk behaviors among gay and bisexual male adolescents. *American Journal of Public Health, 84*(12), 1938–1946.

Ryan, C., & Futterman, D. (1998). *Lesbian and gay youth: Care and counseling.* New York: Columbia University Press.

Woodcock, A., Stenner, K., & Ingham, R. (1992a). Young people talking about HIV and AIDS: Interpretations of personal risk of infection. *Health Education Research: Theory and Practice, 7,* 229–247.

Woodcock, A., Stenner, K., & Ingham, R. (1992b). "All these contraceptives, videos and that": Young people talking about school sex education. *Health Education Research: Theory and Practice, 7,* 517–531.

8

The Experiences of Lesbian, Gay, and Bisexual Youths in University Communities

Nancy J. Evans

The college years are a time of self-exploration, personal growth, and determination of the roles one will assume in society. Lesbian, gay, and bisexual students face the added challenge of resolving issues related to their sexual orientation. Until students develop a sense of themselves as gay, lesbian, or bisexual people, addressing the other developmental tasks is difficult. Career decision making, establishing close friendships and intimate relationships, and determining a personal set of religious beliefs and values are issues greatly influenced by how one chooses to live one's life with regard to sexual orientation. As a result of the hostile climate facing gay, lesbian, and bisexual individuals in our society, the task of lesbian/gay/bisexual identity development and the decisions associated with this process can contribute to significant psychological stress and mental health problems (Buhrke & Stabb, 1995; Evans & D'Augelli, 1996). Isolation and feelings of being different from their heterosexual peers are commonplace among lesbian, gay, and bisexual students (D'Augelli, 1993). Without support, the development of a healthy identity is particularly challenging (Slater, 1993).

Becoming lesbian, gay, or bisexual requires conscious distancing from a heterosexist lifestyle and creating a new identity oriented toward homosocial and homosexual dimensions (D'Augelli, 1994). Individuals change and develop over their entire life span, with development being highly responsive to environmental circumstances as well as individual variables. Individuals are unique in their own development, with self-perception influenced by point in life, setting, interactions with significant others, and historical period. In addition, individuals have an impact on their own development, depending on the choices they make and the meanings they ascribe to those choices.

Since environment plays a crucial role in how individuals come to perceive and identify themselves, examining the impact of specific environments can tell us much about how development occurs. College residence halls are environments that present significant developmental opportunities for all students (Winston & Anchors, 1993). Because they often provide the first living context away from home, offer opportunities for interaction with individuals from different backgrounds, and require that individuals make independent decisions regarding how they will manage their lives, residence halls are an important factor in the transition to adulthood. For lesbian, gay, and bisexual students, living on campus away from their families of origin provides an opportunity to give up their heterosexual identity and more clearly define themselves in homosocial and homosexual terms. Research indicates, however, that the environments of residence halls are often unwelcoming, hostile, and even dangerous places for lesbian, gay, and bisexual students (D'Augelli, 1989b).

In this chapter the experiences of lesbian, gay, and bisexual (LGB) students in university communities will be examined. Existing literature will be augmented with information obtained from a qualitative study involving 20 lesbian, gay, and bisexual students who lived in residence halls at a large research university. The purpose of this study was to examine through in-depth interviews the experiences of students in residence halls, the impact of those experiences on students' behavior, the meaning students made of their experiences, and the factors that influenced those perceptions. The chapter will conclude with a list of recommendations for improving the environments of university residence halls and for additional research.

Previous Research on University Climate for Gay, Lesbian, and Bisexual Students

Homophobia and heterosexism are well-documented problems on college campuses (Obear, 1991). Existing research examining these phenomena can be grouped into four categories: (1) practices related to inclusion of gay and lesbian students, (2) attitudes of heterosexual students toward lesbian and gay male students or about homosexuality in general, (3) experiences of lesbian and gay male students in campus settings, and (4) the impact of homophobia and heterosexism on LGB students. Although the need for research addressing the experiences of bisexual and transgendered individuals has been stressed in the literature (Carter, 2000; Denny, 1994; Pope & Reynolds, 1991; Robin & Hamner, 2000), almost no studies have considered these populations. In addition, in-depth analyses of residence hall climates from the perspectives of LGB students are absent from the literature.

Inclusion Issues for Gay Men, Lesbians, and Bisexuals on College Campuses

Individuals continue to experience discrimination on college campuses because of their sexual orientation (Berrill, 1990). Lesbian and gay students' basic rights to association, access to university services and facilities, funding, and privacy have all been challenged in the courts, sometimes successfully and sometimes unsuccessfully (Liddell & Douvanis, 1994). In at least 10 states conservative political groups were advocating for ballot initiatives to limit the ability of gay organizations to exist on campuses or to prevent them from receiving public funding (Carmona, 1994).

Although creating a diverse and multicultural environment is a stated goal for many colleges and universities, sexual orientation is often intentionally excluded from consideration (Love, 1997). Lesbian, gay, and bisexual topics are taboo and LGB people and issues are invisible. Faculty respondents to McNaron's (1997) study reported that few courses include material related to lesbian, gay, or bisexual topics, and almost no universities have gay and lesbian studies programs. Other studies of the academic climate for LGB students on college campuses are equally disquieting, indicating that LGB material is ordinarily excluded and that heterosexist practices regularly occur (DeSurra & Church, 1994; Pilkington & Cantor, 1996). While over 2,000 LGB student groups exist on college campuses, only 30 campuses have full-time administrators responsible for LGB activities and programs (Gose, 1996). And only 10% of this country's colleges and universities have included sexual orientation as a protected classification in their codes of conduct and employment policies (McDonough & McLaren, 1996).

Attitudes of Heterosexual Students toward LGB Students

Researchers have documented that the attitudes of heterosexual students toward lesbian and gay students are often negative. D'Augelli and Rose (1990) found that white heterosexual first-year students held very negative views of homosexuality, with over half believing that male homosexual behavior is "plain wrong," labeling gay men as "disgusting." Almost all the first-year students expected that harassment of lesbians and gay men would take place on campus. In another study of 976 students at a state university in the South (Globetti, Globetti, Brown, & Smith, 1993), 4 out of 5 students thought that lesbian and gay students "would have a hard time fitting in on campus" (p. 211). Malaney, Williams, and Geller (1997) found that 60% of the students at both a research university and a state college (BA level only) reported knowing people who made anti-LGB remarks, and only one-third would intervene if they saw someone presumed to be LGB being harassed. Simoni (1996) reported lower levels of homophobia among students she surveyed in four Los Angeles college settings, but her study included students in ethnic studies and in women's studies classes, and graduate students, as well as undergraduates.

Resident Assistants (RAs), student staff members who live on residence hall floors and who are perhaps most aware of the climates on their floors (besides LGBT students themselves), validate these findings. In one study, 40% of the female RAs and 39% of the male RAs indicated that they had been required to address some type of issue on their floor related to homosexuality (Bowles, 1981). In a study involving 103 prospective Resident Assistants (D'Augelli, 1989a) *all* of the candidates reported hearing negative comments about lesbians and gay men. Over half of these candidates (58%) believed that victimization of lesbians and gay men was very likely to occur in residence halls.

Background characteristics influence the extent to which individuals hold negative attitudes toward lesbians and gay men. For example, a number of studies (D'Augelli, 1992; D'Augelli & Rose, 1990; Herek, 1988; Malaney et al., 1997; Qualls, Cox, & Schehr, 1992) have found that women students are more accepting of homosexuality than men students. Attitudes of male students toward gay men have been found to be more negative than their attitudes toward lesbians (D'Augelli,1992; D'Augelli & Rose, 1990; Herek, 1988; Simoni, 1996). In contrast, one study found attitudes of women to be more negative toward lesbians than toward gay men (Whitley, 1988). Significant relationships have also been found between attitudes toward homosexuality and attitudes toward racial minorities (Larson, Cate, & Reed, 1983; Qualls et al., 1992), stereotypic gender roles (Black & Stevenson, 1984; Qualls et al., 1992) and religious orthodoxy (Larson et al., 1983). Younger students, those with less education, those whose parents are less educated, and those with low self-esteem are also more likely to be homophobic (Simoni, 1996). In one report, gay and bisexual men in one study viewed fraternity members and athletes as the most homophobic individuals on their campus (Rhoads, 1997).

Studies have consistently shown that students who know someone who is lesbian or gay tend to have less homophobic attitudes (D'Augelli, 1992; D'Augelli & Rose, 1990; Malaney, et al., 1997; Simoni, 1996; Wells & Franken, 1987). Wells and Franken (1987) also demonstrated that individuals who were more knowledgeable about homosexuality were less homophobic. Some evidence exists that educational programs involving exposure of students to individuals who are gay, lesbian, or bisexual can lead to positive attitude change (Croteau & Kusek, 1992; Geasler, Croteau, Heineman, & Edlund, 1995; Stevenson, 1988). However, Green, Dixon, and Gold (1993) found that this was the case only for women.

The Experiences of GLB Students on College Campuses

That a college campus may be a hostile place for lesbian, gay, and bisexual students is evident from students' reports. In 1988, a total of 1,411 anti-gay incidents involving harassment, intimidation, or vandalism were reported to the National Gay and Lesbian Task Force by gay, lesbian, and bisexual student organizations on 34 college campuses (Berrill, 1990). A review of campus climate studies done on 30 colleges and universities across the United States revealed extensive anti-LGBT prejudice including verbal abuse, physical violence, and sexual harassment. Because different methodologies were used in obtaining data, percentages of individuals reporting such behavior range from below 10% to 86%, but in most of the studies in which LGBT students were surveyed directly and anonymously, over half the students reported being harassed in some manner (Rankin, 1998). In a study of 121 lesbian and gay undergraduate students, over three-quarters reported verbal abuse, and one-quarter reported threats of violence (D'Augelli, 1992). Other students were most often the harassers. In an ethnographic study of collegiate gay and bisexual men, Rhoads (1994) found that those who were more actively involved in LGB organizations and activities (and were therefore more visible on campus) were more likely to experience harassment and discrimination.

Personal accounts of lesbian and gay students living in residence halls suggest that they often experience these environments as negative. The gay and bisexual men in Rhoads's (1994, 1995) study who lived in residence halls reported many acts of harassment, including homophobic messages written on bathroom mirrors or messages pads, and gay-related materials ripped off their doors. Similar acts were experienced by LGB students at a private liberal arts college studied by Love (1997), who also reported that the events were ignored by administrators.

Effects of Climate on LGB Students

Given these negative experiences, it is not surprising that in a study of university social climate, Reynolds (1989) found that gay males perceived the climate as less emotionally supportive, less innovative, less intellectual, and less tolerant of change than did heterosexual males. Similarly, LGB students in Love's (1997) study reported feelings of pain, loneliness, and helplessness resulting from the harassment and expressions of hatred they experienced at a private liberal arts college with a strong Catholic tradition.

To deal with the hostile environments they perceive in residence halls, many students choose to keep their sexual orientation hidden. In one study (D'Augelli, 1989b), 80% of the lesbian and gay students surveyed indicated that they had not disclosed their sexual identity to their roommates, and 89% reported that they had not come out to other undergraduates. Another strategy LGB students may employ is to move out of residence halls as soon as possible, or to spend little time there, even when they do "officially" live in the halls.

Support seems to play an important role in the adjustment of LGB students. Slater (1993) found that LGB students who had had more support throughout their lives were better able to cope with victimization they experienced on campus. Buhrke and Stabb (1995) pointed out that the student's stage of LGB identity development is also related to how he or she will interpret and cope with negative experiences. For students who are just beginning to disclose their sexual orientation to others, the amount of support and acceptance they receive from those to whom they come out can greatly influence their self-concept and self-esteem. Rhoads (1994, 1997) reported that the support of the LGB community was particularly important in the coming-out process of gay and bisexual men. Yet on many campuses, especially those that are conservative or religiously affiliated, support is often unavailable (Love, 1997). The lack of LGB role models among faculty and staff is especially troubling to youth who are looking for guidance as they assume a new and oppressed identity (Rhoads, 1997). Lack of support often leads students to isolate themselves and to avoid talking about negative experiences (Rankin, 1998; Savin-Williams & Cohen, 1996). Some students choose to drop out of college because they cannot tolerate the isolation, rejection, and harassment they experience (Love, 1997; Slater, 1993).

The potential role of residence life staff in general and Resident Assistants in particular is an important one when it comes to improving the climate for all students. For example, RAs could work with students to create an atmosphere where heterosexist and homophobic comments and actions are unacceptable. Two factors interfere with the success of this strategy. First, because so few lesbian, gay, bisexual, and transgendered students feel they can be open about these aspects of their identities, residence hall staff may see issues related to homophobia and heterosexism as a minor problem and dismiss the need for education and training to address these concerns (Bourassa & Shipton, 1991). For example, despite the complexity of the issues, the majority of RAs in Bowles's (1981) study believed that they could address whatever concerns might come up on their floors related to sexual orientation.

Second, RAs themselves often are misinformed, hold negative attitudes about LGBT students, and demonstrate homophobic behaviors. For example, Robertson (1990) found that while RAs held less homophobic attitudes than students in general, they still scored within the "homophobic" range on a measure of attitudes toward gays and lesbians. Bowles (1981) found that the mean correct responses on informational items about homosexuality were only 67% for female RAs and 63% for male RAs. In the same study, responses to two open-ended questions designed to gather information about RAs' attitudes toward homosexuality suggested that a large number of the men were openly hostile while the women were somewhat less homophobic. In D'Augelli's (1989a) study of RA candidates, 71% of the students reported that they had made derogatory comments about lesbians and gay men. Since Resident Assistants are highly visible members of the university community and important role models for students on their floors, these findings are particularly troublesome. On a more positive note, a study of the attitudes of professional student affairs administrators found that their average scores on a measure of homophobia were within the low nonhomophobic range (Hogan & Rentz, 1996). It is impossible to tell from this study, however, if these scores indicate the true feelings of the administrators or whether they reflect responses administrators perceive as "politically correct."

In summary, the existing literature indicates that significant homophobia and heterosexism exist on college campuses, and particularly within residence halls. Residence Life staff, along with student residents, often hold negative views of LGB students. While some efforts have been made to provide training and programming to increase knowledge of and sensitivity to the issues facing LGB students, little is really known about the success of these efforts in creating a more positive residence hall environment for all students. Additionally, little is known about the extent of psychological and physical harassment directed at LGB students, nor about LGB students' own experiences in and perceptions of residence hall climates.

The Residence Hall Climate Study

The overall goal of the Residence Hall Climate Study was to examine the experiences of LGB students living in university residence halls, and to determine the impact of these experiences. Based on D'Augelli's (1994) theory, specific goals were (1) to gain information about specific experiences and behaviors of LGB students in the residence halls, (2) to determine how LGB students make meaning of their residence hall experiences, (3) to determine the influence of significant people in residence halls on LGB students' perceptions and behavior, (4) to determine the influence of the university and residence hall setting and climate on LGB students' perceptions and behavior, and (5) to determine unique aspects of LGB students' past and current experience that shape their perceptions of the environment.

Ten men and 10 women participated in the study. They were recruited from various LGB organizations, support groups, and electronic mail listservs, as well as through GLB-themed classes and personal contact. Seven identified as gay men, 5 as lesbian women, 3 as bisexual men, and 5 as bisexual women. Eighteen students were white, one was Asian American, and one was Latino. Two women were exchange students from Great Britain. Eight were seniors, 5 were juniors, 4 were sophomores, and 3 were first-year students. They ranged from minimally to extensively open about their sexual orientation. Half were not involved in organized LGB activities, several participated occasionally, and a number were very active. Participants took part in confidential interviews lasting from 2 to 2½ hours conducted by trained interviewers who were actively involved in LGB-related activities and who had also previously worked in residence halls. Interviews were audiotaped and transcribed. Themes and patterns within and across interviews were identified.

Students in the study reported a wide range of experiences in their residence halls, from very negative to very positive. On the extreme negative end of the continuum, one male student reported that when his roommate found out the student was gay, he threatened to kill him. Another student's roommate engaged in a series of passive-aggressive acts, including playing sexually explicit videos, placing anti-gay signs around the room, and recording and playing anti-gay religious programs. Other negative acts included defacement of signs on doors, placing anti-gay graffiti in bathrooms and on message boards, and doing pranks directed against LGB students. Positive experiences that students reported included having students on the hall accept them when they disclosed their sexual orientation. Several students noted that students and residence life staff in their hall demonstrated active support by attending gay pride rallies, being involved in groups for allies of LGB students, standing up for LGB students when negative comments were made, and presenting educational programming in the halls about LGB issues.

Only a few students reported experiencing direct harassment, such as threats, comments directed specifically at them, or other negative acts such as those mentioned above. However, much indirect harassment occurred in the form of general homophobic comments, use of derogatory language, graffiti, and minimization of the concerns of LGB students by other students. A female bisexual sophomore stated, "Women tend to talk behind other people's backs . . . they're emotionally violent. . . . I think in a lot of ways emotional violence is probably worse [than physical violence]."

While a few students reported receiving personal support from friends and staff, the majority of students experienced support indirectly. They noted that staff were friendly toward them and that they appreciated seeing anti-gay bashing signs posted on the floor or gay-themed bulletin boards displayed. Some students felt supported if they were not actively harassed or attacked.

The prevailing perception among the LGB students interviewed was that they were invisible. Students reported that LGB issues were not addressed in programming and that there was a lack of awareness of LGB issues on the part of other students. A gay junior noted, "No one really wanted to even think about the issue [the climate for LGB students]." Another student stated, "It's worse to be invisible than to be called names." Participants in the study also noted that there were few opportunities for social interaction with other LGB students. LGB students did not know other LGB students in their halls, and they were aware of few LGB-oriented social activities on campus.

Students were in varying stages of coming out, ranging from one who had come out very recently to her roommate and was out to no one else, to activists on campus who frequently found their names in the campus newspaper. Those students who were selectively out to straight friends and to members of the LGB community reported more positive experiences in the halls than did either students who were minimally out or those who were publicly out. Students in the latter two groups expressed considerable fear. A lesbian senior who now lives off-campus talked about her feelings while living in the halls where she was very closeted: "I just didn't feel comfortable coming out to anyone around me. I was almost fearful that people would find out because I didn't feel like there was a whole lot of support there." A man who was very active in the LGB student organization and a public advocate for LGB concerns experienced similar feelings of fear and also moved off campus: "I knew that everyone on the floor knew about me. . . . It was a nerve-racking time because I was constantly living in fear. . . . I was at a high point in terms of my visible outness and activism, so I decided I didn't want to go through that anymore, and I moved off campus."

Making Meaning

Three factors seem to play a role in how students understand their residence hall experiences: minimization of negative experiences, exaggeration of positive experiences, and perceiving anything "not negative" as positive.

Students consistently downplayed negative experiences they might have had in the residence halls. For instance, a gay sophomore provided this amusing, yet poignant example: "You don't feel bad when it [graffiti on a bathroom wall] says, 'Die Fagits.' You figure you've met the enemy and he's illiterate." Several students were well aware that they were minimizing experiences. A bisexual senior active in LGB organizations stated, "I don't internalize negative experiences." Another young woman commented on how she had learned to deal with a negative situation on her floor: "I just let [the comments] pass now, which is kind of a sad reality."

Because LGB students expect to be oppressed and harassed, a positive experience may be seen as a cause for celebration. For instance, students were excited when their RAs were friendly and knew their names. A Residence Life coordinator who helped with a room change, something that would be done for any student, was perceived as "a really cool person." When asked what more Residence Life could do for LGB students, a bisexual senior reasoned, "I always feel like if we ask for anything more, we'll be asking for too much. At least they acknowledge that gay people exist and they try to be friendly about it. I don't really know how much more they could do." Students frequently made positive comments about a lack of negative experiences. Typical statements include the following: "So far the climate has been pretty exceptional. . . . Like I haven't really had any real negative experiences" (from a bisexual first year student); "Nothing absolutely terrible has happened" (from a lesbian senior); and "No one has bashed me yet" (from a gay junior). A junior bisexual woman stated that the best thing about living in the residence halls for her was, "I suppose the fact that I haven't directly come into any kind of conflict with anyone over the issue."

Influential People

Other people in the residence halls played an important role in determining how the LGB students in the study perceived the climate of their halls. Roommates had the most influence, but Residence Life staff were also important in creating a climate in the halls. In addition, the actions of other students on the floor influenced perceptions. In all cases, minimally supportive actions were viewed as positive, including such activities as being friendly, putting up posters about LGB-oriented events, or not engaging in negative actions.

LGB students who had other LGB students as roommates or who had single rooms reported the best experiences. These students felt that they could be themselves in their rooms. They could put up gay-related room decorations, leave gay materials on their desks, have friends visit, and not censor conversations. Those with LGB roommates also had the support of having someone to talk with about their feelings and experiences. Accepting roommates who became allies were also valued, as were roommates who were willing to learn despite holding homophobic views.

In general, Resident Assistants were viewed positively by the students interviewed. Often RAs received positive evaluations for doing little more than being a "nice person." Only those RAs who had made homophobic comments in the direct presence of the student or who had taken some action that reflected homophobic attitudes, such as siding with a homophobic roommate in a conflict situation, were perceived negatively. RAs and other residence life staff who were openly lesbian, gay, or bisexual were particularly valued by LGB students. They were seen as important role models who actively helped to raise awareness in the halls and who provided direct support to LGB students through friendship, connections to the LGB community, and assistance in negotiating the university bureaucracy.

Most LGB students interacted very little with other LGB students in the halls. Many students did not personally know any other LGB student in their hall, and most reported that they interacted with LGB friends in other locations. This phenomenon was lessened in halls with LGB staff and in the one area on campus that housed many LGB students. The presence of other LGB people, then, appeared to facilitate social interaction.

The Influence of Setting and Climate

The specific residence hall setting influenced students' perceptions of the climate. Smaller, coed, and more academically oriented residence halls were generally perceived as more positive settings by LGB students. Such settings tended to produce a greater sense of community, allowed for more extensive interaction, and provided opportunities for students to get to know each other on a personal basis. All of these factors seemed to lead to greater acceptance of LGB students as individuals and more tolerance of diversity in general. In contrast, halls that were large, single-sex, and had no particular focus tended to be viewed negatively. Students in such halls interacted very little with their peers, spent little time in their halls, and experienced them as cold, unwelcoming, and intolerant.

The reputation of the hall and whether the student had chosen to live there also influenced students' evaluations of the climate. If a hall was known as being tolerant of LGB students, and if the student had specifically chosen to live there, the student seemed to anticipate and look for positive experiences to confirm their impressions of the hall. The perceived residence hall climate definitely had an impact on the behaviors and emotional well-being of the LGB students who were interviewed in this study. Affected behaviors included the degree to which problems were confronted, the extent to which students were out, the extent to which students were involved on their floors, and where students sought support. When the hall climate was perceived as positive, students were much more willing to address issues that arose and to bring problems to Residence Life staff. On the other hand, in negatively perceived environments, confrontations were avoided. A 26-year-old gay senior noted, "I mind my own business." A bisexual female exchange student, asked what advice she would pass on to a student about to move into the residence halls, stated, "I would just say, 'Don't aggravate people.'"

Students who found more welcoming climates were more likely to come out to their roommates and other people on their floors. In contrast, one participant perceived the climate of her residence hall as very hostile and was not out to anyone. She stated her feelings very emotionally: "I was so terrified of anybody finding out or knowing. I certainly couldn't tell anybody."

Students who perceived their hall positively tended to become more involved in that hall. For instance, one student mentioned spending a significant amount of time with people on his floor who often accompanied him to gay-oriented events and rallies. Students who experienced their halls negatively withdrew from them. One man commented, "So when I go home, I go home to sleep. I go home to take a shower." He also noted that the second hall he lived in was somewhat better than the first "because I just didn't have an many interactions, and I didn't have to deal with them as much." If a hall is experienced in a positive manner, students were more likely to seek support there. One student's advice to other LGB students included the following comment: "[The halls provide] a great opportunity to meet other people. I would just let them [LGB students] know that there are other people out there and to try to find them. Try to find other gay friends, RAs who may be gay. . . . It's just a matter of finding them and getting to know them." On the other hand, many students who found the residence hall climate to be more negative sought support and friendship elsewhere. One woman noted, "I haven't been hanging out on my floor as much. I've started to surround myself with people who are more accepting." She had found these people in a support group for lesbian and bisexual students run by the university counseling center.

In addition to influencing students' behaviors, the residence hall climate also affected emotional well-being. Students' emotional reactions to their experiences were both positive and negative. One woman reflected on how she felt after coming out to women on her floor: "It's very affirming when people find out and treat me the same." However, a man noted that on his floor, "You're not allowed to express how you actually feel. You have to hide it sometimes. And it makes me feel kind of angry sometimes." A woman reacted more succinctly to feeling that she had to hide her identity, "It made me feel like shit." She also felt that the hostile climate of her residence hall retarded her identity development: "It was very difficult for me to come to terms with myself because of all the negative stuff that was out there."

Some students reported becoming more self-confident and secure. For instance, one male student felt that the best thing about living in the halls was "becoming more self-confident . . . basically the feeling that there's nothing wrong with me." Another student, whose experiences in the halls had been mostly negative, reflected that, "Knowing what I know now gives me strength in terms of how to handle a situation."

Unique Aspects

Several background factors influenced how students perceived the climate of their residence halls and behaved in these settings. These included previous environments and settings in which they had lived, their status in the identity development process, gender, and their degree of involvement with residence life.

The extent to which previous settings had been welcoming influenced students' perceptions of their present environment. For example, two male students had transferred from institutions they found to be much less open and accepting. They were both quite positive about their experiences at their new institution. Another student had been out in high school and found his home community to be very homophobic. He felt much more comfortable at college. In contrast, two British bisexual women had previously attended college in London. Both found the climate stifling in the United States, reporting that they had to be much more closeted to feel safe here.

The point at which students were in their identity development process also affected their perceptions. Students who had only recently begun to identify themselves as LGB were less secure in their identity and more likely to expect, look for, and perceive experiences to be negative. For instance, one woman was newly self-identified as bisexual and had come out only to a few people. She perceived her hall as very hostile. Yet she reported actually hearing negative statements from only two women in the room next to her and she experienced no direct harassment. On the other hand, a lesbian senior who had been active in LGB organizations for a number of years and who was quite secure in her identity was much less critical of the climate, although an outside observer might consider her experiences as being more negative.

While surprisingly few gender differences were apparent in the interviews, two themes did emerge. First, men were more likely to be the targets of harassment than women. Men reported pranks played against them, harassing phone calls, and direct threats, whereas women did not report these experiences. Instead, women noted derogatory comments about LGB people, attitudes of indifference, and a sense of being invisible. Men, perhaps because they were more likely to be attacked directly, were also more aware of the reputations of certain residential areas on campus as more intolerant and more carefully selected where they were going to live.

A final finding was that students who were more involved with the residence life staff and programs were much more likely to be positive about their experiences in the halls. One student was dating an RA, and, as a result, many of her friends were Residence Life staff. She was, therefore, very aware of their efforts to improve the climate for LGB students. Another student was an RA candidate himself at the time of the interview. Although he related many negative experiences in the halls, he was very positive about the efforts being made by residence life to improve the climate.

Implications for Campus Housing Administrators

Croteau and Lark (1995) surveyed 270 members of the American College Personnel Association Standing Committee on Gay, Lesbian, and Bisexual Issues to identify exemplary practices addressing gay, lesbian, and bisexual concerns on college campuses. They identified the following 10 practices: (1) open affirmation of LGB people and confrontation of homophobic remarks; (2) response to homophobic harassment and violence with victim support, sanctions for perpetrators, and education for the community; (3) inclusivity of LGB people in language, programming, media, and policies; (4) equitable treatment of LGB people; (5) attention to the unique developmental and situational needs of LGB people; (6) promotion of a climate in which LGB individuals can be open, and respect for those who choose not to be; (7) provision of staff training and educational programming for students designed to address homophobia; (8) provision of support programs for LGB persons; (9) advocacy for LGB individuals and organizations; and (10) equitable and affirmative employment procedures and benefits.

These practices can assist in developing a welcoming climate in campus residence halls. The following additional recommendations are based upon both the university climate literature and the Residence Life study.

1. RAs have a significant impact. Careful recruitment and selection are crucial to ensure that RAs are open to all forms of diversity and are supportive of lesbian, gay, and bisexual students in particular. In addition, ongoing staff development about LGB issues is needed to ensure that RAs are knowledgeable and trained to handle harassment and conflict situations appropriately.
2. Publicly open LGB Residence Life staff should be hired. Students consistently mentioned the positive impact of known LGB staff on

their level of comfort in the halls. LGB staff play an important role in breaking down stereotypes and educating heterosexual students in the hall.

3. Room changes requested because of homophobic actions should be expedited. The study demonstrated that students tend to minimize negative situations and endure very hostile circumstances without notifying authorities. If a student requests a change, it is fair to conclude that he or she is experiencing significant mental anguish. Every effort should be made to remove the student from the negative situation as quickly as possible, and to locate the student in a context known to be positive.

4. Acts of vandalism, harassment, and homophobic statements should be confronted quickly and visibly. These circumstances can have a powerful negative impact on students' emotional well-being, especially if students are in the early stages of identity development. On the other hand, experiencing support from Residence Life staff in the form of sanctioning such behavior sends an important message of acceptance. In addition, immediate denunciation of homophobic acts provides heterosexual students with a clear statement that such behavior is unacceptable.

5. Special efforts should be made to assist LGB students in identifying LGB-friendly roommates, RAs, and halls. Supportive environments do much to facilitate the development of LGB students and enable them to succeed in the college environment. Yet most students have no way of knowing if their living situations will be positive or negative prior to entering them. A confidential clearinghouse, perhaps in the form of a LGB listserv, might serve to connect LGB students looking for roommates or provide information about gay-friendly halls and staff.

6. Passive programming in the form of bulletin boards, posters, and displays about LGB issues has a significant impact and should be encouraged in residence halls. Many LGB students commented on the positive effect that seeing such materials had on their perceptions of the environment. They also noted that since heterosexual students had to walk past such displays, they could not be as easily avoided as educational programs in the halls.

7. More nonpoliticized support groups for LGB and questioning students are needed. Since they experience little support in their halls, feel that they cannot come out to students or staff in their halls, and know no other LGB students in their halls, many students feel isolated and alone. Support groups in which they can explore their identity would assist them in becoming more confident and help them to develop greater self-esteem.

8. More social outlets are needed for LGB students. As noted above, LGB students are unlikely to know other LGB students in the halls.

They are forced to look elsewhere for connections to the LGB community. Campus-sanctioned social activities would be a positive alternative to off-campus social settings such as bars or parties that center on the use of alcohol.

9. More integration of LGB issues into the curriculum is needed. LGB students consistently mentioned feeling as if their community and its issues were invisible. Attention to LGB issues in the classroom would help to break the silence and normalize LGB people and lifestyles. Curricular integration would send a powerful message to heterosexual students about the importance of inclusivity while providing a significant source of support for LGB students.

10. University officials must not assume that because students do not actively raise issues that the climate on campus is accepting. As is very evident for the Residence Life study, LGB students minimize negative experiences and avoid confrontation. It is incumbent upon all members of the university community to makes themselves aware of the climate for LGB students and to actively address problems they identify.

Future Directions

While the study reported in this chapter provides a start in determining the impact of the college environment on the development of gay, lesbian, and bisexual students, more comprehensive work is needed to investigate the influence of other aspects of college life. This study suggests several additional areas that deserve exploration, including student social and political organizations, classroom environments, and visible programming related to LGB issues.

Evaluation studies to determine the effectiveness of existing programs and services are crucial. For instance, do educational programs offered to students in residence halls result in changes in their attitudes and behavior? Does the training provided to RAs and other Residence Life staff provide them with the skills and knowledge to effectively address homophobic and heterosexist acts in the residence halls? What effect is curricular integration of diversity issues having on students' development and attitudes concerning social justice? Case studies of exemplary programs are particularly important to determine what interventions are having a positive impact and why they are working.

The important role played by supportive others in the residence halls is worthy of further consideration. What factors lead individuals to become allies? How does attitude change related to sexual orientation occur? What can be done to facilitate the process in residence halls and other college settings? Changes in attitudes and behavior of students over time are also important to consider. The increased visibility of sexual orientation issues and increasing numbers of openly LGB staff, faculty, and students on colleges campuses seem to be having a positive impact on the climate for LGB people. This phenomenon deserves careful study.

University environments, particular residence hall environments in which students engage in significant interactions with peers, play a central role in the development of all students. For LGB students, too often these experiences are negative. By acknowledging and addressing the presence and needs of LGB students, Residence Life staff can do much to reverse this situation and create environments that are open and welcoming for all students.

References

Berrill, K. T. (1990). Anti-gay violence and victimization in the United States: An overview. *Journal of Interpersonal Violence, 5,* 274–294.

Black, K. N., & Stevenson, M. R. (1984). The relationship of self-reported sex-role characteristics and attitudes toward homosexuality. *Journal of Homosexuality, 10*(1/2), 83–93.

Bourassa, D., & Shipton, B. (1991). Addressing lesbian and gay issues in residence hall environments. In N. J. Evans & V. A. Wall (Eds.), *Beyond tolerance: Gays, lesbians and bisexuals on campus* (pp. 79–96). Alexandria, VA: American College Personnel Association.

Bowles, J. K. (1981). Dealing with homosexuality: A survey of staff training needs. *Journal of College Student Personnel, 22,* 276–277.

Buhrke, R. A., & Stabb, S. D. (1995). Gay, lesbian, and bisexual student needs. In S. D. Stabb, S. M. Harris, & J. E. Talley (Eds.). *Multicultural needs assessment for college and university student populations* (pp. 173–200). Springfield, IL: Charles C Thomas.

Carmona, J. (1994, March 30). Anti-gay initiatives cause anxiety on state campuses. *Chronicle of Higher Education,* p. A32.

Carter, K. (2000). Transgenderism and college students: Issues of gender orientation and its role on our campuses. In V. A. Wall & N. J. Evans (Eds.), *Toward acceptance: Sexual orientation issues on campus* (pp. 261–282). Washington, DC: American College Personnel Association.

Croteau, J. M., & Kusek, M. T. (1992). Gay and lesbian speaker panels: Implementation and research. *Journal of Counseling and Development, 70,* 396–401.

Croteau, J. M., & Lark, J. S. (1995). A qualitative investigation of biased and exemplary student affairs practice concerning lesbian, gay, and bisexual issues. *Journal of College Student Development, 36,* 472–482.

D'Augelli, A. R. (1989a). Homophobia in a university community: Views of prospective resident assistants. *Journal of College Student Development, 30,* 546–552.

D'Augelli, A. R. (1989b). Lesbians' and gay men's experiences of discrimination and harassment in a university community. *American Journal of Community Psychology, 17,* 317–321.

D'Augelli, A. R. (1992). Lesbians and gay male undergraduates' experiences of harassment and fear on campus. *Journal of Interpersonal Violence, 7,* 383–395.

D'Augelli, A. R. (1993). Preventing mental health problems among lesbian and gay college students. *Journal of Primary Prevention, 13*, 245–261.

D'Augelli, A. R. (1994). Identity development and sexual orientation: Toward a model of lesbian, gay, and bisexual development. In E. J. Trickett, R. Watts, & D. Birman (Eds.), *Human diversity: Perspectives on people in context* (pp. 312–333). San Francisco: Jossey-Bass.

D'Augelli, A. R., & Rose, M. L. (1990). Homophobia in a university community: Attitudes and experiences of heterosexual freshmen. *Journal of College Student Development, 31*, 484–491.

Denny, D. (Ed.). (1994). *Gender dysphoria: A guide to research.* New York: Garland.

DeSurra, C. J., & Church, K. A. (1994, November). *Unlocking the classroom closet: Privileging the marginalized voices of gay/lesbian college students.* Paper presented at the Annual Meeting of the Speech Communication Association, New Orleans, LA.

Evans, N. J., & D'Augelli, A. R. (1996). Lesbians, gay men, and bisexual people in college. In R. C. Savin-Williams & K. M. Cohen (Eds.), *The lives of lesbians, gays, and bisexuals: Children to adults* (pp. 201–226). Fort Worth, TX: Harcourt Brace.

Geasler, M. J., Croteau, J. M., Heineman, C. J., & Edlund, C. J. (1995). A qualitative study of students' expression of change after attending panel presentations by lesbian, gay, and bisexual speakers. *Journal of College Student Development, 36*, 483–491.

Globetti, E. C., Globetti, G., Brown, C. L., & Smith, R. E. (1993). Social interaction and multiculturalism. *NASPA Journal, 30*, 209–218.

Gose, B. (1996, February 9). The politics and images of gay students. *The Chronicle of Higher Education*, pp. A33–A34.

Green, S., Dixon, P., & Gold, N. V. (1993). The effects of a gay/lesbian panel discussion on college student attitudes toward gay men, lesbians and persons with AIDS (PWAs). *Journal of Sex Education and Therapy, 19*, 47–63.

Herek, G. M. (1988). Heterosexuals' attitudes toward lesbians and gay men: Correlates and gender differences. *The Journal of Sex Research, 25*, 451–477.

Hogan, T. L., & Rentz, A. L. (1996). Homophobia in the academy. *Journal of College Student Development, 37*, 309–314.

Larson, K. S., Cate, R., & Reed, M. (1983). Anti-Black attitudes, religious orthodoxy, permissiveness, and sexual information: A study of the attitudes of heterosexuals toward homosexuality. *The Journal of Sex Research, 19*, 105–118.

Liddell, D. L., & Douvanis, C. J. (1994). The social and legal status of gay and lesbian students: An update for colleges and universities. *NASPA Journal, 31*, 121–129.

Love, P. G. (1997). Contradiction and paradox: Attempting to change the culture of sexual orientation at a small Catholic college. *Review of Higher Education, 20*, 381–398.

Malaney, G. D., Williams, E. A., & Geller, W. W. (1997). Assessing campus climate for gays, lesbians, and bisexuals at two institutions. *Journal of College Student Development, 38*, 365–375.

McDonough, P. M., & McLaren, P. (1996). Critical, postmodern studies of gay and lesbian lives in America. *Harvard Educational Review, 66*, 368–382.

McNaron, T. A. H. (1997). *Poisoned ivy: Lesbian and gay academics confronting homophobia.* Philadelphia: Temple University Press.

Obear, K. (1991). Homophobia. In N. J. Evans & V. A. Wall (Eds.), *Beyond tolerance: Gays, lesbians and bisexuals on campus* (pp. 39–66). Alexandria, VA: American College Personnel Association.

Pilkington, N. W., & Cantor, J. M. (1996). Perceptions of heterosexual bias in professional psychology programs: A survey of graduate students. *Professional Psychology: Research and Practice, 27,* 604–612.

Pope, R. L., & Reynolds, A. L. (1991). Including bisexuality: It's more than just a label. In N. J. Evans & V. A. Wall (Eds.), *Beyond tolerance: Gays, lesbians and bisexuals on campus* (pp. 205–212). Alexandria, VA: American College Personnel Association.

Qualls, R. C., Cox, M. B., & Schehr, T. L. (1992). Racial attitudes on campus: Are there gender differences? *Journal of College Student Development, 33,* 524–529.

Rankin, S. (1998). Campus climate for lesbian, gay, bisexual, and transgendered students, faculty, and staff: Assessment and strategies for change. In R. Sanlo (Ed.), *Working with lesbian, gay, and bisexual students: A guide for administrators and faculty* (pp. 277–283). Westport, CT: Greenwood.

Reynolds, A. J. (1989). Social environmental conceptions of male homosexual behavior: A university climate analysis. *Journal of College Student Development, 30,* 62–69.

Rhoads, R. A. (1994). *Coming out in college: The struggle for a queer identity.* Westport, CT: Bergin & Garvey.

Rhoads, R. A. (1995). Learning from the coming-out experiences of college males. *Journal of College Student Development, 36,* 67–74.

Rhoads, R. A. (1997). Implications of the growing visibility of gay and bisexual male students on campus. *NASPA Journal, 34,* 275–286.

Robertson, D. L. (1990). *Resident students' homophobia: Implications for staff selection and training.* Unpublished master's thesis, Western Illinois University.

Robin, L., & Hamner, K. (2000). Bisexuality: Identities and community. In V. A. Wall & N. J. Evans (Eds.), *Toward acceptance: Sexual orientation issues on campus* (pp. 245–259). Washington, DC: American College Personnel Association.

Savin-Williams, R. C., & Cohen, K. M. (1996). Psychological outcomes of verbal and physical abuse among lesbian, gay, and bisexual youths. In R. C. Savin-Williams & K. M. Cohen (Eds.), *The lives of lesbians, gays, and bisexuals: Children to adults* (pp. 181–200) Fort Worth, TX: Harcourt Brace.

Simoni, J. M. (1996). Pathways to prejudice: Predicting students' heterosexist attitudes with demographics, self-esteem, and contact with lesbians and gay men. *Journal of College Student Development, 37,* 68–78.

Slater, B. R. (1993). Violence against lesbian and gay male college students. *Journal of College Student Psychotherapy, 8,* 177–202.

Stevenson, M. R. (1988). Promoting tolerance for homosexuality: An evaluation of intervention strategies. *Journal of Sex Research, 25,* 500–511.

Wells, J. W., & Franken, M. L. (1987). University students' knowledge about and attitudes toward homosexuality. *Journal of Humanistic Education and Development, 26,* 81–95.

Whitley, B. E., Jr. (1988). Sex differences in heterosexuals' attitudes toward homosexuals: It depends upon what you ask. *Journal of Sex Research, 24,* 287–291.

Winston, R. B., Jr., & Anchors, S. (1993). Student development in the residential environment. In R. B. Winston, Jr., S. Anchors, & Associates (Eds.), *Student housing and residential life* (pp. 25–64). San Francisco: Jossey-Bass.

9

The Victimization of Lesbian, Gay, and Bisexual Youths

Ian Rivers and Anthony R. D'Augelli

Recently, there has been a significant increase in empirical research relating to the victimization of lesbian, gay, and bisexual (LGB) youths in both schools and community settings. This chapter reviews the nature of victimization of LGB youths and details some of the findings of recent studies focusing upon the long-term consequences of this victimization. It also focuses on current initiatives designed to address the direct as well as the indirect effects of victimization of LGB youths. Finally, recommendations for future research on the victimization of LGB youths are presented.

Normative Victimization of Lesbian, Gay, and Bisexual Youths

Many stressors in the lives of LGB youths occur only because of their sexual orientation. These distinctive experiences reflect historical and cultural heterosexism. This kind of victimization—through the normalizing of heteroeroticism and the marginalization of homoeroticism—is at the core of the transition to adulthood for LGB youths. The normative victimization adds distinct challenges to the lives of these adolescents, above and beyond the challenges faced by all youths. Three prominent forms of cultural victimization are described below.

Being Made to "Feel Different"

In contrast to the heterosexual youth whose development has been charted by adolescence researchers, LGB youths have few opportunities to explore their developing identities without severe risk. Given the stressors still associated with adult LGB identity in contemporary society, it is not surprising that the earliest phenomenological experience of a young LGB person is a profound sense of difference. This sense of "otherness" results from isolation from those with similar feelings and from messages that homoerotic feelings are shame worthy. A cyclical pattern emerges: feeling different (and often not being able to understand the feeling), youths withdraw from others, or try to act "straight," with varying degrees of success. This widens the gap between private identity and public identity. The process also intensifies social vigilance, lest others figure out one's "true" identity. That such an identity is socially stigmatized can be seen in the results of a national study of sexual harassment in high school, which found that being called "gay" by others was deemed the most psychologically upsetting form of verbal harassment (American Association of University Women, 1993). As a result of discerning others' views, tension and loneliness may increase as LGB youths become increasingly aware of the nature of their "difference." During the initial period of recognition and labeling of homoerotic feelings, LGB youth have little support from peers, who are so crucial during adolescence. Another recent U.S. survey, of male adolescents 15–19 years of age, found that few (12%) felt they could have a gay friend, and most (89%) considered sex between males to be "disgusting" (Marsiglio, 1993).

Atypical Family Stressors

Many problems LGB youths face are exacerbated by the lack of parental, sibling, and extended family support. Research on parental reactions to disclosure of sexual orientation reveals considerable upset among parents, many of whom respond very negatively at first (Savin-Williams, 1994a; Strommen, 1989). Remafedi (1987) found that 43% of a sample of gay male adolescents reported strong negative reactions from parents about their sexual orientation. Rotheram-Borus, Hunter, and Rosario (1994) found that coming out to parents and siblings, being discovered as gay by parents or siblings, telling friends or being discovered by friends, and being ridiculed for being gay were the most common gay-related stressors. Using an adult gay male sample, Cramer and Roach (1988) found that 55% of the men's mothers and 42% of their fathers had an initially negative response. Robinson, Walters, and Skeen (1989) sampled parents of lesbian and gay adults through a national support group for parents, and found that many reported initial sadness (74%), regret (58%), depression (49%), and fear for their child's well-being (74%). Boxer, Cook, and Herdt (1991) studied parents of LGB youths aged 21 and younger. More youths had disclosed to their mothers than fathers. Of the lesbian youths, 63% had disclosed to mothers and 37% to fathers; of the males, 54% to mothers and 28% to fathers. Parents reported considerable family disruption after the initial disclosure. Herdt and Boxer (1993) found that most youths first disclose their orientation to friends, with more males finding this difficult than females. Few received a supportive reaction from families.

HIV/AIDS

Feelings of marginality and conflicts with families have been nearly universal experiences of developing as a LGB person for as long as such themes have been described. The historical anomaly of the HIV/AIDS epidemic adds to these common stressors layers of systemic victimization unknown to LGB people prior to the early 1980s. Issues related to HIV/AIDS are now major normative stressors in the lives of LGB youths, especially males. Sexual identity depends upon sexual behavior; the psychological experience of sexual behavior helps confirms self-identification. Yet for young males who wish to engage in sexual activity with other males, fear of HIV infection can become an overpowering obstacle. Recent studies have documented seroprevalence rates for HIV among young gay men varying from 7% to 12% and unprotected intercourse at rates from 10% to over 40% (Davies et al., 1992; Dean & Meyer, 1995; Lemp et al., 1994; Remafedi, 1994; Rotheram-Borus, Rosario, Meyer-Bahlburg, Koopman, Dopkins, & Davies, 1994; Silvestre et al., 1993; Stall et al., 1992). Hoover et al. (1991) estimate that seronegative 20-year-old gay males have a 20% chance of seroconversion before age 25. Thus, it is a crucial developmental requirement that a young gay or bisexual male know how to negotiate a sexual experience with a new partner. Such a process presumes an advanced level of social skills and well-developed personal assurance, characteristics often lacking in LGB youths who are negotiating complex psychological and social dilemmas.

The burden of feeling that one's sexual orientation puts one at risk for a potentially lethal infection (even though it is one's sexual behavior and drug-using behavior, as well as the serostatuses of one's sexual partners, which literally creates the risk) is but one form of the special stress that HIV/AIDS has superimposed on LGB youth development—a directly experienced pervasive stress. Additional victimization occurs owing to AIDS-related homophobia (Herek & Glunt, 1988).

Bias- and Hate-Motivated Attacks on Lesbian, Gay, and Bisexual Youths

The other primary type of victimization experienced by LGB people are *direct attacks* caused because the attackers know, suspect, or presume that their targets are LGB persons.

Research suggests that young LGB people are often the victims of such assaults (D'Augelli & Dark, 1995; Dean, Wu, & Martin, 1992). Dean et al. (1992) showed that young gay men aged 17–24 in New York were more frequently attacked than older men. Victimization was highest among women aged 17–24 in the National Lesbian and Gay Health Foundation study (Bradford, Ryan, & Rothblum, 1994). Of the entire sample of 1,925, 24% reported that they had been harshly beaten or physically abused while growing up. Among the 17- to 24-year olds, 29% reported physical abuse, 50% reported rape and physical assault, and 18% reported incest. Gross, Aurand, and Addessa (1988) found that 50% of a sample of gay men reported victimization in junior high school and 59% in high school; of lesbians sampled, 12% were victimized in junior high school, and 21% in high school. These findings were corroborated in a later survey (Gross & Aurand, 1992). In a study of New York City LGB youths, 41% had suffered from physical attacks; nearly half of these attacks were provoked by the youths' sexual orientation (Hunter, 1990). LGB youths are more frequently the survivors of childhood physical or sexual abuse than heterosexual youths. In national surveys of victimization, between 19% and 41% of adult lesbians and gay males report family verbal abuse, and between 4% and 7% report family physical abuse (Berrill, 1990). Pilkington and D'Augelli (1995) found that over one-third of their LGB youth sample had been verbally abused by a family member, and 10% Of 1,001 adult gay and bisexual males attending sexually transmitted disease clinics, Doll et al. (1992) found that 37% had been encouraged or forced to have sexual contact (mostly with older men) before age 19. Using the same sample, Barthalow et al. (1994) reported a significant association between earlier sexual abuse and current depression, suicidality, risky sexual behavior, and HIV-positive serostatus. Harry (1989) found that gay males were more likely to be physically abused during adolescence than heterosexual males, especially if they had a history of childhood femininity and poor relationships with their fathers. In comparison to the rates found in these samples, the prevalence estimates for victimization of different kinds in general survey findings are considerably lower (Finkelhor & Dziuba-Leatherman, 1994).

Victimization in the Secondary and High School Setting

Research focusing on the victimization of LGB youths in the school setting has been long overdue. Previous attempts to estimate the nature and extent of harassment and bullying in school have relied upon retrospective data collection techniques where lesbian, gay, and bisexual adults have recounted their experiences to researchers (Berrill, 1990; Gross et al., 1988; Rivers, 1996a). In some cases, more contemporary data have been gathered with the co-operation of community groups and organizations serving LGB youths (Hershberger & D'Augelli, 1995; Pilkington & D'Augelli, 1995; Trenchard & Warren, 1984; Warren, 1984). Although both strategies have been criticized for their methodologies (retrospective studies for their reliance upon the accuracy of participants' memories; and community studies for the biases inherent to their samples [see Muehrer, 1995; Savin-Williams, 1994]), such research provides valuable insight into the experiences and repercussions of victimization within the education system.

One of the first projects to address the issues surrounding LGB youths in secondary school was conducted in the United Kingdom by Trenchard and

Warren in 1984. Overall, 416 young lesbians and gay males completed detailed questionnaires about their experiences at school. Of the entire sample, 39% (164) had experienced some form of bullying or pressure to conform. When these figures were broken down further according to types of bullying or harassment, of the 154 who had specified the exact nature of such experiences, 21% reported having been verbally abused, 13% had been teased, 12% said they had been beaten up, 7% had been ostracized by their peers, and a further 7% said they had been pressurized to change (Warren 1984). In the United States, comparable studies of the school experiences of lesbians and gay men illustrate that homophobic victimization can begin very early in a person's educational career. For example, Gross et al. (1988) found that 50 percent of the gay men and 12 percent of the lesbians surveyed in Philadelphia and in the state of Pennsylvania had been victimized in junior high school, rising to 59% for gay men and 21% for lesbians in high school. According to Berrill (1990), estimates of the extent of school-based victimization for young lesbians and gay men in the United States range from 33% to 49%. Pilkington and D'Augelli (1995) have reported that, of the 194 LGB youths they surveyed (aged 15–21 years), 30% of the males and 35% of the females had experienced some form of harassment or verbal abuse in school, and that this had an effect on their degree of openness about their sexual orientation. Using a representative sample of Massachusetts high school students comparing LGB-identified youths with other youths, Garofalo, Wolf, Kessel, Palfrey, and DuRant (1998) found that one-quarter of the LGB youths said they missed school within the last month because of fear compared to 5% of the non-LGB youths. This finding reflects other differences experienced by the LGB youths compared to their heterosexual peers. Of the LGB youths, one-third said they had been threatened with a weapon at school compared to 7% of the other youths. More than one-third (38%) of the LGB youths were involved with fighting at school, in contrast to 14% of the other students. And half of the LGB youths reported property damage at school compared to 29% of the other youths.

LGB youths clearly undergo victimization at the hands of peers, but they also have few sources of support from teachers and administrators. Warren (1984) observed that when students had disclosed their sexual orientation to teachers in the hope of enlisting their aid, very little help was offered. One young man recalled being told by a teacher that he might be expelled from school if his sexual orientation became public knowledge, and was then asked if he had been dropped on his head as a baby. Rivers (1995a) recounts the story of a 16-year-old male who was "outed" by his teacher in the classroom with the words, "Well, we all know what Matthew is, don't we? He's a homosexual" (p. 47). Such experiences only reinforce the belief of many LGB youths that asking teachers or school counselors for help is futile and can sometimes make matters worse. Pilkington and D'Augelli (1995) found that 7% of the LGB youths in their study reported being hurt by teachers because of the youths' sexual orientation. In that study, over one-quarter said that fear of being physically harmed by peers or teachers influenced their openness about themselves in school settings, and one-third reported fear of verbal harassment as an inhibitor.

Results from a recent study of the long-term impact of peer victimization in school show that the types of behavior remembered by 190 LGB adults (mean age 29 years) were even more varied than had been previously reported in school research (Rivers, 1999). Like many of the studies quoted above, the most common form of harassment was found to be name-calling and labeling (82%); however, participants also recalled being ridiculed openly by other students and by teachers (71%). In addition, 60% reported being hit or kicked by other students regularly, and 59% recalled having rumors spread about them. Other methods of intimidation including teasing (58%); theft (49%); being stared at constantly in class (52%), and being isolated (27%). In a few cases, participants reported being sexually assaulted or raped (11%). Perhaps one of the most worrying aspects about these findings is that not all of the methods of intimidation would be identified by parents and teachers as victimization and, as a result, youths may not have been taken seriously. It is worth remembering that harassment and bullying in schools (including anti-lesbian/gay victimization) is often perceived to be nothing more than "a rite of passage," or, in some cases, an initiation into the subculture of the school where victims learn their places within the social hierarchy. There are, as well, many forms of psychological and physical harassment that would not be observed by teachers and other authorities. The fact that something as innocuous as a look or stare could have a frightening effect was described by Aaron Fricke in his autobiography *Confessions of a Rock Lobster* when he described his persecutor's look as "an uninterrupted gaze that could melt steel" (Fricke, 1981, p. 29). In such an environment, it comes as no surprise that LGB youths describe feeling helpless and isolated at school, and this feeling is made all the more acute in cases where the subjective and often nonverbal nature of victimization results in the school becoming a painful setting rather than one that provides respite from victimization (Rivers, 1995a).

In cases where reports of harassment involve violent attack or sexual assault, it should cease to be an internal matter for the school, and law enforcement officials should become involved. However, some schools are unwilling to bring in outside agencies in cases of violent or sexual assault, preferring to deal with them as internal matters. Where this occurs, LGB youths are often encouraged to conform to avoid attack. Some of the difficulties LGB youths face in school are illustrated by the following extract. This youth describes his final years in compulsory education as being schooled "in the company of wolves":

> On the first day at my new high school I was full of a kind of optimistic trepidation. I was very pleased that I had got this far, and I was happy to be surrounded by boys and girls who seemed just like me. Later in the first year I realized I was homosexual, and I soon came to terms with it and in a way I

was glad I was a little different from the rest—the others were all the same, but I was the one who stood out in the crowd. It [the bullying] started one morning after assembly. A boy in the same year group as me yelled out the word "poofter" and, like a fool, I looked around. From that moment on, I was the subject of beatings, verbal abuse and so-called "queer bashing." I received torrents of verbal abuse and I had things stolen from me not just by other boys, but also by girls. There was no way around it, I was punished for being gay.

The injuries I received were numerous: I had my left arm broken (the bullies said that I was lucky it wasn't my right arm); I was held down while cigarettes were stubbed out on the back of my neck; and I was kicked repeatedly by both boys and girls even when a teacher was nearby. One teacher told me that my problems were my own fault because I refused to deny my sexuality. In retaliation I told him that G.A.Y. stood for "Good As You." I then got detention for insolence.

In this situation, the school failed to act appropriately in stopping a series of violent assaults. However, there have also been cases where schools have failed to report cases of rape or violent sexual assault to police because of the victim's sexual orientation (Rivers, 1996b). In such cases, the perpetrator of the assault is able to break the law without fear of prosecution. This view is supported by Pilkington and D'Augelli (1995), who found that of the 79% of lesbian, gay, and bisexual youths who said they did not report at least one incident of victimization to the authorities, 32% said they had minimalized the experience, 32% feared the embarrassment associated with disclosure of the victimization, 29% felt helpless believing that the authorities would not act, and 8% said they did not know they could report such incidents. This perception of helplessness is not just confined to those who have experienced abuse; without change, it is likely to continue with each new generation of LGB youths.

Victimization at Home

Having a child who is lesbian, gay, or bisexual presents many parents with a number of concerns and dilemmas. In contemporary society, the perception of being gay or bisexual is linked to a fear of HIV/AIDS (Frankham, 1996; Lovell, 1995). When parents find out that their child is lesbian, gay, or bisexual, they must reappraise their own relationships with others: their own parents, partners, their other children, friends and colleagues at work (Lovell, 1995). Coming out to a parent is a significant step in the development of young lesbians, gay men, and bisexual men and women (Savin-Williams, 1998). Not only is it filled with fear of rejection (Borhek, 1988; Cramer & Roach, 1988; Kahn, 1991), disclosure to a parent also marks a turning point in a young person's identity as she or he sheds heterosexual identity and takes up a new, homosexual identity (D'Augelli, 1994). According to Borhek (1988), parents' reactions to the knowledge that their child is lesbian, gay, or bisexual can be mediated by issues such as a lack of information about homosexuality, religious beliefs, and of course homophobia. Furthermore, the perpetuation of popular myths about lesbian, gay, and bisexual lives reinforces perceptions of unnaturalness, and many parents find the knowledge that their child is LGB difficult to cope with.

Thus, the home is often not a safe haven for LGB youths if they tell their families about themselves or if their sexual orientation becomes known. Many parents believe that they have caused their offspring's sexual orientation, a belief that puts the family and the youth in an irresolvable conflict that may lead to estrangement and violence (Hunter & Schaecher, 1987). For many youths, family religious commitments set the stage for rejections of different kinds, ranging from a begrudging acknowledgment to a forceful ejection from the household. In studies of anti-lesbian/gay abuse by relatives, reports indicate that between 19% and 41% of respondents had experienced verbal insults or threats, and 4%–7% had encountered physical violence (Herek & Berrill, 1992). In a study of lesbian and gay youths at a social service agency in New York dedicated to their needs, Hunter (1990) found that 61% of the violence youths reported as related to sexual orientation had occurred in the family. One-quarter said that fear of victimization at home affected their openness about their orientation. The particular family members (e.g., mothers, fathers, siblings, extended family members) who attack LGB youths have not been carefully studied. The National Lesbian and Gay Health Foundation survey (1987) indicated that 70% of all women beaten or abused as children were attacked by unspecified male relatives and 45% by female relatives; of those women raped or sexually attacked as children, 31% were male relatives and 45% were other known males; and of those who ever experienced incest (19% of the total sample), 34% were brothers, 28% were fathers, 27% were uncles, and 18% were cousins.

In their survey of LGB youths, Pilkington and D'Augelli (1995) addressed the issue of victimization in the home. They found that 36% of participants had been insulted by at least one member of their immediate family because of their sexual orientation. When they examined the types of abuse that took place in the home, they found that 22% of young women and 14% of young men had been verbally insulted and significantly more young women than young men had been physically assaulted by a family member (18% and 8%, respectively). When participants were asked about the perpetrators of verbal abuse, the general finding was that mothers (22%) were more abusive than fathers (14%), brothers (16%), or sisters (9%). However, it is worth noting that mothers were also more protective of their LGB children (25%) than fathers (13%), brothers (11%), and sisters (10%). An analysis of youths in this project who resided with their families demonstrated that youths who do not disclose to their families successfully escape victimization by family members (D'Augelli, Hershberger, & Pilkington, 1998). The nondisclosed youths who live at home predicted significantly more negative reactions from their families compared to those who had already disclosed, suggesting that fear of familial victimization is a strong deterrent to telling families.

These results indicate that, contrary to the popular stereotype, fathers may react less negatively to their child's homosexuality than mothers or brothers. Cramer and Roach (1988) found that 21% of the gay men who participated in their study said that their relationships with their fathers improved following disclosure of their sexual orientation. In fact, research suggests that pressure to conform from within the family is greater for lesbians than for gay males, and proportionally more young lesbians contemplate or attempt suicide as a result of their unhappiness (Herdt & Boxer, 1993). In her analysis of the factors affecting the coming out process for lesbians, Kahn (1991) has argued that perceived parental intolerance may in fact interfere with personal development and increase the likelihood of internalized homophobia.

As much of the research focusing on the coming-out process in LGB youths relates to the effect it has upon the individual who is coming out, very little attention has been given to the effect disclosure has on family, friends, or other associates. Yet it is clear that disclosure of sexual orientation affects the entire family, as well as the family's social network. In essence, when one member of the family comes out, the whole family also comes out and must deal with reactions that follow. This point was illustrated by Troix Bettencourt, former leader of a Boston youth coalition, who recalled the aftermath of a speech he had made at a Gay Pride event one year:

> Once people in my hometown who might of heard my name somewhere connected the face with the name, things just skyrocketed. Rumors started flying. People at my mother's work started approaching my parents, saying, "How could your son be gay? It's disgraceful. What kind of parents are you? How could you let him do this?" My friends had people saying things to them like, "Are you gay, too? How can you be friends with him? That's sick." (Bettencourt, 1995, pp. 230–231)

Even when parents say that they have accepted their child's homosexuality, the comments and pressure brought about by members of the extended family, friends, and colleagues can sometimes result in conflict. A son's or daughter's sexual orientation can become an issue in the most unlikely of arguments between parents or between parent and child. As Bettencourt recalled, the argument that led to his being thrown out of his parents' home was actually between his parents and had not involved him initially. However, as he says, "My name came up, and the argument escalated and exploded" (Bettencourt, 1995, p. 231). Bettencourt was fortunate in that he was able to stay at a friend's apartment after his mother had thrown him out. Other LGB youths find themselves homeless. According to Kruks (1991), many of the young LGB people who live on the streets and engage in commercial sex have either been expelled from their homes or been the victims of homophobic abuse and ridicule. They run away from home hoping to find acceptance in metropolitan areas; however, many find only homelessness, exploitation, and despair. Kruks (1991) noted that the rate of attempted suicide among the LGB homeless youths in his study was far higher (53%) than the rate for street youths in general (32%).

In the United Kingdom, very little information is available concerning LGB homeless youths, although one organization, the Albert Kennedy Trust, has been supporting such youths since 1989. The Trust was set up following the death of Albert Kennedy, a 16-year-old boy from Manchester who fell to his death while trying to escape a group of "queerbashers." Young people who come into contact with the Trust have a range of different experiences. Some have left home because they have been rejected by their parents, while others (like Albert Kennedy) have run away from hostels or homes to escape discrimination and abuse. In some cases, young people have voluntarily left their family home to avoid rejection and conflict.

Victimization in the Community

In the pilot study for a project focusing on the long-term consequences of peer victimization in school for LGB adults, Rivers (1995c) found that most participants also recalled being bullied outside the school on the way home, on the school bus, or in shopping malls. Although attitudes toward homosexuality seem to be gradually improving, it is clear that young LGB people continue to experience rejection and ridicule because of their sexual orientation. The fear of what might happen if a young person's homosexuality or bisexuality becomes known generally was demonstrated by Pilkington and D'Augelli (1995). They found that 96% of LGB youths with work experience had hidden their sexual orientation for fear of reprisal, and that 27% feared losing their job if their sexual orientation were revealed at work. On a daily basis, they found that 46% admitted altering their behavior to avoid being victimized, with 73% of females and 55% of males reporting trying to act "straight" in public. In addition, 31% of males and 20% of females deliberately avoided locations or situations where they felt vulnerable or could be identified as being gay (e.g., gay clubs and neighborhoods). In a qualitative study conducted in the United Kingdom, Frankham (1996) also found that some of the gay men interviewed had attempted to change their behavior in order to "fit in" with peers:

> I could put on the act and not appear camp or gay, and just appear to be one of everybody else. And talk about girls, and all the rest of it, which I didn't particularly like but I had to do it at the time to stay in with them and not be shoved out. You had to put on the act at the time, especially in a school like that, so people would accept you. (Frankham, 1996, p. 17)

Others describe the difficulties they had in coming to terms with their sexual orientation because they had been told it was wrong and because they had been brought up to believe they would settle down with a woman, marry, and have children. As one young man states: "I had a basic awareness that being gay was wrong. I didn't know what gay was, you know, it's just a *word*, like murderer or something like that. It didn't have a picture with it, if you like. So it was something that I definitely *wasn't*. None of it could be applicable to me" (Frankham, 1996, p. 7).

The lack of positive lesbian and gay images presented in schools and, indeed, in the wider culture, has had a significant effect upon the social acceptability of homosexuality (Slater, 1988). Both Davies (1996) and Rothblum (1990) suggest that the lack of positive lesbian and gay role models has a negative impact upon feelings of self-worth among LGB youths. Furthermore, the portrayal of homosexuality as amoral or sinful not only reinforces the need to hide from society but also continues to prompt some young people to seek counseling, psychotherapy, or religious guidance in an attempt to change their sexual orientation (Davies & Neal, 1996).

When Pilkington and D'Augelli (1995) examined the degree to which LGB youths disclosed their sexual orientation in public, they found that 52% had hidden their sexuality when they came into contact with a police officer, 38% with a doctor/nurse or dentist, 33% with a lawyer, 31% with a sales clerk, 27% with a counselor and 27% with a waiter/waitress. They also found that white youths were more likely to hide their sexual orientation (57%) than youths of color (41%). In contrast, the number of youths who had actually experienced homophobic abuse from those working in the community was surprisingly low: only 4% of those who had come into contact with police officers reported being hurt by them; 4% had also been hurt by counselors; 3% had been hurt by the reactions of sales clerks, and 2% by the reactions of waiters/waitresses. Only 1% reported a negative reaction on the part of doctors, nurses, or dentists, and no one had been hurt by a lawyer.

The Effects of Victimization

In the last two decades there has been an increasing recognition that the many forms of psychological and physical victimization that occur in school settings can have a devastating effect upon the well-being of youths, and can have detrimental effects upon their parents and siblings as well (Olweus, 1993; Smith & Sharp, 1994). Increasingly, researchers have suggested that victimization and alienation during childhood and adolescence can be associated with mental health problems for lesbian, gay, and bisexual adults (Buhrich & Loke, 1988; Gonsiorek, 1988; Remafedi, Farrow & Deisher, 1991; Rivers, 1995d, in press; Rothblum, 1990; Shaffer, Fisher, Hicks, Parides, & Gould, 1995; Shidlo, 1994). Rivers (1995b) argues that LGB youths who experience considerable peer victimization at school are at a particular risk for suicidal and parasuicidal behaviors in later years. This point is reinforced by Hershberger and D'Augelli (1995) in their study of the impact of victimization upon the mental health and suicidality of LGB youths. Overall, they found that 42% of their sample reported a past suicide attempt, and that only 40% had never considered suicide as an option. In a study conducted in the

United Kingdom, the rates for self-harming behavior and/or attempted suicide among LGB adults who were victimized at school were found to be comparable to Hershberger and D'Augelli's results (Rivers, 1999). Overall, 52% of the total sample reported having contemplated self-harm or suicide as a consequence of repeated victimization while 40% of the total sample said they had made an attempt on at least one occasion. In addition, three-quarters of those reporting an attempt made more than one attempt. For some, the feelings of wanting to escape from life can become stronger after leaving school, as can be seen in this reflection of a 30-year-old gay man in Rivers's (1999) study:

> The strongest feeling I think was not to physically hurt myself. The feeling of wanting to disappear was stronger. There were the odd times when you felt like just closing the door, and just ending it all. I think the feelings have been stronger to do away with my own life since leaving school. . . . I have to take a grip of those [feelings] and say, "What's going on?" That is to do with my own sexuality and coming to terms with it. That may be a weakness in my character, in me. I don't think I'll ever carry them out, but they are there.

Although Hershberger and D'Augelli (1995) did not find a direct link between suicidal ideation and victimization, they note that even those youths who receive a great deal of support from their families and have a high level of self-esteem experience some mental health problems. Rivers (1999) compared the responses of former victims of school-based homophobia who had attempted to take their own lives with those who had not. Significant differences were found between the groups in terms of the total number of sexual partners recalled, with those who had attempted suicide reporting more than three times the number of sexual partners compared to those who had not. Significant differences were also found in terms of levels of anxiety and symptoms associated with post-traumatic stress disorder.

One of the most striking findings in the Rivers (1999) study is the significantly more sexual partners reported by young adults victimized at school. Other research suggests that low levels of self-esteem and feelings of worthlessness (exemplified by measures of internalized homophobia) in lesbians and gay men are correlated with difficulties in the formation of intimate or affectional relationships (Friedman, 1991; George & Behrendt, 1988); unsafe sexual practices (Shidlo, 1994); and avoidant coping strategies with AIDS among HIV seropositive gay men (Nicholson & Long, 1990). Comparison may also be made with research that focuses on heterosexual women who have experienced sexual abuse and rape in childhood and, subsequently, in adulthood. Wyatt, Guthrie, and Notgrass (1992) found that the women who were childhood victims of sexual abuse were likely to have a history of brief sexual relationships and multiple partnerships; they were also more likely to engage in high-risk sexual behaviors and avoided barrier contraception. Gilmartin (1987) reports that none of the heterosexual men who had been victimized by peers in school had a meaningful intimate relationship with a woman, and that the older men in his study (aged 35–50 years) had experienced fewer, if any, close relationships with women than a comparative group of younger men (aged 19–24 years), and that both groups also had had significantly fewer nonsexual relationships than heterosexual single men not bullied in school. Based on these findings, it seems feasible to expect fewer satisfactory social and intimate relationships among LGB youths victimized in school compared to youths who had not been victimized.

Intervention Strategies to Reduce Victimization

The development of approaches that would diminish the common life stressors experienced of LGB youth must be consonant with the core paradox of LGB identity development: that candidness about sexual orientation leads to crucial benefits as well as serious risks. Telling parents, siblings, extended family members, peers, teachers, and so on is difficult in its many practical details, even for adults with supportive resources to call upon. The most effective strategy for preventing mental health problems in this population emphasizes changes in others' attitudes and reactions. Effective approaches must target heterosexism, homophobia, and harassment in the social ecologies of LGB youths. A comprehensive approach to the prevention of heterosexism must operate at several levels: it must address current problems of youths and forestall further deterioration (tertiary prevention); it must specify which LGB youths may be at special risk and address their particular circumstances (secondary prevention); and, finally, it must be poised to create circumstances that prevent the development of heterosexism in the first place (primary prevention). Primary prevention of heterosexism should be the ultimate goal.

   D'Augelli (1993) has written elsewhere that the prevention of mental health problems in LGB youth calls for four strategies: affirmative services development, the development of safe settings, curriculum integration in educational settings, and policy review/legal protection. Ways to implement these general strategies will be briefly discussed below.

Affirmative Services Development

Counseling and mental health services are crucial resources for lesbian, gay, and bisexual youth, given the developmental challenges they face and the years of confusion and conflict they experience. Many of their situations call for professional attention and cannot be adequately addressed by reliance on peer support. Many metropolitan areas in the United States have LGB human services centers that provide professional help, but schools and other mental health/counseling systems must also be prepared to assist LGB youth and their families. To be effective, services must be perceived by the informal community of LGB youths as accessible and helpful; the reputation of an unresponsive system spreads very quickly. Assurance that staff do not display outright homophobia or heterosexism is a necessary but insufficient step. Services must be affirmative; the presence of open LGB staff is evidence of institutional commitment. Just adding an open staff member will not be sufficient; it is necessary that staff participate in experiences that present contemporary views of sexual orientation, and be trained in affirmative modes of helping. Although professional staff may feel capable of seeing LGB youth in their work, training is required for heterosexually oriented staff (Garnets, Hancock, Cochran, Goodchilds, & Peplau, 1991; Graham, Rawlings, Halpern, & Hermes, 1984; Holahan & Gibson, 1994; Ryan, this volume).

In addition to providing unbiased and affirmative counseling, schools (both secondary schools and colleges and universities) should take the initiative in outreach to the LGB youth population. The subpopulations within this large group of young people need specialized programs. For those who are closeted or uncertain of their sexual orientation, general public lectures on human sexuality and sexual orientation are an important method for outreach. Closeted youths are the largest group; they are the neediest and the hardest to reach. An option for such youth is a telephone help-line, which can assure anonymity. Another enormous group are those who have taken some steps to come out to others; this "questioning" group may not consider themselves LGB. For this group, the most useful approach is a support/discussion group with other youth who are clear about their sexual orientation and those who are exploring. Schools and community centers should have semester-long coming-out support groups, given the complex nature of the processes involved. LGB youths can be trained as facilitators and should be supervised by staff. Peer facilitation is most effective; over time, the center can develop a cadre of trained facilitators to meet an increasing need. Finally, a whole array of specialized support groups and educational workshops must be developed. The highest priority should be given to coping with disclosure to family and others, dating and intimacy, and avoiding HIV infection. But attention to vocational development is crucial as well. Clearly, the scope of issues involved is considerable and the need for liaison to the local LGB communities obvious. Because of the demands involved, it is recommended that a staff coordinator of LGB youth services be appointed at local LGB community centers. Within schools, it is useful to assign a professional staff member the responsibility for LGB youth program development.

The Development of Safe Settings

The accumulated evidence of the impact of heterosexism and homophobia provides a strong case for the need to assure "safe spaces" for LGB youths. Much of the victimization of LGB youths takes place in schools, and it may be unrealistic for schools to guarantee privacy and safety; nonetheless, it is important to enhance the school climate for LGB youths. School policies about intolerance and harassment must be inclusive of sexual orientation.

Teachers and other staff must be trained in issues related to sexual orientation, and they must be made aware of their special role in creating a social climate in which expression of anti-lesbian and anti-gay views is unacceptable. LGB youths must be assured that their living spaces are free of harassment and victimization. The problems of persistent victimization of LGB youths in school settings led to the creation of specific high schools dedicated to serving LGB youths, such as the Harvey Milk High School in New York City and the EAGLES Center in California (Battey, 1995). The critical need for safety also led to the development of Project 10 (Uribe & Harbeck, 1992), a high school-based program that provides discussion, support, and advocacy. Since its inception and piloting, many other schools in the United States and Canada have used the Project 10 model. According to Uribe (1983/84), a Project 10–type intervention must consist of eight elements: (1) a district resource center; (2) a paid coordinator for the program; (3) a series of ongoing workshops to train school counselors, teachers, and other members of staff on the needs of lesbian and gay students, and how to tackle institutional homophobia; (4) the development of school based teams to whom students can go for information, advice and support; (5) assistance in expanding library resources to incorporate fiction and nonfiction on lesbian and gay subjects; (6) the enforcement of behavioral codes in school, anti-slur resolutions and nondiscriminatory clauses; (7) support for lesbian, gay, and bisexual rights through commissions, task forces, PTA's and research programs; and (8) networking within the community to open a dialogue with parents, teachers, welfare agencies, educational organizations, and teachers' unions.

In addition to within-school programs such as Project 10 and alternative high schools such as the Harvey Milk School, there has been an exponential growth of community-based LGB youth programs, most of which combine social and recreational opportunities with support and informal counseling. There are as well entire formal human service agencies that provide assistance to LGB youths, with services ranging from counseling to residential care (Mallon, 1992). For most youths, informal programs in community settings are the most appropriate and accessible form of support. Such programs have been expanding rapidly, with most cities and many suburban areas having LGB social, recreational, and support activities (see Gerstel, Feraios, & Herdt, 1989; Singerline, 1994).

Other safe spaces are needed as well. Most college and university campuses have an association or organization for LGB students, and many have a LGB student affairs officer. These groups have historically met all the needs of LGB students because counseling centers and campus housing personnel have paid little attention to the problems of lesbian and gay students until very recently. LGB student organizations play a pivotal role in preventing mental health problems, since they will likely be the only organized groups that most students will access. Much informal counseling and crisis intervention occurs in these organizations. Because of their critical role in mental health prevention, it is important that the LGB student organizations be supported. The administration should provide resources for programs and must allocate adequate meeting space. A large, comfortable office, for instance, is particularly important, since many closeted students will take their first "baby step" out of the closet by stopping by or calling the office of a student organization. This "safe space" literally represents a lifeline for many youth, so it is important that it be accessible. More campuses are supplementing the operations of student organizations with professionally staffed centers for LGB students—units that can engage in a wide variety of support and educational functions for LGB students as well as for others on campus. Given the many years of isolation that LGB youth experience, such a center can be a powerful preventive intervention. Such centers can spearhead the enormous task of addressing the climate for heterosexism on campuses, a role that is legitimately fulfilled by administrative staff, not students. A center can also advocate for administrative and policy changes, which can indirectly prevent heterosexism.

Curriculum Integration

Lesbians, gay, and bisexual people are a hidden population in the curriculum, even in higher education (D'Augelli, 1991). In secondary schools, little material about lesbians and gay men is included in classes, even if it is relevant. For example, few history classes address the gay/lesbian rights movement. Few literature classes mention the sexual orientation of many of the authors covered, so they are presumed to be heterosexual. The only explicit mention of gay men occurs in AIDS education programs, and the message may be a destructive one for LGB youth and a seriously misleading one for heterosexual students. Indeed, this situation may perpetuate the stereotypes that provide the foundation for biases and victimization. Considerable impact on school climate can be affected if teachers include informative discussions of sexual orientation in relevant courses. Such efforts not only help the many LGB youth in these classes (who, perhaps for the first time, find their lives addressed) but also educate heterosexually identified students and help them modify heterosexist assumptions. These events also provide an opportunity for teachers and others to communicate to all students that heterosexism is unacceptable. As more and more schools strive to address issues of diversity, it is crucial that sexual orientation be included (Jennings, 1994; Lipkin, 1993/94). It should be remembered that such inclusiveness will be highly controversial for some segments of the local community.

There are increasing resources for teachers, governors, and parents dealing with homosexuality. One example of the resource materials currently available in the United States comes from the Harvard Graduate School of Education's Gay and Lesbian High School Curriculum and Staff Development Project (Lipkin, 1993/94). The project has produced a series of leaflets and manuals to help those developing a positive lesbian and gay curriculum. The series includes: (1) a staff development manual for anti-homophobia education in secondary schools; (2) strategies for teachers using lesbian and gay related materials in the high school classroom; (3) an 8- to 10-day social studies unit focusing on the Stonewall riots and the history of lesbians and gay men in the United States; (4) a 3- to 5-day unit focusing on current theories surrounding the origins of homosexuality; (5) a pack of study questions focusing on lesbian and gay literature; (6) two reading lists covering gay authors and coming out; (7) a copy of an article for teachers, school administrators, and parents advocating the development of a lesbian and gay curriculum; and (8) an annotated bibliography of literature and resources.

In the United Kingdom, homosexuality remains a controversial and complicated issue within school education. Prior to the introduction of Section 28 of the 1988 Local Government Act, which prohibits the "promotion" of homosexuality by county and borough councils (and their officers), discussions of lesbian, gay, and bisexual people concerning homosexuality had been a feature of the sex education curriculum in a number of schools. However, with the introduction of Section 28, local authorities and the schools understood that homosexuality was not to be represented in a positive manner. Since the introduction of the 1988 Local Government Act, a number of changes have occurred within the education system that have resulted in several schools "opting out" of local government control. Although this has meant, in effect, that Section 28 does not apply to those schools, other educational directives have ensured that a discussion of homosexuality and bisexuality has remained outside the national curriculum. In accordance with Section 241 of the Education Act of 1993, schools in England and Wales now have the power to determine their own policy on sex education. In the case of maintained primary schools, governors have been given the responsibility for deciding whether or not sex education should be included in the curriculum and, if it is included, at what level pupils should receive it. On the other hand, maintained secondary schools are required, by law, to provide sex education for all registered pupils and make their policy known to parents who have also been given the right to withdraw their children from all or part of the sex education program (including the discussion of HIV and AIDS).

Despite the confusion surrounding the discussion of homosexuality in schools in the United Kingdom (Scotland and Northern Ireland each have their own educational system), a number of resource packages have been developed dealing with LGB issues and HIV/AIDS discrimination. One of the first resource packs was produced by the National Union of Teachers (NUT) in conjunction with the City of Leicester Teachers' Association. It sets out the legal implications of Section 28 and describes ways in which teachers could address LGB issues in schools. It defines homophobia and heterosexism and offers advice to teachers on how to teach about sexual orientation. In addition, it uses case study material to illustrate the experiences of LGB students and teachers in schools, and gives an annotated bibliography of literature and audiovisual material for use in the classroom (NUT/City of Leicester Teachers' Association, 1989). More recently, the Camden and Islington Health Authority launched a resources pack for teachers, governors, parents, and care workers called, *Colours of The Rainbow: Exploring Issues of Sexuality and Difference* (Mole, 1995). This pack introduces the concept of difference at a very early age and focuses on concepts such as feeling good about oneself and others, feeling different, variations in human sexuality, and homophobia and its effects.

Many popular concerns relating to the discussion of homosexuality and bisexuality in the classroom are not always reflected in the attitudes of parents. Indeed, in the United Kingdom, the Health Education Authority (1994) found that only one of every eight parents surveyed would consider withdrawing children from classes in which sexual orientation is discussed or where such as discussion was believed to be inappropriate for the age of the students. Overall, the survey revealed that 85% of parents believed that secondary education (11–16 years in the U.K.) has an important role in teaching young people about HIV/AIDS, and 56% believed that a discussion of sexual orientation should be included. However, developing a policy concerning the discussion of sexual orientation and bisexuality and enacting it through the curriculum is not an easy task, especially where there is little support from central or local government. For many school administrators, the easiest solution is to ignore the topic and to introduce a traditional sex education program that focuses only on hygiene, physical growth, parenthood, and childbirth.

In New South Wales, Australia, the inclusion of homophobia into antibullying/harassment initiatives in schools was a significant step forward in ensuring that all young people are educated in a safe and nurturing environment where they learn nonviolent ways of relating and, most important, they learn to appreciate and value difference. Materials such as *Resources for Teaching Against Violence* (NSW Department of School Education, 1996) help students deal with their prejudices as well as prejudices of others through a structured program using video, role play, and worksheets, and by inviting a panel of lesbian and gay speakers into the classroom (where this is not possible an audio tape of a panel interview that is provided can be used). These materials undoubtedly lead the way in challenging the victimization of LGB people, not only within the school environment but also in the local community. Certainly written materials do not constitute an effective intervention and are inadequate in addressing the social climate of a school if it is strongly homophobic. However, modification of the school climate in this regard is the most important goal, and this requires a coordinated effort of school administrators, teachers, coaches, parents, and community leaders dedicated to making schools safe for all youths.

Policy Review and Legal Protection

Educational settings contribute to the way LGB youth are perceived by the nature of their formal policies, especially those that define harassment or intolerance and those that prohibit discrimination in employment and access to services. By including sexual orientation in policy statements institutions break the pattern of denying that LGB people exist. Statement that neither harassment nor discrimination based on sexual orientation will be tolerated conveys the idea that LGB people are part of the community at large. Such statements demand institutional mechanisms for implementation, resulting in direct prevention of victimization and its consequences. In addition to policies about harassment, the overall institutional policy concerning discrimination must include sexual orientation. Without formal protection, LGB faculty or staff can be removed from their jobs without cause. Many of the other suggestions made earlier depend on actions that could be compromised if simple protection from discrimination for employees is not provided. Counseling staff, for example, may hesitate to suggest programs for LGB youth because they fear reprisals. Staff in athletic programs may be hesitant to be "too" supportive since this not only may bring suspicions upon them but also risk career advancement. This aspect of human diversity is least protected by federal, state, and local law. Few institutions include sexual orientation among "protected classes" in prohibiting discrimination. Without formal protection in policy, efforts to develop programs to prevent problems among this population will be jeopardized by fear and hesitancy, much of which may be justifiable. The efforts suggested above cannot be undertaken if professionals are unable to assume leadership roles without fear. Disinhibiting professionals with responsibilities for youth development from helping LGB youth is a crucial step in breaking the cycle of invisibility.

Intervention has not just occurred at the level of individual school or district but also at a state level. In Massachusetts, the passing of House Bill 3353, which incorporates issues of sexual orientation into existing antidiscriminatory legislation, means that young people who identify themselves as lesbian, gay, or bisexual are now protected in public schools (Deitcher, 1995). Although the passing of the bill is a significant step forward in tackling homophobia, its success is marred by decisions in other states to exclude or ignore the issue of homosexuality. For example, in 1995 a school board in New Hampshire passed a regulation forbidding the mention of homosexuality in a favorable light and banned the referral of students to affirmative counseling. In the summer of that year, again in New Hampshire, a teacher was dismissed when she refused to stop teaching from gay books that had been previously approved by the school's administration. More recently, researchers have been following developments in Utah, where a bill was passed that bans all high school clubs in an attempt to deter the creation of alliances of LGB youths and heterosexuals.

Another statutory advance occurred In New South Wales (NSW), Australia, where discrimination on the basis of sexual orientation has been illegal since 1977. For the past several years, the state government has actively sought to curb discrimination on the grounds of sexuality in schools and has produced a number of resource materials to assist teachers and school psychologists counter homophobia and heterosexism (NSW Department of School Education, 1991, 1994, 1996).

Conclusion

From the moment a young person recognizes that she or he may be lesbian, gay, or bisexual, so too comes the realization that she or he will have to hide that sexual orientation from friends, family, and others in the community to avoid victimization. For those LGB youths who come out, not only do they have to contend with the fear of negative parental and peer reactions but they also have face isolation, humiliation, and harassment at school. Schools and community organizations have a valuable role to play in supporting LGB youths and their parents. Teachers, coaches, school counselors, and administrators can work together to ensure that victimization of LGB youths in schools becomes a thing of the past. Currently, many of the initiatives that deal with homophobia are palliative. However, in the long term, only by introducing sexual orientation issues into the educational process and by institutionalizing protections against discrimination and violence will all students grow up appreciating diversity and difference within their schools, their communities, and in society.

References

Albert Kennedy Trust. (1995). *General information guide*. Manchester: Author.

American Association of University Women. (1993). *Hostile hallways: The AAUW survey on sexual harassment in America's schools*. Washington, DC: Author.

American Psychiatric Association. (1994). *Diagnostic and statistical manual of mental disorders* (4th ed). Washington, DC: Author.

Barthalow, B. N., Doll, L. S., Joy, D., Douglas, J. M., Bolan, G., Harrison, J. S., Moss, P. M., & McKirnan, D. (1994). Emotional, behavioral, and HIV risks associated with sexual abuse among homosexual and bisexual men. *Child Abuse and Neglect, 18*, 747–761.

Battey, J. (1995). In their own words. In D. Deitcher (Ed.), *Over the rainbow: Lesbian and gay politics in America since Stonewall* (pp. 223–224). London: Boxtree.

Berrill, K. T. (1990). Anti-gay violence and victimization in the United States: An overview. *Journal of Interpersonal Violence, 5*, 274–294.

Bettencourt, T. (1995). In their own words. In D. Deitcher (Ed), *Over the rainbow: Lesbian and gay politics in America since Stonewall* (pp. 227–233). London: Boxtree.

Borhek, M. V. (1988). Helping gay and lesbian adolescents and their families: A mother's perspective. *Journal of Adolescent Health Care, 9*(2), 123–128.

Boxer, A. M., Cook, J. A., & Herdt, G. (1991). Double jeopardy: Identity transitions and parent-child relations among gay and lesbian youth. In K. Pillemer & K. McCartney (Eds.), *Parent-child relations throughout life* (pp. 59–92). Hillsdale, NJ: Erlbaum.

Bradford, J., Ryan, C., & Rothblum, E. D. (1994). National Lesbian Health Care Survey: Implications for mental health care. *Journal of Consulting and Clinical Psychology, 62*, 228–242.

Buhrich, N., & Loke, C. (1988). Homosexuality, suicide, and parasuicide in Australia. *Journal of Homosexuality, 15*, 113–129.

Cramer, D. W., & Roach, A. J. (1988). Coming out to Mom and Dad: A study of gay males and their relationships with their parents. *Journal of Homosexuality, 15*(3/4), 79–91.

D'Augelli, A. R. (1991). Lesbians and gay men on campus: Visibility, empowerment, and educational leadership. *Peabody Journal of Education, 66*, 124–142.

D'Augelli, A. R. (1993). Preventing mental health problems among lesbian and gay college students. *Journal of Primary Prevention, 13*(4), 1–17.

D'Augelli, A. R. (1994). Identity development and sexual orientation: Toward a model of lesbian, gay, and bisexual development. In E. J. Trickett, R. J. Watts, & D. Birman (Eds.), *Human diversity: Perspectives on people in context* (pp. 312–333). San Francisco: Jossey-Bass.

D'Augelli, A. R., & Dark, L. J. (1995). Vulnerable populations: Lesbian, gay, and bisexual youth. In L. D. Eron, J. H. Gentry, & P. Schlegel (Eds.), *Reason to hope: A psychosocial perspective on violence and youth* (pp. 177–196). Washington, DC: American Psychological Association.

D'Augelli, A. R., Hershberger, S. L., & Pilkington, N. W. (1998). Lesbian, gay, and bisexual youths and their families: Disclosure of sexual orientation and its consequences. *American Journal of Orthopsychiatry, 68*, 361–371.

Davies, D. (1996). Homophobia and heterosexism. In D. Davies & C. Neal (Eds.), *Pink therapy: A guide for counsellors and therapists working with lesbian, gay and bisexual clients* (pp. 41–65). Buckingham: Open University Press.

Davies, D., & Neal, C. (1996). An historical overview of homosexuality and therapy. In D. Davies & C. Neal (Eds.), *Pink therapy: A guide for counsellors and therapists working with lesbian, gay and bisexual clients* (pp. 11–23). Buckingham: Open University Press.

Davies, P. M., Weatherburn, P., Hunt, A. J., Hickson, F. C. I., McManus, T. J., & Coxon, A. P. M. (1992). The sexual behavior of young gay men in England and Wales. *AIDS Care, 4*, 259–272.

Dean, L., & Meyer, I. (1995). HIV prevalence and sexual behavior in a cohort of New York City gay men (aged 18–24). *Journal of Acquired Immune Deficiency Syndrome and Human Retrovirology, 8*, 208–211.

Dean, L., Wu, S., & Martin, J. L. (1992). Trends in violence and discrimination against gay men in New York City: 1984 to 1990. In G. M. Herek & K. T. Berrill (Eds.), *Hate crimes: Confronting violence against lesbians and gay men* (pp. 46–64). Newbury Park, CA: Sage.

Deitcher, D. (Ed.). (1995). *Over the rainbow: Lesbian and gay politics in America since Stonewall*. London: Boxtree.

Department for Education. (1994). *Education Act 1993: Sex education in schools.* London: HMSO.

Department of Health. (1992). *The health of the nation.* London: HMSO.

Doll, L. S., Joy, D., Bartholow, B. N, Harrison, J. S., Bolan, G., Douglas, J. M., Saltzman, L. E., Moss, P. M., & Delgado, W. (1992). Self-reported childhood and adolescent sexual abuse among adult homosexual and bisexual men. *Child Abuse and Neglect, 16,* 855–864.

Finkelhor, D., & Dziuba-Leatherman, J. (1994). Victimization of children. *American Psychologist, 49,* 173–183.

Frankham, J. (1996). *Young gay men and HIV infection.* Horsham: AVERT.

Fricke, A. (1981). *Confessions of a rock lobster.* Boston, MA: Alyson.

Friedman, R. C. (1991). Couple therapy with gay couples. *Psychiatric Annals, 18,* 33–36.

Garofalo, R., Wolf, R. C., Kessel, S., Palfrey, J., & DuRant, R. H. (1998). The association between health risk behavior and sexual orientation among a school-based sample of adolescents. *Pediatrics, 101,* 895–902.

Garnets, L., Hancock, K. A., Cochran, S. D., Goodchilds, J., & Peplau, L. A. (1991). Issues in psychotherapy with lesbians and gay men: A survey of psychologists. *American Psychologist, 46,* 964–972.

George, K. D., & Behrendt, A. E. (1988). Therapy for male couples experiencing relationship problems and sexual problems. *Journal of Homosexuality, 14,* 77–88.

Gerstel, C. J., Feraios, A. J., & Herdt, G. (1989). Widening circles: An ethnographic profile of a youth group. *Journal of Homosexuality, 17,* 75–92.

Gilmartin, B. G. (1987). Peer group antecedents of severe love-shyness in males. *Journal of Personality, 55,* 467–489.

Gonsiorek, J. C. (1988). Mental health issues of gay and lesbian adolescents. *Journal of Adolescent Health Care, 9*(2), 114–122.

Graham, D. L. R., Rawlings, E. I., Halpern, H. S., & Hermes, J. (1984). Therapists' needs for training in counseling lesbians and gay men. *Professional Psychology, 15,* 482–496.

Gross, L., & Aurand, S. K. (1992). *Discrimination and violence against lesbian women and gay men in Philadelphia and the Commonwealth of Pennsylvania.* Philadelphia: Philadelphia Lesbian and Gay Task Force.

Gross, L., Aurand, S., & Adessa, R. (1988). *Violence and discrimination against lesbian and gay people in Philadelphia and the Commonwealth of Pennsylvania.* Philadelphia: Philadelphia Lesbian and Gay Task Force.

Harry, J. (1989). Parental physical abuse and sexual orientation. *Archives of Sexual Behavior, 18,* 251–261.

Health Education Authority (1994). *Parents, schools and sex education.* Slough: NFER.

Herdt, G.H., & Boxer, A. M. (1993). *Children of Horizons: How gay and lesbian teens are leading a new way out of the closet.* Boston: Beacon.

Herek, G. M., & Berrill, K. T. (Eds.) (1992). *Hate crimes: Confronting violence against lesbians and gay men.* Newbury Park, CA: Sage.

Herek, G. M., & Glunt, E. K. (1988). An epidemic of stigma: Public reactions to AIDS. *American Psychologist, 43,* 886–891.

Hershberger, S. L., & D'Augelli, A. R. (1995). The impact of victimization on the mental health and suicidality of lesbian, gay, and bisexual youths. *Developmental Psychology, 31*(1), 65–74.

Holahan, W., & Gibson, S. A. (1994). Heterosexual therapists leading lesbian and gay therapy groups: Therapeutic and political realities. *Journal of Counseling and Development, 72,* 591–594.

Hoover, D. R., Munoz, A., Carey, V., Chmiel, J. S., Taylor, J. M. G., Margoloic, J. B., Kingsley, L., & Vermund, S. H. (1991). Estimating the 1978–1990 and future spread of HIV-1 in subgroups of homosexual men. *American Journal of Epidemiology, 134*(10), 1190–1205.

Hunter, J. (1990). Violence against lesbian and gay male youths. *Journal of Interpersonal Violence, 5,* 295–300.

Hunter, J., & Schaecher, R. (1987). Stresses on lesbian and gay adolescents in schools. *Social Work in Education, 9,* 180–190.

Jennings, K. (Ed.). (1994). *Becoming visible: A reader in gay and lesbian history for high school and college students.* Boston: Alyson.

Kahn, M. J. (1991). Factors affecting the coming out process for lesbians. *Journal of Homosexuality, 21*(3), 47–70.

Kruks, G. (1991). Gay and lesbian homeless/street youth: Special issues and concerns. *Journal of Adolescent Health, 12*(7), 515–518.

Lemp, G. F., Hirozawa, A. M., Givertz, D., Nieri, G. N., Anderson, L., Lindegren, M. L., Janssen, R. S., & Katz, M. (1994). Seroprevalence of HIV and risk behaviors among young homosexual and bisexual men. *Journal of the American Medical Association, 272,* 449–454.

Lipkin, A. (1993/94). The case for a gay and lesbian curriculum. *High School Journal, 77*(1–2), 95–107.

Lovell, A. (1995). *When your child comes out.* London: Sheldon Press.

Mallon, G. P. (1992). Gay and no place to go: Assessing the needs of gay and lesbian adolescents in out-of-home care settings. *Child Welfare, 71* (2), 47–61.

Marsiglio, W. (1993). Attitudes towards homosexual activity and gays as friends: A national survey of heterosexual 15- to 19-year-old males. *Journal of Sex Research, 30,* 12–17.

Mole, S. (1995). *Colours of the rainbow: Exploring issues of sexuality and difference.* London: Camden and Islington Health Authority.

Muehrer, P. (1995). Suicide and sexual orientation: A critical summary of recent research and directions for future research. *Suicide and Life Threatening Behavior, 25* (Supplement), 72–81.

National Lesbian and Gay Health Foundation (1987). National Lesbian Health Care Survey: Mental health implications. Unpublished report submitted to the National Institute of Mental Health. Atlanta: Author.

New South Wales Department of School Education. (1991). *Resources for teaching against violence.* Sydney, NSW: Author.

New South Wales Department of School Education. (1994). *Mates: HIV/AIDS-related discrimination.* Sydney, NSW: Author.

New South Wales Department of School Education. (1996). *Resources for teaching against violence.* Sydney, NSW: Author.

Nicholson, W. D., & Long, B. C. (1990). Self-esteem, social support, internalized homophobia, and coping strategies of HIV-positive gay men. *Journal of Consulting and Clinical Psychology, 58,* 873–876.

NUT/ City of Leicester Teachers' Association. (1989). *Challenging oppression— lesbians and gays in schools: A resources pack.* Leicester: Author.

Olweus, D. (1993). *Bullying at school: What we know and what we can do*. Oxford: Blackwell.

Otis, M. D., & Skinner, W. F. (1996). The prevalence of victimization and its effects on mental well-being among lesbian and gay people. *Journal of Homosexuality, 30*(3), 93–121.

Pilkington, N. W., & D'Augelli, A. R. (1995). Victimization of lesbian, gay, and bisexual youth in community settings. *Journal of Community Psychology, 23*(1), 33–56.

Powell, V. (1996, April). Under attack, *Gay Times, 211*, 12–14.

Remafedi, G. (1987). Homosexual youth: A challenge to contemporary society. *Journal of the American Medical Association, 258*, 222–225.

Remafedi, G. (1994). Predictors of unprotected intercourse among gay and bisexual youths: Knowledge, beliefs, and behavior. *Pediatrics, 94*, 163–168.

Remafedi, G., Farrow, J. A., & Deisher, R. W. (1991). Risk factors for attempted suicide in gay and bisexual youth. *Pediatrics, 87*, 869–875.

Rivers, I. (1995a, May). The best years of our lives. *Attitude, 13*, 44–48.

Rivers, I. (1995b, September). Long-term consequences of peer victimization in school: The development of the LGB Bullying Project. Paper presented at the Youth Research Center, Lund University, Sweden.

Rivers, I. (1995c). The victimization of gay teenagers in school: Homophobia in education. *Pastoral Care in Education, 13*(1), 35–41.

Rivers, I. (1995d). Mental health issues among lesbians and gay men bullied at school. *Health and Social Care in the Community, 3*(6), 380–383.

Rivers, I. (1996a, January). Young, gay and bullied. *Young People Now, 81*, 18–19.

Rivers, I. (1996b, May). The bullying of lesbians and homosexuals and its effects. Paper presented at the Bullying in Schools Seminar, The United Medical and Dental Schools of Guy's and St. Thomas' Hospitals (South East Institute of Public Health), University of London, UK.

Rivers, I. (1999). The psycho-social correlates and long-term implications of bullying at school for lesbians, gay men, and bisexual men and women. Unpublished doctoral dissertation, University of Surrey.

Rivers, I. (in press). Protecting the gay adolescent at school. *Medicine and Mind: Journal of the Philosophy of Medicine and Medical Psychology*.

Rivers, I., & Soutter, A (1996). Bullying and the Steiner school ethos: A case study analysis of a group-centered educational philosophy. *School Psychology International, 17*(4), 359–377.

Robinson, B. E., Walters, L. H., & Skeen, P. (1989). Response of parents to learning that their child is homosexual and concern over AIDS: A national survey. *Journal of Homosexuality, 18*(½), 59–80.

Rothblum, E. D. (1990). Depression among lesbians: An invisible and unresearched phenomenon. *Journal of Lesbian and Gay Psychotherapy, 1*(1), 67–87.

Rotheram-Borus, M. J., Hunter, J., & Rosario, M. (1994). Suicidal behavior and gay-related stress among gay and bisexual male adolescents. *Journal of Adolescent Research, 9*, 498–508.

Savin-Williams, R. C. (1994). Verbal and physical abuse as stressors in the lives of lesbians, gay male and bisexual youths: Associations with school problems, running away, substance abuse, prostitution and suicide. *Journal of Consulting and Clinical Psychology, 62*, 261–269.

Savin-Williams, R. C. (1998). The disclosure to families of same-sex attractions by lesbian, gay, and bisexual youths. *Journal of Adolescent Research, 8,* 49–68.

Shaffer, D., Fisher, P., Hicks, R. H., Parides, M., & Gould, M. (1995). Sexual orientation in adolescents who commit suicide. *Suicide and Life-Threatening Behavior, 25* (Supplement), 64–71.

Shidlo, A. (1994). Internalized homophobia. In B. Greene & G. M. Herek (Eds.), *Lesbian and gay psychology: Theory, research and clinical applications* (pp. 176–205). Thousand Oaks, CA: Sage Publications.

Silvestre, A. J., Kingsley, L. A., Wehman, P., Dappen, R., Ho, M., & Rinaldo, C. R. (1993). Changes in HIV rates and sexual behavior among homosexual men, 1984 to 1988. *American Journal of Public Health, 83,* 578–580.

Singerline, H. (1994). Outright: Reflections on an out-of-school gay youth group. *High School Journal, 77,* 133–137.

Slater, B. R. (1988). Essential issues in working with lesbian and gay male youths. *Professional Psychology: Research and Practice, 19*(2), 226–235.

Smith, P. K., & Sharp, S. (1994). The problem of school bullying. In P. K. Smith & S. Sharp (Eds.), *School bullying: Insights and perspectives* (pp. 1–19). London: Routledge.

Stall, R., Barrett, D., Bye, L., Catania, J., Frutchey, C., Hennessey, J., Lemp, G., & Paul, J. (1992). A comparison of younger and older gay men's HIV risk-taking behaviors: The Communication Technology 1989 Cross-Sectional Survey. *Journal of Acquired Immune Deficiency Syndromes, 5,* 682–687.

Strommen, E. F. (1989). Hidden branches and growing pains: Homosexuality and the family tree. *Marriage and Family Review, 14,* 9–34.

Trenchard, L., & Warren, H. (1984). *Something to tell you.* London: London Gay Teenage Group.

Uribe, V. (1993/94). Project 10: A school-based outreach to gay and lesbian youth. *High School Journal, 77*(1–2), 108–112.

Uribe, V., & Harbeck, K. M. (1992). Addressing the needs of lesbian, gay, and bisexual youth: The origins of Project 10 and school-based intervention. *Journal of Homosexuality, 22*(3–4), 9–28.

Warren, H. (1984). *Talking about school.* London: London Gay Teenage Group.

Wyatt, G. W., Guthrie, D., & Notgrass, C. M. (1992). Differential effects of women's child sexual abuse and subsequent sexual revictimization. *Journal of Consulting and Clinical Psychology, 60*(2), 167–173.

10

Counseling Lesbian, Gay, and Bisexual Youths

Caitlin Ryan

During the past 15 years, a growing body of literature has explored the experiences of lesbian, gay, and bisexual (LGB) youths. Little research to date has been conducted on developing a bisexual identity during adolescence[1] (Ryan & Futterman, 1998; Savin-Williams, 1995), so while the literature may refer to lesbian, gay, and bisexual youths, much of the research has been conducted on gay male youths and less frequently on lesbian youths. Since the mid-1980s, information has increased substantially on identity development and coming out, family interactions, HIV prevention, victimization, suicide, and risk behaviors. But with few exceptions, counseling and clinical care have not kept pace with the rapidly changing experiences of today's generation of LGB youths.

Unlike previous generations of lesbians and gay men who were more likely to come out after they left home for college or began to live on their own, LGB youths are coming out at younger ages and in social environments in which others are more likely to be aware that some youths may be lesbian, gay, or bisexual. Violence and harassment appear to be on the increase, and greater awareness of same-sex sexual orientation—without opportunities for education and discussion—may increase discomfort among heterosexual peers. For example, a 1997–98 survey of outstanding high school students listed in *Who's Who Among American High School Students* found that nearly half (48%) admitted they were prejudiced against LGB people, and two-thirds (66%) said that depiction of same-sex relationships on television or film was offensive (Krouse & Krouse, 1998). This represents an increase from 29% who held similar views during the previous year. Greater visibility of LGB people in the media, arts, and politics has increased awareness that an adolescent may actually be lesbian or gay. When this is coupled with earlier awareness of same-sex attraction, identity consolidation, and coming out at younger ages, LGB youths may become more likely targets for victimization and are in greater need of support.

Comprehensive studies of LGB teens (e.g., D'Augelli & Hershberger, 1993; Herdt & Boxer, 1993) and coming out among lesbian and gay youths (e.g., Savin-Williams, 1990) have shown significant changes in the ages and experiences of same-sex awareness and identity development between earlier and more recent generations of LGB youths, and changes are anticipated in the current generations as well. Thus, more attention is needed on counseling today's generation of LGB youths, with a focus on interventions to address the challenges of greater visibility, the shorter time span between same-sex awareness and coming out, and identity consolidation while living with their parents and families of origin. This chapter will provide an overview of mental health and counseling needs of LGB youths based on a comprehensive review of the literature.

Effects of Stigma and Prejudice

Identity development is a major task for all adolescents, but transforming and managing a stigmatized identity is a primary developmental task for LGB youths, and one that may precipitate the need for counseling. Stigma has social, behavioral, and health-related consequences that can increase high-risk behaviors, such as unprotected sex and substance abuse, and intensify psychological distress and risk for suicide (Ryan & Futterman, 1998). Internalized as low self-esteem or self-hate, stigma requires a range of coping behaviors to deal with increased stress and isolation among LGB youths who may try to "pass" as heterosexual by monitoring their behavior, dating the opposite sex, or even expressing anti-gay sentiment.

Research on adults has shown that lesbians and gay males who have internalized a positive identity show better psychological adjustment (Weinberg & Williams, 1974), greater satisfaction and higher self-concept (Schmitt & Kurdek, 1987), and lower rates of depression (Schmitt & Kurdek, 1987) or stress (Brooks, 1981; Meyer, 1995) than those conflicted about their identity. In one of the few studies that has explored identity satisfaction among adolescents, Hunter (1996) found that self-identified lesbian and gay youths who had made a commitment to their sexual identity had positive attitudes about it, while those who self-identified as bisexual or who were still exploring their sexual identity had more negative attitudes. Hunter also found that adolescents who did not disclose their identity were more socially and emotionally isolated, and that negative attitudes were correlated with less knowledge of the lesbian and gay community. The importance of lesbian and gay communities to psychological well-being and identity development has been discussed elsewhere (D'Augelli & Garnets, 1995), and this connection is especially important for adolescents who lack basic support for emerging sexual identities, and who are coming out at younger ages. For example, Herdt and Boxer (1993) found that lesbian and gay youths were coming out, on average, at age 16 and were first becoming aware of same-sex attraction around age 10, while D'Augelli and Hershberger (1993) reported that self-labeling occurred at age 14, four years after initial awareness of same-sex desires. Other recent studies have reported similar results (Rosario, Meyer-Bahlburg, et al., 1996; Savin-Williams, 1998). Self-identification at younger ages means that youths will be experiencing and expressing same-sex feelings in settings that are ill prepared to deal with their needs and concerns, including school, home, and community settings.

Ethnic and Racial Minority Youths

Although there are clear differences, the task of transforming a stigmatized sexual identity is similar to the developmental tasks faced by ethnic and racial minorities who must transform a stigmatized identity into a positive one. Although little research has been conducted on sexual identity development in lesbians, gay men, and bisexual people of color, a recent study of a multicultural sample of urban LGB youths found that sexual identity is a domain of personal identity, similar to ethnic identity (Hunter, 1996). However, ethnic identity only assumes salience for youths of color, increasing the developmental challenges for ethnic-minority LGB youths. Until recently, models of sexual identity development were based on the experiences of middle- and upper-middle class white lesbians and gay men (Greene, 1994; McCarn & Fassinger, 1996). Ethnic-minority youths face additional stressors and challenges in consolidating sexual, racial, and ethnic identities (Tremble, Schneider, & Appathurai, 1989). Sexuality holds different meanings for each cultural and ethnic group, based on attitudes, values, and beliefs about sexuality; stereotypes about gender and sex roles; responsibilities for childbearing; religious values, degree of acculturation into mainstream society; and the importance of family and ethnic communities in providing acceptance and support (Greene, 1994).

In a society that discriminates on the basis of race and ethnicity, strong connections with family and ethnic community remain essential for survival. However, many ethnic groups perceive being gay or lesbian as a rejection of their ethnic heritage, as a "Western" or white phenomenon (Chan, 1989; Espin, 1993; Greene, 1994; Icard, 1986; Tremble et al., 1989), and adolescents may feel pressure to choose or value one identity over another. Having to manage more than one stigmatized identity increases the adolescent's level of vulnerability and stress (Greene, 1994). To meet their emotional, educational, and practical needs, ethnic minority youths must learn to interact with three separate "communities" that have different and often conflicting values (Morales, 1989). These include their ethnic community, the predominantly white lesbian and gay community, and mainstream society. Each community provides access to important resources, but all devalue part of the youth's identity (Morales, 1989). Because ethnic minority communities provide essential emotional and practical support, LGB youths of color are particularly vulnerable to rejection. As a result, many continue to hide.

Mental Health Concerns of Lesbian, Gay, and Bisexual Youths

Lesbian, gay, and bisexual adolescents experience a range of mental health concerns that affect adolescents in general. In addition, they are at risk for stress and mental health problems related to stigma. Most LGB youths grow up to lead satisfying, productive lives, but some are more vulnerable. Pre-existing vulnerabilities, such as dysfunctional or addicted parents, abuse and neglect, severe stress, and underlying emotional disorders, may make it difficult for some youths to manage the stress associated with their sexual orientation. Hetrick and Martin (1987) have suggested that adolescents with such histories may constitute the majority of youths who attempt suicide or who develop serious substance abuse problems.

Research on the counseling needs and experiences of LGB youths is limited. However, available studies show considerable use of counseling services, when services are available (Coleman & Remafedi, 1989). Nearly three-quarters of 15- to 19-year-old gay males in one study sought help from psychologists or psychiatrists (Remafedi, 1987). And nearly two-thirds of a national sample of lesbians, aged 17–24, reported use of mental health professionals, while 31% used nonprofessionals, such as peer counselors and support groups (Bradford, Ryan, & Rothblum, 1994). Reasons for seeking mental health services commonly included issues related to sexual orientation, family conflicts, concerns with relationships, substance abuse, depression, and anxiety. Nearly half (46%) of young lesbians in the National Lesbian Health Care Survey sought counseling for problems with their families, 29% reported problems with their partners, and 22% cited problems with being a lesbian as a precipitant for seeking mental health services (Bradford & Ryan, 1988). A substantial proportion of two groups of college-age lesbians and gay males reported feeling anxious and depressed (Bradford & Ryan, 1988; D'Augelli, 1991). In his study of gay male youths in college, D'Augelli (1991) found that anxiety was related to coming-out dilemmas, while depression was not. Among these youths, hiding their sexual identity was associated with greater worry about disclosing their identity to parents, co-workers, and heterosexual friends, as well as concerns about AIDS.

Various problems may develop as adolescents struggle to manage the stigma related to an emerging lesbian or gay identity. Adolescents (and adults) who are struggling with their sexual identity may experience intense feelings and psychological reactions (Gonsiorek, 1988). These may include adjustment problems, impaired psychosocial development, family alienation, substance abuse, depression, suicidal ideation, and sexual acting out (Coleman & Remafedi, 1989). Confusion is also a common experience for adolescents who are struggling with their sexual identity (Schneider, 1988).

As with any emotional crisis, coming out is mediated by underlying personality structure, coping resources, and access to support, and some youths are more vulnerable than others. When sexual identity remains troublesome for youths, other problems such as sexual abuse, emotional deprivation, and prolonged external stress may be factors. Increasingly, youths and their parents report a relatively smooth adjustment to coming out; however, this trend has not been documented empirically.

Chronic Stress

Chronic stress is a common theme identified in research and clinical reports on LGB youths, generally linked to harassment, including conflicts, and verbal and physical abuse from family members and peers (see Rivers & D'Augelli, this volume). Verbal and physical abuse is associated with negative outcomes, such as school-related problems, running away from home, conflict with the law, substance abuse, prostitution, and suicide (Savin-Williams, 1994). Like heterosexual male adolescents, gay and bisexual male youths are more likely to externalize stress, thus increasing their visibility and bringing them to the attention of service agencies and institutions. However, some investigators have observed that stress associated with role expectations and pressures to conform may be even greater among young lesbians than gay males though they may be less likely to externalize it (Herdt & Boxer, 1993).

In a study of stressful life events among minority gay and bisexual youths, emotional distress and multiproblem behaviors increased with the number of gay-related stressors (Rosario, Rotheram-Borus, & Reid, 1996). More than three-quarters had experienced at least one gay-related stressful event and an average of six nongay related stressors during the past three months (including problems with family and peers, moving, and major illness or injury). Gay-related stressors were associated with increasing depression, and youths with higher self-esteem experienced less emotional distress, including depression and anxiety. Moreover, gay youth reported three to five times more negative non-gay-related stress than their heterosexual peers. In addition, many non-gay-related stressful events (e.g., arguments with parents, problems at school) may be indirectly linked to sexual identity, thus compounding the stress experienced (Hershberger & D'Augelli, 1995; Remafedi, 1987; Rotheram-Borus, Rosario & Koopman, 1991). LGB youths consistently report significant stress associated with school and related activities. Many describe harassment, verbal and physical abuse, and negative attitudes of both teachers and peers (Malinsky, 1996; Rofes, 1989; Sears, 1991). Anecdotal information suggests that transgendered youths are most frequently abused. While these youth may be heterosexual, lesbian, gay, or bisexual, their visibility often leads to scapegoating, harassment, and persistent verbal and physical abuse from peers.

Depression and Suicide Risk

Many of the studies of lesbian, gay, and bisexual youths have relied on self reports to assess depression and other mental health concerns, but several have used psychological testing (e.g., Herdt & Boxer, 1993) or standardized measures of depressive mood (e.g., D'Augelli & Hershberger, 1993; Rosario, Meyer-Bahlburg, et al., 1996). In the general adolescent population, prevalence studies show rates of clinical depression ranging from 1% to 5% (Tancer & Shaffer, 1992), with higher rates from self-reports in contrast to clinician-generated diagnoses. Petersen et al. (1993) describe prevalence of depressed mood in nonclinical samples of adolescents as 20–35% for boys and 25–40% for girls. Many youths who attempt suicide are depressed, and depressed mood, drug use, and suicidality are strongly related (Petersen et al., 1993).

Adolescent girls, in general, show increases in depressive feelings across adolescence, and are more often diagnosed with depression than males (Kandel & Davies, 1982). Herdt and Boxer (1993) and Hunter (1996) underscore the role of cultural constraints and pressures to conform to "ideal" standards of beauty and sexual attractiveness in girls that may result in greater difficulties for young lesbians during adolescence. In their study of predominantly Hispanic and Black gay and bisexual youths, Rosario, Rotheram-Borus, et al. (1996) reported that gay-related stressful events were related to increasing depression, and youths who were ridiculed reported more depression and phobic anxiety than those who were not. High rates of depression have been found in many community samples of LGB youths. Schneider (1991) and Hershberger and D'Augelli (1995) found that more than half of their samples reported problems with depression, and about 40% of young lesbians in a national sample reported depression (Bradford et al., 1994). While these studies also document other mental health concerns, such as anxiety and feeling overwhelmed, the general association between depression and suicide in adolescence makes this a particularly salient clinical feature in assessment and treatment of LGB youths.

Studies of adolescent suicide show that between 6% and 13% of adolescents report at least one suicide attempt (Garland & Ziegler, 1993), and a history of attempted suicide is a powerful predictor of suicide (Setterberg, 1992). Thus, all suicidal behavior and ideation must be taken seriously. Not all youths who attempt suicide go on to commit suicide. Studies of completed suicides (psychological autopsies that screen records and interview friends and family after death) show that adolescent victims had higher rates of ideation and prior attempts (Brent, Perper & Moritz, 1993; Shaffer, Garland, Gould, Fisher, & Trautman, 1988). More than half had depressive, aggressive, and antisocial symptoms (Setterberg, 1992), and up to half of all suicides were committed under the influence of alcohol and drugs. More than 90% of completed youth suicides had evidence of a psychiatric diagnosis, some of which may co-exist, such as conduct and mood disorders (particularly depression and bipolar illness), substance abuse, and psychoses (Blumenthal, 1990). However, not all were properly diagnosed until after their death. The co-occurrence of depression, substance abuse, and impulsivity is especially lethal (Blumenthal, 1990). Both physical and sexual abuse are more common in families with suicidal adolescents, and youths are often victims of this abuse. Suicide is often precipitated by life events that involve shame or humiliation. Arrests, assaults, or disciplinary incidents at school are also typical events that trigger suicide attempts in vulnerable youths (Blumenthal, 1990; Setterberg, 1992).

Like most information about LGB youths, data on suicide have generally been gathered from youths who are open about their sexual identity and who have sought health, mental health, or social support services. Reported rates of attempted suicide and suicidal ideation are generally very high among LGB adolescents; however, very little information is available on LGB youths who ultimately commit suicide. Of the two forensic community studies that have attempted to identify youths who may be lesbian and gay after their deaths, rates of LGB sexual orientation were quite low (between 2.5 and 5%; Rich, Fowler, Young, & Blenkush, 1986; Shaffer, Fisher, Hicks, Parides, & Gould, 1995). However, trying to identify sexual orientation may be even more difficult after death since sexual identity unfolds over a period of years and fear of disclosure may deepen isolation and prevent youths from discussing feelings of difference or same-sex attraction.

Rates of attempted suicide in community samples of LGB youths range from 20% to 42%, with higher percentages in youths who are homeless, runaways, and victims of sexual abuse or violence (Bradford et al., 1994; D'Augelli & Hershberger 1993; Herdt & Boxer, 1993; Remafedi, 1987; Remafedi, Farrow, & Deisher, 1991; Schneider, Farberow, & Kruks, 1989). Until recently, population-based surveys of adolescents did not include items on sexual identity or same-sex behavior, and community-based studies were criticized for not using representative samples. However, two school-based probability studies have confirmed earlier findings of higher suicide risk among LGB youths. In an analysis of data from a 1987 adolescent health survey of 7th- to 12th-grade high school students in Minnesota, investigators found higher rates of suicide attempts among nonheterosexual youths. Over one-quarter (28%) of gay or bisexual males, 21% of homosexual or bisexual females, 15% of heterosexual females, and 4% of heterosexual males reported suicide attempts (Remafedi, French, Story, Resnick, & Blum, 1998). Moreover, gay or bisexual identity was associated with suicidal intent and attempts for males, but not for females. However, in one of the few community studies to assess suicide in both lesbian and gay youths, lesbians were more than twice as likely to have attempted suicide and to have used more lethal means (Herdt & Boxer, 1993).

Data from the 1995 Massachusetts Youth Risk Behavior Survey found that lesbian, gay, and bisexual youths, and those who reported same-sex experiences, were four times more likely than heterosexual youths to have attempted suicide in the past year (Massachusetts Department of Education, 1995). These youths were also four times more likely than their heterosexual peers to have skipped school during the past month because they felt unsafe or to have been threatened or injured with a weapon at school during the past year. An analysis of the 104 self-identified LGB youths in the sample found that these youths were three-and-a-half times as likely to have attempted suicide during the past year and more likely to engage in other risk behaviors (e.g., alcohol and drug use, sexual intercourse with multiple partners, or to be the victims of forced sexual contact) than were heterosexual youth in the sample (Garofalo, Wolf, Kessel, Palfrey, & DuRant, 1998).

Garofalo et al. (1998) noted but did not comment on how the high proportion of bisexual youths in this subsample (78%) might affect the findings. Although limited data are available on the experiences and risks of bisexual adolescents, some differences have been observed. As noted earlier, Hunter (1996) found that bisexual youths and those who were still exploring their identities reported negative attitudes about their sexuality, as compared to self-identified lesbian and gay youths. Bisexual youths also had less information about sexual orientation and about lesbian and gay communities, which may increase isolation, affect self-esteem, and promote risky behaviors. In a study of 60 lesbian and gay adolescents, Schneider (1991) found that contact with other lesbians and gay males was the most important factor in developing a positive sexual identity. And in a 14-city study of LGB youths, Hershberger, Pilkington, and D'Augelli (1997) found that bisexual youths were more than five times as likely as lesbian and gay youths to have attempted suicide more than once, suggesting that youths who identify as bisexual may experience unusual levels of stress until their sexual identity has stabilized.

Studies of gay and bisexual suicide attempters found that these youths were more likely to have self-identified as gay or bisexual and to come out to others at younger ages (Hershberger & D'Augelli, 1995; Remafedi et al., 1991), to have friends and relatives who attempted or committed suicide (Hershberger & D'Augelli, 1995; Remafedi et al., 1991) or to have been rejected because of their sexual orientation (Schneider et al., 1989). In one of the few studies of attempted suicide among LGB youths, adolescents who attempted suicide reported having more fully disclosed their sexual identity to others, were more often victimized, and lost more friends as a result of their sexual identity (Hershberger et al., 1997). Ethnic minority gay and bisexual youths who attempted suicide were more likely to have dropped out of school, to have been ejected from their homes and to have experienced a higher number of gay-related stressors than nonattempters (Hershberger & D'Augelli, 1995). In another study, nearly half of gay and bisexual youths reported family problems as the precipitating event (Remafedi et al., 1991). One-third of the suicide attempts were related to conflict over sexual identity. Three out of four attempts followed self-labeling as gay or bisexual. Gender-atypical youths and those who used drugs had a three-time higher risk for suicide. Youths who attempted suicide resembled actual suicide victims in terms of substance abuse, high levels of family dysfunction, and antisocial behaviors (Remafedi et al., 1991).

Effects of Victimization and Abuse

Adolescents are frequent victims of violence, with highest rates reported by lesbian and gay youths (see Rivers & D'Augelli, this volume). Nearly half of all rape victims are adolescents (American Academy of Pediatrics, 1988). Most reported crimes involve young women, but males are also victimized, and incidence in males is likely underreported, with shame and fear of being perceived as gay contributing to underreporting (Dimock, 1988). Prevalence studies suggest that 15% to 22% of women have been raped at some time in their lives (Koss, Gidycz, & Wisniewski, 1987). Estimates of sexual abuse prior to age 18 range from 3% to 31% for males (Finkelhor, 1987) and 28% to 36% for females under age 14 (Wyatt & Peters, 1986). Comparable data are not available for lesbian and gay youths, although half of lesbians aged 17–24 in a national survey reported rape or sexual assault (Bradford et al., 1994). In a study of gay males, aged 15–19, 6% reported sexual assault, while an additional 6% reported sexual abuse by family members (Remafedi, 1987). Among college students in one study, 12% of gay males and 31% of lesbians reported sexual assault, compared to rates of 4% and 18% in heterosexual males and females (Duncan, 1990).

Rates of sexual abuse are considerably higher among clinical samples of lesbians and gay men and among heterosexuals who have had higher lifetime exposure to trauma. In a survey of sexual abuse victims who attended sexually transmitted disease (STD) clinics, for example, 37% of gay men reported past sexual abuse as children or adolescents (Bartholow et al., 1994). And in an outcome study of lesbians and gay men who had completed inpatient substance abuse treatment, 44% reported having been sexually abused (37% of males and 67% of females), with abstinence after treatment being much more likely in those who had not experienced earlier abuse (Ratner, Kosten, & McLellan, 1991). Prevalence of sexual abuse appears higher among gay males than heterosexual males (Finkelhor, 1984; Johnson & Shrier, 1985) although gay males may be more willing to report such abuse. Social isolation heightens vulnerability for young gay males, particularly as they explore their sexual identities in environments in which they may be exploited or abused.

Childhood sexual abuse has a range of psychological and behavioral consequences that increase risk for further victimization and health problems. These include depression (Briere & Runtz, 1987), post-traumatic stress disorder (Blake-White & Kline, 1985; Briere, Evans, Runtz, & Wall, 1988), substance abuse (Dimock, 1988; Zierler et al., 1991), suicidal ideation and behavior (Briere et al., 1988), and risk for HIV infection (Bartholow et al., 1994; Zierler et al., 1991). Victims also experience sexual identity confusion, sexual dysfunction, and relationship problems, and are more likely to engage in prostitution (Coleman, 1989; Zierler et al., 1991), to seek counseling, or to be hospitalized for psychiatric problems (Bartholow et al., 1994). In one study, lesbians who had been sexually abused, raped, or victimized were twice as likely to attempt suicide (Bradford & Ryan, 1988), and reported significantly more depression and alcohol abuse than lesbians who had not been victimized (Descamps, Rothblum, Bradford, & Ryan, 1999).

In addition to risk for sexual abuse and assault, LGB adolescents are at high risk for anti-gay violence, including physical attacks, verbal and physical abuse, and harassment because of their sexual orientation (D'Augelli & Dark, 1995; Dean, Wu, & Martin, 1992), and victimization is more common for youths who are openly or stereotypically gay. For example, D'Augelli, Hershberger and Pilkington (1998) found that youths who disclosed their sexual identity were significantly more likely to be victimized at home and in school. And Descamps et al. (1999) found that lesbians who had been victimized reported significantly more daily stress, and alcohol and drug abuse, compared to those who had not. While the psychological, somatic, and behavioral sequelae are similar to those seen in non-bias-related victimization, anti-gay attacks heighten an adolescent's feelings of vulnerability, often intensify conflictual feelings about sexual orientation, and may cause the youth and others to perceive the act as punishment for being gay (Garnets, Herek, & Levy, 1992). Family and peer support are important resources for recovering from trauma; in many cases, an adolescent victim who is lesbian, gay, or bisexual may not have previously come out to parents or to peers. Parents may react to the assault with anger and may "blame the victim" if the adolescent's sexual orientation is initially disclosed as a result of the incident. Rape is especially traumatizing for both males and females, though male rape and sexual abuse victims have additional concerns. Some male victims fear that having been sexually abused by a male might "make them gay," that they were victimized because they are gay, or that family and friends will assume they are gay because of the attack.

Eating Disorders

Although limited data are available, eating disorders have been identified as a concern for young gay males (Siever, 1994). In one study of male and female patients in an inpatient program for eating disorders, male patients were more likely to be gay (Herzog, Norman, Gordon, & Pepose, 1984). In other studies of body image, eating disorders, and weight, gay men were found to be more dissatisfied with body image and appearance than heterosexual men (Brand, Rothblum, & Solomon, 1992; Silberstein, Mishkind, Striegel-Moore, Timko, & Rodin, 1989) or women (Siever, 1994), while lesbians appeared least concerned (Siever, 1994). In one of the few studies of eating disorders in adolescents, based on data from the 1987 Minnesota Adolescent Health Survey, gay male youths were more likely to report poor body image and frequent dieting compared to heterosexual males, while binge eating and purging behaviors were about twice as prevalent in gay and bisexual youths, compared to their heterosexual peers (French et al., 1996). In the same study, lesbian adolescents were less likely to perceive themselves as overweight and were more likely than heterosexual females to report a positive body image.

Substance Abuse

Alcohol and other kinds of drug abuse are the leading causes of disability among adolescents and young adults, and since the 1960s, alcohol and drug use have become widespread among teens (Alderman, Schonberg, & Cohen, 1992). Nine out of 10 high school seniors have used alcohol and consider themselves "drinkers," while 43% have used marijuana (Farrow, 1990). Stimulants, such as cocaine and amphetamines, are the fourth most frequently used drug among adolescents; smokable forms of "crack" and "ice" are accessible, affordable, and highly addictive. Polydrug abuse is common among the majority of youths who use substances.

Substance abuse also increases risk for STDs, including HIV infection. Many adolescents report using alcohol before having intercourse (more than half who drink before sex report having five or more drinks), which impairs judgment and increases potential for high-risk behaviors (Fortenberry, 1995). Use of crack cocaine is highly predictive of HIV infection since crack users often exchange sex for drugs or money to buy drugs. In a cohort of adolescents with HIV infection, two-thirds of girls and more than half of boys used crack; of these, 86% and 80%, respectively, exchanged sex for money, drugs, food, and shelter (survival sex; Futterman, Hein, Ruben, Dell, & Shaffer, 1993).

Although substance abuse has been identified as a health concern for adult lesbians and gay men, investigators have only recently begun to collect data on use in LGB youths. Some studies of urban gay youths show high rates of alcohol and drug use (Remafedi, 1987; Rotheram-Borus et al., 1994) while others do not (Boxer, 1990; Bradford & Ryan, 1988). Findings from a national survey of young lesbians, ages 17–24, showed rates of use that are comparable to heterosexual women, but higher rates of drug use overall (Bradford & Ryan, 1988). One out of three smoked cigarettes daily; 13% were concerned about use of alcohol, and 5.9% and 2.4%, respectively, were concerned about marijuana and cocaine use.

LGB youths use alcohol and drugs for many of the same reasons as heterosexual youths—to experiment, to assert independence, to relieve tension, to increase feelings of self-esteem and adequacy, and to self-medicate for depression or another mood disorder (Ryan & Futterman, 1998). However, vulnerability for LGB youths is enhanced by social isolation and the need to hide their sexual orientation. For these youths, substance use may be motivated by an attempt to manage stigma and shame, to deny same-sex feelings, or as a defense against ridicule and anti-gay violence. Without appropriate assessment and treatment these youths will remain at continued risk for chemical dependency, relapse following treatment, and experience the myriad complications of addictive disease.

Experiences with Families

Most adolescents have strong desires to come out to their parents but fear of rejection and other negative reactions hold many back (Boxer, Cook, & Herdt, 1991; D'Augelli et al., 1998). In a study of family disclosure experiences of 105 LGB youths, D'Augelli et al. (1998) found that most adolescents who came out to their parents did so around age 17 (generally following initial disclosure to friends) and approximately six years after first awareness of same-sex attraction and two years after self-labeling as LGB. Youths who disclosed were more likely to be "out," more readily identified by others as being gay, had more gay and lesbian friends, felt more comfortable about their sexual identity, and were more comfortable disclosing their identity. However, these youths were also more likely to lose friends and to report significantly higher frequency of victimization at home and school than youths who did not disclose their sexual identity. Moreover, youths who came out to their parents were four times more likely than those who did not to attempt suicide (51% vs. 12%), and two-and-a-half times as likely to report more frequent thoughts of suicide (30% vs. 12%), suggesting that coming out while they are still dependent emotionally and financially on their parents may have negative consequences.

Adolescents may decide to come out to their parents for various reasons: to improve relationships, to increase honesty and reduce the stress of passing and deception about their lives, to increase their self-esteem, for political reasons (to increase lesbian/gay visibility), and to provoke confrontation (Boxer et al., 1991). Adolescents who have not come out at home report that fear of negative and abusive responses, including physical violence, is a major deterrent (D'Augelli et al., 1998). Boxer et al. (1991) noted that gay youth are "betwixt and between" different social worlds—the primarily heterosexual and heterosocial world of their families and peers and their newly found lesbian, gay, and bisexual peers and communities. This may result in a double bind since being honest will upset parents, while coming out represents the end of secrecy and the potential for integrating both worlds.

Just as coming out precipitates an emotional crisis for individuals, disclosure of LGB identity to parents generally promotes a family crisis. Parents undergo a kind of multi-stage coming-out process during which they grieve the loss of their child's heterosexual identity and ultimately reframe negative social sanctions and lost expectations into positive experiences of lesbian and gay lives. This process is lengthy; for some parents, it is not achievable, and they will never be able to accept their child as lesbian or gay. Adaptation appears more difficult for parents whose children come out earlier (Boxer et al., 1991). All parents go through some process of adaptation to the disclosure; reactions are predictably more intense when parents accidentally discover their child's sexual orientation, rather than having an opportunity for open discussion. After the initial shock of disclosure, which is often followed by denial, guilt, and various stages of grieving, parents begin to grapple with the stigma associated with homosexuality that their child (and now they) will experience. In searching for information and understanding, they slowly confront and expose myths and misconceptions, learn about the broad support and extensive resources available through the lesbian and gay community, meet successful lesbian and gay role models, and fashion new expectations, hopes, and dreams for their child (Ryan & Futterman, 1998; Herdt & Koff, 2000).

However, acceptance takes time. Only half of mothers and siblings and one-quarter of fathers were fully accepting when a youth initially disclosed his or her sexual identity (D'Augelli et al., 1998); fathers reacted more negatively (Boxer et al., 1991; D'Augelli et al., 1998), particularly with daughters (Boxer et al., 1991); and lesbians were more often threatened and were the victims of physical attacks than gay males, most often by their mothers (D'Augelli et al., 1998). Most parents of lesbian and gay children who participated in a national study compared learning of their child's sexual orientation with mourning a death (Robinson, Walters & Skeen, 1989). Loss of their child's heterosexual identity involves changes in parental expectations for (heterosexual) success, especially marriage, family, and grandchildren (Borhek, 1988; Boxer et al., 1991). With access to accurate information, however, parents develop a new understanding of the reality of lesbian and gay lives that includes options for positive long-term relationships, successful careers, and even parenting. At the same time, parents need information to dispel outmoded, guilt-inducing theories that have previously attributed homosexuality to unhappy childhoods and disturbed relationships with parents, including smothering, seductive mothers, and cold, rejecting fathers (Drescher, 1996; Magee & Miller, 1996).

In a study of adolescent coming out and parental disclosure, parents' primary concerns were for their child's happiness and well-being (Boxer et al., 1991). After working through their initial distress, parents reported that it was not their child's sexual orientation that bothered them, but the implications, such as discrimination, homophobia, and what might happen to their children in old age. Parents of gay males worried about AIDS (Boxer et al., 1991; Robinson et al., 1989). Most reported improved relationships following disclosure; many described feelings of relief that their child's attempts at hiding his or her sexual identity (which they experienced as evasive or secretive) did not conceal something worse, such as drug use or drug dealing.

Most information on the coming-out experiences of adolescents and parents has focused on white, middle-class families. However, some researchers have suggested that coming out may be more difficult for ethnic minority LGB youths (Greene, 1994). Disclosure of sexual orientation may jeopardize family relationships and threaten close-knit association within ethnic communities (Morales, 1989). In a study of the experiences of multicultural lesbian and gay teens, coming out to parents was found to alter the youths' relationship with their ethnic communities (Tremble et al., 1989). To avoid shaming their families, some youths excluded themselves from cultural activities that were important in reinforcing their ethnic identity. Among ethnic minority youths, fear of rejection or reluctance to be seen as rejecting traditional cultural roles that value marriage, child-bearing, and conventional gender roles are primary reasons for not disclosing to parents.

Counseling Lesbian, Gay and Bisexual Youths

Little information was available on counseling lesbian and gay youths prior to the 1980s, when several researchers and practitioners provided guidance for mental health providers based on their clinical experiences (e.g., Coleman & Remafedi, 1989; Gonsiorek, 1988; Schneider, 1988). Since then, publications on LGB youths have increased substantially. However, few new materials have been developed on counseling LGB youths that incorporate the changing social and political environment, practice experience, and recent research. Recent exceptions include an edited book of counseling strategies (Schneider, 1998) and a guide to comprehensive health and mental health care (Ryan & Futterman, 1998), and an analysis of issues faced by LGB youths in residential care (Mallon, 1998).

Counselors who work with adolescents, in general, need to be aware of sexual identity issues since most LGB youths will not disclose their sexual identity until they perceive that it is safe to do so (e.g., the counselor signals his or her knowledge, lack of judgment, and potential for support), and adolescents who are questioning or confused about their sexual identity may be too uncomfortable or unsure to introduce the topic. Counselors and investigators working with LGB youths should approach these youths first as adolescents since developmental tasks related to sexual identity occur in the context of adolescent developmental norms (e.g., risk taking and substance use are rites of passage for adolescents; Ryan & Futterman, 1998).

Counselors' Knowledge and Attitudes

One of the problems in providing appropriate mental health services for LGB youths is a general lack of information and training among counselors, particularly those at the elementary, junior high, and high school levels. Most of the empirical studies of counselors' knowledge, experience, and attitudes about sexual orientation have been conducted on those who work with adults. These studies have frequently documented lack of knowledge, ambivalence, and disdain among providers (DeCrescenzo, 1984; Graham, Rawlings, Halpern, & Hermes, 1984; Rudolph, 1988). A survey of 2,544 members of the American Psychological Association found that practice varied widely, with many incidents of biased and inappropriate care (Garnets, Hancock, Cochran, Goodchilds, & Peplau, 1991). Nearly three-fifths of psychologists surveyed knew of negative or discriminatory care, including incidents where practitioners labeled lesbians or gay men as "sick" and in need of change of their sexual orientation. Providers who knew someone gay were least likely to be homophobic (DeCrescenzo, 1984), while the least stereotypical and negative perceptions of lesbian and gay clients were held by lesbian and gay providers (Bieschke & Matthews, 1996; Rudolph, 1988; Ryan, Bradford, & Honnold, 1999; Smith, 1993). Basic knowledge is often lacking. For example, a probability survey of licensed clinical social workers' and licensed professional counselors' knowledge and attitudes about lesbian clients found that lesbian, gay, and bisexual providers were five times as likely as their heterosexual counterparts to understand that sexual orientation encompasses more than a sexual component (e.g., affectional, emotional, and social) and more than twice as likely to know that coming out has mental health benefits (Ryan et al., 1999).

Use of mental health services is important in helping lesbians, gay men, and bisexual people cope with a hostile environment, obtain support and guidance in managing heterosexism, and developing a positive sexual identity. A recent national survey of the psychotherapy experiences of lesbians, gay men, and bisexual people found that two-fifths (39%) had sought counseling to resolve conflict related to their sexual orientation, and the majority said that counseling had a positive influence on their lives (Jones & Gabriel, 1999). Those who received more counseling (in successive therapeutic episodes), were less conflicted and more likely to select lesbian, gay, or bisexual counselors who would presumably provide more validation for their sexual identity.

Research has shown that graduate training on sexual identity has been minimal for mental health providers (Buhrke & Douce, 1991; Myers, 1982). A survey of accredited social work programs found that only one out of three offered what program directors described as "very strong" content related to sexual orientation (Mackelprang, Ray, & Hernandez-Peck, 1996). And a survey of counselor education programs found that only two-fifths (44%) of departments participating in the survey offered such courses, while only 1 out of 10 schools required them for graduation (Gray, Cummins, Johnson, & Mason, 1989; Murphy, 1992).

Counseling Approaches

Lesbian, gay, and bisexual youths seek counseling for a variety of concerns. However, many report that when a counselor learns their sexual orientation, this becomes the primary focus for counseling (Gonsiorek, 1988).

Schneider (1998) has suggested that counselors consider the needs of sexual minority youths as falling into one of three categories, each of which requires a slightly different approach. First, youths may seek counseling to obtain support for issues related to their sexual identity (e.g., confusion, isolation, distress). However, they also need a social context and connection to other LGB youths to provide socialization and support for developing a positive identity. Second, others may present with general problems that are related to and exacerbated by their sexual identity (e.g., family problems). Underlying these problems, however, may be fears and tension related to undisclosed sexual identity that requires counselors to address the immediate problem within the broader context of distress about their sexual identity. And finally, some youths' problems are unrelated to their sexual orientation. In all instances, Schneider (1998) suggests that counselors consider the impact of stigma on the adolescent's concerns, carefully assessing the role of sexual identity.

In working with LGB youths on problems related to their sexual identity, Schneider (1998) points out that the counselor's tasks are to: create a supportive environment where adolescents can feel good about themselves, help find other environments to enhance self-esteem, help them understand that the stigma they experience is societally induced, and build on their strengths to enhance coping skills to manage homophobia and heterosexism. Much of the counseling with LGB youths is psychoeducational, providing basic information about sexuality and self-care, dispelling myths, helping them understand and manage stigma, developing positive coping skills and help-seeking behaviors. Ryan and Futterman (1998) suggest incorporating the concept of anticipatory guidance into counseling with LGB youths. Anticipatory guidance—providing information about the challenges of adolescence—is a way of making youths and parents aware of typical life events and changes that adolescents and families are likely to experience, and helping them anticipate responses to facilitate development. For LGB youths and their families, this includes providing information related to sexual identity development and disclosure, sexual behavior and prevention, substance use, mental health, relationships, discrimination and anti-gay violence, developing a support system, developing access to lesbian, gay, and bisexual communities, and future plans including career and vocational planning.

HIV-Related Counseling

A vital aspect of counseling LGB youths involves exploring their knowledge, attitudes, practices, and risk behaviors for HIV infection (see Grossman, this volume; Rotheram-Borus et al., 1995). Gay and bisexual male youths are at high risk for HIV infection, in part because sexually active male youths may have older partners who are at high risk for infection. A lack of safe places to socialize increases the likelihood of seeking sexual partners in high-risk environments where risk behaviors are reinforced and youths may be exploited. Lesbian youths are often heterosexually experienced, and may also engage in sex with gay and bisexual males in their social networks, increasing their risk for infection (Hunter, 1996). Lack of accessible information on health risks for LGB youths further deepens cognitive isolation since health promotion and prevention literature often fails to mention lesbians, gay males, or bisexual people. So many LGB youths—who already have internalized misconceptions about their health needs and risks—do not apply prevention messages to their own activities (Ryan & Futterman, 1998). Counselors who have developed rapport with their adolescent clients can play a very important role in helping them identify and understand their risks for HIV infection, develop skills to negotiate safer sex with potential partners, obtain HIV testing (all sexually active adolescents should routinely receive HIV counseling and testing), and make decisions related to care should they become HIV-infected.

Reparative Therapy

Counselors may encounter parents or even some adolescents who seek help in changing the youth's sexual orientation. However, such attempts raise many ethical concerns, often contribute to negative self-esteem and mental health problems, and have not been proved to be successful over time (Haldeman, 1994). Even though the American Psychiatric Association removed homosexuality from its list of mental disorders more than 20 years ago, some practitioners still attempt to change an individual's sexual orientation. Such efforts appear to have intensified in recent years. Attempts by conservative and religious fundamentalist groups to assert that homosexuality is "curable" have resulted in increased media attention on reparative therapy and efforts to increase the availability of such services. For example, a 1997 conference on Homosexuality and American Public Life at Georgetown University included psychiatrists, psychologists, and clinical social workers who advocate and practice reparative therapy. Panelists recommended the development of pro-active "preventive homosexuality" initiatives to identify potentially gay adolescents and to provide early intervention treatment to prevent the development of homosexuality.

The increased public debate about reparative therapy has prompted professional associations to issue statements on reparative therapy. In 1993, the American Academy of Pediatrics stated that, "Therapy directed specifically at changing sexual orientation is contraindicated, since it can provoke guilt and anxiety while having little or no potential for achieving changes in sexual orientation" (American Academy of Pediatrics, 1993, p. 633). Moreover, the American Psychiatric Association states that "there is no published scientific evidence supporting the efficacy of 'reparative therapy' as a treatment to change one's sexual orientation" (American Psychiatric Association, 1997, p. 1). In its resolution related to therapeutic approaches to changing sexual orientation (DeLeon, 1998, pp. 934–935), the American Psychological Association cautions psychologists not to "make false or deceptive statements concerning . . . the scientific or clinical basis . . . for their services," and requires them to obtain appropriate informed consent before providing such services. And most recently, the American Psychiatric Association noted that it "opposes any psychiatric treatment, such as 'reparative' or 'conversion' therapy which is based upon the assumption that homosexuality per se is a mental disorder or based upon a prior assumption that the patient should change his/her homosexual orientation" (American Psychiatric Association, 1998, p. 1).[2] Counselors should caution parents against referring the adolescent for "reparative therapy" and instead should recommend treatment from mental health providers who will help the adolescent manage fears and confusion, while providing support for the youth's developmental processes.

Victimization and Assault

Counseling following victimization and assault is important for both the family and the adolescent. Recovery will take time and talking about the experience is a crucial part of resolving the trauma. LGB youths also need to talk about how the assault affects their self-esteem, their evolving sexual identity, and their sense of vulnerability in a homophobic society.

Counselors working with rape and assault victims should assess the adolescent's support system and connections to the organized lesbian and gay community. Decisions will need to be made about bringing charges against the assailant (which can help facilitate recovery for some people). The adolescent will need support to interact with the legal system and with law enforcement personnel who may be judgmental or dismissive. Referral to a supportive counselor who is knowledgeable about lesbian and gay community resources can help the youth obtain appropriate support. Increasingly, lesbian or gay anti-violence projects that provide victim advocacy and counseling are available in large cities (see, for example, Wertheimer, 1992).

Working with Families

Since youths are coming out at younger ages, parents and families are more likely to learn about their child's sexual identity during adolescence and to require guidance and support in dealing with this new, and generally distressing, information. Counselors can assist families in a variety of ways in dealing with the disclosure or discovery of an adolescent's lesbian or gay identity by providing individual or family counseling or mediation; providing accurate information, including written materials on LGB issues; and, making referrals to family counselors and community support groups, such as Parents, Families and Friends of Lesbians and Gays (PFLAG), a national organization with chapters in every state that sponsors support groups and educational activities to help parents and family members deal with their feelings and concerns. Parents have reported that contact with other parents of lesbian and gay children is extremely helpful in working through their distress and in debunking negative myths and misconceptions about homosexuality.

Need for Appropriate Referrals

In addition to general mental health concerns and problems related to social stigma and developing a positive sexual identity, some LGB youths may experience serious mental health disorders. Counselors may need to refer such youths for inpatient or outpatient psychiatric care or treatment for chemical dependency. Because many providers and agencies have limited knowledge and experience serving openly LGB youths (many do not disclose their sexual identity to health and mental health workers), counselors should assess the agency's or provider's capacity and level of support for lesbian and gay adolescents before making a referral. In particular, counselors should assess their treatment philosophy and prior experience in working with LGB youths; policies on working with LGB patients; availability of openly LGB staff; and linkages to other programs serving LGB youths. Many providers and agencies are still guided by outdated information based on inappropriate treatment philosophies that continue to view homosexuality as pathological or maladaptive (Mallon, 1998). Moreover, some youths are at risk for misdiagnoses of gender identity disorder and inappropriate treatment related to their sexual identity (Ryan & Futterman, 1998). While such approaches are harmful to adults, they can be even more damaging to adolescents who have fewer resources and options, and who are dependent on adults for support. Providers and adults frequently perceive homosexuality in adolescents as "just a passing phase" and consider adolescents too young to be able to develop a LGB identity, or to be sure that they are not heterosexual.

Increasingly, resources are available for youths in communities that lack specific services for LGB youths, including online support groups. The National Youth Advocacy Coalition provides referral information for providers and support services around the country (www.nyacyouth. org). Youth Guardian Services, a web-based network for nonheterosexual adolescents, provides supervised online support groups for teens, grouped by age (www.youthguard.org), and Youth Resource, a web page for LGB and transgendered youths offers health, mental health, and prevention information; referrals and links to youth services and online information (www.youthresource.com). Even in communities with support services for lesbian, gay, and bisexual youths, online resources offer anonymity, ready access, and opportunities to connect with youths in other areas. Together with infolines and hotlines, these provide critical access points to services and support for youths who may lack other resources.

Future Directions

As the experiences of LGB youths continue to change, their need for counseling and support services will also change. In the past few youths came out in junior high school or high school, and by the time they came out, many had left home. As a result, youths had more freedom to explore their emerging sexual identities, to find and access supportive communities, to openly date same-sex partners, and to explore lesbian and gay culture. Most adolescents struggling to integrate a positive sexual identity must do so in secrecy, since relatively few have reported satisfactory responses from parents when they disclosed their identity. Even though coming out during adolescence offers many benefits, coming out to parents and to peers appears to have a number of costs. Because most adolescents are still dependent on their parents for emotional and financial support, counselors should caution youths to carefully consider the consequences of coming out while they are still living at home, are still in school, and remain dependent on their parents.

Few clinicians who work with LGB youths are writing about the changing nature of youths' experiences, including greater visibility, wider availability of information and resources, and emerging counseling needs. In addition, research is needed in several key areas:

- Longitudinal studies on the development and evolution of sexual identity and life course outcomes, including the impact of stigma, ethnic background, and sexual identity among ethnic and racial minority youths.
- Studies of coping behaviors and adjustment in LGB youths who come out at various stages of adolescence, and the role of families and institutions in their identity development.
- Comparative studies of mental health and psychosocial adjustment among LGB youths, including suicide risk and prevention.
- Studies of help-seeking behaviors for health and mental health care, including accessing HIV-related services and care.
- Studies of strategies to enhance the mental health of LGB youths.

Additional research is required on the training needs and barriers to training for school counselors on working with LGB youths. Training should be provided for counselors at elementary and middle schools, as well as junior high and high schools. Other important targets include pediatricians (who are often asked by parents to make referrals and to help with sexual identity issues) and other key providers who serve children and adolescents such as workers in residential care facilities. Ironically, while media attention on LGB youths has increased and support services are more widely available even in many nonurban areas, the lack of attention to their health and mental health needs remains a major barrier to accessing appropriate and quality care.

Notes

1. The limited prospective research on adolescent sexual identity, to date, has provided very little information on developing a separate, bisexual cultural identity during adolescence. However, several patterns of behavior have been observed: many lesbian and gay youths have heterosexual experiences before identifying as lesbian or gay; some may identify as "bisexual" for a period of time, while consolidating a lesbian or gay identity, perceiving "bisexual" as a less stigmatizing label; while others who have same-sex experiences as adolescents and predominantly heterosexual experiences as young adults may later report both opposite-sex and same-sex experiences.

2. Policies are available from the American Psychiatric Association, Committee on Lesbian, Gay, and Bisexual Concerns, 1400 K Street, NW, Washington, DC 20005, and the American Psychological Association, 750 First Street, NW, Washington, DC, 20002.

References

Alderman, E. M., Schonberg, S. K., & Cohen, M. I. (1992). The pediatrician's role in the diagnosis and management of substance abuse. *Pediatrics in Review, 13*, 314–318.

American Academy of Pediatrics (1988). Rape and the adolescent. *Pediatrics, 81*, 595–597.

American Academy of Pediatrics. (1993). Homosexuality and adolescence. *Pediatrics, 92*, 631–634.

American Psychiatric Association. (1994). Gay and lesbian issues: Fact sheet. Washington, DC: Author.

American Psychiatric Association (1997). Homosexual and bisexual issues. Fact Sheet. Washington, DC: Author.

American Psychiatric Association. (1998). Position statement on psychiatric treatment and sexual orientation. Washington, DC: Author.

Bartholow, B. N., Doll, L. S., Joy, D., Douglas, J. M., Bolan, G., Harrison, J. S., Moss, P. M., & McKirnan, D. (1994). Emotional, behavioral and HIV risks associated with sexual abuse among adult homosexual and bisexual men. *Child Abuse and Neglect, 18*, 747–761.

Bieschke, K. J., & Matthews, C. (1996). Career counselor attitudes and behaviors toward gay, lesbian, and bisexual clients. *Journal of Vocational Behavior, 48*, 243–255.

Blake-White, J., & Kline, C. M. (1985). Treating the dissociative process in adult victims of childhood incest. *Social Casework, 66*, 394–402.

Blumenthal, S. J. (1990). Youth suicide: Risk factors, assessment and treatment of adolescent and young suicidal patients. *Psychiatric Clinics of North America, 13*, 511–556.

Borhek, M. V. (1988). Helping gay and lesbian adolescents and their families: A mother's perspective. *Journal of Adolescent Health Care, 9*, 123–128.

Boxer, A. (1990). Life course transitions of gay and lesbian youth: Sexual identity development and parent-child relationships. Unpublished doctoral dissertation, University of Chicago.

Boxer, A. M., Cook, J. A., & Herdt, G. (1991). Double jeopardy: Identity transitions and parent-child relations among gay and lesbian youth. In K. Pillemer & K. McCartney (Eds.), *Parent-child relations throughout life* (pp. 59–92). Hillsdale, NJ: Erlbaum.

Bradford, J., & Ryan, C. (1988). National Lesbian Health Care Survey: Final report. Washington, DC: National Lesbian and Gay Health Foundation.

Bradford, J., Ryan, C., & Rothblum, E. (1994). National Lesbian Health Care Survey: Implications for mental health care. *Journal of Consulting and Clinical Psychology, 62*, 228–242.

Brand, P. A., Rothblum, E. D., & Solomon. L. J. (1992). A comparison of lesbians, gay men and heterosexuals on weight and restrained eating. *International Journal of Eating Disorders, 11*, 253–259.

Brent, D. A., Perper, J. A., & Moritz, G. (1993). Psychiatric risk factors for adolescent suicide: A case control study. *Journal of the American Academy of Child and Adolescent Psychiatry, 32*, 521–529.

Briere, J., Evans, D., Runtz, M., & Wall, T. (1988). Symptomatology in men who were molested as children: A comparison study. *American Journal of Orthopsychiatry, 58*, 457–461.

Briere, J., & Runtz, M. (1987). Post-sexual abuse trauma: Data and implications for clinical practice. *Journal of Interpersonal Violence, 2*, 367–379.

Brooks, V. R. (1981). *Minority stress and lesbian women.* Lexington, MA, Lexington Books.

Buhrke, R. A., & Douce, L. A. (1991). Training issues for counseling psychologists in working with lesbians and gay men. *Counseling Psychologist, 19*, 216–234.

Chan, C. S. (1989). Issues of identity development among Asian-American lesbians and gay men. *Journal of Counseling and Development, 68*, 16–20.

Coleman, E. (1989). The development of male prostitution activity among gay and bisexual adolescents. *Journal of Homosexuality, 18*, 131–149.

Coleman, E., & Remafedi, G. P. (1989). Gay, lesbian and bisexual adolescents: A critical challenge to counselors. *Journal of Counseling and Development, 68*, 36–40.

D'Augelli, A. R. (1991). Gay men in college: Identity processes and adaptations. *Journal of College Student Development, 32*, 140–146.

D'Augelli, A.R., & Dark, L. J. (1995). Vulnerable populations: Lesbian, gay and bisexual youth. In L. D. Eron, J. H. Gentry, & P. Schlegel (Eds.), *Reason to hope: A psychosocial perspective on violence and youth* (pp.177–196). Washington, DC: American Psychological Association.

D'Augelli, A. R., & Garnets, L. D. (1995). Lesbian, gay and bisexual communities. In A. R. D'Augelli & C. J. Patterson (Eds.), *Lesbian, gay and bisexual identities over the lifespan: Psychological perspectives* (pp. 294–320). New York: Oxford University Press.

D'Augelli, A. R., & Hershberger, S. L. (1993). Lesbian, gay and bisexual youth in community settings: Personal challenges and mental health problems. *American Journal of Community Psychology, 21*, 421–448.

D'Augelli, A. R., Hershberger S. L., & Pilkington, N. W. (1998). Lesbian, gay and bisexual youth and their families: Disclosure of sexual orientation and its consequences. *American Journal of Orthopsychiatry, 68*, 361–371.

Dean, L., Wu, S., & Martin, J. L. (1992). Trends in violence and discrimination against gay men in New York City: 1984 to 1990. In G. M. Herek & K. T. Berrill (Eds.), *Hate crimes: Confronting violence against lesbians and gay men* (pp. 46–64). Newbury Park, CA: Sage.

DeCrescenzo, T. A. (1984). Homophobia: A study of attitudes of mental health professionals toward homosexuality. *Journal of Homosexuality, 2,* 115–136.

DeLeon, P. H (1998). Proceedings of the American Psychological Association, Inc., for the legislative year 1997: Minutes of the annual meeting of the Council of Representatives, August 14 and 17, Chicago, IL; and June, August, and December 1997 meetings of the Board of Directors. *American Psychologist, 53,* 882–939.

Descamps, M. J., Rothblum, E., Bradford, J., & Ryan, C. (1999). Mental health impact of child sexual abuse, rape, intimate partner violence and hate crimes in the National Lesbian Health Care Survey. Manuscript submitted for publication.

Dimock, P. T. (1988). Adult males sexually abused as children. *Journal of Interpersonal Violence, 3,* 203–221.

Drescher, J. (1996). Psychoanalytic subjectivity and male homosexuality. In R. P. Cabaj & T. S. Stein (Eds.), *Textbook of homosexuality and mental health* (pp. 173–189). Washington, DC: American Psychiatric Press.

Duncan, D. (1990). Prevalence of sexual assault victimization among heterosexual and gay/lesbian university students. *Psychological Reports, 66,* 65–66.

Espin, O. M. (1993). Issues of identity in the psychology of Latina lesbians. In L. Garnets & D. Kimmel (Eds.), *Psychological perspectives on lesbian and gay male experiences* (pp. 348–363). New York: Columbia University Press.

Farrow, J. A. (1990). Adolescent chemical dependency. *Medical Clinics of North America, 74,* 1265–1274.

Finkelhor, D. (1984). *Child sexual abuse: New theory and research.* New York: The Free Press.

Finkelhor, D. (1987).The sexual abuse of children: Current research reviewed. *Psychiatric Annals, 17,* 233–241.

Fortenberry, J. D. (1995). Adolescent substance use and sexually transmitted diseases risk: A review. *Journal of Adolescent Health, 16,* 304–308.

French, S. A., Story, M., Remafedi, G., Resnick, M. D., & Blum, R. W. (1996). Sexual orientation and prevalence of body dissatisfaction and eating disordered behaviors: A population-based study of adolescents. *International Journal of Eating Disorders, 19,* 119–126.

Futterman, D., Hein, K., Ruben, N., Dell, R., & Shaffer, N. (1993). HIV-infected adolescents: The first 50 patients in a New York City program. *Pediatrics, 91,* 730–735.

Garland, A. F., & Ziegler, E. (1993). Adolescent suicide prevention: Current research and social policy implications. *American Psychologist, 48,* 169–182.

Garnets, L., Hancock, K. A., Cochran, S. D., Goodchilds, J., & Peplau, L. A. (1991). Issues in psychotherapy with lesbians and gay men: A survey of psychologists. *American Psychologist, 46,* 964–972.

Garnets, L., Herek, G. M., & Levy, B. (1992). Violence and victimization of lesbians and gay men: Mental health consequences. In G. M. Herek & K. Berrill (Eds.), *Hate crimes: Confronting violence against lesbians and gay men* (pp. 207–226). Newbury Park, CA, Sage.

Garofalo, R., Wolf, R. C., Kessel, S., Palfrey, J., & DuRant, R. H. (1998). The association between health risk behaviors and sexual orientation among a school-based sample of adolescents. *Pediatrics, 101,* 895–902.

Gonsiorek, J. C. (1988). Mental health issues of gay and lesbian adolescents. *Journal of Adolescent Health Care, 9,* 114–122.

Graham, D. L., Rawlings, E. I., Halpern, H. S., & Hermes, J. (1984). Therapists' needs for training in counseling lesbians and gay men. *Professional Psychology: Research and Practice, 15,* 482–496.

Gray, L. A., Cummins, E. J., Johnson, B. P., & Mason, M. J. (1989). Human sexuality instruction in counselor education curricula. *Counselor Education and Supervision, 28,* 305–317.

Greene, B. (1994). Ethnic minority lesbians and gay men: Mental health treatment issues. *Journal of Consulting and Clinical Psychology, 62,* 243–251.

Haldeman, D. (1994). The practice and ethics of sexual orientation conversion therapy. *Journal of Consulting and Clinical Psychology, 62,* 221–227.

Herdt, G., & Boxer, A. (1993). *Children of Horizons: How gay and lesbian teens are leading a new way out of the closet.* Boston: Beacon Press.

Herdt, G., & Koff, B. (2000). *Something to tell you: How parents grow beyond a myth to integrate gay and lesbian children into families.* New York: Columbia University Press.

Hershberger, S. L., & D'Augelli, A. R. (1995). The impact of victimization on the mental health and suicidality of lesbian, gay, and bisexual youths. *Developmental Psychology, 31,* 65–74.

Hershberger, S. L., Pilkington, N. W., & D'Augelli, A. R. (1997). Predictors of suicide attempts among gay, lesbian, and bisexual youths. *Journal of Adolescent Research, 12,* 477–497.

Herzog, D. B., Norman, D. K., Gordon, C., & Pepose, M. (1984). Sexual conflict and eating disorders in 27 males. *American Journal of Psychiatry, 141,* 989–990.

Hetrick, E. S., & Martin, A. D. (1987). Developmental issues and their resolution for gay and lesbian adolescents. *Journal of Homosexuality, 13,* 25–43.

Hunter, J. (1996). Emerging from the shadows: Lesbian, gay and bisexual adolescents: Personal identity achievement, coming out, and sexual risk behaviors. Unpublished doctoral dissertation, City University of New York.

Icard, L. (1986). Black gay men and conflicting social identities: Sexual orientation versus racial identity. *Journal of Social Work and Human Sexuality, 4,* 83–93.

Johnson, R., & Shrier, D. (1985). Sexual victimization of boys. *Journal of Adolescent Health Care, 6,* 372–376.

Jones, M. A., & Gabriel, M. A. (1999). The utilization of psychotherapy by lesbians, gay men, and bisexuals: Findings from a nationwide survey. *American Journal of Orthopsychiatry, 69,* 209–219.

Kandel, D. B., & Davies, M. (1982). Epidemiology of depressive mood in adolescents. *Archives of General Psychiatry, 39,* 1205–1212.

Koss, M. P., Gidycz, C. J., & Wisniewski, N. (1987). The scope of rape: Incidence and prevalence of sexual aggression and victimization in a national sample of higher education students. *Journal of Consulting and Clinical Psychology, 55,* 162–170.

Krouse, J., & Krouse, P. (1998). *Who's who among American high school students: 29th annual survey of high achievers.* Lake Forest, IL: Educational Communications, Inc.

Mackelprang, R. W., Ray, J., & Hernandez-Peck, M. (1996). Social work education and sexual orientation: Faculty, student and curriculum issues. *Journal of Lesbian and Gay Social Services, 5,* 17–31.

Magee, M., & Miller, D. C. (1996). Psychoanalytic views of female homosexuality. In R. P. Cabaj & T. S. Stein (Eds), *Textbook of homosexuality and mental health* (pp. 191–206). Washington, DC: American Psychiatric Press.

Malinsky, K. P. (1996). Learning to be invisible: A qualitative study of lesbian students in Florida's public high schools. Unpublished doctoral dissertation, University of Sarasota.

Mallon, G. P. (1998). *We don't exactly get the welcome wagon: The experiences of gay and lesbian adolescents in child welfare systems.* New York: Columbia University Press.

Massachusetts Department of Education (1995). Massachusetts Youth Risk Behavior Survey. Unpublished data.

Meyer, I. (1995). Minority stress and mental health in gay men. *Journal of Health and Social Behavior, 36,* 38–56.

McCarn, S., & Fassinger, R. (1996). Re-visioning sexual minority identity formation: A new model of lesbian identity and its implications for counseling and research. *The Counseling Psychologist, 24,* 508–534.

Morales, E. S. (1989). Ethnic minority families and ethnic minority gays and lesbians. *Marriage and Family Review, 14,* 217–239.

Murphy, B. C. (1992). Educating mental health professionals about gay and lesbian issues. *Journal of Homosexuality, 22,* 229–246.

Myers, R. A. (1982). Education and training—The next decade. *The Counseling Psychologist, 10,* 39–44.

Petersen, A. C., Compas, B. E., Brooks-Gunn, J., Stemmler, M., Ey, S., & Grant K. E. (1993). Depression in adolescence. *American Psychologist, 48,* 155–168.

Ratner, E. F., Kosten, T. K., & McLellan, A. T. (1991). Treatment outcome of Pride Institute patients. Unpublished paper.

Remafedi, G. (1987). Adolescent homosexuality: Psychosocial and medical implications. *Pediatrics, 79,* 331–337.

Remafedi, G., Farrow, J. A., & Deisher, R. W. (1991). Risk factors for attempted suicide in gay and bisexual youth. *Pediatrics, 87,* 869–875.

Remafedi, G., French, S., Story, M., Resnick, M. D., & Blum, R. (1998). The relationship between suicide risk and sexual orientation: Results of a population-based study. *American Journal of Public Health, 88,* 57–60.

Rich, C. L., Fowler, R. C., Young, D., & Blenkush, M. (1986). San Diego suicide study: Comparison of gay to straight males. *Suicide and Life Threatening Behavior, 16,* 448–457.

Robinson, B., Walters, L. H., & Skeen, P. (1989). Response of parents to learning their child is homosexual and their concern over AIDS: A national study. *Journal of Homosexuality, 18,* 59–80.

Rofes, E. (1989). Opening up the classroom: Responding to the educational needs of gay and lesbian youth. *Harvard Education Review, 59,* 444–453.

Rosario, M., Meyer-Bahlburg, H. F. L., Hunter, J., Exner, T. M., Gwadz, M., & Keller, A. M. (1996). The psychosexual development of urban lesbian, gay, and bisexual youths. *The Journal of Sex Research, 33*(2), 113–126.

Rosario, M., Rotheram-Borus, M. J., & Reid, H. (1996). Gay-related stress and its correlates among gay and bisexual male adolescents of predominantly black and Hispanic background. *Journal of Community Psychology, 24,* 136–159.

Rotheram-Borus, M. J., Hunter, J., & Rosario, M. (1995). Coming out as lesbian or gay in the era of AIDS. In G. Herek & B. Greene (Eds.), *AIDS, identity and community: The HIV epidemic and lesbians and gay men* (pp. 150–168). Thousand Oaks, CA: Sage.

Rotheram-Borus, M. J., Rosario, M., & Koopman, C. (1991). Minority youths at high risk: Gay males and runaways. In M. E. Colten & S. Gore (Eds.), *Adolescent stress: Causes and consequences* (pp. 181–200). New York: Aldine de Gruyter.

Rotheram-Borus, M. J., Rosario, M., Meyer-Bahlburg, H., Heino, F. L., Koopman, C., Dopkins, S. C., & Davies, M. (1994). Sexual and substance use acts of gay and bisexual male adolescents in New York City. *Journal of Sex Research, 31,* 47–57.

Rudolph, J. (1988). Counselors' attitudes toward homosexuality: A selective review of the literature. *Journal of Counseling and Development, 67,* 165–168.

Ryan, C., Bradford, J., & Honnold, J. (1999). Social workers' and counselors' understanding of lesbian needs. *Journal of Lesbian and Gay Social Services, 9*(4), 1–26.

Ryan, C., & Futterman, D. (1998). *Lesbian & gay youth: Care & counseling.* New York: Columbia University Press.

Savin-Williams, R. C. (1990). *Gay and lesbian youth: Expressions of identity.* New York: Hemisphere.

Savin-Williams, R. C. (1994). Verbal and physical abuse as stressors in the lives of lesbian, gay male and bisexual youths: Associations with school problems, running away, substance abuse, prostitution and suicide. *Journal of Consulting and Clinical Psychology, 62,* 261–269.

Savin-Williams, R. C. (1995). Lesbian, gay male and bisexual adolescents. In A. R. D'Augelli & C. J. Patterson (Eds.), *Lesbian, gay and bisexual identities over the lifespan: Psychological perspectives* (pp. 165–189). New York: Oxford University Press.

Savin-Williams, R. C. (1998). *". . . and then I became gay": Young men's stories.* New York: Routledge.

Schmitt, J.P., & Kurdek, L.A. (1987). Personality correlates of positive identity and relationship involvement in gay men. *Journal of Homosexuality, 13,* 101–109.

Schneider, M. (1988). *Often invisible: Counselling gay and lesbian youth.* Toronto: Central Toronto Youth Services.

Schneider, M. (1991). Developing services for lesbian and gay adolescents. *Canadian Journal of Community Mental Health, 10,* 133–151.

Schneider, M. (1998). Pride, prejudice and lesbian, gay, and bisexual youth. In M. Schneider (Ed.), *Pride & prejudice: Working with lesbian, gay, and bisexual youth* (pp. 11–27). Toronto: Central Toronto Youth Services.

Schneider, S. G., Faberow, N. L., & Kruks, G. N. (1989). Suicidal behavior in adolescent and young adult gay men. *Suicide and Life-Threatening Behavior, 19,* 381–394.

Sears, J. (1991). Educators, homosexuality, and homosexual students: Are personal feelings related to professional beliefs? *Journal of Homosexuality, 22,* 29–79.

Setterberg, S. (1992). Suicidal behavior and suicide. In S.B. Friedman, M. Fisher, & S. K. Schonberg (Eds.), *Comprehensive adolescent health care* (pp. 862–867). St. Louis, MO: Quality Medical Publishing.

Shaffer, D., Garland, A., Gould, M., Fisher, P., & Trautman, P. (1988). Preventing teenage suicide: A critical review. *Journal of the American Academy of Child and Adolescent Psychiatry, 27,* 675–687.

Shaffer, D., Fisher, P., Hicks, R. H, Parides, M., & Gould, M. (1995). Sexual orienta-
    tion in adolescents who commit suicide. *Suicide and Life-Threatening Behav-
    ior, 25 (Suppl.)*, 64–71.
Siever, M. D. (1994). Sexual orientation and gender as factors in socioculturally
    acquired vulnerability to body dissatisfaction and eating disorders. *Journal
    of Consulting and Clinical Psychology, 62*, 252–260.
Silberstein, L. R., Mishkind, M. E., Striegel-Moore, R. H., Timko, C., & Rodin, J.
    (1989). Men and their bodies: A comparison of homosexual and heterosexual
    men. *Psychosomatic Medicine, 51*, 337–346.
Smith, G. B. (1993). Homophobia and attitudes toward gay men and lesbians by
    psychiatric nurses. *Archives of Psychiatric Nursing, 7*, 377–384.
Tancer, N. K., & Shaffer, D. (1992). Depression. In S. B. Friedman, M. Fisher, &
    K. Schonberg (Eds.), *Comprehensive adolescent health care* (pp. 853–861). St. Louis,
    MO: Quality Medical Publishing.
Tremble, B., Schneider, M., & Appathurai, C. (1989). Growing up gay or lesbian in
    a multicultural context. *Journal of Homosexuality, 17*, 253–267.
Weinberg, M. S., & Williams, C. J. (1974). *Male homosexuals: Their problems and adap-
    tations*. New York: Oxford University Press.
Wertheimer, D. (1992). Treatment and service interventions for lesbian and gay male
    crime victims. In G. M. Herek & K. T. Berrill (Eds.), *Hate crimes: Confronting
    violence against lesbians and gay men* (pp. 227–240). Newbury Park, CA: Sage.
Wyatt, G. E., & Peters, S. D. (1986). Issues in the definition of child sexual abuse in
    prevalence research. *Child Abuse and Neglect, 10*, 231–240.
Zierler, S., Feingold, L., Laufer, D., Velentgas, P., Kantrowitz Gordon, I., & Mayer,
    K. (1991). Adult survivors of childhood sexual abuse and subsequent risk of
    HIV infection. *American Journal of Public Health, 81*, 572–575.

11

Educational Reform and Sexual Identity

Conflicts and Challenges

Janice M. Irvine

School reform to include discussion of sexual orientation constitutes a bold strategy of the post-Stonewall movement. Marxists, feminists, and other critical theorists have noted that schools, as social institutions, serve a political function by their support of traditional arrangements of race, class, and gender. A critical scholarship has emerged that deconstructs the complexities of traditional schooling (Bowles & Gintis, 1976; Freire, 1971; Giroux, 1981; Weiler, 1988; Weis & Fine, 1993). The theory and practice of lesbian and gay school reform foregrounds a critique of the institutional, discursive, and social production and reproduction of heterosexism by the educational system. Like schooling itself, however, lesbian and gay school reform is neither neutral nor inconsequential. Such efforts must also be scrutinized, since ideology inheres in the various strategies for its implementation.

School reform represents a contemporary political contest over social and sexual ideologies. Both supporters and opponents deploy a range of discursive strategies, or claims, in an attempt to characterize the nature of issues related to lesbian, gay, bisexual, and transgender youths, and public education. In this chapter, I will examine the claims of both school reformers and their opponents as a site in which ideas about homosexuality, sexuality, and identities are shaped and reconstituted.

Initiatives on Sexual Orientation in Public Education

School reform has assumed increasing importance for the lesbian, gay, and bisexual civil rights movement during the last decade, despite formidable obstacles. Many educators, for example, had to overcome the fear that they would be accused of recruitment of young people in their classrooms. Activists often resisted school-based initiatives owing to a reluctance to revisit the pain of their own adolescence. Nonetheless, reforming public education has taken its place along with ending discrimination in the military and seeking equity for domestic partnerships as a key site for lesbian and gay social reform.

The need for safety and tolerance propelled the first school programs. Project 10 was the first major school-based program developed to provide education and counseling to students on the subject of sexual orientation. Its formation in Los Angeles in 1985 was prompted by the harassment of an openly gay male student who eventually dropped out of school. This incident heightened faculty and staff awareness of homophobia in the schools and eventually resulted in the implementation of Project 10. Since its inception, Project 10 has been the subject of extensive publicity and has been routinely characterized by its opponents as a program for seducing innocent children (Uribe & Harbeck, 1991). Currently there are a range of other programs throughout the country that either teach about lesbian, gay, and bisexual issues or offer counseling and support to youth. Sexual orientation is increasingly integrated into both comprehensive sexuality education and AIDS education programs, although this is hardly universal in secondary education. Other initiatives mention lesbians and gay men in the context of multicultural education. Public schools have developed support groups, such as the increasingly common Gay/Straight Alliances. Project 10 East, in Cambridge, Massachusetts, was developed after the suicide of a gay youth. Massachusetts is also home to the nation's first Commission on Lesbian and Gay Youth. Constituted in 1992 by Republican Governor William Weld, the commission's first task was a series of projects conducted under the rubric, "Making Schools Safe for Gay and Lesbian Youth."

These educational programs are of central importance for several reasons. They represent an unprecedented opportunity for a new generation of schoolchildren to learn that lesbian, gay, and bisexual identities are common and viable. In effective educational systems, schools become an opportunity for social invention, a place where "people think themselves into being" (Thompson & Sangeeta, 1993, p. xxxi). The power of programs that teach about sexual orientation is this awareness that they encourage. They allow for the recognition of lesbian, gay, and bisexual lives, and teach tolerance for diversity. For some students, such programs may facilitate the construction and emergence of lesbian, gay, or bisexual identities. Finally, these programs challenge "recruitment myths" and the historical taboos against lesbian and gay visibility in the classroom.

The very potential of these programs is, of course, the reason for their controversial status. Debates concerning the integration of sexual orientation in public school curricula occur routinely. Social conservatives, especially the religious right, have focused their efforts on opposing these initiatives in public schools. Some critics have invoked what they call "the gay agenda in public education" to reinforce old myths about "the homosexual as child molester." Some national organizations have triggered moral panics in school districts across the country. For example, in Des Moines, Iowa, fundamentalist Christian groups defeated a proposal to add sexual orientation to the curriculum, and in a highly contested and publicized campaign, ousted a prominent school board president who disclosed that he was gay during the controversy (Zuniga, 1995). Encouraged by conservative groups, leaders of the U.S. House of Representatives held hearings on the "promotion" of homosexuality in public schools (Chibbaro, 1995). And the children's book *Daddy's Roommate* (Willhoite, 1990) has topped the American Library Association Office for Intellectual Freedom's Most Challenged Titles list for two years, while other gay-themed books like *Heather Has Two Mommies* (Newman, 1989) continue to generate controversy.

Nationally, then, school reform efforts has been less about the education of children and youths and more about political differences between social movements. Both sides deploy specific discursive strategies in order to launch or defeat these programs. In the following sections, I will examine two pedagogic frames by which educators have made claims for programs or curricula addressing sexual orientation. I call these the "culture-based model" and the "public health model." Using a program that exemplifies each model, I will examine its pedagogic significance, its ideological and theoretical implications, and the grounds on which opponents have attacked it.

Teaching Children about Culture

Multiculturalism has been a vehicle for the inclusion of lesbian and gay issues into public education. As schools develop curricula and programs to more accurately reflect a racially, ethnically, and gender diverse world, many educators have understandably organized for the addition of content concerning the diversity of sexual identities. The culture-based model discursively locates lesbians and gay men on a comparative status with racial and ethnic minorities.

The culture-based model is powerful for several reasons. First, it allows for the teaching of lesbian and gay issues in the context of education about other important human differences. Since multicultural curricula are the primary venue by which children learn about people who are different, it is a practical and logical vehicle in which to insert lesbian, gay, and bisexual lives. Second, it does not ghettoize sexual orientation into a single unit or lesson. Multicultural programs, at their best, seek transformation of the curriculum and broader diffusion of diverse perspectives. Third, the culture-based model is normalizing, not pathologizing. It asserts that lesbians and gay men constitute a minority group like many others.

Perhaps the most widely known example of the culture-based model is the Children of the Rainbow curriculum in New York City. It is a case that exemplifies some of the common counterclaims against this discursive strategy. In September 1992, a group of protesters gathered at City Hall Park in New York City. Holding placards that read, "No way, José, Don't Teach Our Children to be Gay," "God Made Adam and Eve, Not Adam and Steve," and "Don't Brainwash Our Children," they expressed opposition to the implementation of a new multicultural curriculum for first-graders. The Rainbow Curriculum, as it was later termed, was intended to promote tolerance and to facilitate an appreciation for diversity among the city's school-children. Designed as a guide for teachers, it contained lessons on the artifacts, folk songs, and holidays of other cultures. It was based on the premise that children could be taught basic lessons in math, grammar, and reading by utilizing the games, songs, and dances from a wide range of cultures.

The document might have simply faded into obscurity were it not for some sections included at the last minute. The controversy over the curriculum centered on six relatively short entries in the 443-page document that discussed lesbian and gay families. One section noted that "The issues surrounding family may be very sensitive for children. Teachers should be aware of varied family structures, including two-parent or single-parent households, gay or lesbian parents, divorced parents, adoptive parents, and guardians or foster parents. Children must be taught to acknowledge the positive aspects of each type of household and the importance of love and care in family living" (Board of Education, 1991, p. 145). It goes on to note that children growing up in families headed by heterosexual adults "may be experiencing contact with lesbians/gays for the first time . . . teachers of first graders have an opportunity to give children a healthy sense of identity at an early age. Classes should include references to lesbians/gay people in all curricular areas. Educators have the potential to help increase the tolerance and acceptance of the lesbian/gay community and to decrease the staggering number of hate crimes perpetrated against them" (p. 372). The curriculum emphasized the recognition of lesbian and gay culture; there was no mention of sexual behavior.

The opposition to the curriculum was fierce, preying on parents' prejudices and anxieties. Distortions and hyperbole were the weapons in what television news magazine *60 Minutes* reporter Ed Bradley characterized as "a battle for the hearts and minds of New York City's first-graders" ("The Rainbow Curriculum," 1993). Counterclaim-making in this battle, which focused almost exclusively on opposition to the inclusion of sexual orientation content, was mobilized on two related fronts. First, critics attacked lesbians and gay men on the grounds of immorality and their aberrant "lifestyle." Second, they challenged the viability of lesbian and gay culture as appropriate for a multicultural curriculum.

The moral panic assumed familiar dimensions. One assemblyman asserted that homosexuals were "a sin against mankind," while a state senator described them as "pure evil and wickedness" (Minkowitz, 1992). As the controversy escalated, the informal consensual reality shared by the opponents was that the curriculum was "homosexual/lesbian propaganda" that was "teaching sodomy to first graders" (Myers, 1992, p. 6). Passions were inflamed by images of first graders learning about oral and anal sex, while critical parents and school board members described the contents of the multicultural curriculum as perverted, filthy, and deviant. Opponents of the idea of a lesbian and gay culture deployed a simple but powerful tactic to argue that it should be excluded from the multicultural curriculum. They juxtaposed the allegedly stable and indisputable cultural categories of race and ethnicity, and the purportedly fictive notion of lesbian and gay culture. "They want to teach my kid that being gay fits in with being Italian and Puerto Rican!" one parent cried (Tabor, 1992). Some African-American critics were incensed by comparisons of lesbian and gay politics and culture to the black civil rights movement. At one community school board meeting, a parent (who was also a teacher) said:

> Years of being thrown in jail for demonstrating against racism and being sprayed by fire hoses taught me something. I ask you where was the gay community when school children died in Mobile, Alabama? Where was the gay community when many of us were beaten at a lunch counter? Is this the only way we can be included in the curriculum? To allow the gay community to piggyback off our achievement? (D'Angelo, 1992)

For others, the outrage was fueled by the contention that, unlike African Americans or members of other racial groups, lesbians and gay men share no common cultural symbols or artifacts. The chair of the curriculum committee of one local school board was vehement during a *60 Minutes* broadcast on the Rainbow Curriculum:

> How dare they compare themselves to the Blacks, who've had to struggle going over—for over 250 some years? They have no special language, no special clothing, no special food, no special dress wear, so what—what makes them a culture? They don't fit into any definition of what a culture is. They are using the racial issue as a way to open doors. How dare they? ("The Rainbow Curriculum," 1993)

When Bradley suggested that lesbians and gay men have a minority identity, Banks fumed, "You're doing it again. You're putting—you're putting a sexual orientation on the same level of a race, and . . . that's unacceptable to this person sitting here." The limitations of the culture-based model emerge in the contours of this conflict. This paradigm forces the square pegs of lesbian and gay identities into the round holes of fixed, essentialized definitions of culture that are common in traditional multicultural programs (see Banks, 1991). There are several related complications to this. First, despite widespread colloquial use of the term "gay culture," there is a vibrant debate over whether lesbians and gay men can be best described as a culture, community, ethnic group, lifestyle, or sexual minority (see, e.g., Epstein, 1987; Irvine, 1994; Warner, 1993). Scholarship that questions the very notion of stable, unified cultural categories—either racial or sexual—has raised the stakes in this definitional debate.

Second, activists in the Rainbow Curriculum controversy were promulgating rigidly essentialist definitions of both race and sexuality at a moment when scholars and theorists were questioning those ideas by asserting the socially constructed nature of identity categories and rejecting false universalisms and ahistorical essentialisms. Much popular opposition to the idea of gay culture rests on lingering traces of biologism from the social sciences that cast racial culture as a fixed and natural essence. From this perspective, we are all born into culture, and race and ethnicity are the quintessentially authentic cultures. One's social location in a racial culture is secured at birth, and, as Banks (1991) implies, allows one entry into a stable system of shared language, dress, clothing, and other cultural signifiers. The popular conviction that cultural status is biologically and generationally transmitted inevitably excludes lesbians and gay men, who cannot indisputably lay such claims. Nevertheless, the bitterness of the Rainbow Curriculum controversy left gay activists with no option but to argue that they do constitute a culture. As one gay man insisted on *60 Minutes*, "We do have a culture. We do have our own literature. We have our own artworks. We have music that would be identifiable to lesbian and gay people." When the paradigm of multiculturalism is the only vehicle for addressing social differences, lesbians and gay men must fit themselves, however awkwardly, into that model. However unintentionally, in this context, the assertion of certain social preferences resembles a universal claim.

Third, the discursive positioning of lesbian and gay culture as equivalent to racial and ethnic culture allows for conflict by exploiting historical tensions among groups, fanning feelings of injustice, marginality, and competition for resources. As illustrated above, critics greet the suggestion of a lesbian and gay culture not simply with opposition but also with the fear that such recognition would somehow diminish their own social position or erode whatever legitimacy they have garnered from years of civil rights efforts. The borders of identities stiffen. For example, in conflicts over the Rainbow Curriculum, African-American parents yelled "White faggots" at ACT UP members, and ACT UP men yelled back, "Black racists" (Lee, Murphy, & North, 1994). One white school board president described how the Latino community responded to Children of the Rainbow in his district: "They said, 'We're a culture, and you [whites, liberals, gay people] are being culturally insensitive to our beliefs about sexuality, homosexuality, explicitness of sexual discussion, by pushing this curriculum'" (interview with Norman Fruchter, October 31, 1994). The culture-based model, then, can generate futile and destructive political contests over who constitutes a "legitimate" culture, and thereby polarize (allegedly white) lesbians and gay men against (allegedly heterosexual) communities of color.

The culture-based model has not escaped attack by the religious right. Counterclaims are mounted on several fronts. Opponents individualize and repathologize homosexuality, ridicule the notion of gay culture by making invidious comparisons, and position themselves as defenders of racial and ethnic groups.

Rainbow Curriculum opponents were strategically canny in framing the debate as exclusively about the (typically male) sexually deviant individual. One highly visible school board president charged that Children of the Rainbow was "aimed at promoting acceptance of sodomy" (it was informally dubbed "the sodomy curriculum"). When questioned on *60 Minutes*, she insisted, "What is homosexuality except sodomy? . . . There's no difference. Homosexuals are sodomists." Her lawyer in the battle against the Rainbow Curriculum extended this argument by invoking the dark specter of untold "deviants" stalking the halls of public schools:

> I do have a problem when homosexuality and lesbianism are portrayed as a culture. If homosexuality and lesbianism is a culture, then so is drug abuse. So is alcohol abuse. So is being a Nazi skinhead. There are all sorts of groups and lifestyles in the world, but it's highly misleading, and I think unhealthy to treat them as cultures in the same sense as Hispanic culture or Afro-American culture or Italian American culture. . . . If diversity is to be worshipped without limit, then presumably we should have Ku Klux Klan clubs in high schools, or we should have cocaine clubs in high schools. And no one should be excluded because we worship diversity and there are no limits on diversity. Ax murderers would be honored and respected. (interview with John Hartigan, October 18, 1994)

Finally, the argument that lesbians and gay men are not a culture enabled the religious right to mobilize communities of color by arousing fear and hatred. A white organizer could become the defender of racial and ethnic minorities while simultaneously spearheading the campaign that ultimately undermined the implementation of the entire multicultural curriculum. The same school board president mentioned above declared, "I will not demean our legitimate minorities, such as Blacks, Hispanics and Asians, by lumping them together with homosexuals in that curriculum" (Meyers, 1992). Yet she ultimately rejected not only the Rainbow Curriculum but also the entire mandate for a multicultural curriculum. She had a separate program crafted for her district, an area which is overwhelmingly Asian American, Latino, and African American. Her "Reaching Out" program features a story about a fictional town where all the inhabitants are squares, circles, triangles, and rectangles. All the shapes eventually come together and form a wagon, a development that is "the way to teach [children] to understand about differences and getting along" (interview with John Hartigan, October 18, 1994).

In sum, the culture-based model is enormously complex in its theoretical and practical consequences. Obviously we cannot generalize to all multicultural programs on the basis of the set of controversies that greeted the Rainbow Curriculum in New York City. All cities have their own unique histories of political accommodation and conflict. Yet in addition to its strengths, culture-based claims carry with them a particular configuration of vexing dilemmas. These difficulties are not necessarily resolved in what have been termed anti-bias or diversity programs, since opponents read these initiatives as thinly veiled culture-based models. In contrast, a different set of discursive strengths and limitations inhere in what I call the public health model.

Making Schools Safe: The Public Health Model

Various strategies fall under the rubric of the public health model. One common initiative is the integration of sexual orientation issues into sexuality or health education curricula, and building programs around safety and danger concerns. This model also includes counseling and support programs for youths such as Project 10 and its offshoots. In addition, many schools have implemented teacher training that emphasizes the enhanced risks of lesbian, gay, and bisexual youths for such problems as suicide, violence, or substance abuse. These myriad programs share a health promotion and risk prevention frame.

Educators in Massachusetts have most skillfully deployed public health claims. In the past several years, the state has far surpassed any other in its institutionalization of comprehensive lesbian, gay, and bisexual educational reform in public schools. Through an emphasis on data that suggest a high rate of lesbian and gay youth suicide attempts, activists persuaded Republican Governor William Weld to impanel a Commission on Lesbian and Gay Youth. In its first years, the commission held public hearings, issued widely publicized reports on the status of lesbian and gay youths in the educational and mental health systems, and implemented a statewide program of teacher training on sexual orientation, called "Making Schools Safe." The Massachusetts success story is all the more striking in that these reforms were undertaken at about the same time as New York City's Children of the Rainbow controversies.

In addition to their emphasis on protection and the risk of suicide, Massachusetts educators' success with the public health model has been enhanced by their strategic use of claims by lesbian and gay youths themselves. Through their active participation, these young people brought the issue alive, helped diffuse controversy, and made a compelling case for reform. For example, they launched an extraordinary lobbying effort to enact a landmark piece of legislation, the Gay and Lesbian Student Rights Law. One thousand students descended on the State House of Representatives to talk with their legislators. A 17-year-old senior told about the time his soccer team attacked him. "They spit on me and threw things at me and called me faggot, homo." Another student lobbied for weeks with a sign: "Gays Make up 30 percent of Completed Teen Suicides." In 1993, the legislation was passed, making Massachusetts the first state to outlaw discrimination against gay and lesbian students in schools.

There are powerful strengths to the public health model. First, many lesbian, gay, and bisexual youths face specific risks, and therefore need assistance and prevention efforts. Although social worker Paul Gibson's chapter in the infamous 1989 Department of Health and Human Services report on youth suicide (Gibson, 1989) has been criticized as anecdotal and derivative in the estimate that lesbian and gay adolescents are three times more likely than heterosexuals to attempt suicide, most current research supports that figure (e.g., D'Augelli & Hershberger, 1993). Furthermore, studies estimate that close to half of lesbian and gay youths have experienced school victimization in the form of verbal harassment or physical violence (Hershberger & D'Augelli, 1995; Hunter, 1990). Dropping out of school, substance abuse, homelessness, and HIV infection are also clear risks (Remafedi, 1987; Savin-Williams, 1994). It is a legitimate role of the schools to educate teachers and counselors about these problems.

A second strength of this model lies in its ability to put a human face on discrimination. In their appearances at hearings, lobbying days, and trainings, lesbian and gay youths make educational reform vital and tangible. Ideology recedes, at least momentarily, in the face of adolescents recounting self-doubt and victimization so severe that they prompt suicide attempts.

Finally, public health claims in Massachusetts have at least temporarily stymied opposition from social conservatives. Opponents have admitted to some difficulty finding ground on which to criticize these prevention programs, which have suicide prevention as their goal. It is reasonable to assume that opposition is inevitable. In fact, there has been town-by-town opposition, as well as statewide legislative initiatives to prevent student involvement in gay-related programs without parental consent. While it is too early to tell, it may be that the greatest strength of this model has been the time it allowed for mobilizing statewide grassroots support through the Making School Safe team-building approach. This support, sorely lacking for Children of the Rainbow, may ultimately thwart whatever opposition arises.

As with the culture-based model, the drawbacks of the public health model are the obverse of its strengths. First, sexual orientation concerns risk being ghettoized in ancillary health education, family life, and after-school programs. This contrasts with the culture-based model, which effects integration throughout the curriculum. Educational activists ideally seek the diffusion of sexual orientation topics throughout the curriculum, from science to English. As one teacher proposed, "There should be, well 'Robert wants to date Pierre.' It needs to be incorporated on that level where being gay is not an issue. The issue is what is the correct conjugation of the verb 'to date'" (interview with Kevin Jennings, November 7, 1994). The public health model can unintentionally reinforce segregation of sexual orientation issues from the curriculum.

A second important limitation of this model is that it leaves intact, and may even strengthen, a pathologized representation of lesbian, gay, and bisexual lives. The overriding concentration on suicide, substance abuse, and victimization has led some lesbian and gay youths and educators to speak out against the unmitigated use of what one student dubbed, "the horror stories." Some call for an emphasis on youths' strengths and successes (Harbeck, 1993). Yet by definition the public health model highlights the risks and dangers to youths, and a reformulation undermines its very strength in engendering sympathy in parents and duty in teachers and administrators.

In fact, the safety discourse of the public health model has prompted a reciprocal danger discourse from counterclaimants. Conservative and religious opponents of these educational programs fold concerns about gay, lesbian, and bisexual youth suicide or substance abuse into their longstanding demonization of homosexuality. As one critic put it, the available data support the contention that homosexuality is a dangerous and destructive lifestyle, or, in his terms, a "death-style" from which children should be protected (Personal communication, John Hartigan, October 18, 1994). In this view, of course, it is homosexuality itself, not cultural heterosexism, that causes youth suicide or other problems.

Conservative critics mount their "death-style" arguments in a consistent and predictable fashion. This often entails a solemn recitation by a seemingly authoritative older white male (sometimes a physician) of grim alleged facts about gay men and lesbians related to diseases or death. Dr. Stanley Monteith's appearance in the highly publicized propaganda video *The Gay Agenda* is a prime example. Monteith intones a list of statistics designed to repulse Mr. and Mrs. Middle America about supposed percentages of "homosexuals" who engage in different sexual activities. *The Gay Agenda*, which is widely used throughout the country by opponents of gay rights initiatives, was the subject of an expose by the *L.A. Times*, which reported that Monteith's statistics were derived from a study of only 41 men conducted by the long-discredited anti-gay psychologist Paul Cameron (Colker, 1993). Cameron's ideologically driven and methodologically unsound research is used by many opponents of lesbian and gay educational reform. He notes that he is "the wellspring of right wing data in that area" (Personal communication, Paul Cameron, November 9, 1994). For instance, his study, "The Longevity of Homosexuals," which compares obituaries from gay newspapers to those of mainstream newspapers, concludes that lesbians and gay men have an abbreviated lifespan (Cameron, Playfair, & Wellum, 1994).

Cameron's work has been used by critics of lesbians and gay men. John Hartigan, an attorney who played a central role in the defeat of Children of the Rainbow, is a major architect of the death-style rhetoric. Hartigan's method is to braid together questionable data from Cameron's studies with statistics on HIV and sexually transmitted diseases from well-respected medical journals. Another propaganda video, *The Gay Agenda in Public Education*, features Hartigan listing high HIV infection rates among gay men in urban areas as reported by the *New York Times*. He then concludes, "If that isn't dangerous, if that isn't frightening, then nothing in the world is. And it's criminal for the New York City public school's chancellor to publish a book [Children of the Rainbow] telling teachers that they should urge children not to view homosexuality as frightening when that's the medical reality" (The Report, 1993).

In danger discourse, then, lesbians and gay men are cast as depraved and diseased individuals who die an early death. These are claims clearly designed to persuade an uninformed public to oppose lesbian and gay rights and educational reform. It is a formidable response to efforts aimed at keeping youths healthy and safe—what one critic of such programs dubbed "public safety as a Trojan Horse" (Pertman & Atkinson, 1993), a metaphor that evokes warfare and destruction.

The shortcomings of both the culture-based model and the public health model do not represent criticisms of either set of claims. Given both the political climate and definitional dilemmas inherent to sexual orientation, there is no vehicle by which integration of lesbian and gay issues into public education is not somehow problematic. The political climate, discussed below, understandably fuels a defensive tone as reformers must defend complex conceptualizations of sexual orientation: for example, we are a legitimate culture we have music, we have literature); we're a different kind of "different" than skinheads or ax murderers; we're born this way, your kids won't catch it; and protect lesbian and gay youth or they'll kill themselves. Theoretical dilemmas aside, it is the case that some critics would oppose these school reforms no matter what conceptual frameworks might be crafted.

Moral Panics in the Schools

The intense attacks of opponents are, in part, testimony to the enormous success of educational reformers in implementing programs nationwide. The backlash represents an irresolvable conflict not just over educational, social, and sexual ideologies but also over a broader national social and political vision. These controversies reflect the widespread cultural tensions of this century. They are the inevitable result of a clash between two important movements. First, there have been rapid changes in social life and cultural values over the last hundred years, a growing secularization and liberalization sometimes labeled modernity. An increasingly sexualized society, in which sex is valued less for reproduction and more for pleasure and satisfaction, is part of this trend. Feminism, lesbian and gay liberation, and comprehensive sexuality education are reflections of this movement. Second, religious evangelical organizations have coalesced throughout the century in reaction to the changes of modernity. Although for decades they were determinedly apolitical, evangelical groups have emerged as a powerful political force in the last 30 years (see, e.g., Ammerman, 1987; Liebman & Wuthrow, 1983; Marty & Appleby, 1991, 1993). Their opposition to lesbian and gay educational reform stems from a profound moral objection to ho-mosexuality and to sexual liberalism, but also from a recognition that such controversies serve as potent political vehicles by which to recruit and gal-vanize members. Lesbian and gay educational reform, then, has become an important and volatile battleground for two competing, irreconcilable worldviews: a fundamentalist religious belief in universal, moral absolutes; and a secular move toward social tolerance, diversity, and openness. In rec-ognition of the depth of these conflicts, the board president of one school district in New York that was torn apart by debates over Children of the Rainbow said, "We're going to have the equivalent of warfare for awhile" (interview with Norman Fruchter, October 31, 1994).

Controversies over teaching about sexual orientation reflect both literal and symbolic concerns. It is important to examine the very tangible ques-tions and anxieties that inform the opposition to lesbian and gay school re-form. Parents, for example, may object to what they see as the public schools' usurpation of their rights to teach sexual values to children. Other parents worry that teachers might not be adequately trained to teach about sensi-tive subjects, or that certain topics may be broached at an inappropriate age.

Certainly homophobia underpins some opposition to lesbian and gay school reform. Some parents, for religious or other reasons, oppose homo-sexuality (and sexual freedom in general) and resent that the topic is raised with their children. They may worry that their children will be somehow seduced or persuaded into becoming lesbian or gay, or they simply believe in the importance of the traditional heterosexual, nuclear family. They may fear recruitment or molestation of their children, or they worry about dis-eases and substance abuse in what they have heard is the "death-style" of homosexuality. For many parents, it is simply that, as journalist Anne Roiphe succinctly put it, "When it comes to their own little Heather's fate, they would rather keep gender choice on the straight path" (Roiphe, 1992). There are a range of interests specific to homosexuality itself that fuel counterclaims against such education. In many cases, however, these community contro-versies are driven by longstanding resentments and conflicts in local com-munity settings that have little to do with sexuality or homosexuality. It is important to understand when sexuality curriculum battles become meta-phors for other problems.

Certain themes recirculate in community debates over teaching about sexuality. First, controversies over sexuality curricula often trigger famil-iar conflicts over the role of the public schools. These debates over whose values will be taught arise in a range of other subjects such as drug educa-tion, death education, multiculturalism, and any other "values clarifica-tion" programs. Opponents may complain that the state, under the aus-pices of the public school, is undermining parental power and control and imposing an unacceptable value system. In this instance, opposition to lesbian and gay school reform is merely another plank, albeit a powerful one, in a larger platform of attack on public education (Provenzo, 1990).

Second, frustrations over incomplete or inadequate educational reform efforts may drive opposition to gay-inclusive curricula. In New York City, for example, the efforts to introduce the Children of the Rainbow Curriculum were complicated by an unwieldy system of both local and central control of schools. Not surprisingly, when communities viewed the supportive school system chancellor as imposing a curriculum on them, some resisted. When a local school board president refused the curriculum, the media portrayed it as "David vs. Goliath battle of local interests versus centralized authority."

Third, sexuality curricula debates may be fueled by anger over inequalities in unequal access to resources. Opposition to sexuality education may reflect a sense of powerlessness in relation to larger social institutions engendered by race, ethnicity, and social class. In the Children of the Rainbow controversies, for example, anger about unequal access was a frequent subtext of the opposition from within communities of color. Parents raged that their children were not being adequately taught basic academic skills, yet they were being taught "sodomy." In addition, many members of communities of color objected to the inclusion of lesbians and gay men in a multicultural curriculum since they did not constitute a "real" culture or minority. Much of this resentment flowed from the sense of a "special interest" group trying to benefit from years of hard work to achieve multiculturalism in the schools. Thus, competition over status and resources underpinned the debate over the curriculum.

Finally, many parents feel an overwhelming sense of powerlessness in the face of a host of potential dangers to their children. Sexuality education can be perceived as threatening in an environment in which drugs, violence, and sexual assault are felt to be constant problems. This was the sentiment shared by many opponents of Children of the Rainbow, such as this staff member of a gay/lesbian social service agency:

> I mean, you're already living in New York and your locus of control isn't too good, because your kid's going out in the street, and you're worried about if they're going to come home alive, and now someone wants to teach faggotry to them. And you're like, "That's it, Gladys. We're going down to the school board." (interview with Andy Humm, September 27, 1994)

Simply being taught about homosexuality may serve as a metaphor for unwanted intrusion and the inability to keep children safe. It can be the last straw for the fictional Gladys and her very real counterparts, for whom a protest at the school board can represent an assertion of personal control.

These aspects are important in that they highlight the many different sources of support or opposition to lesbian and gay school reform. In terms of interventions or resolutions to these community controversies, it is crucial to tease out which objections are specific to lesbian and gay educational initiatives and which are symptomatic of broader social, political, and economic tensions.

Lesbian and gay educational reform faces an uphill battle in this broader context of both displaced concerns and religious right opposition. Consequently, the conceptual strategies and claims that educators deploy often reflect pragmatic opportunities and political realities more than theoretical consensus. For example, many educational reformers are ambivalent about whether lesbians and gay men constitute a culture. Yet when the multicultural curriculum is the central vehicle for discussion of difference, it becomes imperative to include homosexuality.

Similarly, advocates for lesbian and gay initiatives in public education often mount "arguments of reassurance." In order to assuage parental fears and deep cultural anxieties about children being encouraged to explore homosexuality through programs in public schools, they insist sexual orientation is not a choice but a congenital status. Some use research on the "gay brain" and "gay genes," studies that have been questioned by many (see Hershberger, this volume), to reassure parents that their children cannot be socialized into homosexuality.

Arguments of reassurance are difficult to resist. Even skeptics sometimes fall back on them in politically charged moments. One activist in the Children of the Rainbow controversy told me that sexual orientation is not clearly biological and that the research is inconclusive. Yet in a letter he wrote to an African-American leader at the height of the Rainbow conflict, he claimed that sexual orientation was biological. "All current scientific evidence," he wrote, " points toward the fact that it is an innate human characteristic that is most certainly not chosen as you suggest." There were two unstated subtexts to this letter. First, "your child won't catch it." And second, sexual orientation, since it is an immutable biological characteristic, it should be accorded the same respect and protections given to racial and ethnic minorities.

Conclusion

At this early stage of lesbian and gay educational reform initiatives, the most pressing priority may well be simply to implement programs addressing sexual orientation. As I suggested earlier, however, there is no strategy that will be free of controversy. With that in mind, it may be useful to consider the broader ideological messages in lesbian and gay school initiatives. The claims may either reproduce or challenge social stereotypes, operating as an assertion about "the homosexual" as a biological entity or a cultural creation, reinforcing particular political identities and subjectivities. As we have seen, some claims leave lesbians and gay men vulnerable to being labeled as disordered, while others put them in a specific relationship to other disempowered groups in ways that may generate resentment. We may do well to consider the "hidden curricula" in these various programs designed to reform the "hidden heterocentric" curriculum.

References

Ammerman, N. T. (1987). *Bible believers: Fundamentalists in the modern world*. New Brunswick, NJ: Rutgers University Press.

Banks, J. (1991). *Teaching strategies for ethnic studies*. Boston: Allyn and Bacon.

Board of Education (1991). *Children of the Rainbow: First grade*. New York: Board of Education of the City of New York.

Bowles, S., & Gintis, H. (1976). *Schooling in capitalist America*. New York: Basic Books.

Cameron, P., Playfair, W., & Wellum, S. (1994). The longevity of homosexuals before and after the AIDS epidemic. *Omega: Journal of Death and Dying, 29,* 249–272.

Chibbaro, L. (1995, September 8). House panel postpones hearing on schools. *The Washington Blade*, p. 21.

Colker, D. (1993, February 22). Anti-gay video highlights church's agenda. *Los Angeles Times*.

D'Angelo, L. (1992, September 6). Repercussion continue after school board vote. *Staten Island Sunday Advance*.

D'Augelli, A. R., & Hershberger, S. L. (1993). Lesbian, gay, and bisexual youth in community settings: Personal challenges and mental health problems. *American Journal of Community Psychology, 21,* 421–448.

Epstein, S. (1987). Gay politics, ethnic identity: The limits of social constructionism. *Socialist Review, 93–94,* 9–54.

Freire, P. (1971). *Pedagogy of the oppressed*. New York: Harper & Row.

Gibson, P. (1989). Gay male and lesbian youth suicide. In ADAMHA, *Report of the Secretary's Task Force on Youth Suicide* (Vol. 3, pp. 110–142). (DHHS Pub. No. (ADM) 89-1623). Washington, DC: Government Printing Office.

Giroux, H. (1981). *Ideology, culture, and the process of schooling*. Philadelphia: Temple University Press.

Harbeck, K. (1993). Invisible no more: Addressing the needs of gay, lesbian, and bisexual youth and their advocates. *The High School Journal, 77,* 169–176.

Hershberger, S. L., & D'Augelli, A. R. (1995). The impact of victimization on the mental health and suicidality of lesbian, gay, and bisexual youth. *Developmental Psychology, 31,* 65–74.

Hunter, J. (1990). Violence against lesbian and gay male youths. *Journal of Interpersonal Violence, 5,* 295–300.

Irvine, J. M. (1994). A place in the rainbow: Theorizing lesbian and gay culture. *Sociological Theory, 12,* 232–248.

Lee, T., Murphy, D., & North, L. (1994). Sexuality, multicultural education, and the New York City public schools. *Radical Teacher, 45,* 12–16.

Liebman, R., & Wuthnow, R. (1983). *The new Christian right*. New York: Aldine.

Marty, M., & Appleby, R. S. (1991). *Fundamentalisms observed*. Chicago: University of Chicago Press.

Marty, M., & Appleby, R. S. (1993). *Fundamentalisms and society: Reclaiming the sciences, the family, and education*. Chicago: University of Chicago Press.

Meyers, S. L. (1992, December 13). How a "Rainbow Curriculum" turned into fighting words. *The New York Times*.

Minkowitz, D. (1992, October 21). It felt like a Nazi rally. *New York Newsday*.

Myers, S. L. (1992, December 2). Queens school board suspended in fight on gay-life curriculum. *The New York Times*.

Newman, L. (1989). *Heather has two mommies*. Boston: Alyson Wonderland.

Pertman, A., & Atkinson, L. (1993, May 20). Some say gay-pupil policy unneeded. *The Boston Globe*.

Provenzo, E. (1990). *Religious fundamentalism and American education: The battle for the public schools*. Albany, NY: State University of New York Press.

"The Rainbow Curriculum" (1993, April 4). *60 Minutes*.

Remafedi, G. (1987). Adolescent homosexuality: Psychosocial and medical implications. *Pediatrics, 79*, 331–337.

Roiphe, A. (1992, January 11). Promoting gayness? No—just basic decency. *The New York Observer*.

Savin-Williams, R. C. (1994). Verbal and physical abuse as stressors in the lives of lesbian, gay male, and bisexual youths: Associations with school problems, running away, substance abuse, prostitution, and suicide. *Journal of Consulting and Clinical Psychology, 62*, 261–269.

Tabor, M. (1992, September 6). S. I. drops gay issues from student guide. *The New York Times*.

The Report (1993) *The gay agenda in public education* [Video]. Available from Accuracy in Media, 4455 Connecticut Ave. NW, Suite 330, Washington, D.C. 20008.

Thompson, B., & Sangeeta, T. (Eds.). (1993). *Beyond a dream deferred: Multicultural education and the politics of excellence*. Minneapolis: University of Minnesota Press.

Uribe, V., & Harbeck, K. M. (1991). Addressing the needs of lesbian, gay, and bisexual youth: The origins of Project 10 and school-based intervention. *Journal of Homosexuality, 22*(3/4), 9–28.

Warner, M. (Ed.). (1993). *Fear of a queer planet: Queer politics and social theory*. Minneapolis: University of Minnesota Press.

Weiler, K. (1988). *Women teaching for change: Gender, class, and power*. New York: Bergin & Garvey.

Weis, L., & Fine, M. (Eds.). (1993). *Beyond silenced voices: Class, race, and gender in United States schools*. Albany, NY: SUNY Press.

Zunigà, J. (1995, September 15). Christian Right gives Iowa's Wilson defeat. *The Washington Blade*, p. 24.

12

Social Change, Sexual Diversity, and Tolerance for Bisexuality in the United States

Gilbert Herdt

Whenever society ushers in a new and potentially revolutionary period of change, we can expect to find dramatic transformations in how the culture represents—and individuals negotiate—their sexuality and gender roles, dress and adornment, body images, and social relations. Such a time is now, as we approach the 21st century, wherein technological and global expansion of borders and systems of information create what Martin (1994) has called "flexible bodies." These historical changes are challenging the received traditions of sex/gender, allowing more leeway for human development and reducing heterosexism and homophobia, and thus promoting tolerance for diversity in sexual identities and communities. This chapter focuses on these changes, particularly generational differences in representation and the practice of bisexuality in American society over the past three decades.

Changes in society and within individual subjectivities do not always occur in synchrony: sometimes they complement; other times they collide (Gagnon, 1990; Herdt, 1990; Laumann, Gagnon, Michael, & Michaels, 1994). A change in the culture can occur without necessary changes in individual representations or behaviors, or it may be slow to occur within developmental subjectivities, as sometimes happens in politics and ideology. The influence of the feminist movement on American gender roles and social life provides many examples (Chodorow, 1992; Stimpson, 1996). Likewise, changes in individual perceptions and actions may occur rapidly, but not be mirrored in cultural transformations, at least not in all aspects or for some time, as evidenced in the gay and lesbian movement and its challenge to such basic policy formation as the American military's discrimination against gays and lesbians (Herek, Jobe, & Carney, 1996). Changes in sexual identities and the formation of new sexual communities over the past century in Western countries have provided many fascinating examples of these cultural and individual changes (Weeks, 1985).

The increasing contestation of heterosexuality in its various elements (e.g., marriage between opposite sexes, having children, sexual and partner commitment for life, etc.) has opened the way for new sexual/gender formations, at home and then abroad. Virtually all of these new formations pose a challenge to "heteronormativity," the cultural idea that to be "normal" in human development means being only heterosexual. However, these changes have had a very different impact on two adjacent generations: the baby boomers, who led the sexual revolution of the 1960s and founded feminism and the gay and lesbian movements in their contemporary versions; and, generation X, which came of age during the time of AIDS, in the 1980s and early 90s, and has borne the brunt of the radical resocialization regarding sexual risk behavior. It is this cohort that is pushing the next wave of attitude change in body perception, gender roles, and tolerance for bisexuality. While the evidence for the latter assertion is admittedly incomplete, reflections on research on gay and lesbian youths, and the Chicago Horizons study (Herdt & Boxer, 1993), offers sufficient grounds to think further on the issues.

The change in attitudes and practices regarding bisexuality can be taken as a litmus test of these generational differences. In my own generation of the middle-class baby boomers, it was unusual to find tattoos, body piercing, and gender-blending in growing up. Indeed, many came to see such alternations of the "natural" body as repugnant. Gender and sexual roles in society were too rigid to permit such performances, save in the movies or in the liminal circumstances of Halloween parties. Today we are witness to the emergence of huge variability in the population regarding matters of tattooing and body piercing, androgyny, and bisexuality, which seem far more attractive to younger cohorts than before (Weeks & Holland, 1996). Generation X registers notions of "queering" and "gender-blending" in bodies and practices to a degree unimaginable to the baby boomers (Elkins & King, 1996). The idea that major league team basketball star Dennis Rodman would rise to celebrity status by becoming a national spectacle, through the display of exotic tattoos, extensive body piercing, red and green dyed hair, and occasional gender-blended transvestite crossing, complete with fur boas, is remarkable to the baby boomers and remains repugnant to many of them—heterosexual and homosexuals as well (Coplan, 1996).

I am convinced that the social changes spelled out above are precipitated by the marked decline in heterosexism and homophobia in our society, which is facilitating the emergence of new sexual minorities—not to mention the 15 minutes of fame Rodman enjoyed as a antihegemonic cultural icon, the muscleman in drag. I will consider the broader implications of how such changes enable increasing numbers of American youths to embark upon new and uncharted waters as members of emergent sexual minorities, including "bisexuality."

The Historical Emergence of New Sexual and Gender Identities

Before the concept of homosexuality was invented, somewhere around 1870, or perhaps a decade or more later, depending upon where one was living— whether in New York or New Caledonia—desires that diverged from a focus on the opposite sex had to contend with the existential problem of what Roland Barthes might call "unclassifiable feelings." In the absence of marked categories of sexual identity, the classification of persons was by individual design, less than by cultural difference; by their sexual and gendered acts, not by "sexual identities," for these identities awaited invention. Likewise, the distinctions between homosexual and heterosexual had to await the time of new social distinctions, with rewards (heterosexuality) and punishments (homosexuality) meted out along the way. The stigma and prejudice inherent in this cultural discourse were not ignored; another century was needed for invention of the concept of homophobia (Weinberg, 1972), an index of hatred and fear of homosexuality now better thought of as a component of heterosexism (Herek, 1993).

Through all this historical change, bisexuality remained a kind of lumping category, a grab bag of biological and psychological traits. Of course it mattered whether one spoke of bisexual men *or* women, since the inescapable "sexual drive" ideology of male desire and behavior provided a different target for "bisexual" representations than for women's behavior, which tended to be depicted by conceptions of love and motherhood (unless they were morally "fallen" into prostitution; D'Emilio & Freedman, 1988). In the 19th century, individual women were attracted to other women or fell in love with them. They had no words to describe their feelings precisely, and even if they had, the discourse of their times would not have given voice to such a "Boston marriage," intimate and erotic but not necessarily physically sexual (Smith-Rosenberg, 1985). Hermaphroditism became a common gloss for "bisexuality" at some level of abstraction; Freud's notion of the bisexual "invert" as a "psychic hermaphrodite" is one such expression (Foucault, 1980). And by the early part of the 20th century, bisexuality became more of a gloss for "male homosexuality," less popular in medical and cultural representation since homosexuality became more explicitly developed as "deviance." What remained for "bisexuality" was the residual sense of an organic or biological origin for sexual dimorphism, with ramifications for brain, social role, and even soul. Categories of "third sex" and third gender belong to this area of "unclassifiable feelings" in our cultural tradition, continuing up to the present (Herdt, 1994). However, what changed in the past generation for bisexuality as a category was its gradual transition from the hermaphroditic realm into mainstream conceptions of human development.

The United States is noted for its long historical tradition of expressive individualism and the rise of cultural minorities as a contentious but integral product of liberal democracy formation (Bellah, Madsen, Sullivan, Swidler, & Tipton, 1985; Herdt, 1997b). Historical, sociological, and psychological study of lesbians and gay men over the past two decades has demonstrated the importance of understanding how societal changes in cultural representations of homosexuality have influenced declarations of same-sex desires in American society at large (Murray, 1996). Lesbian and gay culture is a further sociopolitical extension of this basic process (D'Emilio & Freedman, 1988), albeit one that staked its claims to cultural authenticity on new sexual rights (Herdt & Boxer, 1993). For example, lesbian, gay, and bisexual adolescents in the 1980s felt morally justified in "coming out," wanting to live their sexual lives openly in the contexts of the relationships that mattered (family, school, peers, and work). The ones my colleagues and I studied in Chicago felt that it was a moral wrong against their being when they were denied this privilege. Such a cultural construct is a dramatic change from the past, since prior representations of same-sex desire were derived from negative ideas of homosexuality as sin, degeneracy, and disease, the meanings of which were subsumed under psychopathology and the marginality of disease discourse (Adam, 1986; Bayer, 1987).

Heterosexual normativity remains a profound cultural and psychological force in the United States, and it merits being sufficiently detailed to realize the stakes in the struggle for tolerance of sexual diversity. Among the key cultural goals or lifeways privileged as "normative heterosexuality" could be listed the following: (1) being attracted only to the opposite sex (never to the same sex or to both sexes); (2) having the ceremony of a religiously sanctioned wedding that officially validates love, romance, and sexual relations with someone of the opposite sex; (3) parenting biological children with only an opposite-sex partner; (4) living with this partner the rest of one's life to the exclusion of other romantic or sexual partners; and (5) enjoying the status of grandparent in one's later years, a final step in the development of full social personhood in the Western tradition (Herdt, 1997b). This is a cultural ideal, of course, a script we learn in growing up. It resonates most strongly in family life, in school and peer groups, in television soap operas and Hollywood movies, and in religious functions. In the lives of many heterosexuals growing up in our society, this social myth of perfect heterosexuality may be a source of parental guidance, psychological comfort, and social support. For others who are unable, for whatever reason, to live up to these goals, either because they find themselves attracted to the same sex or both sexes, because they prefer to remain unmarried, because they cannot or chose not to have children, because they become separated, divorced or widowed, or finally, because they do not have grandchildren, the myth of the happy heterosexual life may be experienced as a burden (Herdt & Koff, 2000).

These social changes gave rise to a range of new identities that we are presently saddled with, as well as others that were to follow. The contrast set—homosexual and gay (reviewed in Herdt & Boxer, 1992)—is misunderstood and still conflated in popular culture and social science. (For instance, Sullivan [1996] lumps them together in his recent essay.) However, homosexuals and gays or lesbians remain distinct as category labels that people themselves use in reference to themselves or by attribution to others. Older Americans still prefer "homosexual," while younger cohorts prefer "gay" (Herdt 1997a; Herdt & Boxer, 1993). We should think of these not only as labels but also as distinctive sexual ontologies instilled through divergent developmental pathways of desires, beliefs, and values to accompany social roles as scripted performances on the stage of society (Gagnon, 1990; Herdt, 1997b).

The outlines of the major identity categories that emerged from this history are as follows:

1. *The closet homosexual*, an identity from the 19th century that signifies and practices same-sex erotic relations, but hides these signifiers from significant others and does not identify with or participate in gay culture (Sedgwick, 1990).
2. *The gay/lesbian distinction*, a marked cultural identity that involves a process of coming-out rituals, leading to self-disclosure of one's same-sex desires to all significant others, ideally in all domains of life (work, family, school, etc.). This emerged earlier in the century, perhaps as early as the "fairy" category of metropolitan New York (Chauncey, 1995), but it did not rise to prominence until the 1960s.
3. *The "queer,"* historically dating from the last century (perhaps earlier; see Trumbach, 1994), but in its present meaning, a new marked identity that is associated with sexual activism and active involvement in social movements, including Queer Nation, Radical Faeries, etc., that are not exclusively same-sex desired, but for many actors permit the expression of such desires.
4. *Transgenders*, associated with gender-blending, and a variety of social activist movements, which typically undermine absolute male/female sex typing.
5. *The bisexual*, a person who engages in relationships with one or both sexes, although not necessarily at the same period of the life course (Herdt & Boxer, 1995). Though the term "bisexuality" is used in some fashion of historical continuity with the past, in fact there is reason to believe that the meanings of bisexual identity in current use differ by historical generation (Ryan & Futterman, 1998; Rust, 1995; Weinberg, Williams, & Pryor, 1994). These distinctions are increasingly common in different cohorts of American cultural discourse, and while they should be thought of as ideal types, nonetheless these are personal and cultural templates for many individuals in our society.

Contemporary "Bisexuality" Emerges among Youths

A generation ago it was common to find American young adults whose careers as gay and lesbian persons would begin with a transitional phase of self-labeling as "bisexuals." They would leave home, often going off to college, and there they would "experiment" with different sexual encounters, gradually to come out and self-identify as gay or lesbian (Herdt, 1989). In the Horizons study of the 1980s I conducted with Andrew Boxer (Herdt & Boxer, 1993), we found a new variant of that pattern. Using anthropological and psychological methods, we studied the community and its institutions, conducting interviews with 202 male and female youths between the ages of 14 and 20 who self-identified as gay and lesbian. The Horizons group were the vanguard of a new cultural and developmental cohort: youths who came out in their adolescent years.

The boys and girls who found the Horizons center came in search of a safe place to discuss their sexuality, and to come out as openly gay and lesbian they were dealing with four fundamental psychocultural preconceptions as old as our society:

1. Homosexuality is disease, madness.
2. Homosexuality is gender inversion.
3. Homosexuality is self-hatred.
4. Homosexuality is de-individuation and giving up of the personal self.

The undoing of these preconceptions required nothing less than resistance to any ambiguity of identities, including opposition to bisexuality as a potential outcome of sexual development.

We found that by age 9½, on the average, boys and girls in our study had experienced their first attraction to the same sex (Herdt & Boxer, 1993, especially chap. 5). This means that they were aware and in some cases excited or aroused by another person, typically a peer or friend. By age 11, boys and girls had begun to have fantasies about the same sex. By age 13 for boys and 15 for girls, they had already experienced homoerotic activity of some kind, such as masturbation. Their desires and actions were now inclining in a direction that perpetually took the same sex as their preferred and most exciting romantic and sexual object. By age 16, both sexes had typically disclosed their attractions for the same sex, with the ensuing problems leading them to search for a new context for discussing and understanding their emerging adult lives. AIDS may have further accentuated the developmentally early age by injecting a massive media blitz and sex education program that enabled the country to learn of alternative sexualities and gender variations (Paul, Hays, & Coates, 1995).

A historically unique cohort of self-identified gay, lesbian, and bisexual adolescents were coming out—during the adolescent period—for the first time in the history of our society. They did not typically wait to leave home or go to college, but began the experimentation and change during the high school years while still living at home with their families (Boxer, Cook, & Herdt, 1991). Soon these adolescents would experience intense pressures from peers to stop being "bisexual" and start acting out their "true identities"—as the teens themselves referred to them—and declare themselves to be gay or lesbian. This social performance was not only applauded by the adult gay and lesbian community but also regarded as fundamental in the teenager's own ritual passage into gay culture. No one who refused to march in the Pride Parade, as a self-identified gay or lesbian, would be credited with the full citizenship of the gay culture (Herrell, 1992).

Many of the Horizons' youths experienced a time when they saw themselves as bisexual, although they did not typically communicate their dual desires as their cultural identity. We found that of all Horizons' youths, many engaged in sexual relations with both genders in growing up, with a higher number of girls having their first sexual experience with the opposite sex and a higher number of boys having an exclusive history of same-sex relations. Their risk-taking was found to be a function of their experience with or ignorance of sexual intercourse with the same or opposite sex. Experimentation with the other sex was typically with their friends in the group. By "trying out" or "testing" their desires, as the youths put it, they were in a period of behavioral bisexuality, even as their cultural view of the behavior was gay and lesbian defined (Herdt & Boxer, 1995).

In fact, the ideology did not accord with individual developmental histories in some cases and differed significantly as a function of gender, as well. There is a powerful gender difference in the sexual pathways of boys and girls in the Horizons study. Girls typically had more heterosexual experience in their histories, with two-thirds having had significant heterosexual contact before they came to Horizons. Since the mean age of our sample was 19 years, it is easy to infer that early on, between the ages of 13 and 17, girls are being inducted into sexual relations with boys. We face here the problem of what is socially necessary and what is preferred. Only a third of the boys had heterosexual experience, and 40% of them had had no sexual experience with girls. For most of these boys, their sexual contact with girls was restricted to "safe" lesbian-identified girlfriends at the Horizons center. When one interrogates youths' narratives, one discovers that powerful gender-role pressures were exerted on girls to conform to the wishes of parents, siblings, peers, and boyfriends. So while there were pressures on boys to perform, there were greater pressures on girls to conform. The latter case, to use Chodorow's (1992) phrase, creates a compromise in their desires in order to conform to heterosexuality. But, as was seen in Fine's (1992) work in the New York City schools, girls at Horizons were not able to explore and express their desires until they located a safe space that enabled them to think through their sexual decisions. In fact, they could not become the agents of their own desires until they had located the gay and lesbian youth group in the high school. There, some of them had to admit, contrary to their prior stereotypes, that they found the gay and lesbian youths more accepting and open to "diversity" than their peers, adult teachers, or parents.

We generally found that there was a generational divide between attitudes regarding bisexuality in our Horizons study. The adult advisors were nearly all lesbian or gay. The teens were generally ambiguous about their desires and identities at first. Their "confusion" was generally attributed to internalized homophobia by the adult advisors, who ranged in age from 22 to 55. The adults, however, also tended to think of bisexuality as confusion. It was strongly believed that when a bisexual support group in Chicago (called Biways) did its annual presentation, to quote one advisor, "the kids were a little crazy for a week or two after that." Asked why, it was commonly stated that the presenting bisexual adults were themselves confused. In fact, I shared their opinion at the time. I was, after all, of the same baby-boom generation as the advisors, and I sympathized with their plight in wanting to provide a secure environment for the youths. The youths, however, had a much more catholic view. Approximately a fourth of them typically self-identified as bisexual, but this expression was muted in meetings, largely owing to the ideological opposition to being bisexual. In short, there was a strong wave of cultural politics working in favor of declaring one's desires to be either lesbian, gay, or heterosexual, not in-between.

I have written before of this resistance and dislike that many of the adult advisors of the youth group had for bisexuals (Herdt & Boxer, 1993). Indeed, it was even objectified as the "problem of bisexuality" in the internal discourse of the institution, as I believe was so common to the times throughout the United States. We found that the adult gay and lesbian-identified advisors were strongly disposed to think of bisexuality as a "closet defense"— a stage of sexual adjustment immaturity—before the "real thing"—being gay or lesbian—was accepted by the self and performed on the stage of society. This was all the more remarkable because the same cultural terms and idioms were resisted when it came to the hegemonic attribution that being gay or lesbian was just a defense against heterosexuality or a "stage of confusion" that would pass on the way to being mature. I did not find the opposition reported by some of greater hostility by lesbians toward bisexuals (Rust, 1992; Weinberg et al., 1994). I did find, however, that gay men had a more difficult time than their lesbian colleagues in accepting the bisexual expressions of the youths. However, we must be careful not to generalize from such ethnographic studies, owing to the great differences to be found by ethnicity, gender, and social class (D'Augelli, 1996; Hunter & Schaecher, 1995).

A New Vision of Bisexual Identities

The problem of many youths today is not what it was for gay and lesbian-defined adolescents from even a decade ago: a "confusion" in their identities, which in the prior generation was strongly attacked as a manifestation of disease, or illness, or madness, or criminality, a sign and symptom of nature gone astray, of sinful and antisocial appetites that threatened chaos to the social order. The youths we studied at Horizons came to have sufficient resources and role models that they could get beyond the story of confused identities and focus on how to express their desires and identities in a homophobic society.

Today a variety of studies suggest that a new view of bisexuality is required (Ryan & Futterman, 1998). New research suggests that bisexuality is a more attractive option than before, though the declaration bisexual identity still presents social problems for the person. The recent and important sociological study of Weinberg et al. (1994) has demonstrated the stigma that continues to surround bisexuality. The book reports on a significant convenience sample of adult bisexuals studied in the late 1960s and early 70s, whom we can call "baby boomers." Much variation is found in the life course and sexual experiences of these people. The authors noted the persistence of confusion in the identities of bisexually identifed persons, both before the period of their active bisexuality and later. "Most bisexuals reported pervasive feelings of confusion and uncertainty about their sexuality at some point in their lives" (Weinberg et al., 1994, p. 8). The stability of their identities was also in flux during the period of study. The authors found that about two-thirds of all the men and women who identified as bisexual at the beginning of the 1980s had shifted or altered their identities by the end of that decade. It was reported that the bisexuals were routinely suspected of being closeted; even in "San Francisco, the bastion of sexual freedom" (Weinberg et al., 1994, p. 8), they experienced hostility and discrimination. Nevertheless, it also true that many of the respondents in the study were proud of their bisexuality and found their identity pathway rewarding.

The historically earlier reaction of gays and lesbians can now be placed in cultural perspective. I think that we might reinterpret the bias of the baby-boom pioneer generation of gays and lesbians as a necessary by-product of the struggle for acceptance of gay and lesbian causes in the United States (Sullivan, 1996). Intimate citizenship in the gay and lesbian culture required a strident emphasis on being different and on telling a story of coming out that was political and social (Plummer, 1996). Obviously, the liberationist baby-boom ideology committed that generation to "come out of the closets and into the streets," resisting any effort to reduce homosexuality or bisexuality to "confusion" in terms of the received medicalized sexology of the day.

It is the incredible social change in the United States that has provided the basis for this change. While many persons may have become involved in culture-building activities or activism as part and parcel of their own personal identity formation, others did so only later, after having consolidated a new identity; at least this was the case until the later 1970s and early 1980s, prior to the AIDS pandemic publicity (Levine, Nardi, & Gagnon, 1997). Their preparation for this cultural renaissance assisted the work of gay and lesbian community institutions in many American urban centers and smaller cities (Gagnon & Nardi, 1997; Herdt, 1997a). This social activism was the basis of gay and lesbian causes—a necessary cultural politics promoting the acceptance of diverse American sexual communities and identities.

As lesbian and gay culture grew in force, then, it was possible for the first time that a cohort of youths could self-identify as gay or lesbian. Thus, during the past generation, in which the gay and lesbian community has come to power and paved the way for the emergence of a new cohort of youths who could self-identify as gay, lesbian, or bisexual in adolescence, American youths have grown up with the idea that sexuality is much less binary or dichotomous than had earlier cohorts. The role that bisexuality played in this change was always controversial and remains so. Gays and lesbians, and to a certain extent, feminist lesbians in particular, may have been more hostile to those who self-identified as bisexual rather than as gay or lesbian (Rust, 1992). But we must recognize this as a matter of context and as a particular generation's struggle to achieve acceptance and tolerance. Today's youths, who gender-blend, or transcend by transgender, have only a tenuous notion of the cultural history of the United States that led up to the acceptance of sexual diversity, and hence, of bisexual expression.

During the quarter-century in which these changes occurred, new and important sexual communities, or sexual minorities, have emerged in the United States and Western Europe, not to mention the Third World (Herdt, 1997b; Manderson & Jolly, 1997). These new sexual cultures have created the social and psychological impetus for expansion of the concept of sexual diversity as part of an expanded concept of "human sexual nature." The effect has been a new challange to homophobia and heterosexism in its various forms. This has had the tendency to provide for greater acceptance of bisexuality as an alternative sexual and gender identity formation. American youths today are thus growing up with a broader range of sexual, friendship, and social relations than before.

AIDS has played a decisive role in these processes of change in the United States, as many observers have argued (Levine et al., 1997). As the epidemic spread, two strands of social activism were born, one related to HIV and illness, exemplified by the organization ACT UP; the other to Queer nationalism (Queer Nation) and future-oriented utopian causes (Radical Faeries). At the time of the Horizons study, these strands were just beginning to unravel, with some effects on intergenerational relations (Herdt, 1997a). Queer nationalism was thus born in the cradle of the gay and lesbian movement and was nurtured by its cultural politics and rising good fortunes.

However, in the same manner that socialization for AIDS sexual risk reduction is enhanced through social institutions such as Horizons, and the absence of such leads to less education and prevention, we must raise a concern about the effect of "cool bisexuality" as a sexual formation among the current coming-of-age adolescents and young adults (Ryan & Futterman,

1998). In general, there are fewer concerned and supportive caretakers for bisexually identified youths to step in and offer the sort of positive safer-sex education provided by gay and lesbian organizations, or in some instances public schools and clinics (Herdt & Boxer, 1996). The example of the bisexual center studied by Weinberg et al. (1994) in San Francisco is instructive, since AIDS education had not yet appeared on the scene, and the center closed soon after their study was completed. It is well known that bisexuality received bad press because of the epidemic (Paul et al., 1995).

Other changes of a more global nature have impacted upon the very definition of sexuality and personhood. As I argue elsewhere (Herdt, 1997b), sexual diversity in human development is primarily a matter of the limitations imposed upon people as they are born into and grow up in a particular sexual culture. All things being equal, the more their sexual culture restricts the range of "normal and natural" human behavior, the more restrictions and the less experimentation we will find in individual sexual histories. Sexual cultures manage this restriction through norms, rules, beliefs, and sanctions imposed on sexual behavior in the course of child development, imposed at the time of puberty (whether socially or biologically defined) and then cemented through the customs of courtship and mating, which lead up to socially approved and judicially defined marriage. In all human communities, with few and unusual exceptions (e.g., certain orders of monks or nuns), full personhood is defined by heterosexual marriage and child-rearing, and the rights and duties of personhood are denied to those who fail to achieve these milestones of the life course. These are the ways in which sexual variation is controlled in many sexual cultures around the world (Herdt, 1997b). However, once variation is introduced and the restrictions are minimized or removed, as has occurred in American society since the sexual revolution of the 1960s, we find greater acceptance of new forms of sexuality, and greater diversity in sexual behavior (Laumann et al., 1994).

Today a whole range of new sexual movements and minorities have begun to classify and make socially acceptable what previously was thought to be hidden, taboo, strange, freakish, and generally beyond the range of "human sexual nature." Gender-blending, transgenders, she/man, queer movements, Radical Faeries, and the many alternative sexual cultures in Third World countries that deploy their own local concepts fall into this realm of innovations. These formations suggest the basis for a new counterformation in American society: the resistance to heteronormativity. The emergence of divergent sexual cultures, or sexual minorities, is critical to the change. As these sexual cultures have sprung up, and as new age-cohorts have come of age during the same historical period, the sense that there are more alternatives for sexual and gender identity development has grown. Thus, bisexuality has become increasingly accepted by a generation of younger people who resist identification with the main categories of sexual identity.

In general, we can think of these new sexualities as "social constructions"—that is, as social experiments in human culture and development.

Of course, they appeal to the flexibility of the human condition and take advantage of the great range of adaptations that globalization brings. They are thus not "biological" innovations in the narrow sense; and because they are social experiments in learning, they can also quickly disappear from the social landscape. As an anthropologist, I do not believe that people are born with sexual identities, or gender roles, any more than they are born to be Russians or Spanish or Americans or Sambians. This does not mean, however, that they do not grow up with intrinsic desires and particular classes of objects that attract them. Their desires, as distinct from their sexual identities (whose meanings are defined in their key parameters by their cultures), do not depend upon the existence of culture to create them, but culture is required for their expression (Herdt & Boxer, 1995; McClintock & Herdt, 1996).

Such a view suggests that, in general, as sexual prejudice declines, we can expect the range of variation in sexual behavior to increase throughout the world. This means that alternative sexualities will flourish. Bisexuality—when conceived of as a general descriptor that denotes behavior that is neither purely heteronormal nor homonormal—will become increasingly visible and durable over time. This does not mean that heterosexuality and the traditional nuclear family will dissipate, or that the lesbian and gay community will cease to hold its symbolic grasp as positive force against homophobia. However, it might be said that the lesbian and gay movement will become a victim of its own success. Thus, acceptance of sexual variation is diagnostic of a change in fundamental mainstream attitudes, suggesting that within one or two generations, the sexual classification of the modern period will have become obsolete or at least will have hold only in the corners of the provinces. One of the implications of this prediction for gay and lesbian theorists, researchers, developmentalists, and policy experts is to reconsider the limitations of our implicit ideology of human nature and human development (Herdt 1990). Paul and his colleagues (1995, p. 377) have suggested that a sea change has occurred in relations between gays and bisexuals.

> This recognition of bisexuals by both the general public and the gay community as a distinct subgroup (although they might be denigrated as either sexual anarchists or diseased pariahs) coincided with the development of a more organized bisexual movement protesting the enforced invisibility and the stereotyping of bisexuals both in society at large and in the gay community. The growing acceptance of this life-style and label within the gay community is evidenced by number of organizations that have shifted to the more inclusive term "lesbian, gay, and bisexual" versus "lesbian and gay," as well as the broader meanings given to the term "queer." (Paul et al., 1995, p. 377)

I recently completed a preliminary study of older lesbians and gays in Chicago, which has implications for one aspect of this issue (Herdt, Beeler, & Rawls, 1997). We found a strong tendency in the cohort of people over

age 50—men and women—to be skeptical of bisexuality as an outcome or "final product" of development. More than 90% of our sample self-identified as gay or lesbian. They typically expressed the idea that having a community center or providing services for youths or older people should be restricted to those in need—gays and lesbians who have committed themselves to being of and building up a community. This finding suggests that the baby-boom generation that is now headed into retirement is still culturally and psychologically anchored in the categories of identity experienced in their youth. And as our society ages and the mantle passes to the next generation, we might expect to see a different attitude, more inclusive of a broad spectrum of sexual diversity, come into mainstream cultural politics.

Conclusions

At the beginning of the gay and lesbian movement in the 1960s, a set of events that are symbolized by the Stonewall riots but by no means limited to them, it was unimaginable to divide a still hidden population into "gay youth" and "older gays." Looking back at the progress of the past quarter-century has made us appreciate the extraordinary sense in which we are witness to a revolution in lesbian and gay lives. Indeed, the development of gay and lesbian culture over the past several decades has seen the rise of many extraordinary community organizations and services that have done much social good. By promoting positive gay and lesbian attitudes the community has sought to fight homophobia at the most fundamental level; and its political, social, and economic efforts have been notable. In the early years of the gay and lesbian movement the emphasis was primarily upon coming out and being open in affirming same-gender love, sexual relationships, and life partnerships. Within a few years, the emphasis shifted to HIV/AIDS education and prevention efforts. Soon, and in part as a result of the AIDS effort, another initiative occurred in the creation of support groups for lesbian and gay young people. In recent years, however, the awareness has grown that a whole area of need exists for the support of older lesbians and gay men. Thus far, this need has been largely subordinated to these earlier goals of coming out, preventing the spread of AIDS, and the support of younger people. As our society ages, and the baby boomers mature, self-identified gay men and lesbians are growing into their retirement years. As the younger generations, including generation X, moves into its place, we can expect even greater diversity of identities and sexual cultures and greater respect accorded for bisexuality than ever before.

As bisexuality becomes more culturally routine we are sure to find other dramatic changes in the more intimate aspects of human development, too. What people enjoy and find pleasurable, what they regard as repugnant in beliefs and practices, are matters of the cultural politics of the era that shapes their developmental subjectivities and positions of power on the stage of society. These involve us in rethinking what is at stake in the concept of homophobia. In this regard, I recall Sedgwick's (1991) ironic essay, "How to Bring Up Your Child As Gay." Gay men and lesbians were upbraided for not being more courageous in actively "socializing" the new generation of gay and lesbian youths into the culture of gay institutions. Fearing the end-less assaults of right-wing rhetoric, gay men dreaded being accused of brain-washing children into homosexuality, and thus being charged as guilty—again—of recruitment, a charge which haunts so many policy discussions surrounding the welfare and education of younger lesbians, gays, and bi-sexuals. Sedgwick, herself a kind of pansexual/heterosexual, offered the criticism in the spirit of promoting tolerance of sexual diversity in identities and in communities. And yet this is a difficult process, both to teach and to learn, owing to the intense homophobia of our society, so deeply ingrained in adult lesbians and gay men (Herdt & Boxer, 1996).

Gay and lesbian citizens should take courage from the utopian visions that came down from the 19th century and fan the flames of aspirations for positive change across the generations. Our efforts to support the younger cohort of gays and lesbians in their nascent struggles of coming out, coping with homophobia, promoting tolerance, and living with HIV/AIDS are generative not only of a commitment to the intentional project of gay and lesbian culture building but also of the very finest legacy of American lib-eral democracy. This is an expansion of bisexuality concepts as well, beyond the cultural stereotypes of the past. Maybe we cannot resonate with all the sexual and gender changes of generations today. The baby-boom genera-tion finds itself distressed at times that youths refer to themselves as "bi," not gay or lesbian. But that is a harbinger of things to come in the multiplic-ity of sexual formations and diverse sexual cultures proliferating around the world. These declarations are often meant to support affirmative action and sexual diversity in a land that still debates its own ideology of equal-ity. By lending support and criticism in equal measure, we might find new intergenerational dialogues. These discussions will not be dull, and they will, at times, even excite utopian visions of past married to future.

References

Adam, B. (1986). Age-structured homosexual organization. In E. Blackwood (Ed.), *Anthropology and homosexual behavior* (pp. 1–34). New York: Haworth.

Bayer, R. (1987). *Homosexuality and American psychiatry: The politics of diagnosis.* Princeton: Princeton University Press.

Bellah, R. N., Madsen, R., Sullivan, W. M., Swidler, A., & Tipton, S. T. (1985). *Hab-its of the heart: Individualism and commitment in American life.* Berkeley: Uni-versity of California Press.

Boxer, A. M., Cook, J. A., & Herdt, G. (1991). To tell or not to tell: Patterns of self-disclosure to mothers and fathers reported by gay and lesbian youth. In

K. Pillemer and K. McCartney (Eds.), *Parent-child relations across the lifespan* (pp. 59–93). New York: Oxford University Press.

Chaucey, G. (1995). *Gay New York*. New York: Basic.

Chodorow, N. J. (1992). Heterosexuality as a compromise formation: Reflections on the psychoanalytic theory of sexual development. *Psychoanalysis and Contemporary Thought, 15,* 267–304.

Coplon, J. (1996, April 21). Legends. Champions? *New York Times Magazine,* 32–54.

D'Augelli, A. R. (1996). Enhancing the development of lesbian, gay and bisexual youths. In E. D. Rothblum & L. A. Bond (Eds.), *Preventing heterosexism and homophobia* (pp. 124–150). Thousand Oaks, California: Sage.

D'Emilio, J. D., & Freedman, E. B. (1988). *Intimate matters: A history of sexuality in America*. New York: Harper and Row.

Elkins, R., & King, D. (Ed.). (1996). *Blending genders: Social aspects of cross-dressing and sex-changing*. New York: Routledge.

Fine, M. (1992). *Disruptive voices: The possibilities of feminist research*. Ann Arbor: University of Michigan Press.

Foucault, M. (1980). *The history of sexuality*. New York: Viking.

Gagnon, J. (1990). The implicit and explicit use of the scripting perspective in sex research. *Annual Review of Sex Research, 1,* 1–44.

Gagnon, J., & Nardi, P. (Eds.). (1997). Introduction. In M. P. Levine, P. M. Nardi, & J. H. Gagnon (Eds.), *In changing times: Gay men and lesbian encounter HIV/AIDS* (pp. 1–19). Chicago: University of Chicago Press.

Herdt, G. (1989). Gay youth, emergent identities, and cultural scenes at home and abroad. In G. Herdt (Ed.), *Gay and lesbian youth* (pp. 1–42). New York: Harrington Park Press.

Herdt, G. (1990). Developmental continuity as a dimension of sexual orientation across cultures. In D. McWhirter, J. Reinisch, & S. Sanders (Eds.), *Homosexuality/heterosexuality: Concepts of sexual orientation* (pp. 208–238). New York: Oxford University Press.

Herdt, G. (Ed.). (1994). *Third sex, third gender: Beyond sexual dimorphism in culture and history*. New York: Zone Books.

Herdt, G. (1997a). Intergenerational relations and AIDS in the formation of gay culture in the United States. In M. P. Levine, P. M. Nardi, & J. H. Gagnon (Eds.), *In changing times: Gay men and lesbians encounter HIV/AIDS* (pp. 245–282). Chicago: University of Chicago Press.

Herdt, G. (1997b). *Same sex, different cultures*. New York: Westview Press.

Herdt, G., & Boxer, A. (1992). Introduction: Culture, history, and the life course of gay men. In G. Herdt (Ed.), *Gay culture in America* (pp. 1–28). Boston: Beacon Press.

Herdt, G., & Boxer, A. (1993). *Children of Horizons: How gay and lesbian teens are leading a new way out of the closet*. Boston: Beacon Press.

Herdt, G., & Boxer, A. (1995). Toward a theory of bisexuality. In R. Parker & J. Gagnon (Eds.), *Conceiving sexuality: Approaches to sex research in a postmodern world* (pp. 69–84). New York: Routledge.

Herdt, G., & Boxer, A. (1996). Epilogue: Growing up gay and lesbian in the time of AIDS. In G. Herdt & A. Boxer (Eds.), *Children of Horizons*. Boston: Beacon Press.

Herdt, G., Beeler, J., & Rawls, T. W. (1997). Life course diversity among older lesbians and gay men: A study in Chicago. *Journal of Gay, Lesbian, and Bisexual Identity, 2,* 231–246.

Herdt, G., & Koff, B. (2000). *Something to tell you: How parents grow beyond a myth to integrate gay and lesbian teens into their families*. New York: Columbia University Press.

Herek, G. M. (1993). The context of antigay violence: Notes on cultural and psychological heterosexism. In L. Garnets & D. C. Kimmel (Eds.), *Psychological perspectives on lesbian and gay male experiences* (pp. 89–108). New York: Columbia University Press.

Herek, G. M., Jobe, J. B., & Carney, R. M. (Eds.). (1996). *Out in force: Sexual orientation and the military*. Chicago: University of Chicago Press.

Herrell, R. (1992). The symbolic strategies of Chicago's gay and lesbian pride day parade. In G. Herdt (Ed.), *Gay culture in America* (pp. 225–252). Boston: Beacon Press.

Hunter, J., & Schaecher, R. (1995). Gay and lesbian adolescents. In R. L. Edwards (Ed.), *Encyclopedia of social work* (19th ed., pp. 1055–1063). Washington, DC: NASW Press.

Laumann, E. O., Gagnon, J. H., Michael, R. T., & Michaels, S. (1994). *The social organization of sexuality: Sexual practices in the United States*. Chicago: University of Chicago Press.

Levine, M., Nardi, P., & Gagnon, J. (Eds.). (1997). *In changing times: Gay men and lesbians encounter HIV/AIDS*. Chicago: University of Chicago Press.

Manderson, L., & Jolly, M. (Ed.). (1997). *Sites of desire and economies of pleasure: Sexualities in Asia and the Pacific*. Chicago: University of Chicago Press.

Martin, E. (1994). *Flexible bodies: Tracking immunity in American culture from the days of polio to the age of AIDS*. Boston: Beacon Press.

McClintock, M. K., & Herdt, G. (1996). Rethinking puberty: The development of sexual attraction. *Current Directions in Psychological Science, 5,* 178–183.

Murray, S. O. (1996). *American gay*. Chicago: University of Chicago Press.

Paul, J. B., Hays, R. B., & Coates, T. J. (1995). The impact of the HIV epidemic on the U. S. gay male community. In A. R. D'Augelli & C. Patterson (Eds.), *Lesbian, gay, and bisexual identities over the lifespan* (pp. 347–397). New York: Oxford University Press.

Plummer, K. (1996). Intimate citizenship and the culture of sexual story telling. In J. Weeks & J. Hollands (Eds.), *Sexual cultures: Communities, values, and intimacy* (pp. 34–52). New York: St. Martin's Press.

Rust, P. C. (1992). The politics of sexual identity: Sexual attraction and behavior among lesbian and bisexual women. *Social Problems, 39,* 366–386.

Rust P. C. (1995). *Bisexuality and the challenge to lesbian politics: Sex, loyalty, and revolution*. New York: New York University Press.

Ryan, C., & Futterman, D. (1998). *Lesbian and gay youth: Care and counseling*. New York: Columbia University Press.

Sedgwick, E. K. (1990). *Epistemology of the closet*. Berkeley: University of California Press.

Sedgwick, E. K. (1991). How to bring your kids up gay. *Social Text, 29,* 18–27.

Smith-Rosenberg, C. (1985). *Disorderly conduct*. New York: Knopf.

Stimpson, C. R. (1996). Women's studies and its discontents. *Dissent, 43,* 67–75.

Sullivan, A. (1996). *Virtually normal: An argument about homosexuality*. New York: Knopf.

Trumbach, R. (1994). London's Sapphists: From three sexes to four genders in the

making of modern culture. In G. Herdt (Ed.), *Third sex, third gender: Beyond sexual dimorphism in culture and history* (pp. 111–136). New York: Zone Books.

Weeks, J. (1985). *Sexuality and its discontents*. New York: Routledge.

Weeks, J., & Holland, J. (Eds.). (1996). *Sexual cultures: Communities, values and intimacy*. New York: St. Martin's Press.

Weinberg, G. (1972). *Society and the healthy homosexual*. New York: St. Martin's Press.

Weinberg, M. S., Williams, C. J., & Pryor, D. W. (1994). *Dual attraction: Understanding bisexuality*. New York: Oxford University Press.

Index

284